CRITICAL SURVEY
OF
LONG FICTION

Picaresque Novelists

Editor

Carl Rollyson
Baruch College, City University of New York

SALEM PRESS
Ipswich, Massachusetts • Hackensack, New Jersey

Cover photo:
Gulliver's Travels (© Stefano Bianchetti/Corbis)

Copyright ©2012, by Salem Press, A Division of EBSCO Publishing, Inc.
All rights in this book are reserved. No part of this work may be used or reproduced in any manner whatsoever or transmitted in any form or by any means, electronic or mechanical, including photocopy, recording, or any information storage and retrieval system, without written permission from the copyright owner. For information, contact the publisher, EBSCO Publishing, 10 Estes Street, Ipswich, MA 01938.

978-1-4298-3680-7

CONTENTS

Contributors iv

The Picaresque Novel 1

Sholom Aleichem 12
Saul Bellow 18
T. Coraghessan Boyle 36
Miguel de Cervantes 46
Daniel Defoe 57
Denis Diderot 74
Henry Fielding 88
Nikolai Gogol 104
Hans Jakob Christoffel von Grimmelshausen 115
Franz Kafka 129
Alain-René Lesage 141
Joaquim Maria Machado de Assis 153
Frederic Prokosch 166
Salman Rushdie 175
William Saroyan 191
Tobias Smollett 204
Jonathan Swift 214
Voltaire 224
John Wain 240

Bibliography 254
Glossary of Literary Terms 257
Guide to Online Resources 269
Geographical Index 274
Subject Index 275

CONTRIBUTORS

Michael Adams
CUNY Graduate Center

Allan Chavkin
Texas State University-San Marcos

John R. Clark
Original Contributor

Mark Conroy
Original Contributor

Paul J. deGategno
Original Contributor

Stefan Dziemianowicz
Bloomfield, New Jersey

Robert J. Forman
St. John's University

Stephen M. Hart
University College London

Irma M. Kashuba
Original Contributor

Anna B. Katona
Original Contributor

Rebecca Kuzins
Pasadena, California

Lawrence F. Laban
Original Contributor

Avril S. Lewis
Original Contributor

Leon Lewis
Appalachian State University

Charles E. May
California State University, Long Beach

Richard A. Mazzara
Original Contributor

Laurence W. Mazzeno
Alvernia College

Carole Moses
Original Contributor

Allene Phy-Olsen
Original Contributor

Rosemary M. Canfield Reisman
Charleston Southern University

Victor Anthony Rudowski
Original Contributor

Dale Salwak
Original Contributor

Walter Shear
Original Contributor

Jack Shreve
Original Contributor

Stan Sulkes
Original Contributor

Victor Terras
Original Contributor

David Allen White
Original Contributor

The Picaresque Novel

The Spanish words *picaresque* and *picaro* achieved currency in Spain shortly after 1600. Today they are terms in literary criticism, sometimes misused because of the vague meaning attached to them. The revival of the genre in the twentieth century was accompanied by an increased critical interest in this type of novel, with the result that some critics try to stretch the definition of the picaresque while others attempt to restrict it. Still, some features are generally accepted as distinct characteristics of the picaresque, including a loose, episodic structure; a rogue-hero (the picaro) who is on the move and goes through a series of encounters with representatives of a hostile and corrupt world; a first-person narrative; and a satirical approach to the society in which the adventures occur.

The typical social background of the picaresque involves a disordered, disintegrating world in which traditional values are breaking down. The instability of the social structure permits the emergence of the picaro, a resilient rogue but not a criminal, a person of low birth or uncertain parentage, an outsider whose adventures take him or her from innocence to experience. In this sense, the picaresque novel has affinities with the bildungsroman, but unlike the protagonist of the latter, the picaro is a fixed character. While he (traditionally a "he") learns survival techniques from his adventures, he does not change inwardly; he remains faithful to his healthy instincts without questioning the larger order of things. Pressured by circumstances to choose between integrity and survival, the picaro makes the pragmatic choice and learns to adjust to the corrupt values of his environment.

Sixteenth Century Spain

The picaresque genre emerged in sixteenth century Spain, an age of turmoil and upheaval when medieval homogeneity and social stability were giving way to Renaissance mobility and a greater emphasis on the importance of the individual. All Spanish picaresque novels present a low-life character passing from master to master in search of some financial stability, thus providing a splendid occasion for the author to give an overall picture of Spain in an age of disintegrating values. The differences between the two first examples of the genre, however, already indicate its protean nature.

Lazarillo de Tormes, published anonymously in 1554 (English translation, 1576), presents a picaro, a victim of tricksters who by necessity becomes a trickster himself. The novel's anonymous author was the first to employ a realistic first-person narrator, creating a countergenre to the fastidious courtly literature of the period. Some critics suggest that both the anonymous author of *Lazarillo de Tormes* and Mateo Alemán, the writer of the second Spanish picaresque, were Jews or converted Jews, outsiders to the mainstream of Spanish society; in any case, the picaresque view of life is an outsider's point of view as far as protagonist and author are concerned.

Fear of starvation and anger are Lazarillo's true masters. The lesson he draws from his experience of privation and exploitation is not one of resistance or revolt; on the contrary, it is one of conformity. His is a kind of success story because, at the end of the novel, he finds a secure job as a town crier, but this is qualified success, since he pays for it with his honor, marrying the archpriest's mistress. He accepts the archpriest's advice to concern himself only with his own advantage. The advice, of course, reflects the hypocritical standards of Spanish society. Lazarillo is more than ready to heed the counsel; his bitter adventures have taught him to be content with low expectations. The feeling of being defenseless and unprotected against the wickedness of the world lends a tragic note to the story of his childhood and adolescence. Though most of his adventures make the reader laugh, anguish and despair prevail throughout the novel. The comic and the serious exist side by side, adding a note of ambiguity. *Lazarillo de Tormes* is a mixture of childish immaturity, innocence, and bitter cynicism; it excels in a fusion of modes and attitudes. At the end, Lazarillo compares his rising fortunes to Spain's rising political power; consequently, the unknown author not only puts his picaro's story in an ambiguous light but also extends that ambiguity to the whole empire of Charles V.

A DIFFERENT PICARO

King Charles V was succeeded by Philip II and Philip III; disillusionment followed triumph in the history of the empire. The picaresque novel, from the beginning a protean genre, adjusted to the new demands. Despair and anguish are present already in Lazarillo's story, but the picaro protagonist in Mateo Alemán's *Guzmán de Alfarache* (1599, 1604) is first of all a tormented soul. As an investigator of the prison system, Alemán was well acquainted with prison life. In Guzmán he presents a repentant sinner. The confessions reveal a lower-class character whom a dehumanizing society has forced to adjust to its corrupt values; the emphasis is not on Guzmán's adventures, however, but rather on his tormented soul. He is a kind of psychological picaro, one very much concerned with his soul. Guzmán compares the human predicament to warfare: an existence without any certainty or truth, a life full of hypocrisy and instability.

In spite of the many hilarious tricks played by the rogues on their masters, the Spanish picaresque novels were not intended to be amusing. There is a subtle balance of comedy and seriousness in *Lazarillo de Tormes* and *Guzmán de Alfarache*; at the same time, however, through the encounters of the rogue-hero with various masters—all of them representing the hypocritical, materialistic standards of contemporary Spanish society—these picaresque novels give a fragmented but valid and realistic picture of a society in change.

FRANCE AND GERMANY

The protean nature of the picaresque novel made it easy for the genre to spread rapidly through Europe. Adaptations of *Lazarillo de Tormes* soon appeared in France and England. *Guzmán de Alfarache* soon appeared in Germany. The Spanish original blended in each country with the native tradition, and the Spanish picaro turned into the English rogue, later a foundling; into the German *Schelm*; and in France, into a *gentilhomme*. Despite differences in each of these countries, the picaresque consistently performed the function of a countergenre, making legitimate the serious attention given to low-life characters. With the advance of capitalism, the middle class grew in size and influence, and its members found pleasure in a genre that centered on the plight of a low-life character seeking upward mobility. At the same time, printing techniques improved, and booksellers, in order to boost their profits, encouraged more and more printings of picaresque fiction because of its appeal to the taste of the bourgeoisie. In the following centuries the genre came to be adopted to reflect a bourgeois world view rather than a truly picaresque outlook. With the optimistic attitudes of the Enlightenment, the picaresque novel lost its quality of despair; the former picaro, though in different degrees and in different ways, came to be integrated into the mainstream of society.

In Germany, the Spanish picaresque merged with the native tradition of tales about false beggars. The most significant German novel of the picaresque type is Hans Jakob Christoffel von Grimmelshausen's *Der abenteuerliche Simplicissimus* (1669; *The Adventurous Simplicissimus*, 1912). The background of the book fits the requirements of the picaresque atmosphere: The Thirty Years' War was certainly a period of disorder and disintegration in German history. Simplicius Simplicissimus, as his name implies, is a naïve, simple, ignorant boy; his peasant background emphasizes this feature. He is almost another Parzival, a "pure fool," but the war destroys his pastoral life. His picaresque wanderings eventually lead him to live the life of a hermit. Compared to what is considered normal and sane in the gambling, warring, drinking, whoring society of contemporary Germany, the seemingly foolish idealism of the hermit is perhaps the only truly sane attitude amid universal madness. While society may consider Simplicissimus mad, his madness makes more sense than the reality created by the so-called respectable people. The German picaro, by tearing off the masks, shows the real face of society behind the facade.

In France, the Spanish picaresque merged with the tradition of criminal biographies and books on vagabonds; in the seventeenth century the genre came to be exploited by writers such as Charles Sorel and Paul Scarron, whose comic, realistic novels functioned as a countergenre to the improbable romances that flooded the market. The French picaro, born into the middle class, uses his tricks to unmask the society to which he belongs by birth; in consequence, the social criticism always implicit in the genre becomes more obvious. By far the most famous French picaresque novel is Alain-René Lesage's *Histoire de Gil Blas de Santillane* (1715-1735; 4 vols.; *The History of Gil Blas of Santillane*, 1716, 1735; better known as *Gil Blas*, 1749, 1962). Though the adventures of this son of humble parents take place in Spain, Gil Blas is different from the original Spanish picaro. Influenced by Molière and La Bruyère, satirists of morals and manners, Lesage turned his Gil Blas into an observer of rogues rather than a participant in roguery. Indeed, Gil Blas is a noble-hearted adventurer who, in view of his virtuous behavior, deserves the success he achieves in the end.

England

In England, the first translation of *Lazarillo de Tormes* appeared in 1576, the work of David Rowland; the first English *Guzmán de Alfarache* appeared in 1622. Soon thereafter, the Spanish picaresque merged with the native tradition of anatomies of roguery. The best early English picaresque is Thomas Nashe's *The Unfortunate Traveller: Or, The Life of Jack Wilton* (1594). *Guzmán de Alfarache* was very popular with translators; Richard Head's and Frances Kirkman's *The English Rogue* (1665, 1668) is the best among English adaptations of the original *Guzmán de Alfarache*.

In the eighteenth century, a kind of picaresque enjoyed a boom in English literature. Most of Tobias Smollett's fiction is in the picaresque vein. In his outstanding novel *The Adventures of Roderick Random* (1748), the protagonist, an orphan, foreshadows the English picaro as a foundling. He is a decent young person, and his inherent virtues contrast sharply with the cruelty and viciousness of most of the other characters in the novel. They stand for the attitudes of a dehumanized society that subjects the young protagonist to all kinds of hardships and misfortunes on land and on sea. Resilient, in the true picaresque spirit, Roderick Random bounces back after each misadventure. Although his personal fortunes are straightened out in the end when he finds his father and is happily married, on the whole, Smollett presents a rather gloomy view of the human condition.

Daniel Defoe's *The Fortunes and Misfortunes of the Famous Moll Flanders, Written from Her Own Memorandums* (1722) is an episodic fictional autobiography of a picara, a female rogue. She is a true criminal whose crimes are rooted in capitalistic attitudes. Indeed, Moll is a bourgeois picara; inspired by the spirit of profit and investment, she acquires the fortune necessary for investment in the New World by the only means available to her: thievery and prostitution. Her behavior and standards reflect on the materialistic values of the society to which she wants to conform.

Henry Fielding's *The History of Tom Jones, a Foundling* (1749) illustrates better than any other novel of the eighteenth century the transformation of the picaro from a roguish outsider to a belonger. Tom Jones is a foundling and thus an outsider—as a true picaro is expected to be—and in the course of the novel he must take to the road, where he undergoes various adventures. There is no doubt, however, that by the end of his journey he will be integrated into society. As a matter of fact, Tom Jones is a kind of vanishing picaro on his way to becoming the traditional English fictional hero. This hero always ultimately conforms to accepted norms. Tom Jones's place in the world of Allworthy is only being questioned in order to provide adventures for the amusement of the reader. The element of economic necessity is entirely lacking; in consequence, ambiguity and despair vanish and the adventures provoke wholehearted, easy laughter.

The next step on the path of the vanishing English picaro falls in the nineteenth century. In Charles Dickens's *Pickwick Papers* (1836-1837, serial; 1837, book), the picaresque structure is nothing more than a form of convenience. The rogue is Jingle, yet the hero of the adventure-series is the most respectable Mr. Pickwick. He is the picaro turned respectable, in an age when respectability, exemplified by Queen Victoria and the Prince Consort, dominated British society. Mr. Pickwick goes through a series of hilariously comic adventures, gains experience, and even goes to prison, but in the end he returns to society. Integration, so important in British fiction, is achieved at the end of the adventures.

THE UNITED STATES

The American development of the picaresque followed a radically different course. American dark humor, born on the pioneer frontier, recalls in its mixture of laughter and terror the atmosphere of the early Spanish picaresque. The early American, a lonely figure on a vast, unknown, and possibly hostile continent, is a distant cousin of Lazarillo and Guzmán. It is not surprising, then, that the novel from which, according to Ernest Hemingway, all American literature derives, Mark Twain's *Adventures of Huckleberry Finn* (1884), is an American picaresque story not only in the obvious picaresque pattern of Huck's adventures but also in the elements of loneliness and terror that fill up the frame.

Huck is an outsider, belonging to the lowest rank of whites in his society; he recognizes that society pays only lip service to ideals and decides to stay true to his own conscience. While the adventures of his trip down the Mississippi match Lazarillo's experiences of near starvation, the haunting experience with his own conscience over the case of Jim, the runaway black slave, makes Huck a relative of Guzmán, tortured about his soul. Huck, the American picaro, is a rogue with a conscience who chooses to listen to his own heart rather than follow the sham values of society.

THE PICARO IN MODERN FICTION

Many features of the original Spanish picaresque pattern and of its picaro-rogue hero correspond to trends in modern fiction and to the concept of the modern limited hero or antihero. The episodic, open-ended plot is an appropriate device for the modern writer, who knows "only broken images" for presenting the fragmented reality of a disorderly, chaotic universe. The picaro is not unlike the modern alienated individual, born into a world turned upside down. Many critics, therefore, consider the picaresque mode to be one of the most characteristic in twentieth century fiction, while others speak of a picaresque renaissance.

Irish writer James Joyce's *Ulysses* (1922), the archetype of modern fiction, shows striking similarities with the picaresque. Joyce's "joco-serious" recalls the unbalanced Spanish picaresque atmosphere of half-comical and half-serious attitudes. Leopold Bloom, a Jew in Ireland, is an outsider in society; as a betrayed husband, he also is an outsider in his family. Both *Ulysses* and the Spanish picaresque present a series of experiences rather than a coherent narrative. They present a roguelike hero, who is no criminal but still less than an example of virtue and whose life is a hard-luck story.

Bloom experiences a despair and anxiety which was alien to the more respectable picaros of the eighteenth and nineteenth centuries but which recalls the mood of *Lazarillo de Tormes*.

The English writer Joyce Cary also used the picaresque genre for his first trilogy, which concerns the life of the artist Gulley Jimson, a rascally but appealing picaro. Interestingly, only the first and third volumes can qualify as picaresque novels, for the narrator of the second book, *To Be a Pilgrim* (1942), is Thomas Wilcher, who does not fit the definition of a picaro. Wilcher is a member of the establishment, a rich, respectable lawyer who believes himself to be on the way to the Heavenly City. However, the first novel in the trilogy, *Herself Surprised* (1941), is narrated by a picara worthy to be classed with Moll Flanders; she not only habitually disregards the moral laws but also has no difficulty justifying even the most flagrant betrayal of trust—for instance, systematically stealing from Mr. Wilcher while she pretends to be the perfect housekeeper. Like Moll, Sara is eventually caught; *Herself Surprised* is written from prison. Gulley, who was probably the most important man in Sara's life, also falls victim to the law. *The Horse's Mouth* (1944, 1957), which he narrates, begins with his release from prison, an old man, but still adept at lying, cheating, stealing, and justifying his sins as necessitated by his art. Nevertheless, Gulley's zest for life and his ability to laugh both at the world and at himself make him a particularly appealing picaro.

The picaresque pattern also emerged in the novels of Britain's Angry Young Men in the 1950's. The angry picaresque novel of postwar Great Britain resulted from serious discontent with the welfare state. The decade found England in unsettled conditions, with the empire falling to pieces and the class system only slowly weakening in its traditional rigidity. Just as the Spanish picaresque novel arose in part as an expression of the social resentment of the underdog against the privileged classes, so Kingsley Amis's *Lucky Jim* (1954), John Wain's *Hurry on Down* (1953), and Alan Sillitoe's *Saturday Night and Sunday Morning* (1958) reject the values of the phony middle class. Yet their protagonists share Lazarillo's dream of belonging; in consequence, the angry picaresque stays within the pattern of integration characteristic of British fiction.

The American picaresque novel of the twentieth and twenty-first centuries may describe a restless small-town youth, as in John Updike's *Rabbit, Run* (1960), or a wild drive across the continent, as in Jack Kerouac's *On the Road* (1957). The present-day American rogues display an old American attitude; they try to recapture the heroic spirit of the frontier and confront the nature of humanity, of the self. The modern American picaro is an outsider; he may be a sensitive adolescent shunning the phony world, like Holden Caulfield in J. D. Salinger's *The Catcher in the Rye* (1951), or a man fighting the military in order to survive, like Yossarian in Joseph Heller's *Catch-22* (1961); he may be a member of a minority group—African American, like Ralph Ellison's Invisible Man in his novel *Invisible Man* (1952); Irish, like Ken Kesey's McMurphy in *One Flew over the Cuckoo's Nest* (1962); or Jewish, like Saul Bellow's Augie March in *The Adventures of Augie March* (1953).

Augie March is the product of the Chicago ghetto, the son of Jewish immigrants forced by his dehumanizing environment into a picaro attitude. A servant to many masters, resilient and ready to adjust, Augie ultimately refuses any attempt to be adopted and preserves his outsider status. Practical and pragmatic, he is able to do almost anything. While he is open to any new experience, he remains faithful to his own self, considering all his adventures as means to find his true identity. The Invisible Man, who is black, learns to accept his invisibility in white America; his picaresque experiences take him through a series of rejections at the end of which he emerges as a truly protean individual and even a trickster.

A PICARESQUE RENAISSANCE

Despite the protests of purists, who felt that the term "picaresque" was being applied too loosely, in the last three decades of the twentieth century novels thus described appeared in ever-increasing numbers, as did scholarly articles about specific works and books in which the genre was discussed more generally. Not surprisingly, much of the scholarship focused on the literature of Spain and Latin America, where the tradition has always flourished, and to a lesser degree on fiction from England and America. Occurrences of the picaresque novel were also found in some unexpected places, such as Morocco and Japan.

If the latter part of the twentieth century did see not only the preservation of the genre but also a very real picaresque renaissance, it can be explained by the fact that the form is so adaptable. Danny Deck, the successful writer-protagonist in Larry McMurtry's *All My Friends Are Going to Be Strangers* (1972), has little in common with the drug-dependent drifter in Jay McInerney's *Bright Lights, Big City* (1984), which is one of the few picaresque novels written in the second person. In *All My Friends Are Going to Be Strangers*, Danny travels from Texas to California and back to Texas, sometimes stopping for a time but always moving on, until at the end of the book he comes to a halt in the borderland between Texas and Mexico, his future uncertain. By contrast, all the adventures of McInerney's picaro take place in Manhattan over the course of one week, with frequent flashbacks into the past, and his story ends with his realizing that he must reclaim the values he was taught in childhood.

The quest of the picaro-narrator in Paul Auster's *Moon Palace* (1989) is also successful, though it takes some time for the aptly named Marco Stanley Fogg to realize that his own lack of purpose is rooted in his knowing nothing about his father and little about his mother, who is now dead. The scope of the novel is broadened geographically, temporally, and thematically by an interpolated narrative, a story told by the elderly man for whom Fogg works, which with the customary picaresque dependence upon happy coincidence enables the hero to identify his father and propels the hero westward across the continent to his own rebirth. The American Western novel, long a genre that easily accommodated the picaresque, reached what may be considered its literary pinnacle with the work of Cormac McCarthy, whose teenage runaway protagonist known only as "the kid" animated *Blood Meridian: Or, the Evening Redness in the West* (1985). In McCarthy's Western trilogy—the National Book Award winner *All the Pretty Horses* (1992), *The Crossing* (1994), and *Cities of the Plain* (1998)—each novel is a picaresque story of a young man on the move, facing tests and facing challenges from other men.

The historical picaresque

Interjected narratives, letters, and diaries have sometimes extended the time frame of picaresque novels a short distance into the past, but as long as one aim of the genre was to satirize a corrupt society, it did not occur to writers to set such works in the distant past. Late in the twentieth century, however, a new form appeared, in which a fictional picaro operates within a historical setting. In his introduction to *Flashman* (1969), British writer George MacDonald Fraser pretends to have discovered the papers of a minor character in Thomas Hughes's *Tom Brown's School Days* (1858). In *Flashman* and in the twelve that followed it, including *Flashman on the March* (2005), Harry Paget Flashman exposes himself as an unprincipled rogue, a lecher, and a coward who not only seduces every woman who catches his eye but also survives such episodes as the Indian Mutiny, the Charge of the Light Brigade, China's Taiping Rebellion, John Brown's raid on Harper's Ferry, and Little Big Horn, winning a reputation as a hero and eventually rising to the rank of brigadier general. Fraser's plots are exciting, but the secret of his popularity is the character of Flashman, perhaps because no matter how much he deceives others, he is always honest with himself.

In other picaresque novels, however, the picaro is very different from Lazarillo de Tormes or Flashman. A first-person narrator with a need to survive, the picaro candidly relates his adventures, while also serving as an observer. Having attached himself to a historical figure, the picaro talks with and observes him or her, thus presenting the author's interpretation of history. In E. L. Doctorow's *Billy Bathgate* (1989), for example, the title character is involved with the Depression-era gangster Dutch Schultz, and in Larry McMurtry's *Anything for Billy* (1988), the inept train robber Ben Sippy develops a real affection for Billy Bone, or Billy the Kid, the legendary outlaw of the Old West. The primary goal of both narrators is to survive, Billy by finding a way out of the slums, Ben by fleeing from a household of females and the stifling life of a Philadelphia gentleman. However, they also have a boundless curiosity, and they knowingly risk their lives in order to satisfy it. The protagonist in *Johnny One-Eye: A Tale of the American Revolution* (2008), by Jerome Charyn, is a double agent who encounters historical figures on both sides of the conflict: George Washington, Alexander Hamilton, Lord Admiral Richard Howe, and Benedict Arnold. Like the other picaresque heroes, he is a close observer of the world around him, and he describes everything in detail as he moves through the war and through the island of Manhattan looking for the identity of his father.

The Feminist Picaresque

Another new development in the late twentieth century picaresque renaissance was the novel with a feminist slant. Though picaras had appeared in earlier works, such as *Moll Flanders*, now picaresque novels written by women and about women began to proliferate. They varied widely in content and in tone. Rita Mae Brown's semiautobiographical *Rubyfruit Jungle* (1973) is both a moving description of what it is like to be rejected by society and a defiant celebration of lesbian sexuality, as is Sarah Waters's *Tipping the Velvet* (1998), a lighthearted picaresque of lesbian love. Margaret Atwood's *Lady Oracle* (1976) features another kind of rebel, one who would be seen more and more frequently in fiction during the years that followed: a mature woman who becomes a runaway. Atwood's heroine, Joan Foster, a writer, is so tired of her marriage, her ongoing affair, and her fans that she decides to fake her own death and run off to Italy. By the time she is found out and forced to return, this picaresque heroine has made some important decisions about the direction her life will take. Bella, the protagonist of Helen Zahavi's *Dirty Weekend* (1991), is on the run from a neighbor who has molested her, and in her flight she meets and kills seven abusive men.

Picaresque novels by women have taken many different shapes. There are dozens of fantasies by writers such as Marion Zimmer Bradley, Jo Clayton, Sharon Green, Tanith Lee, Anne Maxwell, Anne McCaffrey, and Janet Morris, all of which are feminist in philosophy and picaresque in form. The picaresque is also allied with Magical Realism, as in Isabel Allende's *Eva Luna* (1987; English translation, 1988), in which the title character survives one crisis after another with the aid of unseen powers and the force of her own imagination. Erica Jong's *Fanny: Being the True History of Fanny Hackabout-Jones* (1980) is much more like the picaresque novels of the eighteenth century, the period in which it is set. The author uses not only the language, capitalization, and punctuation of novels written in that era but also a huge cast of characters and a plot dependent on mistaken identities, chance meetings, and improbable coincidences. As in the historical novels already mentioned, the fictional Fanny meets and comments on real people; among her customers in a brothel are Dean Swift, William Hogarth, and John Cleland, whose *Fanny Hill: Or, Memoirs of a Woman of Pleasure* (1748-1749) Jong insists is an inaccurate account of Fanny Hill's life. *Fanny* could well have been written in the eighteenth century, as it appears to be, were it not for the fact that the author's twentieth century sensibility and, specifically, her feminism are evident in every one of Fanny's pronouncements.

A Genre of Lasting Value

One of the reasons for the widespread use of the picaresque form at the end of the twentieth century was obviously its flexibility. It has been utilized by writers from very different cultures, representing a wide range of literary traditions, from the historical novel to Magical Realism and fantasy. Picaresque works can be confessional, autobiographical, philosophical, or savagely satirical, and their protagonists can range from the unfortunate to thoroughgoing scoundrels. Some picaros and picaras even reform. What they all share with their Spanish originals is an exuberant love of life and a determination to survive in order to enjoy it.

The picaresque renaissance can also be attributed to the times themselves. The disorder, instability, and chaotic nature of the age may remind one of the transitional character of the sixteenth century. Modern men and women, dwarfed by an awareness of their lack of control over events in the outside world as well as over their own behavior, cannot hope for heroism; the best they can achieve is a kind of picaro status—an unwilling conformist, a rebel-victim, a picaresque saint. In the protean genre of the picaresque, sixteenth century Spanish writers created a fictional form appropriate for presenting the human predicament in an age of turmoil and instability.

Anna B. Katona
Updated by Rosemary M. Canfield Reisman

BIBLIOGRAPHY

Benito-Vessels, Carmen, and Michael Zappala, eds. *The Picaresque: A Symposium on the Rogue's Tale.* Newark, N.J.: University of Delaware Press, 1994. Specific picaresque works are discussed in most of these essays, while others deal with more general topics, such as translation. In their preface, the editors explain the ongoing disagreements about what constitutes picaresque literature.

Bjornson, Richard. *The Picaresque Hero in European Fiction.* Madison: University of Wisconsin Press, 1977. History of the picaresque through the eighteenth century, presented through the examination of major works such as *Moll Flanders* and *The Adventures of Roderick Random*. Includes illustrations.

Dunn, Peter N. *The Spanish Picaresque Novel.* Boston: Twayne, 1979. Traces the development of the picaresque novel in Spain, from the sixteenth century's *Lazarillo de Tormes* through seventeenth century tales written by Miguel de Cervantes and others. Explains distinctive qualities of the genre and demonstrates how these continued in novels during the development of realistic fiction.

Friedman, Edward H. *The Antiheroine's Voice: Narrative Discourse and Transformations of the Picaresque.* Columbia: University of Missouri Press, 1987. Feminist and deconstructionist analysis of the effect of an author's gender and outlook on a novel with a picara as first-person narrator. Highly theoretical but thought-provoking.

Gutiérrez, Helen Turner. *The Reception of the Picaresque in the French, English, and German Traditions.* New York: Peter Lang, 1995. Explores ways a common tradition is adapted in various countries in Europe to meet the needs of individual writers and the expectations of the reading public. Discusses the development of the picaresque in three countries, examining examples from the sixteenth through the twentieth centuries.

Kaler, Anne K. *The Picara: From Hera to Fantasy Heroine.* Bowling Green, Ohio: Bowling Green State University Popular Press, 1991. After outlining the relationship among the picara, the picaro, and picaresque literature, the author considers the six characteristics that differentiate a picara from a picaro. Kaler points to many picaras in contemporary literature, notably in fantasies.

Miller, Stuart. *The Picaresque Novel.* Cleveland, Ohio: Press of Case Western Reserve University, 1967. Scrutinizes six works in order to arrive at a definition of the genre. Although dated, this book is still valuable for Miller's comments about technical matters and for its accessibility.

Monteser, Frederick. *The Picaresque Element in Western Literature.* Tuscaloosa: University of Alabama Press, 1975. Traces the picaresque novel from its Spanish beginnings into France, Germany, Britain, Latin America, and the United States, but concludes that American society is now constituted so as to make the existence of a picaro impossible. Includes a chronological list of works.

Sherrill, Rowland A. *Road-Book America: Contemporary Culture and the New Picaresque.* Urbana: University of Illinois Press, 2000. Explores American fiction and nonfiction about life on the road, arguing these particular forms define a "new" picaresque. Novelists discussed include John Steinbeck and E. L. Doctorow.

Viviès, Jean. *English Travel Narratives in the Eighteenth Century: Exploring Genres.* Burlington, Vt.: Ashgate, 2002. Focuses on the travel journals of James Boswell, Laurence Sterne, and Tobias Smollett to demarcate the line between fiction and nonfiction. Chapter four examines "The Vagaries of the Picaresque."

Wicks, Ulrich. *Picaresque Narrative, Picaresque Fictions: A Theory and Research Guide.* New York: Greenwood Press, 1989. In the first part of this important volume, the author examines the picaresque from a theoretical standpoint and provides a comprehensive list of secondary sources. In the second section, Wicks analyzes more than sixty picaresque fictions, films as well as novels, in alphabetical order.

SHOLOM ALEICHEM

Born: Pereyaslav, Russia (now Pereyaslav-Khmelnitsky, Ukraine); March 2, 1859
Died: New York, New York; May 13, 1916
Also known as: Sholom Naumovich Rabinowitz

PRINCIPAL LONG FICTION
Natasha, 1884
Sender Blank und zayn Gezindl, 1888
Yosele Solovey, 1890 (*The Nightingale*, 1985)
Stempenyu, 1899 (English translation, 1913)
Blondzne Shtern, 1912 (*Wandering Star*, 1952)
Marienbad, 1917 (English translation, 1982)
In Shturm, 1918 (*In the Storm*, 1984)
Blutiger Shpas, 1923 (*The Bloody Hoax*, 1991)

OTHER LITERARY FORMS

Sholom Aleichem (ah-LAY-kehm) is best known for his short narratives, impressionistic sketches, and literary slices of life. The stories surrounding two of his characters—Tevye, the milkman, and Menahem-Mendl, the unsuccessful jack-of-all-trades—are frequently brought together in collections that form episodic but coherent wholes. The adventures of a third character, Mottel, the cantor's son, are sometimes published as young adult fiction, though divisions of Aleichem's audience according to age distinctions are artificial. Aleichem's stories have been published throughout Europe, in Israel, and in the United States. At least eight separate compilations are now available in English.

Some of Aleichem's writings, descriptions, or reactions to events and people are difficult to classify and are sometimes labeled simply "miscellany." Even his autobiography—*Fun'm yarid*, 1916 (*The Great Fair: Scenes from My Childhood*, 1955)—contains as much fantasy as fact. Although he had planned the book for many years, it was left incomplete at his death and covers only his youth.

ACHIEVEMENTS

Sholom Aleichem is regarded as one of the founders of Yiddish literature and is perhaps the most beloved writer in that language. While his longer fiction adds little to the development of the novel, even these works demonstrate the strengths for which he is loved throughout the Jewish world. Although, like most educated East European Jews of his time, he began by writing in Hebrew, the language of sacred learning and of scholarship, he soon discovered that Yiddish was the proper vehicle for relating the exploits of people like those he had known in his youth. The wisdom, the humor, and even the foolishness of these folk could be fully captured only as they actually spoke. In his hands, this despised "jargon" became a vivid, lively, literary instrument. Fluent in the Russian language, and a correspondent with Leo Tolstoy and Anton Chekhov, Aleichem brought to Yiddish fiction the compassion for the insulted and injured that was such a dominant note in classic Russian fiction.

By the end of the twentieth century, Yiddish was spoken only in small pockets of the United States, East Europe, and Israel, and was spoken chiefly by older people. The Yiddish newspapers had almost disappeared, and the theater was preserved only as a relic. Though much of the humor was lost in translation, Aleichem's writing survived and reached large Gentile as well as Jewish audiences in English, Russian, Hebrew. and other languages. Aleichem's fictional characters were introduced to even wider audiences with the popularity of his Broadway musical *Fiddler on the Roof* (pr. 1964), adapted from his Tevye tales, and an operatic adaptation of the novel *The Nightingale* (music by Noam Elkies and libretto by Jeremy Dauber), which was performed at Harvard University in 1999.

Aleichem's central value, though, is his preservation in fiction of a milieu that has vanished, of a people dispersed through pogroms, immigration, revolution, assimilation, and the Holocaust. His books are populated by rabbis, cantors, religious teachers, and kheder students, and yet his books have social and political dimensions. The society of the shtetl (a small Jewish townlet) is already changing in these writings. Revolutionaries who identify themselves as Russians more than as Jews and seek to rid their lives of czars, bishops, and rabbinical tyrants alike begin to appear in his novels. Other characters dream of wealth in America, while Zionists preach a return to the land of their spiritual ancestors.

Along with a large continuing readership, Aleichem has received many posthumous honors, including, in his name, statues in Russia's Kiev and Moscow and a street in New York City. His likeness is also on postage stamps in East Europe and Israel. His home in Kiev is now a place of literary pilgrimage.

Biography

Sholom Aleichem was born Sholom Naumovich Rabinowitz in 1859 in Pereyaslav, Russia (now in Ukraine), to a family of means, although family fortunes fluctuated during his childhood as they did throughout his entire life. His family moved to Voronkov, a small town nearby, which would be the model for his fictional town of Kasrilevke. Even though he received a traditional Jewish religious education, his father was aware of his talents and made sure they were supplemented by training at a Russian secondary school.

Sholom was thirteen years old when his beloved mother died. According to Jewish custom, it was not long before he had a stepmother; in this case, she could have stepped from the tales of the Brothers Grimm. However, she inspired his first published Yiddish work, a dictionary of humorous curses commonly uttered by stepmothers.

Because of the precarious financial situation of his family, young Sholom accepted a position as a government rabbi, an elected but despised functionary who mediated between the czarist government and the Jewish community. Later he was able to find more congenial employment as tutor to Olga Loyeff, daughter of a wealthy Jewish family. Falling in love and fearing her father's disapproval, Aleichem and Loyeff eloped. Their marriage lasted until his death.

Around 1883, Sholom wrote a humorous sketch that appeared in a Yiddish paper under the pseudonym Sholom Aleichem, a Hebrew greeting meaning "Peace unto you." He used the pseudonym initially as an apology for not writing in Hebrew, but he would come to use this pen name exclusively, just as he would continue to write in Yiddish. As business concerns and stock-market speculation took him to cities such as Kiev, Odessa, Paris, and Vienna, his writing continued, with brief narratives, character sketches, extended anecdotes, and even poems. Also a skilled reader, he was soon in demand as a performer, reading his own stories.

As times became ever more difficult in the Pale of Settlement (the area of the czarist empire in which Jews were permitted to live), immigration to the United States became an attractive possibility. In 1905, a devastating pogrom in which many Jews perished convinced Aleichem to relocate his family to the United States, where he was widely read and the Yiddish theater promised a decent livelihood.

It was in his later years that Aleichem aspired to be a playwright. His ear for the rhythms of speech of many different personalities, along with his imaginative portrayal of different character types, would seem to have fitted his work for the stage. However, he had limited success in the American Yiddish theater.

Even as his sales mounted on two continents, Aleichem, who was not an especially skilled businessman, received limited royalties and often was compelled to earn his living with lectures and readings. Never fully at home in the United States, he died in New York City in 1916. Enormous crowds attended his funeral, acknowledging him as a folk hero. His plays met with some acclaim after his death.

Analysis

Sholom Aleichem excelled in character development. The personalities of his protagonists unfold through their thoughts, desires, dreams, worries, and hopes; their interactions with others; and, most of all, through their speech. Their language—a lively, colloquial Yiddish—is rhythmic and rustically poetic. They curse one another, express affection, identify with animals, misquote Scripture, and misuse Talmudic lore, though, even in their innocent, or calculated, mangling of Scripture and tradition, they often reveal a higher folk wisdom.

Because Aleichem was basically a writer of short impressionistic sketches, it is difficult to diagram a clear plot in his narratives. He was largely indifferent to the literary architecture required of longer works. His novels, often picaresque, are therefore disjointed and episodic. He may introduce a character, leave him or her for several chapters, take up another character, and only later return to the first. The natural environment is rarely or only briefly described, yet the little towns and bustling cities through which his characters move come alive as they struggle to survive in whatever setting God has placed them.

The most famous Aleichem characters struggle with poverty, dream of what it would be like to be rich, and ultimately accept their plight. They are not, however, above arguing with the Deity. There is frequently a nearly magical, even mystical element in some of Aleichem's writing, which may reflect the influence of his grandfather, a Hasidic Jew and Kabbalistic mystic.

Preferring the epistolary narrative form or the monologue, Aleichem allows his protagonists to speak for themselves. Sometimes they address their unseen listener respectfully, but the author appears rarely to interfere with them. This encourages the reader to laugh with rather than at the characters so compassionately presented. In his novels, Aleichem appears to be telling rather than writing a story.

It has been customary to refer to Aleichem as the Jewish Mark Twain. There is a story, almost certainly apocryphal, of his meeting with the American humorist: When introduced, Twain is modestly rumored to have said "I understand that I am the American Sholom Aleichem." Certainly, in their use of first-person narrative, often in dialect, to individualize their fictional creations and bring out the humor of situations, the two are similar. They are alike in their kindly satire, as they comment on the foibles of society. However, Aleichem, as several critics have suggested, might more appropriately be compared to Charles Dickens, who displays, as does Aleichem, a stoic quality of writing and a "laughter through tears" humor.

In the Storm

An early short novel presented as if it were a two-act play, *In the Storm* is a story of three different families who live together at one address in Russia in 1905. In the background are revolution, pogroms, and riots. The characters try to cope through assimilation, religion, and rebellion against tradition. Jews of three different social classes further represent different economic orders. One family is headed by a prosperous businessman who bullies his way through the Jewish community; another father is a struggling druggist, trying to assimilate. The third head of household is a shoemaker, very conscious of his poverty. Although there is little sustained action, the novel is a fine mirror of its time and place.

Stempenyu

Stempenyu, the novel's title character, is a fiddler, with the soul of an artist. He has made an unfortunate marriage to Friedl, a shrew. He meets the gentle Rachel, and the two fall in love. She, too, is unhappily married, to a rich young man who ignores her in his enthusiasm for Talmudic study. Stempenyu and Rachel meet only a few times, once significantly against a monastery wall, and their love is never consummated. Rachel's virtue is, in fact, rewarded, when her husband is exhorted by his mother that his family is as important as his religion. While the chief interest of the novel is its examination of Jewish life in the Pale of Settlement, with its arranged marriages, the narrative also enables Aleichem to express his rejection of sentimental romances and the adulterous tradition of "love in the Western world." In Jewish life, readers are reminded, love comes in marriage, not before or apart from it.

WANDERING STAR

Aleichem's final attempt at sustained fiction allowed him to express his opinion of actors, the Yiddish stage, and theatrical promoters. This novel is strung together by a thin love story about two youths who escape their oppressive homes to become wandering performers. The main interest of *Wandering Star*, however, resides in descriptions of the magic of theater, reflections on the differences between sacred and secular music, and a lively review of the history of Yiddish theater. Aleichem focuses on the theater's origins in Romania to its degeneration in New York City at the hands of impresarios more interested in money than in Jewish folk art.

THE BLOODY HOAX

The Bloody Hoax is a novel based on a real event, known as the Beiliss affair, in which a Ukrainian Jew was accused of a ritual murder in 1911. In Aleichem's recasting of events, two friends, one Jewish and the other Gentile, decide to exchange places in order to expand their experience of life. The Gentile boy initially encounters problems through his inability to speak Yiddish, but his trouble really begins with the surfacing of "the blood libel," an unfounded but pervasive accusation made against Jews in times of persecution. He is accused of using Gentile blood to make Passover bread. Despite its serious subject, the novel is marketed as a comedy, and it is especially notable in its treatment of Russian Jewish intellectuals and the Zionist movement at the beginning of the twentieth century.

 Allene Phy-Olsen

OTHER MAJOR WORKS

SHORT FICTION: *Tevye der Milkhiger*, 1894-1914 (*Tevye's Daughters*, 1949; also known as *Tevye the Dairyman*); *Menakhem-Mendl*, 1895 (*The Adventures of Menachem-Mendl*, 1969); *Der farkishnefter Shnayder*, 1900 (*The Bewitched Tailor*, 1960); *Mottel, Peyse dem Khazns*, 1907-1916 (*The Adventures of Mottel, the Cantor's Son*, 1953); *Jewish Children*, 1920; *The Old Country*, 1946; *Inside Kasrilevke*, 1948; *Selected Stories of Sholom Aleichem*, 1956; *Stories and Satires*, 1959; *Old Country Tales*, 1966; *Some Laughter, Some Tears*, 1968; *Holiday Tales of Sholem Aleichem*, 1979; *The Best of Sholom Aleichem*, 1979 (Irving Howe and Ruth R. Wisse, editors); *Tevye the Dairyman and the Railroad Stories*, 1987; *The Further Adventures of Menachem-Mendl*, 2001.

PLAYS: *A Doktor*, pr. 1887 (*She Must Marry a Doctor*, 1916); *Yakenhoz*, pr. 1894; *Mazel Tov*, pr. 1904; *Tsuzeyt un Tsushpreyt*, pr. 1905; *Die Goldgreber*, pr. 1907; *Samuel

Pasternak, pr. 1907; *Stempenyu*, pr. 1907; *Agenten*, pb. 1908; *Az Got Vil, Shist a Bezem*, pb. 1908; *Konig Pic*, pb. 1910; *Shver Tsu Zein a Yid*, pb. 1914; *Dos Groyse Gevins*, pb. 1915 (*The Jackpot*, 1989); *Menshen*, pb. 1919; *Der Get*, pr. 1924; *The World of Sholom Aleichem*, 1953; *Fiddler on the Roof*, pr. 1964.

NONFICTION: *Fun'm yarid*, 1916 (*The Great Fair: Scenes from My Childhood*, 1955); *Briefe von Scholem Aleichem und Menachem Mendl*, 1921.

BIBLIOGRAPHY

Butwin, Joseph, and Frances Butwin. *Sholom Aleichem*. Boston: Twayne, 1977. A general review of the life and work of Aleichem, with insightful descriptions of all major writings and critical reactions to them. Part of Twayne's World Authors series.

Halberstam-Rubin, Anna. *Sholom Aleichem: The Writer as Social Historian*. New York: Peter Lang, 1989. A scholarly consideration of Aleichem's reconstruction of his native East European Jewish community written as a background study for the Broadway production of *Fiddler on the Roof*.

Howe, Irving. *World of Our Fathers: The Journey of the East European Jews to America and the Life They Found and Made*. New York: Simon & Schuster, 1976. A thorough examination of East European Jewish immigrants in the United States, the role of Yiddish in their lives, and their love of the Yiddish theater and Yiddish writers. This is the world Aleichem entered in his later years.

Liptzin, Solomon. *A History of Yiddish Literature*. New ed. Middle Village, N.Y.: Jonathan David, 1985. A thorough survey of the entire sweep of Yiddish literature and Aleichem's dominant place within it. Especially helpful are the discussions of characteristic Yiddish humor and the problems of translation. Equally pertinent is the examination of the rise and ultimate decline of Yiddish as a language of literature, theater, and cultural exchange.

Samuel, Maurice. *The World of Sholom Aleichem*. New York: Random House, 1973. A readable reconstruction of the world about which Aleichem wrote, the towns and villages of the Jewish Pale of Settlement. Illustrations are taken from the writings of Aleichem, in a demonstration of the ways in which fiction can imaginatively recapture an actual time and place now vanished.

Silverman, Erica, and Mordicai Gerstein. *Sholom's Treasure: How Sholom Aleichem Became a Writer*. New York: Farrar, Straus and Giroux, 2005. An illustrated biography aimed at younger readers. Covers events of the author's early life, including his problems with a difficult stepmother and his fascination with Jewish folklore.

Waife-Goldberg, Marie. *My Father, Sholom Aleichem*. New York: Schocken Books, 1971. A loving, carefully prepared biography of the author by his youngest daughter. Waife-Goldberg discusses the reception of Aleichem's works, the fluctuations in his career, and his sometimes-precarious financial situation even after he became famous as a writer.

SAUL BELLOW

Born: Lachine, Quebec, Canada; June 10, 1915
Died: Brookline, Massachusetts; April 5, 2005

PRINCIPAL LONG FICTION
Dangling Man, 1944
The Victim, 1947
The Adventures of Augie March, 1953
Seize the Day, 1956
Henderson the Rain King, 1959
Herzog, 1964
Mr. Sammler's Planet, 1970
Humboldt's Gift, 1975
The Dean's December, 1982
More Die of Heartbreak, 1987
A Theft, 1989
The Bellarosa Connection, 1989
The Actual, 1997 (novella)
Ravelstein, 2000
Novels, 1944-1953, 2003 (includes *Dangling Man*, *The Victim*, and *The Adventures of Augie March*)
Novels, 1956-1964, 2007 (includes *Seize the Day*, *Henderson the Rain King*, and *Herzog*)

OTHER LITERARY FORMS

In addition to his many novels, Saul Bellow published short stories, plays, and a variety of nonfiction. His stories have appeared in *The New Yorker*, *Commentary*, *Partisan Review*, *Hudson Review*, *Esquire*, and other periodicals, and his collections of short stories include *Mosby's Memoirs, and Other Stories* (1968) and *Him with His Foot in His Mouth, and Other Stories* (1984). His full-length play *The Last Analysis* was produced for a short run on Broadway in 1964, and three one-act plays, *Orange Soufflé*, *A Wen*, and *Out from Under*, were staged in 1966 in the United States and Europe. Another one-act play, *The Wrecker*, was published, though not staged, in 1954. Throughout his career, Bellow wrote numerous articles on a variety of topics. In 1976, he published an account of his trip to Israel, *To Jerusalem and Back: A Personal Account*.

ACHIEVEMENTS

Often described as one of America's most important novelists, Saul Bellow earned enormous critical praise and a wide readership as well. He was awarded the Nobel Prize in

Saul Bellow
(The Nobel Foundation)

Literature in 1976. His popularity is, perhaps, surprising, because his novels do not contain the usual ingredients one expects to find in best-selling fiction—suspense, heroic figures, and graphic sex and violence. In fact, his novels are difficult ones that wrestle with perplexing questions, sometimes drawing from esoteric sources such as the anthroposophy of Rudolf Steiner and the psychology of Wilhelm Reich. One of America's most erudite novelists, Bellow often alluded to the work of philosophers, psychologists, poets, anthropologists, and other writers in his fiction. He once stated that modern novelists should not be afraid to introduce complex ideas into their work. He found nothing admirable about the anti-intellectualism of many modern writers and believed that most of them failed to confront the important moral and philosophical problems of the modern age. Opposed to the glib pessimism and the "complaint" of the dominant tradition of modern literature, Bellow struggled for affirmation at a time when many writers viewed such a possibility as merely an object of ridicule.

In contrast to many other American writers, who produced their best work when they were young and then wrote mediocre or poor fiction as they grew older, Bellow is known for the consistent high quality of his work. Moreover, his fiction reveals an immense versatility. In his work, one finds highly structured Flaubertian form as well as picaresque narrative, naturalistic realism as well as romance.

Bellow earned a reputation as a master of narrative voice and perspective, a great comic writer (perhaps the best in America since Mark Twain), and a fine craftsman whose remarkable control of the language allowed him to move easily from the highly formal to the colloquial. Most important, his novels illuminate the dark areas of the psyche and possess immense emotional power. Bellow once complained that many contemporary authors and critics are obsessed with symbolism and hidden meanings. A literary work becomes an abstraction for them, and they contrive to evade the emotional power inherent in literature. Bellow's novels do not suffer from abstraction; they deal concretely with passion, death, love, and other fundamental concerns, evoking the whole range of human emotions for his readers.

Biography

Saul Bellow was born Solomon Bellows (he later dropped the "s" from his last name) in Lachine, Quebec, Canada, on June 10, 1915, the youngest of four children. Two years before, his parents, Abraham and Liza (Gordon) Bellows, had emigrated to Canada from St. Petersburg, Russia. The family lived in a very poor section of Montreal, where Bellow learned Yiddish, Hebrew, French, and English. In 1923, Bellow was diagnosed with tuberculosis and spent half a year in Montreal's Royal Victoria Hospital. When he was nine years old, the family moved to Chicago, where they lived in the tenements of Humboldt Park.

In 1933, after graduating from Tuley High School, Bellow entered the University of Chicago. Two years later he transferred to Northwestern University, where he received a bachelor's degree with honors in sociology and anthropology. In 1937, he entered the University of Wisconsin at Madison to study anthropology but left school in December to marry Anita Goshkin and to become a writer. He was employed briefly with the Works Progress Administration Writers' Project and then led a bohemian life, supporting himself with teaching and odd jobs. During World War II, he served in the merchant marine and published his first novel, *Dangling Man*.

After publishing his second novel, *The Victim*, Bellow was awarded a Guggenheim Fellowship in 1948, which enabled him to travel to Europe and work on *The Adventures of Augie March*, parts of which he published in various periodicals before publishing the novel in 1953. This third novel won the National Book Award for fiction in 1953 and established Bellow as one of America's most promising novelists.

After his return from Europe in 1950, Bellow spent a large part of the next decade in New York City and Duchess County, New York, teaching and writing before moving back to Chicago to publish *Herzog*. While *Seize the Day* and *Henderson the Rain King* did not receive the critical attention they deserved, *Herzog* was an enormous critical and financial success, even becoming a best seller for forty-two weeks and selling 142,000 copies, making Bellow wealthy for the first time in his life. *Herzog*, which prompted several thousand readers to send letters to the author pouring out their souls, is not only Bellow's masterpiece but also the most autobiographical of his novels. The impetus for the novel was the breakup of his second marriage, to Sondra Tschacbasov, because of her affair with his best friend, the writer Jack Ludwig. Although the novel reveals all of the important episodes of Bellow's life up to the time of the writing of *Herzog*, its primary focus is on the triangle of Herzog (Bellow), an academic suffering from writer's block, his beautiful and strong-willed wife Madeleine (Sondra), and the flamboyant charlatan Valentine Gersbach (Ludwig). The shameless Gersbach pretends to be Herzog's best friend and even provides marital counseling for the despondent husband while cuckolding him.

The next two novels, *Mr. Sammler's Planet* and *Humboldt's Gift*, helped increase Bellow's reputation but also created some controversy. *Mr. Sammler's Planet* was critical of the excesses of the late 1960's, and some complained that Bellow had become a reactionary. Although Bellow opposed the Vietnam War, he found it difficult to identify with the "counterculture." *Humboldt's Gift* disturbed some critics, who complained that Bellow's interest in the ideas of Austrian social philosopher Rudolf Steiner indicated that he was becoming an escapist; it was a mistaken assumption. An ardent supporter of Israel, Bellow traveled to that country in 1975 and published an account of his journey, *To Jerusalem and Back*. In 1976 he was awarded the Nobel Prize in Literature. Winning the Nobel Prize did not result in a loss of Bellow's creativity, and he published important books in the 1980's and 1990's, especially *The Dean's December, More Die of Heartbreak*, and *The Actual*, which challenge conventional thinking on political, aesthetic, and philosophical matters. His final novel, *Ravelstein*, published in 2000, prompted controversy, as it revealed that Bellow's close friend Allan Bloom (Abe Ravelstein in the novel) was gay and probably died as a consequence of acquired immunodeficiency syndrome (AIDS).

Bellow was married five times; he had three sons by his first three wives and, at the age of eighty-four, a daughter by his fifth wife. After living in Chicago for many years, he moved to Massachusetts in 1994, where he became a professor of literature at Boston University. Bellow died in Brookline, Massachusetts, in 2005 at the age of eighty-nine.

Analysis

Saul Bellow's mature fiction can be considered a conscious challenge to modernism, the dominant literary tradition of the age. Bellow viewed modernism as a "victim literature" because it depicts alienated individuals who are conquered by their environments. According to Bellow, this "wasteland" tradition originated in the middle of the nineteenth century with the birth of French realism and culminated in the work of Samuel Beckett and other nihilistic contemporary writers. This victim literature reveals a horror of life and considers humanist values useless in a bleak, irrational world. Modernism assumes that the notion of the individual self that underlies the great tradition of the novel is an outmoded concept and that modern civilization is doomed.

First novels

Bellow's first two novels owe a large debt to the wasteland modernism that he would explicitly reject in the late 1940's. *Dangling Man* is an existentialist diary that owes much to Fyodor Dostoevski's *Notes from the Underground* (1864). The demoralized protagonist, Joseph, is left "dangling" as he waits to be drafted during World War II. A moral casualty of war, he has no sense of purpose and feels weary of a life that seems boring, trivial, and cruel. Excessively self-conscious and critical of those around him, he spends most of his time alone, writing in his journal. He can no longer continue his past work, writing biographical essays on philosophers of the Enlightenment. Although he is alienated, he does realize that he should not make a doctrine out of this feeling. The conclusion of the novel reveals Joseph's ultimate failure to transcend his "victimization"; he is drafted and greets his imminent regimentation enthusiastically.

Bellow's next novel, *The Victim*, also depicts a passive protagonist who is unable to overcome his victimization. As Bellow admitted, the novel is partially modeled on Dostoevski's *The Eternal Husband* (1870) and uses the technique of the doppelgänger as Dostoevski does in *The Double* (1846). Bellow's novel presents the psychological struggle between Asa Leventhal, a Jew, and Kirby Allbee, his Gentile "double." A derelict without a job, Allbee suggests that Leventhal is responsible for his grim fate. Leventhal ponders the problem of his guilt and responsibility and tries to rid himself of his persecuting double. Despite his efforts to assert himself, he is still "dangling" at the end of the book—still a victim of forces that, he believes, are beyond his control.

The Adventures of Augie March

After his second novel, Bellow became disenchanted with the depressive temperament and the excessive emphasis on form of modernist literature. He had written his first two novels according to "repressive" Flaubertian formal standards; they were melancholy, rigidly structured, restrained in language, and detached and objective in tone. Rebelling against these constricting standards, Bellow threw off the yoke of modernism when he began to write his third novel. The theme, style, and tone of *The Adventures of Augie March* are very different from those of his earlier novels, for here one finds an open-ended picaresque narrative with flamboyant language and an exuberant hero who seeks to affirm life and the possibility of freedom. Whereas the environment has a profound influence on Joseph and Asa Leventhal, Augie refuses to allow it to determine his fate. During the course of many adventures, a multitude of Machiavellians seek to impose their versions of reality on the good-natured Augie, but he escapes from them, refusing to commit himself.

With his third novel, then, Bellow deliberately rejected the modernist outlook and aesthetic. The problem was to find an alternative to modernism without resorting to glib optimism. It seems that he found an alternative in two older literary traditions—in nineteenth century English Romantic humanism and in a comedy that he considered typically Jewish. Unlike the fiction of the modernists, which denigrates the concept of the individual, Bellow's fiction asserts the potential of the self and its powerful imagination, which can redeem ordinary existence and affirm the value of freedom, love, joy, and hope.

While comedy in Bellow's fiction is a complex matter, its primary function seems to be to undercut the dejection that threatens his heroes. The comic allows Bellow's protagonists to cope with the grim facts of existence; it enables them to avoid despair and gain a balanced view of their problematic situations. Comedy, the spirit of reason, allows them to laugh away their irrational anxieties. Often Bellow seems to encourage his worst anxieties in order to bring them out into the open so that he can dispose of them through comic ridicule.

SEIZE THE DAY

Whereas *The Adventures of Augie March* presents Bellow's alternative to a "literature of victimization," his subsequent novels can be regarded as probing, exploratory studies in spiritual survival in a hostile environment. *Seize the Day* is a much more somber novel than *The Adventures of Augie March*. Bellow felt that his liberation from Flaubertian formalism had gone too far, and that he must use more restraint in his fourth novel. He realized that Augie was too effusive and too naïve. The protagonist of *Seize the Day* is similar to the protagonists of the first two novels, but while Tommy Wilhelm is a "victim," Bellow's attitude toward him is different from his attitude toward Joseph and Asa Leventhal. In his fourth novel, Bellow sought to show the spiritual rebirth of such a "victim."

The short novel, divided into seven parts, presents the day of reckoning in the life of Wilhelm, a forty-four-year-old former salesman of children's furniture whose past consists of a series of blunders. Living in the Hotel Gloriana (which is also the residence of his wealthy father, Dr. Adler), Wilhelm feels that he is in a desperate situation. He is unemployed and unable to obtain money from his unsympathetic father. He gives his last seven hundred dollars to be invested for him by the mysterious psychologist Dr. Tamkin, a man who has become not only his surrogate father and financial adviser but also his instructor in spiritual and philosophical matters. Furthermore, Wilhelm's wife, Margaret, from whom he is separated, is harassing him for money. Depressed and confused by the memories of his failures in the past and absorbed by his problems in the present, Wilhelm needs love and compassion. Dr. Adler, Dr. Tamkin, and Margaret all fail him.

Seize the Day is a harsh indictment of a money-obsessed society, where a father is unable to love a son who is unsuccessful. Tamkin's speech on the two souls, no doubt the most important passage in the novel, helps clarify Bellow's social criticism. The psychologist argues that there is a war between a person's "pretender soul," the social self, and the "real soul." When the pretender soul parasitically dominates its host, as is common in modern society, the individual becomes murderous. If the individual is true to the real soul, however, and casts off the false pretender soul, he or she can learn to love and "seize the day."

Bellow shows that all of the characters in the novel are products of an exploitative, materialistic society—all are dominated by their pretender souls. Dr. Adler has fought his way up the economic ladder to success. Revered by the residents of the Hotel Gloriana, he is full of self-love. He desires to spend his remaining years in peace and refuses to acknowledge his paternal obligation to his desperate son. Wilhelm's appeals for money are actually pleas for some sign of paternal concern. He provokes his father, trying to disturb the polite barrier of aloofness that the old man has constructed to prevent any kind of real communication between father and son. While Wilhelm is a difficult son for a father to cherish, Dr. Adler is a coldhearted man who has no real affection for his son, or for anyone else except himself. When, at the end of the novel, Wilhelm begs his father for some kind of sympathy, the hard-boiled Adler brutally rejects him, revealing his hatred for his "soft" son.

Dr. Adler's failure as a father results in Wilhelm's turning to the strange psychologist Dr. Tamkin. Down on his luck, Tamkin is a confidence man hoping to make easy money. He is another one of Bellow's eccentric fast-talkers, full of fantastic stories and philosophical and psychological insights. Wilhelm is attracted to Tamkin not only because he is a father figure who promises to save him from his dire financial crisis but also because he is one man in a cynical society who speaks of spiritual matters. The direct result of Tamkin's advice is the loss of Wilhelm's money, but while the doctor is a phony whose flamboyant personality enables him to dupe the naïve ex-salesman, he does indirectly allow Wilhelm to obtain a kind of salvation.

Wilhelm is the only character in the novel who is able to forsake his pretender soul. He is a product of society as the other characters are, but he is different from them in his instinctive distaste for the inveterate cynicism at the heart of society. Accepting society's definition of success, he considers himself a failure. He suffers immensely and constantly ponders his life and his errors in the past, yet while he can at times degenerate into a buffoon indulging in self-pity and hostility, he is also attracted to the idealism that Tamkin occasionally expounds.

A significant moment occurs near the end of the novel when Wilhelm suddenly feels a sense of brotherhood with his fellow travelers in the New York subway. For once he has transcended his self-absorption, though he is immediately skeptical of this intuitive moment. At the very end of the novel, another heightened moment occurs in which he does make the breakthrough foreshadowed in the subway scene. Having lost all of his money, he pursues into a funeral home a man who resembles Tamkin. Suddenly he finds himself confronting a corpse, and he begins to weep uncontrollably. He weeps not merely out of self-pity, as some have suggested, but for humankind. Understanding that death and suffering are an inextricable part of the human condition, he feels humility and is able to overcome his excessive self-absorption. He is finally able to cast off his pretender soul. The work concludes with a powerful affirmation and suggests an alternative to the spiritual death of a materialistic, predatory society.

HENDERSON THE RAIN KING

Bellow's next novel, *Henderson the Rain King*, is the first fully realized work of his maturity. It is Bellow's first novel of which one can say that no other writer could have conceived it, much less written it. Although it has some characteristics of the picaresque, the fable, and the realistic novel, *Henderson the Rain King* assumes the most widely used form for longer works during the English Romantic era—the quest romance. The tone of the novel is somewhat different from that typically found in the quest romance, however; it is exuberant and comic, and the book is full of wit, parody, farce, and ironic juxtapositions.

The novel might be seen as Bellow's version of Joseph Conrad's *Heart of Darkness* (1902). Like Conrad's Marlow, Eugene Henderson recalls his journey into the heart of Africa and his bizarre adventures there, which culminate in his meeting with a Kurtz-like instructor who has a profound influence on him. Whereas Kurtz reveals to Marlow the human potential for degradation, Dahfu conveys to Henderson the human promise of nobility. With its allusions to William Wordsworth, Samuel Taylor Coleridge, Percy Bysshe Shelley, and William Blake, the novel affirms the possibility of the individual's regeneration by the power of the human imagination; it is a trenchant rejection of Conrad's pessimism.

The novel can be divided into three basic parts: Chapters 1-4 depict Henderson's alienation; chapters 5-9 present his journey to the African tribe of the Arnewi; and chapters 10-22 portray his journey to the African tribe of the Wariri and his spiritual regeneration. The first section presents Henderson's discursive recollections of his life before he set out for Africa, in which he attempts to reveal the reasons for the journey. While these chapters provide a plethora of information about him, he is never able to articulate the reasons for his "quest," as he calls it. Bellow is suggesting in this section that there are no clear-cut reasons for the African journey. Henderson leaves his wife and family for the African wilderness because of his dissatisfaction with his meaningless existence. A millionaire with tremendous energy but no scope for it, Henderson has spent most of his life suffering or making others suffer. Middle-aged, anxious about his mortality, and unable to satisfy the strident inner voice of "I want, I want," he leaves for Africa, hoping to burst "the spirit's sleep," as he phrases it, echoing Shelley's *The Revolt of Islam* (1818).

With his loyal guide Romilayu, he first visits the Arnewi tribe. These people are "children of light" who represent a healthy existence; they are gentle, peaceful, and innocent. Queen Willatale, who rules the tribe, informs Henderson that man wants to live—"grun-tu-molani." It is an important message for Henderson, but he soon demonstrates that he is unable to follow Willatale's wisdom. Desiring to help the tribe, whose water supply has been infested by frogs, he decides to kill the creatures. His bomb is too powerful and destroys the cistern as well as the frogs. Henderson has violated the code of the Arnewi, who abhor violence and have love for all living creatures.

After Henderson leaves the Arnewi, he visits the Wariri, "the children of darkness," who are violent and hostile, reminiscent of the predatory society of Bellow's earlier novels. He does meet one extraordinary individual, however, and establishes a friendship with him. King Dahfu is a noble man who completes Henderson's education begun with the Arnewi. He perceptively observes that Henderson's basic problem is his avoidance of death: He is an "avoider." Dahfu helps him by persuading him to go down into a lion's den to overcome his anxiety over mortality. Dahfu believes, too, that Henderson can absorb qualities of the lion and slough off his porcine characteristics. Dahfu is another one of Bellow's eccentric teachers who speaks both wisdom and nonsense. His greatest importance for Henderson is that he embodies the nobility of human beings, who can by the power of the imagination achieve spiritual regeneration. At the end of the novel, Henderson finally bursts the spirit's sleep and leaves Africa for America. He has a sense of purpose and can love others. He plans to become a physician and will return home to his wife.

Herzog

Herzog is by most accounts Bellow's best and most difficult novel. It is a retrospective meditation by a middle-aged professor who seeks to understand the reasons for his disastrous past. A complex, discursive work, pervaded by sardonic humor, it defies traditional labeling but owes a debt to the novel of ideas, the psychological novel, the epistolary novel, and the romantic meditative lyric. *Herzog* is a meditative work in which the protagonist compulsively remembers and evaluates his past, striving to avoid complete mental breakdown. There are reminiscences within reminiscences, and the story of Moses Herzog's life is related in fragments. Bellow's method enables the reader to see how Herzog's imagination recollects and assembles the fragments of the past into a meaningful pattern.

Distraught over his recent divorce from his second wife, Madeleine, Herzog has become obsessed with writing letters to everyone connected with that event as well as to important thinkers, living and dead, who concern him. He associates his domestic crisis with the cultural crisis of Western civilization, and therefore he ponders the ethics of Friedrich Nietzsche as well as those of his psychiatrist, Dr. Edvig. Herzog's letter writing is both a symptom of his psychological disintegration and his attempt to meditate on and make sense of suffering and death.

At his home in the Berkshires, Herzog recalls and meditates on the events of his recent past; the five-day period of time that he recalls reveals the severity of his psychological deterioration. His mistress, Ramona, believes that a cure for his nervous state can be found in her Lawrentian sexual passion, but he considers her "ideology" to be mere hedonism; impulsively, he decides to flee from her to Martha's Vineyard, where he has friends. After arriving there, the unstable professor leaves almost immediately and returns to New York.

The next evening he has dinner with Ramona and spends the night with her, waking in the middle of the night to write another letter. The following morning he visits a courtroom while waiting for a meeting with his lawyer to discuss a lawsuit against Madeleine. Hearing a brutal child-abuse and murder case causes the distraught professor to associate Madeleine and her lover with the brutal child murderers; he flies to Chicago to kill them. As he spies on them, he realizes his assumption is absurd and abandons his plan. The next morning he takes his young daughter Junie for an outing but has a car accident and is arrested by the police for carrying a gun. He confronts an angry Madeleine at the police station and manages to control his own temper. Later, he is released and returns to his run-down home in the Berkshires, and the novel ends where it began.

Interspersed within these recollections of the immediate past are memories of the more distant past. By piecing these together, one learns the sad story of Herzog's domestic life. Feeling a vague dissatisfaction, the successful professor divorced his first wife, Daisy, a sensible midwestern woman, and began affairs with a good-natured Japanese woman, Sono, and the beautiful, bad-tempered Madeleine. After marrying Madeleine, Herzog purchased a house in the Berkshires, where he intended to complete his important book on the Romantics. Soon they returned to Chicago, however, where both saw a psychiatrist, and Madeleine suddenly announced that she wanted a divorce. The shocked Herzog traveled to Europe to recuperate, only to return to Chicago to learn that Madeleine had been having an affair with his best friend and confidant the whole time their marriage had been deteriorating.

Herzog's grim past—his disastrous marriages and the other sad events of his life that he also recalls—becomes emblematic of the pernicious influence of cultural nihilism. Herzog is devoted to basic humanist values but wonders if he must, as the ubiquitous "reality instructors" insist, become another mass man devoted to a brutal "realism" in the Hobbesian jungle of modern society. His antipathy for the wastelanders' cynicism is strong, but he knows his past idealism has been too naïve. Repeatedly, the "reality instructors" strive to teach ("punish") Herzog with lessons of the "real"—and the "real" is always brutal and cruel. Sandor Himmelstein, Herzog's lawyer and friend, proudly announces that all people are "whores." It is an accurate description not only of Himmelstein but also of his fellow reality instructors. Their cynical view is pervasive in modern society, in which people play roles, sell themselves, and seduce and exploit others for their own selfish ends.

The turning point of the novel is Herzog's revelation in the courtroom episode. Intellectually, he has always known about evil and suffering, but emotionally he has remained innocent. His hearing of the case in which a mother has mistreated and murdered her son while her lover apathetically watched is too much for him to bear; here is a monstrous evil that cannot be subsumed by any intellectual scheme. In a devastating moment the professor is forced to realize that his idealism is foolish.

At the end of the novel, Herzog has achieved a new consciousness. He recognizes that he has been selfish and excessively absorbed in intellectual abstractions. A prisoner of his private intellectual life, he has cut himself off from ordinary humanity and everyday existence. He sees that his naïve idealism and the wastelanders' cruel "realism" are both escapist and therefore unacceptable attitudes; they allow the individual to evade reality by wearing masks of naïve idealism or self-serving cynicism. The exhausted Herzog decides to abandon his compulsive letter writing and to stop pondering his past. The threat of madness has passed, and he is on the road to recovery.

Mr. Sammler's Planet

Mr. Sammler's Planet is a meditative novel of sardonic humor and caustic wit. The "action" of the novel centers on the protagonist's recollection of a brief period of time in the recent past, though there are recollections of a more distant past, too. Once again the mental state of the protagonist is Bellow's main concern. Like Herzog, Artur Sammler has abandoned a scholarly project because he finds rational explanations dissatisfying; they are unable to justify suffering and death. The septuagenarian Sammler is yet another of Bellow's survivors, a lonely humanist in a society populated by brutal "realists."

This seventh novel, however, is not merely a repetition of Bellow's previous works. Sammler is detached and basically unemotional, yet he reveals a mystical bent largely absent in Bellow's other protagonists. He is drawn to the works of Meister Eckhart and other thirteenth century German mystics. While he does not literally believe in their ideas, he finds reading their works soothing. His religious inclination is a recent phenomenon. Sammler had been reared in a wealthy, secular Jewish family in Kraków, Poland. As an adult, he became a haughty, cosmopolitan intellectual, useless to everyone, as he readily admits. On a visit to Poland in 1939, when the Germans suddenly attacked, he, his wife, and others were captured and ordered to dig their own graves as the Nazis waited to murder them. Although his wife was killed in the mass execution, miraculously Sammler escaped by crawling out of his own grave. After the war ended, Sammler and his daughter Shula were rescued from a displaced persons camp by a kind nephew, Dr. Elya Gruner, who became their patron.

The experience of the Holocaust destroyed what little religious inclination Sammler possessed, but in his old age he has become concerned with his spiritual state. Unfortunately, it is difficult to pursue spiritual interests in a materialistic society hostile to them. The basic conflict in the novel is between Sammler's need to ponder the basic questions of existence—a need accentuated by the dying of the noble Gruner—and the distractions of modern-day society. In the primary action of the novel, Sammler's main intention is to visit the dying Gruner, who finds Sammler a source of great comfort. Several "accidents" distract Sammler from his goal, and on the day of his nephew's death, he arrives too late.

The "accidents" that encumber Sammler reveal clearly the "degraded clowning" of contemporary society. Sammler is threatened by a black pickpocket who corners the old man and then exposes himself. In the middle of a lecture he is shouted down by a radical student who says that Sammler is sexually defective. His daughter Shula steals a manuscript from an Indian scholar, and Sammler must waste precious time to recover it. Even Gruner's self-centered children, who have little compassion for their dying father, distract Sammler by their thoughtless actions.

Opposed to Gruner, who is part of the "old system" that esteems the family, the expression of emotion, and the traditional humanist values, is the contemporary generation, a kind of "circus" characterized by role-playing, hedonism, amorality, self-centeredness, and atrophy of feeling. Despite its flaws, Bellow sympathizes with the "old system." The novel concludes after Sammler, despite the objections of the hospital staff, goes into the postmortem room and says a prayer for Gruner's soul.

HUMBOLDT'S GIFT

As in Bellow's previous novels, the tension and the humor of *Humboldt's Gift* have their origins in the protagonist's attempt to free himself from the distractions of contemporary society and pursue the needs of his soul. The protagonist, Charlie Citrine, strives to define for himself the function of the artist in contemporary America. He tries to come to terms with the failure and premature death of his onetime mentor, Von Humboldt Fleisher, who had the potential to be America's greatest modern poet but achieved very little. Charlie wonders if the romantic poet can survive in a materialistic society; he wonders, too, if he can overcome his fear of the grave and exercise his imagination. A writer who has squandered his talent, Charlie has intimations of terror of the grave and intimations of immortality. He spends much time reading the anthroposophical works of Rudolf Steiner; although he is skeptical of some of Steiner's more esoteric teachings, he is sympathetic to the spiritual worldview of anthroposophy, even finding the notion of reincarnation persuasive.

The primary nemesis of Charlie's spiritual life is Ronald Cantabile, a small-time criminal. Renata, Charlie's voluptuous mistress, Denise, his ex-wife, and Pierre Thaxter, a confidence man, are also major distractions. When Charlie, on the advice of a friend, refuses to pay Cantabile the money he owes him from a poker game, the criminal harasses him. In fact, the proud, psychopathic Cantabile refuses to leave Charlie alone even after he agrees to pay him the money. He continually humiliates Charlie and even tries to involve him in a plot to murder the troublesome Denise.

Denise, Renata, and Thaxter also distract Charlie from pondering the fate of Humboldt and meditating on fundamental metaphysical questions. Hoping Charlie will return to her, Denise refuses to settle her support suit and continues to demand more money. When Charlie is forced to put up a two-hundred-thousand-dollar bond, he is financially ruined, and the loss of his money results in the loss of the voluptuous Renata, who decides to marry a wealthy undertaker. A third disillusioning experience involves Thaxter, who has apparently conned Charlie. Charlie had invested a small fortune in a new journal, *The Ark*, which was supposed to restore the authority of art and culture in the United States.

Thaxter, the editor of *The Ark*, never puts out the first issue and has, it appears, stolen the money. His confidence game symbolizes America's lack of respect for art and culture, impractical subjects in a practical, technological society.

Charlie does, however, overcome these "distractions." Humboldt's posthumously delivered letter, accompanied by an original film sketch (his "gift") and a scenario that the two had written at Princeton years before, provides the genesis for Charlie's salvation. The original film idea and the scenario of their Princeton years enable Charlie to attain financial security, but, more important, Humboldt's letter provides the impetus for Charlie's decision at the end of the novel to repudiate his past empty life and pursue the life of the imagination. Humboldt's ideas, bolstered by the poetry of Blake, Wordsworth, and John Keats, enable Charlie to avoid the fate of the self-destructive artist. He decides to live in Europe and meditate on the fundamental questions—in short, to take up a different kind of life.

When, at the end of the novel, Charlie gives Humboldt and the poet's mother a proper burial, Bellow suggests that Charlie's imagination is ready to exert itself and wake him from his self-centered boredom and death-in-life. The final scene of the novel promises Charlie's spiritual regeneration.

THE DEAN'S DECEMBER

Bellow's 1982 novel *The Dean's December* is "a tale of two cities," Chicago and Bucharest, in which the protagonist, a dean at an unnamed college in Chicago, ponders private and public problems. Albert Corde experiences at first hand the rigid penitentiary society of the Communist East as well as the anarchic society of the non-Communist West, which seems on the verge of disintegration. The novel is a protest against the dehumanization of the individual. The East has enslaved its population, while the West has "written off" its doomed "Underclass." Like *Humboldt's Gift*, this novel can be seen as a kind of retrospective crisis meditation in which the protagonist attempts to come to terms with an immensely complex and threatening "multiverse," as Augie March calls it.

The complicated plot defies a succinct summary, but the basic situation can be outlined. The dean and his wife, Minna, arrive in Romania to visit her dying mother. Corde tries to help his despairing wife, who is unable to reconcile herself to the grim reality of her mother's death. He also ponders the controversy that he has provoked in Chicago. The dean has published two articles in *Harper's* in which he has commented on the political and social problems of the city. The articles outrage the powerful members of Chicago society, and the administration of his college disapproves of the controversy that the dean has provoked. Moreover, Corde creates another controversy when he pressures the police to solve the murder of a white graduate student, Rickie Lester. A sensational trial, a "media circus," is the result of the dean's search for justice.

While, more than any other novel by Bellow, *The Dean's December* is concerned with contemporary public issues, especially the vile conditions of the inner city, it is also concerned with the spiritual state of the individual. In fact, Bellow suggests that there is a connection between the spiritual malady of the individual and the spiritual anarchy of society. The novel is a protest against not only people's lack of political freedom but also the spiritual enslavement that is the result of their inability to see clearly and to experience reality. Corde implies that this inability to experience reality is largely a product of "seeing" the world with a kind of reductive journalism completely lacking in imagination. Disgusted with contemporary journalism that provides only substitutes for reality, Corde intends to incorporate "poetry" into writing. The novel suggests that in Corde's kind of poetic vision there is hope for the spiritual rebirth of the individual and society.

MORE DIE OF HEARTBREAK

Three years after the publication of his collection *Him with His Foot in His Mouth, and Other Stories*, Bellow published *More Die of Heartbreak*. This comic novel does not have a highly structured plot; rather, it might be best described as an elaborate monologue from the overstimulated mind of the bachelor narrator, Kenneth Trachtenberg. Kenneth, an expert in Russian history and culture, is preoccupied with his uncle, Benn Crader, a renowned botanist. The only important "action" in the novel revolves around the attempt of Dr. Layamon, his daughter Matilda, and her fiancé Benn Crader to "extort" money from Benn's relative, Harold Vilitzer, a political racketeer in bad health. Years before, Vilitzer had cheated the Crader family in a real estate deal. The greedy Dr. Layamon sees his daughter's marriage to Benn as a marvelous opportunity to acquire a fortune if Benn will agree to pressure Vilitzer for the money the corrupt politician stole from the Crader family. Although he wants to please his beautiful fiancé and her father, Benn is not enthusiastic about the plan. As the narrator suggests, Benn is a man who should be in search of "higher meanings." At the end of the novel, Benn flees from the Layamons to the North Pole to carry out his research. The implication is that now he will be able to pursue his neglected aesthetic and metaphysical goals.

A THEFT

After being rejected by two periodicals because it was "too long," the short novel *A Theft* was published in 1989 as a paperback original. Like so many of Bellow's works, the plot of this 109-page novel is subordinate to Bellow's interest in character. Just as *Seize the Day* might be considered an intimate psychological exploration of Wilhelm, *A Theft* is a detailed exploration of the soul of the heroine, Clara Velde. Clara was brought up on old-time religion but has led a disorganized life, including disappointing love affairs, suicide attempts, and four marriages. Her fourth marriage is not successful, and she is actually in love with an "old flame," Ithiel Regler, a Henry Kissinger-like high-powered adviser to statesmen. For Clara, transcendent love between her and Ithiel is symbolized by an emerald ring that he gave her years ago. When this ring is stolen, Clara finds herself in a troubling search for it and experiences a kind of spiritual quest as well. She feels a special sense of kinship with her self-possessed au pair, Gina. In its epiphany-like quality, the conclusion of the novel is reminiscent of *Seize the Day*.

THE BELLAROSA CONNECTION

Another paperback original, the short novel *The Bellarosa Connection* is narrated by the wealthy founder of the Mnemosyne Institute in Philadelphia. The institute instructs businesspeople and others in the use of memory. The narrator, a retired widower, focuses his immense powers of recollection on two relatives who haunt him—Harry and Sorella Fonstein. Harry narrowly escaped the Nazi death camps, thanks to the Broadway producer Billy Rose, who made use of his gangster connections in Italy to help Fonstein and others escape to freedom. Billy Rose's generosity is particularly noteworthy, the narrator implies, because the Broadway producer has a sleazy reputation.

In the United States, Harry marries the intelligent, capable Sorella and becomes successful but is frustrated by Rose's repulsing Harry's repeated attempts to meet him and express his gratitude. The central scene of the novel is the dramatic encounter between Sorella and Rose, in which the determined woman attempts to coerce the stubborn producer into meeting her husband by threatening to reveal sordid details of Rose's private life. Despite Sorella's "blackmail," Rose refuses to meet Harry.

Bellow in this short novel is pondering how the assimilation of Jews into American life can corrupt not only their values but also their souls. Sorella reflects: "The Jews could survive everything that Europe threw at them. I mean the lucky remnant. But now comes the next test—America." Apparently the United States proves "too much" for at least some of them.

THE ACTUAL

The novella *The Actual* is narrated by Harry Trellman, an introspective man in his sixties who grew up in a lower-middle-class Jewish neighborhood in Chicago. His father was a simple carpenter; his mother's family was wealthy. Harry was put in an orphanage despite the fact that both his parents were alive because his hypochondriacal mother did not have the time to care for him; she spent much time abroad and in the United States at various sanitariums looking for a cure for her disease of the joints. The bills for sojourns abroad and at home were paid by the mother's family; her brothers were successful sausage manufacturers who could pay for the cures she took at Bad Nauheim or Hot Springs, Arkansas. After the Korean War, the government sent Harry to study Chinese at a "special school." He spent a number of years in the Far East, the final two in Burma, where he made business connections, and then returned to Chicago, where he had "unfinished emotional business."

Although the precise source of Harry's income is not clear, apparently he is well-off. Semiretired and without financial concerns, Harry is nevertheless far from being content. For more than four decades he has loved Amy Wustrin, whom he first knew in high school. When Harry returned to Chicago after his Far East sojourn, he and Amy met again. Despite for Harry a momentous sexual encounter in which he kissed Amy "under the breast and inside the thigh," the relationship did not progress. After divorcing her first husband, Amy married Jay Wustrin, Harry's best friend in high school. Neither Jay nor Amy paid much heed to the marriage vows, and the result was a bitter divorce that culminated in Jay's playing tapes in divorce court of Amy's adulterous lovemaking in which one could hear her orgasmic cries. None of this disheartening history dampened Harry's ardent love for Amy.

Harry and Amy are brought together by the ninety-two-year-old billionaire Sigmund Adletsky, for whom Amy is working as an interior decorator and Harry as adviser in his "brain trust." Harry accompanies Amy in her emotionally arduous task of exhuming Jay's body from his cemetery plot next to the grave of Amy's mother so that Amy can bury her father there. (A practical joker with nihilistic proclivities, Jay had purchased the plot from Amy's father.) In the grave scene that concludes the novel, the withdrawn intellectual Harry takes decisive action by confessing his love for Amy and asking her to marry him. This scene is reminiscent of the conclusion to *Humboldt's Gift*, when the protagonist in the cemetery achieves an epiphany and the work ends with the implication that the protagonist, keenly aware of mortality and the death-in-life of his past existence, will be spiritually reborn.

RAVELSTEIN

Bellow's final novel, *Ravelstein*, is heavily autobiographical and explores the relationship between the narrator Chick (Bellow) and his good friend Abe Ravelstein, a fictional portrait of Allan Bloom, whose book *The Closing of the American Mind* (1987) was a surprise best seller and made the University of Chicago professor wealthy and famous. This novel prompted some controversy when it was published because it revealed that Bloom was gay and probably died of complications from AIDS. Some people felt that Bellow acted unethically by "outing" Bloom and invading his privacy. Bellow seems to have anticipated this objection to the writing of *Ravelstein*, for early in the novel the dying Ravelstein encourages his friend Chick to write a book about him after he dies and be as ruthless as Chick wants in exposing his flaws and weaknesses. It is likely that the iconoclastic Bloom encouraged Bellow to write a candid book about him that would eschew all romanticizing and sentimentality.

The form of the novel owes debts to the genres of biography, memoir, and roman à clef. In addition to the narrator and Ravelstein, other characters in the novel also have real-life counterparts, including Bellow's fifth wife, Janis Freedman, as Rosamund; his Romanian-born fourth spouse, Alexandra Tulcea, as Vela; the conservative thinker Leo Strauss as Davaar; the sociologist Edward Shils as Rakhmiel Kogon; former assistant secretary of state Paul Wolfowitz as Philip Gorman; and political scientist Werner Dannhauser as Ravelstein's close friend Morris Herbst.

Unlike *The Victim* or many of Bellow's other stories, plot is unimportant in this novel; portrayal of character and the exploration of ideas are the primary interests. Bellow is concerned, too, with exploring the interior life of the narrator, who is preoccupied with the problem of nihilism in its various forms and disguises. The narrator wrestles with the problem of how a good person should react to evil in the modern world. Chick seems to regard Ravelstein as his mentor—this dying intellectual comes to embody Jewish humanism that places the highest importance on the worth of human life and the value of the individual; in contrast is the murderous nihilism of the World War II period that resulted in the horrors of the Holocaust. The meandering meditative mind of the narrator repeatedly returns to the anti-Semitism of the twentieth century, which represents the evil that is the opposite of the goodness that Ravelstein embodies.

Ravelstein is a death-haunted book that describes not only the final illness of the narrator's dear friend but also the illness that comes very close to killing the narrator. Like Bellow, who nearly died from an illness similar to the narrator's, the narrator survives to write this portrait of his friend. The book concludes with the narrator's recollection of his and Ravelsteins's discovery of a huge flock of tropical parrots surviving in the midwestern winter. This epiphany suggests that the narrator has finally reconciled himself to the profound loss of his friend and that he can affirm existence in all its inexplicable strangeness and mysterious beauty.

Allan Chavkin

OTHER MAJOR WORKS

SHORT FICTION: *Mosby's Memoirs, and Other Stories*, 1968; *Him with His Foot in His Mouth, and Other Stories*, 1984; *Something to Remember Me By: Three Tales*, 1991; *Collected Stories*, 2001.

PLAYS: *The Wrecker*, pb. 1954; *The Last Analysis*, pr. 1964; *Under the Weather*, pr. 1966 (also known as *The Bellow Plays*; includes *Out from Under*, *A Wen*, and *Orange Soufflé*).

NONFICTION: *To Jerusalem and Back: A Personal Account*, 1976; *Conversations with Saul Bellow*, 1994 (Gloria L. Cronin and Ben Siegel, editors); *It All Adds Up: From the Dim Past to the Uncertain Future*, 1994.

EDITED TEXT: *Great Jewish Short Stories*, 1963.

BIBLIOGRAPHY

Atlas, James. *Bellow: A Biography*. New York: Random House, 2000. Full and accessible biography was written with the cooperation of its subject. Includes bibliography and index.

Bach, Gerhard, ed. *The Critical Response to Saul Bellow*. Westport, Conn.: Greenwood Press, 1995. Substantial collection presents two to five reviews and essays on each of Bellow's novels. Includes an informative editor's introduction, a chronology, and an interview with Bellow.

Bigler, Walter. *Figures of Madness in Saul Bellow's Longer Fiction.* New York: Peter Lang, 1998. Examines the psychological makeup of Bellow's characters. Includes bibliographical references.

Bloom, Harold, ed. *Saul Bellow.* New York: Chelsea House, 1986. Omnibus of reviews and essays on Bellow's work gives a good sense of the early critical responses. Includes commentary by writers such as Robert Penn Warren, Malcolm Bradbury, Tony Tanner, Richard Chase, and Cynthia Ozick.

Cronin, Gloria L. *A Room of His Own: In Search of the Feminine in the Novels of Saul Bellow.* Syracuse, N.Y.: Syracuse University Press, 2001. Approaches Bellow's novels from the perspective of French feminist theory, providing many provocative insights on gender in the works and analyzing Bellow's characters with attention to the nuances of language. Unlike some critics, Cronin avoids a reductionist reading of Bellow's work that sees the novels as the product of a biased male point of view.

Freedman, William. "Hanging for Pleasure and Profit: Truth as Necessary Illusion in Bellow's Fiction." *Papers on Language and Literature* 35 (Winter, 1999): 3-27. Argues that Bellow's realism is a search for truth, not the discovery of it. Discusses how Bellow deals with the question of whether the individual is isolated or a member of a human community. Contends that for Bellow the value of literature is the ceaseless search for truth in a world that promises truth but seldom provides it.

Halldorson, Stephanie S. *The Hero in Contemporary American Fiction: The Works of Saul Bellow and Don DeLillo.* New York: Palgrave Macmillan; 2007. Juxtaposition of the works of two major American writers who are rarely linked results in an insightful examination of the meaning of the hero and the antihero in modern culture.

Kiernan, Robert. *Saul Bellow.* New York: Continuum, 1989. Provides a useful chronology of Bellow's life and production. Traces the writer's development from *Dangling Man* to *More Die of Heartbreak.* Among the best books on Bellow for the general reader.

Leroux, Jean-Francois. "Exhausting Ennui: Bellow, Dostoevsky, and the Literature of Boredom." *College Literature* 35, no. 1 (Winter, 2008): 1-15. Explores the theme of ennui, a major element in Bellow's work, and the influence of the novels of Fyodor Dostoevski on Bellow's outlook.

Miller, Ruth. *Saul Bellow: A Biography of the Imagination.* New York: St. Martin's Press, 1991. Traces Bellow's travels, linking the author's life to his work. Contains useful appendices, a bibliography, a listing of interviews, and a table of contents from *The Noble Savage,* a journal edited by Bellow.

T. CORAGHESSAN BOYLE

Born: Peekskill, New York; December 2, 1948
Also known as: Thomas John Boyle; T. C. Boyle

PRINCIPAL LONG FICTION
Water Music, 1981
Budding Prospects: A Pastoral, 1984
World's End, 1987
East Is East, 1990
The Road to Wellville, 1993
The Tortilla Curtain, 1995
Riven Rock, 1998
A Friend of the Earth, 2000
Drop City, 2003
The Inner Circle, 2004
Talk Talk, 2006

OTHER LITERARY FORMS

In addition to his novels, T. Coraghessan Boyle has published several collections of mostly satirical short stories that generally address the same themes seen in his longer fiction.

ACHIEVEMENTS

T. Coraghessan Boyle's novels have been praised for their originality, style, and comic energy. At a time when his contemporaries seem obsessed with the mundane details of everyday life—presented in a minimalist style—Boyle approaches fiction as an iconoclastic storyteller who embraces and borrows from the entire history of narrative literature, celebrating the profane, often-absurd complexities of human endeavors. His first collection of short stories won the St. Lawrence Award for Short Fiction, *Water Music* received the Aga Khan Award, and the PEN/Faulkner Award for Fiction was given to *World's End*. Boyle also has been a recipient of the PEN short story award. A film adaptation of *The Road to Wellville* by director and screenwriter Alan Parker was released in 1994.

BIOGRAPHY

Born into a lower-middle-class family in Peekskill, New York, in 1948, Thomas John Boyle was a rebellious youth who played drums, sang in a rock-and-roll band, and drove fast cars. He did not get along with his father, a school-bus driver whose alcoholism killed him at age fifty-four in 1972. Boyle's mother, a secretary, was also an alcoholic and died of liver failure. Assuming the name T. Coraghessan Boyle at the State University of New

York at Potsdam, Boyle studied saxophone and clarinet until he realized that he lacked the necessary discipline for music and drifted into creative writing. After college, to avoid military service during the Vietnam War, he taught English for two years at Lakeland High School in Shrub Oak, New York, while increasing his use of drugs, including heroin.

In 1972, Boyle entered the creative-writing program at the University of Iowa, where he studied under Vance Bourjaily, John Cheever, and John Irving. He also studied nineteenth century English literature and received a Ph.D. in 1977, with a short-story collection, later published as *Descent of Man* (1979), serving as his dissertation. He became head of the writing program at the University of Southern California and settled in Woodland Hills, a suburb of Los Angeles, with his wife, Karen Kvashay (whom he met when they were both undergraduates), and their children, Kerrie, Milo, and Spencer. In 1992 the Boyles moved to Montecito, near Santa Barbara, and a 1909 house designed by Frank Lloyd Wright.

Analysis

T. Coraghessan Boyle's novels concern the misconceptions that people of different sexes, races, nationalities, and backgrounds have about one another and the misunderstandings—some violent—that result. The clashes between Britons and Africans in *Water Music*, drug entrepreneurs and Northern California rednecks in *Budding Prospects*, Indians and Dutch settlers in New York in *World's End*, Americans and a half-American Japanese in *East Is East*, privileged white Southern Californians and destitute illegal Mexican immigrants in *The Tortilla Curtain*, environmentalists and timber companies in *A Friend of the Earth*, hippies and straights in *Drop City*, and a deaf woman whose identity has been stolen and law-enforcement authorities in *Talk Talk* all allow Boyle to satirize the prejudices, eccentricities, and excesses of several cultures as well as groups within those cultures. Boyle's ironic fiction is populated by a multitude of diverse characters, all convinced that theirs is the only possible way of perceiving and dealing with a complex, changing, often-hostile world. Boyle alternates the viewpoints of these protagonists to present events and issues from all possible sides and increase the irony of the situations. He writes both in a straightforward, economical style and in more ornate prose resembling that of such popular writers as John Barth and Thomas Pynchon. Far from being didactic, Boyle's serious fiction entertains through masterful storytelling and through the author's control of his vivid style.

WATER MUSIC

Water Music alternates between the stories of Scottish explorer Mungo Park and London criminal Ned Rise until their destinies converge in Africa. Park (1771-1806), the first white man to see the Niger River, wrote a best-selling account of his adventures, *Travels in the Interior Districts of Africa* (1799), led a larger expedition into the interior of Africa, and drowned in the rapids of the Niger during an attack by natives. Boyle uses the fictionalized Park and the lowborn Rise to contrast the levels of English society and attitudes toward the British Empire.

Park, a public hero, is less than heroic as imagined by Boyle. He thinks he has had unique experiences because he is unable to recognize the humanity of the Africans he encounters. He selfishly ignores Ailie, his long-suffering fiancé and later devoted wife, thinking nothing of leaving her behind for years while he strives for glory. Park is less concerned with any benefits to humankind resulting from his expeditions than with mere adventure and fame. This need leads him to distort and romanticize his experiences in his writings. The irony of these exploits is that Park would be totally lost without the assistance of such nonwhites as Johnson, born Katunga Oyo. Sold into slavery in America, Johnson learns to read, wins his freedom, becomes a highly respected valet in London, and translates Henry Fielding's *Amelia* (1751) into Mandingo before returning to Africa. His earthy yet sophisticated realism contrasts strongly with Park's muddled idealism. Park's moral blindness suggests some of the causes of the collapse of the Empire.

Ned Rise, on the other hand, is a victim in the tradition of the picaros created by Fielding, Daniel Defoe, and Charles Dickens. (Dickens's mixture of colorful characterizations, humor, and moral outrage, as well as his use of odd names, seems to be a major influence on Boyle.) Rise is stolen from his mother at birth and forced to become a beggar when old enough. He has his right hand mutilated by a cleaver, is nearly drowned, is robbed, is wrongfully imprisoned and hanged—coming back to life as he is about to be dissected— loses his true love, Fanny Brunch, is imprisoned again, and is shipped to Africa to become part of Park's fatal expedition. Park's Britain represents culture and privilege; Ned's stands for the poverty and depravity at the extreme other end of the social scale. The ironically named Rise learns to survive, however.

In the tradition of such classics of the American picaresque novel as John Barth's *The Sot-Weed Factor* (1960) and Thomas Berger's *Little Big Man* (1964), *Water Music* is an enormously entertaining black comedy, a deliberately anachronistic, self-conscious narrative that frequently calls attention to its form and style. Boyle's delight in being a literary show-off, a tendency he has subdued as his career has progressed, led some of the novel's reviewers to dismiss it as a stunt, but *Water Music* quickly developed a cult following and has come to be seen as a clear announcement of the debut of an original, irreverent talent.

BUDDING PROSPECTS

Boyle presents another ill-conceived adventure, though on a much smaller scale, in *Budding Prospects: A Pastoral*. Its thirty-one-year-old protagonist, Felix Nasmyth, is a chronic failure given another shot at success by the mysterious Vogelsang, a Vietnam War veteran and sociopath. With the assistance of Boyd Dowst, holder of a master's degree in botany from Yale University, Felix is to grow marijuana in rural Northern California. Vogelsang promises the desperate Felix that he will earn half a million dollars from the enterprise.

Felix and his inept friends Phil and Gesh experience culture shock in isolated Willits, a town whose aggressively antagonistic citizens consider themselves morally superior to the rest of the decadent world. Obstacles to raising a productive marijuana crop include rain, fire, a hungry bear, a 320-pound alumnus of the state mental hospital's violent ward, and John Jerpbak, a menacing policeman who, like everyone in Willits, knows what Felix is doing. The comedy of *Budding Prospects* results from the dogged perseverance of Felix and friends in this doomed endeavor.

Beside his usual theme of individuals out of their element in a strange environment, Boyle offers a satire of the American free-enterprise system. As he interprets it, the system is motivated primarily by greed, with success coming less through intelligence or hard work than through luck. The dubious morality of Felix's project only adds to the irony. He and his friends want to get rich quickly and are honest only in admitting that they care about nothing but money. That they work harder to fail in an illegal business than they would to earn money honestly is yet another irony in a highly ironic tale. Felix's unreliable narration as he constantly compares himself to the pioneers who settled America adds comic hyperbole. Such humor keeps Boyle's examination of the materialistic side of the American Dream from being preachy.

WORLD'S END

Boyle returned to a larger canvas with *World's End*, his most ambitious and least comic novel, a consideration of America's self-destructive impulse. The Van Brunts, Dutch settlers in what is now northern Westchester County, New York, in the late seventeenth century, experience conflicts with a hostile nature and the voracious Van Warts, the patroons who own the land they farm. The lives of the Van Brunts become intertwined with those of the Kitchawanks, their Indian neighbors. The greedy machinations of the Van Warts lead to misery for the settlers and Indians and death for several of them.

Boyle alternates chapters about these characters with chapters dealing with their twentieth century descendants, including Jeremy Mohonk, the last of the Kitchawanks, whose efforts to regain his birthright (stolen by the Van Warts) earn for him seventeen years in prison. Truman Van Brunt betrays his friends and relatives to save himself, just as one of the original Van Brunts had done. The protagonist of the twentieth century chapters is Walter Van Brunt, reared by communists after Truman runs away and his mother dies. In the late 1960's, Walter is torn between the countercultural life led by his friends and the wealth and social position of the Van Warts. After losing his wife when she finds him in bed with Mardi Van Wart and losing both his feet in separate motorcycle accidents, Walter tracks down his lost father in Barrow, Alaska, to discover that Truman has spent years researching his family's history to justify his actions. Walter returns home thoroughly disillusioned, and Jeremy Mohonk gains revenge against his enemies by impregnating the wife of the current Van Wart, ironically allowing the despised line to continue.

In *World's End*, Boyle shows how people of different races, sexes, and social and economic backgrounds exploit, betray, and fail one another. The characters either are desperate to control their destinies or consider themselves the victims of fates they are incapable of overcoming. Almost everyone is self-deluding, from the right-wing fanatic Dipe Van Wart, in his pathetic attempts to resist change, to Walter, who sees himself as an alienated, existential antihero in the tradition of Meursault in Albert Camus's *L'Étranger* (1942; *The Stranger*, 1946). Walter thinks that his life will fall into place if he can understand his father, but finding Truman leads only to confusion.

As Boyle rifles English literary traditions as part of his satire in *Water Music*, in *World's End* he draws on the mythical views of America espoused by such writers as Washington Irving, James Fenimore Cooper, Nathaniel Hawthorne, Herman Melville, and William Faulkner. From the destruction of the virgin wilderness to the exploitation of the Indian to the curses inflicted on several generations of characters to fatal obsession with the inexplicable, the novel is virtually a catalog of traditional American literary themes.

World's End represents a new maturity in Boyle as an artist. In this novel he eschews the too-easy irony and too-obvious satire that occasionally weaken his earlier fiction, while he confirms his skill at storytelling. Though *World's End* is a sprawling novel with more than one hundred characters, Boyle exerts masterful control over his complicated, overlapping plots, expecting his readers to share his joy in the manipulation of so many coincidences, parallels, and ironies.

EAST IS EAST

The inability of people of different backgrounds to understand one another is even more at the center of *East Is East* than it is in Boyle's other novels. Hiro Tanaka, a twenty-year-old cook on a Japanese ship, jumps overboard off the coast of Georgia. Hiro, another Boyle orphan, has never known his father, an American rock musician who loved and left Hiro's mother, an eventual suicide. Ostracized by Japanese society for being half American, Hiro longs to lose himself in the great melting pot but unfortunately washes ashore on isolated Tupelo Island, site of Thanatopsis House, an artists' colony.

After a series of confused encounters with the natives, Hiro finds refuge in the cottage of Ruth Dershowitz. A mediocre writer from California, Ruth is at Thanatopsis thanks to her being the lover of Saxby Lights, son of Septima Lights, the colony's founder. Ruth pities the hungry, frightened fugitive from immigration authorities but also longs to incorporate Hiro into a short story with which she is having difficulty. Saxby finds out about Hiro, who is imprisoned, escapes to the Okefenokee Swamp, and is arrested again when near death.

Both the white and the black residents of Tupelo Island are frightened by their Japanese visitor, who is equally bewildered by them. Detlef Abercorn, the immigration official sent to find Hiro, is from Los Angeles and feels totally alienated in the South. An albino, he, like Hiro, has never truly fit in anywhere. Abercorn is assisted by Lewis Turco, a veteran of covert operations in Southeast Asia, who prides himself on being in control in any environment, but he is so paranoid that he creates nothing but chaos. No one in *East Is East* understands or trusts anyone else. The writers, painters, sculptors, and composers at Thanatopsis, who should be able to transcend the cultural differences that handicap the others, are instead so self-absorbed and crippled by petty jealousies that they are totally ineffective as human beings.

Hiro is another Boyle innocent destroyed by his inability to deal with the world's complexities and hostilities and by his own foolishness. Hiro has a system of beliefs—based on Japanese writer Yukio Mishima's theory of the samurai—to help guide him, but Mishima's teachings prove tragicomically ineffective in the Georgia swamps. Hiro trusts Ruth, to a degree, because he has no one else, and although she genuinely wants to help, her needs must come first. Ruth, the most fully developed female character in Boyle's early novels, ironically finds success through being caught harboring an illegal immigrant, for she then lands a book contract to tell her story. In this novel, the unscrupulousness of supposedly sensitive artists is as much the target of Boyle's satirical ire as are cultural differences.

THE ROAD TO WELLVILLE

Similar to each other in scheme and scope, *The Road to Wellville* and *Riven Rock* elaborate the wry appraisal of human nature and American values found in *Budding Prospects* and *East Is East* in period tales whose vivid historical tableaux call to mind Boyle's achievement in *Water Music* and *World's End*. *The Road to Wellville* is a farcical examination of the career of Dr. John Harvey Kellogg, inventor of cornflakes and other "gastrically correct" natural foods. A devout vegetarian and zealous promoter of physical culture, Kellogg opens his Battle Creek Sanitarium to men and women at the beginning of the twentieth century, hoping to win them over to his vision of a healthier lifestyle through carefully restricted diets, vigorous exercise regimens, and crackpot medical interventions that include yogurt enemas and sinusoidal baths.

Kellogg's "Temple of Health," as some deem it, is a magnet for celebrities, socialites, eccentrics, and connivers who represent a cross section of Boyle's America. Among them is Eleanor Lightbody, an independent woman and self-proclaimed "Battle Freak" whose sense of liberation is tied to her willing embrace of Kellogg's instruction. Intelligent and principled, Eleanor is blind to the absurdity of Kellogg's methods and to the misery they cause her sickly husband, Will, who suffers the increasingly dangerous indignities of rehabilitation at the sanitarium out of love for his wife. Boyle interweaves the adventures of the Lightbodys with those of Charlie Ossining, a likable scalawag who has squandered the money given him by a patron to establish a competing health-food company in Battle Creek. Ossining's inept efforts to duplicate Kellogg's products through cheap and eventually devious means offer a comic reflection on the underside of entrepreneurialism and the free-enterprise system.

The most interesting character is George Kellogg, one of Dr. Kellogg's numerous adopted children and a symbol of the Kellogg method's failure. George spends most of the novel dissipated and disorderly, deliberately embarrassing his father to extort money from him. He embodies the tendency toward entropy that undermines the best-laid plans in all of Boyle's novels and the irrepressible primitive appetites that get the better of even the most sophisticated characters.

RIVEN ROCK

Boyle develops these character types and traits further in *Riven Rock*. Set at approximately the same time as *The Road to Wellville*, *Riven Rock* portrays another American captain of industry whose personal shortcomings reflect an inherent flaw in the human condition. Stanley McCormick, heir to the McCormick Reaper fortune, is afflicted with an apparently hereditary schizophrenia that manifests as sexual psychopathy. He spends most of the novel locked away at Riven Rock, a family retreat in Santa Barbara, deprived of the company of women—his wife included—because a mere glimpse of a woman provokes him into profane and lewd attacks. In flashbacks, Boyle portrays Stanley as a naïve and sensitive young man who has perhaps been driven mad by the pressure of family responsibilities, and almost certainly by the insensitivity of the women in his life, including his domineering mother and his crusading wife.

As in his other panoramic novels, Boyle refracts the central conflicts and issues through the experiences of a number of characters. Chief among these is Stanley's wife, Katherine, a caring but ambitious woman who bears a striking resemblance in her attitudes to Eleanor Lightbody of *The Road to Wellville*. Educated and fiercely independent, Katherine is dedicated to Stanley's rehabilitation partly out of affection, but also as part of her selfish quest to have a child and know the fulfilled expression of her privilege and will. Edward O'Kane, Stanley's nurse and caretaker, complements Katherine. Sexually profligate and perpetually hostage to his lusts, he impregnates several women over the course of the novel, which leads to repeated comic complications with their families and his employer. In their own ways, Katherine and O'Kane embody the same appetites that govern Stanley. Boyle emphasizes this point through the efforts of Stanley's doctors to cure him by studying the insatiable sex drives of monkeys brought to the secluded estate. *Riven Rock* is possibly Boyle's most direct attempt to present the competing interests and compelling drives behind a culture and citizens as an expression of Darwinian biological imperatives.

The anger in Boyle's novels is tempered by the comedy. Even a relatively somber work such as *World's End* has moments of sublime silliness, as Dipe Van Wart fights middle-age depression by eating dirt from beneath his ancestral home—a fitting comic metaphor for his family's neuroticism and mindless consumption of the land. Boyle's fiction is also notable for the diversity of his style, which changes not only from novel to novel but also from chapter to chapter. Boyle understands well how to play on the natural rhythms of convoluted sentences and when to resort to the subtler joys of simpler ones, has a vocabulary rivaling Vladimir Nabokov's, and delights in parody. *East Is East* offers the mock Faulkner appropriate to a comic novel set in the South, but it avoids the overkill occasionally seen in Boyle's short stories and earlier novels. *The Road to Wellville* and *Riven Rock* are kaleidoscopic narratives in the style of Charles Dickens and William Makepeace Thackeray; their broad historical context accommodates their sweeping social satire. Most important is Boyle's ability to create believable, usually sympathetic, characters caught in absurd quests for truths they are incapable of understanding.

A Friend of the Earth

A Friend of the Earth is both a satire of environmentalism and an attack on those who stand by while the planet is being decimated. Boyle tells parallel stories about Ty Tierwater and Andrea, his second wife. In the 1989-1997 chapters, Ty, owner of a shopping center established by his late father, is converted to saving nature from the excesses of human greed by the charismatic Andrea. In 2025-2026, all their work has been wasted, with the United States experiencing extreme weather conditions, especially blazing heat and endless rain. Forests are barren and most animal species extinct. After many years apart, Andrea is reunited with her seventy-five-year-old husband, who cares for a menagerie of exotic animals rescued by legendary rock star Maclovio Pulchris on his Northern California estate. The twentieth century chapters explain how Ty, Andrea, and the earth came to be the way they are.

In 1989, Sierra, Ty's teenage daughter from his first marriage, has an epiphany while taking part in a protest against a logging operation's destruction of the Oregon forests. Her commitment to the cause leads her to spend three years squatting in a redwood. Meanwhile, Ty goes to prison, first for kidnapping Sierra after she is taken from him by the authorities and later for setting fire to logging equipment. His increasing fanaticism places a huge strain on his relationship with Andrea.

Boyle is that rare writer who cares passionately about social and political issues yet is never didactic. Rather than lecturing about environmental causes, he makes the reader care about his fully developed, deeply flawed characters. As his career has developed, Boyle has become increasingly skilled at descriptive writing, and the passages in *A Friend of the Earth* about the effects of the high temperatures and resulting sandstorms, the muddy terrain left by the rains, the tree Sierra sees as almost human, and the confusion of the soon-to-be-extinct animals underscore what the characters say about their cause.

Boyle's vivid vision of the near future is pessimistic. Eating and drinking options are limited, with catfish the only available fish species and sake the only alcoholic drink. Outbreaks of a super flu are a constant threat. Baby boomers such as Ty and Andrea are left without Social Security and carry out tenuous existences. Only the ultrarich can live what once passed for normal lives. Environmental organizations such as Earth First!, which Andrea has helped guide, have failed miserably. Solace comes only through family, friendship, and love.

DROP CITY

Boyle returns to the milieu of *Budding Prospects* with *Drop City*. Paulette Starr, who calls herself Star, and her friend Ronnie Sommers, who prefers Pan, travel west from New York in 1970 to join the Drop City commune near Sonoma, California. Star and Ronnie feel at home in the ostensibly utopian community created by Norm Sender, though they find themselves growing apart. Ronnie wants to experience everything possible, while the less adventurous Star begins a relationship with the more stable Marco Connell.

Boyle alternates between the lives of the characters in Drop City and the lives of a completely different set of outsiders in Boynton, Alaska. Living alone in a remote wilderness, Cecil "Sess" Harder, a fur trapper, is the winner when Anchorage native Pamela McCoon comes to Boynton to audition three potential suitors. Sess has a live-and-let-live attitude toward everything but bush pilot Joe Bosky, who once stole Sess's girlfriend, shot his sled dogs, and makes obscene advances to Pamela. When Drop City begins collapsing into anarchy, Norm decides to move the group to Alaska, where the two strands of the story merge. While many in Boynton are horrified by the hippies, Sess and Pamela are more sympathetic, becoming friends with Star and Marco, while Ronnie gravitates to Joe, with dire results.

As Boyle contrasts the two communities, it becomes increasingly clear that he favors Sess's more workmanlike existence. The self-obsessed Drop City residents are too casual and undisciplined to survive the harsh Alaskan winter. They would rather smoke marijuana, have sex, and listen to music than try to ensure there is enough food for everyone. When Norm leaves, the leaderless community becomes even more chaotic. Sess and Pamela, on the other hand, know how to adjust to the demands of their lonely isolation. They have chosen to exist apart from others, knowing what sacrifices and skills are needed. Star and Marco can prosper only by following their examples.

A gentler satire than usual for Boyle, *Drop City* is another of his examinations of the American quest for individual freedom and the pitfalls awaiting those who embark on such an adventure. The communal scenes recall *The Road to Wellville*, while the scenes set in the Alaskan wild resemble *A Friend of the Earth*. Although nature (rivers, mountains, wild animals) has been a consistent concern of Boyle's from the beginning of his career, none of his novels has captured nature's haunting beauty and primitive danger as well as *Drop City*.

Michael Adams
Updated by Stefan Dziemianowicz

OTHER MAJOR WORKS

SHORT FICTION: *Descent of Man*, 1979; *Greasy Lake, and Other Stories*, 1985; *If the River Was Whiskey*, 1989; *Without a Hero*, 1994; *T. C. Boyle Stories: The Collected Stories of T. Coraghessan Boyle*, 1998; *After the Plague: Stories*, 2001; *Tooth and Claw*, 2005.

EDITED TEXT: *Doubletakes: Pairs of Contemporary Short Stories*, 2003.

Bibliography

Boyle, T. Coraghessan. "According to Boyle." Interview by Louisa Ermelino. *Publishers Weekly*, June 19, 2006. Boyle discusses the inspiration and research for *Talk Talk* and his love for language.

_____. "Rolling Boyle." Interview by Tad Friend. *The New York Times Magazine*, December 9, 1990. Boyle portrays himself as a missionary for literature who promotes himself to ensure that his work is read. He comments on the new maturity and reality in some of his fiction but admits that the absurd and bizarre are more natural for him.

_____. "T. C. Boyle: Errant Punk." Interview by Gary Percesepe. *Mississippi Review* 35 (Fall, 2007): 21-43. Boyle talks about the themes of his novels and about being a creative-writing student and teacher.

Hicks, Heather. "On Whiteness in T. Coraghessan Boyle's *The Tortilla Curtain*." *Critique* 45 (Fall, 2003): 43-64. Discusses Boyle's treatment of ethnic identity and compares it with that of William Faulkner in *Light in August* (1932).

Hume, Kathryn. *American Dream, American Nightmare: Fiction Since 1960*. Urbana: University of Illinois Press, 2000. Boyle's work is discussed in an extensive study of the tension between utopian and dystopian tendencies in late twentieth century American fiction.

Kammen, Michael. "T. Coraghessan Boyle and *World's End*." In *Novel History: Historians and Novelists Confront American's Past (and Each Other)*, edited by Mark C. Carnes. New York: Simon & Schuster, 2001. Discusses Boyle's fictional use of history and historical characters, particularly in *World's End*. Followed by a response from Boyle.

Schäfer-Wünsche, Elisabeth. "Borders and Catastrophes: T. C. Boyle's California Ecology." In *Space in America: Theory, History, Culture*, edited by Klaus Benesch and Kerstin Schmidt. Atlanta: Rodopi, 2005. Compares Boyle's treatments of environmental issues in *The Tortilla Curtain* and *A Friend of the Earth*.

Schenker, Daniel. "A Samurai in the South: Cross-Cultural Disaster in T. Coraghessan Boyle's *East Is East*." *Southern Quarterly* 34 (Fall, 1995): 70-80. Presents an in-depth analysis of the cultural clashes and intransigence that inform the tragicomic vision of Boyle's novel.

Vaid, Krishna Baldev. "Franz Kafka Writes to T. Coraghessan Boyle." *Michigan Quarterly Review* 35 (Summer, 1996): 533-549. Using the form of a letter from Franz Kafka, Vaid discusses Boyle's work, investigates the similarity between the two writers, and argues that the reader could grow as tired of Kafka's logic as of Boyle's broad panoramas.

MIGUEL DE CERVANTES

Born: Alcalá de Henares, Spain; September 29, 1547
Died: Madrid, Spain; April 23, 1616
Also known as: Miguel de Cervantes Saavedra

PRINCIPAL LONG FICTION

La Galatea, 1585 (*Galatea: A Pastoral Romance*, 1833)
El ingenioso hidalgo don Quixote de la Mancha, 1605, 1615 (*The History of the Valorous and Wittie Knight-Errant, Don Quixote of the Mancha*, 1612-1620; better known as *Don Quixote de la Mancha*)
Novelas ejemplares, 1613 (*Exemplary Novels*, 1846)
Los trabajos de Persiles y Sigismunda, 1617 (*The Travels of Persiles and Sigismunda: A Northern History*, 1619)

OTHER LITERARY FORMS

Miguel de Cervantes (sur-VAHN-teez) never sought acclaim as a writer of fiction. He longed for the more popular success and financial rewards offered by the stage and hoped to gain a more prestigious literary reputation as a great poet, as evidenced by the time and dedication he committed to his long derivative poem *Viaje del Parnaso* (1614; *The Voyage to Parnassus*, 1870). These ambitions were unrealized. In fact, he admits in the poem of 1614 that heaven never blessed him with the poetic gift. His efforts in the theater did not bring him success at the time but did produce some significant work. Cervantes contributed to the Spanish theater not only by writing plays but also by stirring critical debate. In chapter 48 of the first part of *Don Quixote de la Mancha*, Cervantes attacked the Spanish stage and certain kinds of popular plays. This attack prompted a response from Lope de Vega Carpio, *Arte nuevo de hacer comedias en este tiempo* (1609; *The New Art of Writing Plays*, 1914) that was the central piece of dramatic theorizing of the Golden Age of Spanish theater. Cervantes also wrote one epic tragedy, *El cerco de Numancia* (wr. 1585, pb. 1784; *The Siege of Numantia*, 1870), a play praised in later centuries by Johann Wolfgang von Goethe, Percy Bysshe Shelley, Friedrich Schlegel, and Arthur Schopenhauer, and he published a collection of eight comedies and eight interludes in 1615. These works were never performed in the author's lifetime. The eight interludes, one-act farces that would have been performed as intermission pieces, are original, dynamic, and highly theatrical. They rank with the finest work in the one-act form by Anton Chekhov, August Strindberg, and Tennessee Williams.

ACHIEVEMENTS

Cervantes belongs to that elite group of supreme literary geniuses that includes Homer, Vergil, Dante, Geoffrey Chaucer, and William Shakespeare. The first to establish his

Miguel de Cervantes
(Library of Congress)

greatness as a writer through the medium of prose fiction, Cervantes is acknowledged as an influential innovator who nurtured the short-story form and, more important, shaped the novel, sending it into the modern world. The list of succeeding masters of the novel who paid homage to Cervantes either through direct praise or imitation is awesome—among them Daniel Defoe, Tobias Smollett, Henry Fielding, Laurence Sterne, Jonathan Swift, Sir Walter Scott, Charles Dickens, Voltaire, Stendhal, Honoré de Balzac, Gustave Flaubert, Victor Hugo, Goethe, Thomas Mann, Ivan Turgenev, Nikolai Gogol, Fyodor Dostoevski, Washington Irving, Herman Melville, Mark Twain, William Faulkner, and Saul Bellow; all of these authors recognized an indebtedness to the Spanish writer who, at the end of a lifetime of failure and disappointment, created the unlikely Knight of La Mancha and sent him out into the Spanish landscape with his equally unlikely squire, Sancho Panza. *Don Quixote de la Mancha* remains Cervantes' greatest gift to the world of literature.

If Cervantes became a giant in world literature by creating his mad knight, he also gave Spanish literature its greatest work. Cervantes' life and career spanned the glory days of Spain's eminence as a great empire as well as the beginning of its fall from world power.

Cervantes re-created this Spain he knew so well in his great work. His love of his native Spain is evident in the generosity of detail with which he created the backdrop of his novel—the inns, the food, the costumes, the dusty roads, the mountains, the rogues, the nobility, the arguments, the laughter. The superb realization of his world set a standard that has guided novelists for centuries; Cervantes' rendering of his native Spain has by extension given us the England of Dickens, the Paris of Balzac, the Russia of Dostoevski.

Cervantes' imaginative depiction of his native land also has influenced subsequent Spanish literature. Most Spanish writers feel an indebtedness to Cervantes and regard his work with awe. Such modern masters of Spanish literature as José Ortega y Gasset and Miguel de Unamuno have written extensive studies and detailed commentaries on his great novel, treating it with a reverence usually reserved for religious writings. Cervantes, in creating Don Quixote, gave Spain its greatest masterpiece, and his figure has loomed majestically over all subsequent Spanish literature.

Cervantes' contributions to the development of the novel form are considerable. In addition to re-creating the texture of daily life in the Spain of his day, he became an innovator in the form of the novel. *Don Quixote de la Mancha* is a strange kind of prose epic, with its singularly odd hero with his visions of virtue and glory riding into a mundane and common world. From the first, Cervantes saw how the richness of the older epic form might be adapted to the new prose form to create a new vision, grand and common, eloquent and humorous, ideal and real, all at once. Cervantes quickly mastered the ability to elevate the common; the greatest of all later novelists have also mastered this unlikely duality—a large ideal vision that must find expression within the confines of a real world, whether that world be the streets of London, an American whaling vessel, or a Russian prison camp.

Cervantes also freed his characters to exist within a more real world and to behave as more realistic human beings. The Don in all of his madness is still rooted in the Spain of his day, and Sancho Panza is the embodiment of a class as well as an attitude toward life. The characters also relate to one another through recognizable conversation. Cervantes made dialogue an integral part of the novel form, allowing his characters to speak their minds with the same freedom with which they travel the roads of Spain. Such conversations have been a part of most novels ever since.

Finally, and perhaps most important, Cervantes bequeathed to humankind a compelling vision of itself—man as committed idealist combined with man as foolish lunatic. Don Quixote rides out of the pages of the novel with a magnetic presence that has fascinated many subsequent artists. Honoré Daumier, Pablo Picasso, and many other painters have put him on canvas; Richard Strauss has placed him in an orchestral tone poem; Jules-Émile-Frédéric Massenet and Manuel de Falla have rendered him on the opera stage; and Tennessee Williams has brought him into American drama. The fascinating figure of the foolish knight continues to command the attentions of other artists. The Don remains a popular figure, too, appearing on the Broadway musical stage and in television commercials. The novel that Cervantes created is second only to the Bible in the number of different languages into which it has been translated, but the appeal of the title character extends beyond literature into the dream life of humankind.

Biography

In the most interesting of the full-length comedies by Miguel de Cervantes published in 1615, *Pedro de Urdemalas*, the title character dreams ambitiously of becoming all the great personages that a man can become: pope, prince, monarch, emperor, master of the world. After a career that is typical of a picaro or any other adventurous Spanish rogue of the time, Pedro finds his wishes realized when he becomes an actor and enters imaginatively into the ranks of the great. In much the same way, Cervantes' great ambitions in life were never realized; the only satisfaction he found was in a world he himself created.

In one sense, Cervantes' greatest adventure was his own life. Born Miguel de Cervantes Saavedra in a small university city not far from Madrid, he traveled constantly with his family in his early years. His father, an impoverished and impractical man who attempted to earn a living as a surgeon, kept the family moving, from Valladolid to Córdoba, from Seville to Madrid. Cervantes learned the life of the road and the diversity of city life in Spain as a youth. In his twenties, he journeyed to Italy, perhaps fleeing from arrest as a result of a duel; there, he entered the service of Cardinal Aquaviva. In 1569, he enlisted in the Spanish army and went to sea. Cervantes was present at the Battle of Lepanto in 1571, serving under the command of Don John of Austria in the famous victory against the Turks. Cervantes rose from his sickbed to join in the battle and was twice wounded, one wound leaving his left hand permanently incapacitated. With his brother, Rodrigo, he embarked for Spain in 1575, but their ship was seized by Turkish pirates, and Cervantes spent five years in captivity as a slave.

Ransomed by monks, Cervantes returned to Spain, but not to glory and acclaim. With his military career at an end because of his paralyzed hand, Cervantes fell into poverty and moved from one failure to another, including an apparently unhappy marriage in 1584. Moving about Spain as in his youth, he again gained an education in the character and behavior of the Spanish lower classes, an education that continued when he was imprisoned twice in Seville, once in 1597 and again in 1602, both times, it is assumed, the result of financial difficulties. Despite a life of bad luck, missed opportunities, and little reward for his talent, Cervantes did achieve a popular success when the first part of *Don Quixote de la Mancha* was published in 1605, although his finances saw only minor improvement. In 1615, the second part of the novel appeared, to challenge the "false" sequels being produced by other writers seeking to capitalize on the book's success. Cervantes died in Madrid in 1616, at peace, having received the Sacraments.

Analysis: Don Quixote de la Mancha

Many critics maintain that the impulse that prompted Miguel de Cervantes to begin his great novel was a satiric one: He desired to satirize chivalric romances. As the elderly

Alonso Quixano the Good (if that is his name) pores over the pages of these books in his study, his "brain dries up" and he imagines himself to be the champion who will take up the vanished cause of knight-errantry and wander the world righting wrongs, helping the helpless, defending the cause of justice, all for the greater glory of his lady Dulcinea del Toboso and his God.

As he leaves his village before dawn, clad in rusty armor and riding his broken-down nag, the mad knight becomes Don Quixote de la Mancha. His first foray is brief, and he is brought back home by friends from his native village. Despite the best efforts of his friends and relations, the mad old man embarks on a second journey, this time accompanied by a peasant from his village, Sancho Panza, who becomes the knight's squire. The Don insists on finding adventure everywhere, mistaking windmills for giants, flocks of sheep for attacking armies, puppet shows for real life. His squire provides a voice of down-to-earth reason, but Quixote always insists that vile enchanters have transformed the combatants to embarrass and humiliate him. Don Quixote insists on his vision of the ideal in the face of the cold facts of the world; Sancho Panza maintains his proverbial peasant wisdom in the face of his master's madness.

In their travels and adventures, they encounter life on the roads of Spain. Sometimes they are treated with respect—for example, by "the gentleman in green" who invites them to his home and listens to Quixote with genuine interest—but more often they are ridiculed, as when the Duke and Duchess bring the knight and squire to their estate only for the purpose of mocking them. Finally, a young scholar from Quixote's native village, Sampson Carrasco, defeats the old knight in battle and forces him to return to his home, where he dies peacefully, having renounced his mad visions and lunatic behavior.

THEMES

While it is necessary to acknowledge the satiric intent of Cervantes' novel, the rich fictional world of *Don Quixote de la Mancha* utterly transcends its local occasion. On the most personal level, the novel can be viewed as one of the most intimate evaluations of a life ever penned by a great author. When Don Quixote decides to take up the cause of knight-errantry, he opens himself to a life of ridicule and defeat, a life that resembles Cervantes' own life, with its endless reversals of fortune, humiliations, and hopeless struggles. Out of this life of failure and disappointment Cervantes created the "mad knight," but he also added the curious human nobility and the refusal to succumb to despair in the face of defeat that turns Quixote into something more than a comic character or a ridiculous figure to be mocked. Although there are almost no points in the novel where actual incidents from Cervantes' life appear directly or even transformed into fictional disguise, the tone and the spirit, the succession of catastrophes with only occasional moments of slight glory, and the resilience of human nature mark the novel as the most personal work of the author, the one where his singularly difficult life and his profoundly complex emotional responses to that life found form and structure.

If the novel is the record of Cervantes' life, the fiction also records a moment in Spanish national history when fortunes were shifting and tides turning. At the time of Cervantes' birth, Spain's might and glory were at their peak. The wealth from conquests of Mexico and Peru returned to Spain, commerce boomed, and artists recorded the sense of national pride with magnificent energy and power. By the time *Don Quixote de la Mancha* was published, the Spanish Empire was beginning its decline. A series of military disasters, including the defeat of the Spanish Armada by the English and the revolt of Flanders, had shaken the once mighty nation. In the figure of Don Quixote, the greatest of a richly remembered past combines with the hard facts of age, weakness, and declining power. The character embodies a moment of Spanish history and the Spanish people's own sense of vanishing glory in the face of irreversible decline.

Don Quixote de la Mancha also stands as the greatest literary embodiment of the Counter-Reformation. Throughout Europe, the Reformation was moving with the speed of new ideas, changing the religious landscape of country after country. Spain stood proud as a Catholic nation, resisting any changes. Standing alone against the flood of reform sweeping Europe displayed a kind of willed madness, but the nobility and determination of Quixote to fight for his beliefs, no matter what the rest of the world maintained, reflects the strength of the Spanish will at this time. Cervantes was a devout and loyal believer, a supporter of the Church, and Don Quixote may be the greatest fictional Catholic hero, the battered knight of the Counter-Reformation.

The book also represents fictionally the various sides of the Spanish spirit and the Spanish temper. In the divisions and contradictions found between the Knight of the Sad Countenance and his unlikely squire, Sancho Panza, Cervantes paints the two faces of the Spanish soul: The Don is idealistic, sprightly, energetic, and cheerful, even in the face of overwhelming odds, but he is also overbearing, domineering Sancho, who is earthy, servile, and slothful. The two characters seem unlikely companions and yet they form a whole, the one somehow incomplete without the other and linked throughout the book through their dialogues and debates. In drawing master and servant, Cervantes presents the opposing truths of the spirit of his native land.

CHARACTERIZATION

The book can also be seen as a great moment in the development of fiction, the moment when the fictional character was freed into the real world of choice and change. When the gentleman of La Mancha took it into his head to become a knight-errant and travel through the world redressing wrongs and winning eternal glory, the face of fiction permanently changed. Character in fiction became dynamic, unpredictable, and spontaneous. Until that time, character in fiction had existed in service of the story, but now the reality of change and psychological energy and freedom of the will became a permanent hallmark of fiction, as it already was of drama and narrative poetry. The title character's addled wits made the new freedom all the more impressive. The determination of Don Quixote, the impact of his vision on the world, and the world's hard reality as it impinges on the Don make for shifting balances and constant alterations in fortune that are psychologically believable. The shifting balance of friendship, devotion, and perception between the knight and his squire underlines this freedom, as does the power of other characters in the book to affect Don Quixote's fortunes directly: the niece, the housekeeper, the priest, the barber, Sampson Carrasco, the Duke, and the Duchess. There is a fabric of interaction throughout the novel, and characters in the novel change as they encounter new adventures, new people, and new ideas.

One way Cervantes chronicles this interaction is in dialogue. Dialogue had not played a significant or defining role in fiction before *Don Quixote de la Mancha*. As knight and squire ride across the countryside and engage in conversation, dialogue becomes the expression of character, idea, and reality. In the famous episode with windmills early in the first part of the novel (when Quixote views the windmills on the plain and announces that they are giants that he will wipe from the face of the earth, and Sancho innocently replies, "What giants?"), the dialogue not only carries the comedy but also becomes the battleground on which the contrasting visions of life engage one another—to the delight of the reader. The long exchanges between Don Quixote and Sancho Panza provide priceless humor but also convey two different realities that meet, struggle, and explode in volleys of words. In giving his characters authentic voices that carry ideas, Cervantes brought to fiction a new truth that remains a standard of comparison.

The Narrator

Don Quixote de la Mancha is also as modern as the most experimental of later fiction. Throughout the long novel, Cervantes plays with the nature of the narrator, raising constant difficult questions as to who is telling the story and to what purpose. In the riotously funny opening page of the novel, the reader encounters a narrator not only unreliable but also lacking in the basic facts necessary to tell the story. He chooses not to tell the name of the village where his hero lives, and he is not even sure of his hero's name, yet the narrator protests that the narrative must be entirely truthful.

In chapter 9, as Don Quixote is preparing to do battle with the Basque, the narrative stops; the narrator states that the manuscript from which he is culling this story is mutilated and incomplete. Fortunately, some time later in Toledo, he says, he came upon an old Arabic manuscript by Arab historian Cide Hamete Benengeli that continues the adventures. For the remainder of the novel, the narrator claims to be providing a translation of this manuscript—the manuscript and the second narrator, the Arab historian, both lacking authority and credibility. In the second part of the novel, the narrator and the characters themselves are aware of the first part of the novel as well as of a "false Quixote," a spurious second part written by an untalented Spanish writer named Avallaneda who sought to capitalize on the popularity of the first part of *Don Quixote de la Mancha* by publishing his own sequel. The "false Quixote" is on the narrator's mind, the characters' minds, and somehow on the mind of Cide Hamete Benengeli. These shifting perspectives, the multiple narrative voices, the questionable reliability of the narrators, and the "false" second part are all tricks, narrative sleight of hand as complex as anything found in the works of Faulkner, Vladimir Nabokov, or Jorge Luis Borges. In his *Lectures on Don Quixote* (1983), Nabokov oddly makes no reference to Cervantes' narrative games; perhaps the old Spanish master's shadow still loomed too close to the modern novelist.

None of these approaches to the novel, however, appropriate as they may be, can begin to explain fully the work's enduring popularity or the strange manner in which the knight and his squire have ridden out of the pages of a book into the other artistic realms of orchestral music, opera, ballet, and painting, where other artists have presented their visions of Quixote and Sancho. A current deeper and more abiding than biography, history, national temper, or literary landmark flows through the book and makes it speak to all manner of readers in all ages.

Early in the novel, Cervantes begins to dilute his strong satiric intent. The reader can laugh with delight at the inanity of the mad knight but never with the wicked, unalloyed glee that pure satire evokes. The knight begins to loom over the landscape; his madness brushes sense; his ideals demand defense. The reader finds him- or herself early in the novel taking an attitude equivalent to that of the two young women of easy virtue who see Quixote when he arrives at an inn, which he believes to be a castle, on his first foray. Quixote calls them "two beauteous maidens . . . taking air at the gate of the castle," and they fall into helpless laughter, confronted with such a mad vision of themselves as "maidens." In time, however, because of Quixote's insistence on the truth of his vision, they help him out of his armor and set a table for him. They treat him as a knight, not as a mad old fool; he treats them as ladies, and they behave as ladies. The laughter stops, and, for a pure moment, life transforms itself and human beings transcend themselves.

CONTRADICTIONS

This mingling of real chivalry and transcendent ideals with the absurdity of character and mad action creates the tensions in the book as well as its strange melancholy beauty and haunting poignancy. The book is unlike any other ever written. John Berryman has commented on this split between the upheld ideal and the riotously real, observing that the reader "does not know whether to laugh or cry, and does both." This old man with his dried-up brain, with his squire who has no "salt in his brain pan," with his rusty armor, his pathetic steed, and his lunatic vision that changes windmills into giants and flocks of sheep into attacking armies, this crazy old fool becomes a real knight-errant. The true irony of the book and its history is that Don Quixote actually becomes a model for knighthood. He may be a foolish, improbable knight, but with his squire, horse, and armor he has ridden into the popular imagination of the world not only as a ridiculous figure but also as a champion; he is a real knight whose vision may often cloud, who sees what he wants to see, but he is also one who demonstrates real virtue and courage and rises in his rhetoric and daring action to real heights of greatness.

Perhaps Cervantes left a clue as to the odd shift in his intention. The contradictory titles he assigns to his knight suggest this knowledge. The comic, melancholy strain pervades "Knight of the Sad Countenance" in the first part of the novel, and the heroic strain is seen in the second part when the hero acquires the new sobriquet "Knight of the Lions." The first title comes immediately after his adventure with a corpse and is awarded him by his realistic companion, Sancho. Quixote has attacked a funeral procession, seeking to avenge the dead man. Death, however, cannot be overcome; the attempted attack merely disrupts the funeral, and the valiant knight breaks the leg of an attending churchman. The name "Knight of the Sad Countenance" fits Quixote's stance here and through much of the book. Many of the adventures he undertakes are not only misguided but also unwinnable. Quixote may be Christlike, but he is not Christ, and he cannot conquer Death.

The adventure with the lions earns for him his second title and offers the other side of his journey as a knight. Encountering a cage of lions being taken to the king, Quixote becomes determined to fight them. Against all protest, he takes his stand, and the cage is opened. One of the lions stretches, yawns, looks at Quixote, and lies down. Quixote proclaims a great victory and awards himself the name "Knight of the Lions." A delightfully comic episode, the scene can be viewed in two ways—as a nonadventure that the knight claims as a victory or as a genuine moment of triumph as the knight undertakes an outlandish adventure and proves his genuine bravery while the king of beasts realizes the futility of challenging the unswerving old knight. Quixote, by whichever route, emerges as conqueror. Throughout his journeys, he often does emerge victorious, despite his age, despite his illusions, despite his dried-up brain.

When, at the book's close, he is finally defeated and humiliated by Sampson Carrasco and forced to return to his village, the life goes out of him. The knight Don Quixote is replaced, however, on the deathbed by Alonso Quixano the Good. Don Quixote does not die, for the elderly gentleman regains his wits and becomes a new character. Don Quixote cannot die, for he is the creation of pure imagination. Despite the moving and sober conclusion, the reader cannot help but sense that the death scene being played out does not signify the end of Don Quixote. The knight escapes and remains free. He rides out of the novel, with his loyal companion Sancho at his side, into the golden realm of myth. He becomes the model knight he hoped to be. He stands tall with his spirit, his ideals, his rusty armor, and his broken lance as the embodiment of man's best intentions and impossible folly. As Dostoevski so wisely said, when the Lord calls the Last Judgment, man should take with him this book and point to it, for it reveals all of man's deep and fatal mystery, his glory and his sorrow.

David Allen White

OTHER MAJOR WORKS

PLAYS: *El trato de Argel*, pr. 1585 (*The Commerce of Algiers*, 1870); *Ocho comedias y ocho entremeses nuevos*, 1615 (includes *Pedro de Urdemalas* [*Pedro the Artful Dodger*,

1807], *El juez de los divorcios* [*The Divorce Court Judge*, 1919], *Los habladores* [*Two Chatterboxes*, 1930], *La cueva de Salamanca* [*The Cave of Salamanca*, 1933], *La elección de los alcaldes de Daganzo* [*Choosing a Councilman in Daganzo*, 1948], *La guarda cuidadosa* [*The Hawk-Eyed Sentinel*, 1948], *El retablo de las maravillas* [*The Wonder Show*, 1948], *El rufián viudo llamada Trampagos* [*Trampagos the Pimp Who Lost His Moll*, 1948], *El viejo celoso* [*The Jealous Old Husband*, 1948], and *El vizcaíno fingido* [*The Basque Imposter*, 1948]); *El cerco de Numancia*, pb. 1784 (wr. 1585; *Numantia: A Tragedy*, 1870; also known as *The Siege of Numantia*); *The Interludes of Cervantes*, 1948.

POETRY: *Viaje del Parnaso*, 1614 (*The Voyage to Parnassus*, 1870).

BIBLIOGRAPHY

Bloom, Harold, ed. *Cervantes*. New York: Chelsea House, 1987. Collection of essays addresses topics such as the picaresque, the trickster figure, Cervantes' biography and use of language, and his attitude toward realism and the literary tradition. Includes an informative introduction, a chronology, a bibliography, and an index.

_____. *Cervantes's "Don Quixote."* Philadelphia: Chelsea House, 2001. Collection reprints essays about the novel written by well-known authors and critics, including Thomas Mann, Franz Kafka, W. H. Auden, Vladimir Nabokov, and Mark van Doren. Includes an introduction by Bloom, bibliographical references, and index.

Cascardi, Anthony J., ed. *The Cambridge Companion to Cervantes*. New York: Cambridge University Press, 2002. Collection of essays places Cervantes' life and work within historical and social context and discusses Cervantes' relation to the Italian Renaissance and his influence on other writers. An essay titled "*Don Quixote* and the Invention of the Novel" focuses on the well-known work.

Castillo, David R. *(A)wry Views: Anamorphosis, Cervantes, and the Early Picaresque*. West Lafayette, Ind.: Purdue University Press, 2001. Looks at anamorphosis, or visual perception, in the writings of Cervantes and other works of Spanish picaresque literature from the sixteenth and seventeenth centuries. Includes bibliography and index.

Close, A. J. *Cervantes and the Comic Mind of His Age*. New York: Oxford University Press, 2000. Analyzes ideas about comedy and comedic writing in the Spanish Golden Age and describes how Cervantes' works reflected those ideas. Includes bibliography and index.

Durán, Manuel. *Cervantes*. New York: Twayne, 1974. Provides a sound introduction to the author, with chapters on Cervantes' life and his career as a poet, playwright, short-story writer, and novelist. Includes notes, chronology, and annotated bibliography.

Hart, Thomas R. *Cervantes' Exemplary Fictions: A Study of the "Novelas ejemplares."* Lexington: University Press of Kentucky, 1994. Presents a reading of *Exemplary Novels* within the literary conventions of other popular novels of the seventeenth century, drawing on the literature not only of Spain but also of France, Italy, and England. Argues that novels in that era were meant to elicit readers' surprise or wonder and describes how Cervantes' work attains that goal.

McCrory, Donald P. *No Ordinary Man: The Life and Times of Miguel de Cervantes*. Chester Springs, Pa.: Peter Owen, 2002. Thorough biography is based, in part, on original research and unpublished material. Places Cervantes' life within the context of sixteenth and seventeenth century Spanish history. Includes bibliographical references and index.

Mancing, Howard. *Cervantes' "Don Quixote": A Reference Guide*. Westport, Conn.: Greenwood Press, 2006. An excellent companion for undergraduate students and for general readers. Individual chapters explore themes, criticism, language and style, publishing history, and other topics. Select bibliographies make this an important resource.

Nabokov, Vladimir. *Lectures on "Don Quixote."* Edited by Fredson Bowers. New York: Harcourt Brace Jovanovich, 1983. College lectures by a great twentieth century novelist are divided into portraits of Don Quixote and Sancho Panza, the structure of the novel, the use of cruelty and mystification, the treatment of Dulcinea and death, and commentaries on Cervantes' narrative methods. An appendix contains sample passages from romances of chivalry.

Riley, E. C. *Cervantes's Theory of the Novel*. 1962. Reprint. Newark, Del.: Juan de la Cuesta, 1992. Provides a detailed examination of Cervantes' views on questions of literary practice in terms of traditional issues in poetics, such as art and nature, unity, and purpose and function of literature. Includes bibliography and indexes of names and topics.

Weiger, John G. *The Substance of Cervantes*. London: Cambridge University Press, 1985. Provides valuable insights into Cervantes' craft as a writer by exploring questions such as the relationship of art and reality, the functions of authors and readers, the elusive nature of truth, the dynamics of society, and the significance of the individual and of communication between individuals. Augmented by a bibliography and an index.

Williamson, Edwin, ed. *Cervantes and the Modernists: The Question of Influence*. London: Tamesis, 1994. Collection of essays explores the novelist's impact on such twentieth century writers as Marcel Proust, Thomas Mann, Primo Levi, Carlos Fuentes, and Gabriel García Márquez.

DANIEL DEFOE

Born: London, England; 1660
Died: London, England; April 26, 1731
Also known as: Daniel Foe

PRINCIPAL LONG FICTION

The Life and Strange Surprizing Adventures of Robinson Crusoe, of York, Mariner, Written by Himself, 1719 (commonly known as *Robinson Crusoe*)
The Farther Adventures of Robinson Crusoe: Being the Second and Last Part of His Life, 1719
The History of the Life and Adventures of Mr. Duncan Campbell, a Gentleman Who, Tho' Deaf and Dumb, Writes Down Any Stranger's Name at First Sight, with Their Future Contingencies of Fortune, 1720
The Life, Adventures and Pyracies of the Famous Captain Singleton, 1720
Memoirs of a Cavalier: Or, A Military Journal of the Wars in Germany, and the Wars in England, from the Year 1632 to the Year 1648, 1720
Serious Reflections During the Life and Surprising Adventures of Robinson Crusoe with His Vision of the Angelick World, 1720
The Fortunes and Misfortunes of the Famous Moll Flanders, Written from Her Own Memorandums, 1722 (commonly known as *Moll Flanders*)
The History and Remarkable Life of the Truly Honourable Col Jacque, Commonly Call'd Col Jack, 1722 (commonly known as *Colonel Jack*)
A Journal of the Plague Year, 1722 (also known as *The History of the Great Plague in London*)
The Fortunate Mistress, 1724 (also known as *Roxana*)
The Memoirs of an English Officer Who Serv'd in the Dutch War in 1672, to the Peace of Utrecht in 1713, by Capt George Carleton, 1728 (also known as *A True and Genuine History of the Last Two Wars* and *The Memoirs of Cap George Carleton*)

OTHER LITERARY FORMS

Although Daniel Defoe (dih-FOH) is mainly remembered as the author of *The Life and Strange Surprizing Adventures of Robinson Crusoe, of York, Mariner, Written by Himself*, more commonly known as *Robinson Crusoe*, he did not begin to write fiction until he was fifty-nine years old. He spent the earlier part of his writing career primarily in producing essays and political pamphlets and working for strongly partisan newspapers. He also wrote travel books, poetry (usually on political or topical issues), and biographies of rogues and criminals.

Daniel Defoe
(Library of Congress)

Achievements

Daniel Defoe's principal contribution to English literature is in the novel, and he has been called the first English novelist. The extent of his contribution, however, has been debated. A contemporary of Defoe, Charles Gildon, wrote an attack on *Robinson Crusoe*, criticizing, in part, inconsistencies in the narrative. Such problems are not infrequent in Defoe's long and episodic plots. Nevertheless, readers of almost any of Defoe's works find themselves in real and solid worlds, and Defoe's constant enumeration of *things*—such as, in *Moll Flanders*, the layettes for Moll's illegitimate children, the objects she steals, even her escape routes through London—has earned for the author a reputation as a realist and for his style the label "circumstantial realism." To see Defoe as a photographic realist, however, is also to see his limitations, and some of his critics argue that the formlessness of his novels shows his lack of the very shaping power that belongs to great art. Further, even his circumstantial realism is not of the visual sort: Once Moll has named an object, for example, she rarely goes on to describe it in such detail that the reader may visualize it.

In the late twentieth century, Defoe's novels underwent a reassessment, and critics started to see him as more than a mere assembler of objects. Although these critics diverge widely in their interpretation of his techniques, they do agree that Defoe consciously developed themes and used his narratives to shape these themes, all of which center on the conflict between spiritual and earthly values. Instead of viewing Defoe as a plodding literalist, some critics see a keen irony in his work: Moll's actions and her commentary on those actions, they argue, do not always agree. The reader is thus allowed to cultivate a certain ironic detachment about Moll. While few readers would judge Defoe to be a deeply psychological novelist, this double perspective does contribute to a rudimentary analysis of character. Others see a religious vision in his works, one that underwrites an almost allegorical interpretation of his novels: The ending of *Robinson Crusoe*, the killing of the wolves, is seen as Crusoe slaying his earthly passions. While such a reading may seem forced, one should perhaps remember that John Bunyan was a near contemporary of Defoe—he even preached at Morton's Academy at Stoke Newington while Defoe was a student there—and that readers in his time were accustomed to reading allegorically.

Part of the fascination—and achievement—of Defoe may well lie in the tension between realism and allegory that informs his work. Using natural dialogue and a kind of realistic detail, Defoe can yet go beyond these to create events and characters that are, finally, mythic.

Biography

Daniel Defoe was born Daniel Foe in the parish of St. Giles, London, the son of James Foe, a Dissenter and a tallow chandler. (Only after the age of forty did Defoe change his last name, perhaps to seem more aristocratic.) The date of his birth is conjectural: In 1683, he listed his age on his marriage license as twenty-four, but since his sister, Elizabeth, was born in 1659, it is probable that Defoe was born the next year. Not much is known of his early childhood, but his education was certainly important in molding his interests. Being a Dissenter, Defoe was not allowed to attend Oxford or Cambridge; instead, he went to a dissenting academy presided over by the Reverend Charles Morton. While offering a study of the classics, the academy also stressed modern languages, geography, and mathematics, practical subjects neglected at the universities. This interest in the practical seems to have stayed with Defoe all his life: When his library was sold after his death, the advertisements listed "several hundred Curious, Scarce Tracts on . . . Husbandry, Trade, Voyages, Natural History, Mines, Minerals, etc." Defoe's appreciation of the objects and processes by which one is enabled to live in the world is obvious: After making a table and chair, Crusoe reflects that "by stating and squaring everything by reason and by making the most rational judgment of things, every man may be in time master of every mechanic art."

Although his father intended him for the ministry, Defoe became a merchant after leaving school and probably traveled on the Continent as part of his business. In 1684, he married the daughter of another dissenting merchant, and she brought him a considerable dowry. Defoe's fortunes seemed to be rising, but in 1685, he was briefly involved in the duke of Monmouth's rebellion, a Protestant uprising. Although he escaped the king's soldiers, this event illustrates Defoe's willingness to espouse dangerous political causes: Three former schoolmates who joined the rebellion were caught and hanged. While his affairs seemed to prosper during this time, there were disquieting lawsuits—eight between 1688 and 1694, one by his mother-in-law, whom he seems to have swindled—that cast doubt on both Defoe's economic stability and his moral character. In fact, by 1692 he was bankrupt, a victim of losses at sea and his own speculations. Defoe's character is always difficult to label; while the lawsuits show his unsavory side, he did make arrangements after his ruin to repay his creditors, which he seems to have done with surprising thoroughness.

Defoe then began building a brick factory on some land that he owned in Tilbury. This enterprise went well and, with William and Mary on the throne, Defoe could praise the government with a clear conscience. He admired William's religious toleration, foreign policy, and encouragement of English trade. He wrote several pamphlets supporting William's policy of containing Louis XIV's political aspirations, a policy not always popular in England. When William's followers from Holland were harassed by the English, Defoe wrote *The True-Born Englishman: A Satyr* (1701), a long poem arguing that the English are themselves a mixed race who cannot afford to deride other nationalities.

With the accession of Queen Anne of England in 1702, the Dissenters—and Defoe—suffered serious political grievances. Fiercely loyal to the Church of England, Anne looked with disfavor on other religious groups, and bills were introduced to limit the freedom of Dissenters. While both houses of Parliament debated the Occasional Conformity Bill in 1702—a bill that would have effectually prevented Dissenters from holding political office—Defoe published "The Shortest Way with the Dissenters," an ironic pamphlet urging the government to annihilate this group entirely. At first it was taken at face value and applauded by the High Church party, but when its irony was perceived, a warrant was issued for Defoe's arrest, and he went into hiding.

Fearful of imprisonment and the pillory, Defoe sent letters to Daniel Finch, second earl of Nottingham, the secretary of state, trying to negotiate a pardon: He would raise a troop of horses for the government at his own expense; he would volunteer to fight—and possibly die—in the Netherlands. Nottingham was inflexible, however, and when Defoe was found, he was imprisoned in Newgate, the scene of Moll's incarceration. Two months later, he was fined two hundred marks, forced to stand in the pillory three times, imprisoned at the queen's discretion, and forced to provide sureties for his good behavior for the next seven years. This experience helps, perhaps, to explain Defoe's later political views, which seemed to his contemporaries based on expediency rather than conviction: In a letter to a friend, he said that, after Newgate, he would never feel himself maligned if called a coward. When Defoe describes Moll's stay in prison, he knows whereof he speaks.

How long Defoe might have remained in Newgate at the queen's discretion cannot, of course, be known; certainly the government showed no sign of releasing him during the summer or in the fall. He appealed to Robert Harley, a man destined to take Nottingham's place when the latter had been dismissed by the queen. After leisurely negotiations—perhaps to render Defoe more grateful when his pardon finally did come—Harley obtained Defoe's release in November, 1703, the queen even going so far as to send money to Mrs. Defoe and another sum to Defoe to settle his debt.

Harley continued to be influential in Defoe's life; indeed, popular opinion seems to have been that Defoe prostituted himself, abandoning all political ideals for Harley. Still, it is hard to imagine how a forty-three-year-old ruined businessman, with a wife and seven children to support, could begin life over if not with the help of a powerful ally. Defoe's letters to Harley also suggest that Harley sometimes kept him short of funds on purpose, perhaps to make him more compliant. In any case, Defoe's career was definitely the writing of political pamphlets—usually in favor of Harley's policies—and he also edited and wrote most of *A Weekly Review*, which ran from 1704 to 1713. Perhaps Defoe's most significant work for Harley was the establishment of a spy system in England to determine what the national sentiment was for the government. This project—which was Defoe's own idea—began in 1704 when Harley sent Defoe on a preliminary reconnaissance trip through the country. This was the first of several such trips, including one to Edinburgh, Scotland, in 1706 to determine local opinion about the proposed union of the English and Scottish parliaments. On all these trips, Defoe had to assume fictitious identities, and he seems to have relished this subterfuge; it is perhaps significant that Defoe's characters usually are forced to assume many varied disguises in the course of their eventual lives. Even Defoe's tracts and pamphlets bear witness to his fascination with assuming various roles: One critic has estimated that Defoe created eighty-seven personae in these works.

After Harley's political decline and Queen Anne's death, Defoe continued to work for the government, characteristically, in a role requiring deception. Pretending to be a Tory out of favor with the government, he obtained a job on *Mist's Weekly Journal*, one of the most influential Tory papers. In this way, he was able to temper the writing so that the paper's attacks on the government became less virulent. Defoe's shadowy activities are difficult to follow, but it seems that he was also performing the same service to the government on other papers: *Dyer's News-Letter, Dormer's News-Letter,* and *Mercurius Politicus*. Defoe's easy transition from Harley's Tory government to the succeeding Whig regime angered many people, who claimed that he had no principles. Defoe's reply, difficult to counter, was always that he was working for moderation, no matter on which side.

Only toward the end of his life did Defoe begin to write prose fiction: *Robinson Crusoe* and its sequels, *The Life, Adventures and Pyracies of the Famous Captain Singleton, The Fortunes and Misfortunes of the Famous Moll Flanders, Written from Her Own Memorandums* (commonly known as *Moll Flanders*), *A Journal of the Plague Year, The History and Remarkable Life of the Truly Honourable Col Jacque, Commonly Call'd Col Jack,* and *The Fortunate Mistress* (also known as *Roxana*). Even after completing this enormous output, he continued to produce biographies of criminals and imaginary biographies of soldiers and sailors.

To all appearances, Defoe seemed to embark on a comfortable old age; Henry Baker, his son-in-law, reported that Defoe had retired from London to a handsome house in Stoke Newington, where he lived a leisurely life, growing a garden, pursuing his studies, and writing. In 1730, however, Defoe vanished from his home and, in a rather cryptic letter to Baker, wrote about his "Load of insupportable Sorrows," a "wicked, perjur'd, and contemptible Enemy," and the "inhuman dealing of my own son," who reduced his "dying Mother to beg . . . Bread at his Door." The enemy seems to have been Mary Brooke, the wife of one of Defoe's former creditors. Although Defoe appears to have paid Brooke—at least Brooke's executor accepted Defoe's story—Brooke died before destroying his record of the debt, and his wife was determined to collect it. Once again, Defoe was being hounded by a creditor. His reference to his unnatural son is a bit more puzzling but may show that he had transferred most of his money and property to his son to keep it out of Mary Brooke's hands; if so, his son seems to have abused the trust placed in him. Defoe died in April, 1731, while hiding in a lodging house in Ropemaker's Alley.

Although Defoe's colorful life almost calls too much attention to itself—some critics have tried to deduce his exact birth date through events in his characters' lives—it is hard not to see a link between the elements of disguise and trickery in so many of his novels and his own eventful life, spent, in large part, in fabricating identities for himself in his government work. Like his character Moll Flanders, Defoe had personal experience with Newgate, and his biographies of criminals and rogues show a fascination with the inventive powers that allow one to thrive in a treacherous world. In this respect, Defoe and his characters seem to have a great deal in common: They are all survivors in an often hostile environment. This sense of alienation may also have a link with Defoe's religion, a creed that was sometimes tolerated but rarely encouraged by the Crown.

ANALYSIS

Although *A Journal of the Plague Year* is not Daniel Defoe's first work of fiction, it offers an interesting perspective from which to examine all of the author's novels. Purporting to be a journal, one man's view of a period in a city's history, this work shows especially well the nexus between realistic reporting and imaginative invention that is the hallmark of Defoe's novels.

A JOURNAL OF THE PLAGUE YEAR

Defoe himself lived through one siege of the plague, and although he was only five years old when the disease swept through London, he presumably would have retained some recollections of this catastrophic event, even if only through conversations he would have heard among family members. In *A Journal of the Plague Year*, he also refers frequently to the mortality list, drawing on actual documents of the time to give his narrative a sense of reality. In spite of the realistic foundations of the work, however, its imaginative—not to say fantastic—elements outweigh its realism. Defoe, in fact, often shows a surprising interest in the occult or grotesque for one who is supposedly forging the realistic novel in English. Dreams and premonitions often assail his characters—Crusoe's dream of the angel, Moll's telepathic contact with her Lancashire husband, Roxana's precognitive vision of the dead jeweler—and the utter incomprehensibility of the plague takes this work far beyond cause-and-effect realism.

Perhaps the main thing to consider in *A Journal of the Plague Year* is the narrator, H. L., who, like many of Defoe's characters, is divided spiritually: He must decide whether to flee London or stay and trust God's divine Providence. Like Crusoe, H. L. in times of stress opens the Bible randomly and applies its words to his immediate situation. A problem with theme—often Defoe's weakness—immediately arises, for while the passage that he finds in the Bible convinces him to stay, by the end of the novel he has decided that flight is the only sensible option. His stay in the city is not developed as a moral flaw, however, although, given the religious concerns of the novel, it seems as though it should be: Some critics even see him as guilty of overstraining God's Providence. This view seems inconsistent with the overall sympathetic character of H. L., and one feels that Defoe is not, perhaps, completely in control of his theme.

Even more significant for theme is the origin of the plague. H. L., a sensible, levelheaded man, insists that the plague's cause is natural; he is just as insistent, however, that God has used natural means to bring about the plague. In fact, he makes frequent biblical references that, if not providing specific emblematic types for the plague, do give it a resonance beyond that of a mere disease. Thus, the narrator's insistence on seeing all the horrors of the plague for himself—even though he admits he would be safer at home—has led some critics to see his curiosity as a desire to understand God's workings directly. Again, one encounters an awkward thematic problem. Is H. L. really curious about God's wisdom, or is his seeming inability to stay home simply a narrative necessity? There would, after all, be no journal without an eyewitness. Like many thematic problems in Defoe's works, this becomes one only in retrospect; H. L.'s emphasis on the particulars he describes can be so interesting—even if gruesome—that it is not until the reader has finished the book that these problems surface.

Two episodes from this work show how effective Defoe can be with detail. The first involves H. L.'s journey to the post office. Walking through silent and deserted streets, he arrives at his destination, where he sees "in the middle of the yard . . . a small leather purse with two keys hanging at it, with money in it, but nobody would meddle with it." There are three men around the courtyard who tell H. L. that they are leaving it there in case the owner returns. As H. L. is about to leave, one of the men finally offers to take it "so that if the right owner came for it he should be sure to have it," and he proceeds to carry out an elaborate process of disinfection. This episode, on the surface merely straightforward description, is fraught with drama and ambiguity.

While it is realistic for the streets to be deserted as people take to the safety of their houses, the silence lends an eerie backdrop to this scene. Furthermore, the men's motivations are hardly straightforward. Are they leaving the purse there out of honesty or are they fearful of contamination? Are they simply playing a waiting game with one another to see who leaves first? Does one man finally take the purse to keep it for the owner or for himself? Finally, why does he have all the disinfecting materials—including red-hot tongs—immediately available? Was he about to take the purse before H. L. arrived? H. L.'s remarks about the money found in the purse—"as I remember . . . about thirteen shillings and some smooth groats and brass farthings"—complete this episode: The particularity of the amount is typical of Defoe's realism, and H. L.'s hesitant "as I remember" also persuades the reader that he or she is witnessing the mental processes of a scrupulously honest narrator. In fact, this whole passage is so effective that one tends to overlook an internal inconsistency: Early in the paragraph H. L. says that the sum of money was not so large "that I had any inclination to meddle with it," yet he only discovers the sum at the end of this episode. Defoe is prone to narrative slips of this kind, but, like this one, they are usually unimportant and inconspicuous.

Another vivid episode concerns H. L. going to check on his brother's house while he is away. Next to the house is a warehouse, and as H. L. approaches it, he finds that it has been broken into and is full of women trying on hats. Thievery is by no means uncommon during the plague, although the women's interest in fashion does seem bizarre. What is remarkable about this description, however, is its ambience: Instead of grabbing the hats and fleeing, the women are behaving as if they are at a milliner's, trying on hats until they find those that are most becoming. This scene shows Defoe ostensibly writing realistically when, in fact, he is creating a picture that borders on the surreal.

A Journal of the Plague Year does not always achieve the degree of success that these two episodes display; much of the book is filled with descriptions of the cries and lamentations the narrator hears as he walks the streets. Even horror, if undifferentiated, can become monotonous, and Defoe does not always know how to be selective about details. One device that he employs to better effect here than in his other works is the keeping of lists. Defoe's characters often keep balance sheets of their profits and expenditures, and while this may indicate, as Ian Watt contends, Defoe's essentially materialistic bias, these lists often seem examples of the crudest form of realism. In *A Journal of the Plague Year*, however, the mortality lists scattered throughout are rather more successful and provide almost a thudding rhythm to what is being described: God's terrible visitation.

ROBINSON CRUSOE

Robinson Crusoe, like *A Journal of the Plague Year* and much of Defoe's fiction, is based on a factual event: Alexander Selkirk, a Scottish sailor, lived for four years on the island of Juan Fernandez until he was rescued in 1709. Defoe supplemented accounts of Selkirk's adventures with information from travel books: Richard Hakluyt's *The Principall Navigations, Voiages, and Discoveries of the English Nation* (1589, 1598-1600), William Dampier's *New Voyage Round the World* (1697), and Robert Knox's *An*

Historical Relation of Ceylon (1681). Nevertheless, it is as fiction—not a pastiche of other people's books—that *Robinson Crusoe* engrosses the reader.

Because the story centers on one character, it depends on that character for much of its success, and critics have tended to divide into two groups: those who see Crusoe as the new middle-class economic man with only perfunctory religious feelings and those who see him as a deeply spiritual person whose narrative is essentially that of a conversion experience. The answer, perhaps, is that both views of Crusoe coexist in this novel, that Defoe was not sure in this early work exactly where his story was taking him. This ambiguity is not surprising given that the same problem surfaces in *Moll Flanders*; it was not until *Roxana* that Defoe seems to have worked out his themes fully.

The opening frame to Crusoe's island adventure provides a logical starting point for examining his character. Writing in retrospect, Crusoe blames his shipwreck and subsequent sufferings on his "propension of nature," which made him reject his father's counsel of moderation and prompted him to go to sea. His father's speech seems to echo the idea of a great chain of being: Crusoe's life belongs to the "middle state," and he should not endanger himself by reckless acts. If Crusoe's filial disobedience seems trivial to modern readers, it was not to Defoe: His *The Family Instructor, in Three Parts* (1715) and *A New Family Instructor* (1727) make clear how important the mutual obligations of parents and children are. Crusoe himself, recounting his exile from the perspective of old age, talks about his father in biblical terms: After Crusoe's first shipwreck, his father is "an emblem of our blessed Saviour's parable, [and] had even killed the fatted calf for me." When Crusoe reflects, then, on his sinful and vicious life, the reader has to accept Defoe's given: that Crusoe's early giddy nature is a serious moral flaw.

Even with this assumption, however, the reader may have problems understanding Crusoe's character. Throughout the novel, for example, images of prison and capture recur. This makes sense, for the island is both a prison and, if the reader believes in Crusoe's conversion, a means of attaining spiritual freedom. Crusoe himself is imprisoned early in the novel by some Moors and escapes only after two years (the events of which, like the events that take place over many long stretches of time in Defoe's novels, are only briefly summarized) with a boy named Xury, a captive who soon becomes Crusoe's helpmate and friend. Once Crusoe is free, however, he sells Xury willingly and misses him only when his plantation grows so large that he needs extra labor. Indeed, it is indicative of his relations with other people that when Crusoe meets Friday, Friday abases himself to Crusoe, and Crusoe gives his own name as "Master." Perhaps one should not expect enlightened social attitudes about slavery or race in an eighteenth century author. Even so, there seems pointed irony—presumably unintended by Defoe—in Crusoe gaining his freedom only to imprison others; Crusoe's attitude does not seem sufficient for the themes and imagery that Defoe himself has woven into this work.

Crusoe does not behave appreciably better with Europeans. When he rescues Friday and his father, he also rescues a Spaniard who, with a group of Spaniards and Portuguese, has been living peaceably with Friday's tribe. Crusoe begins to think about trying to return to civilization with the Europeans and sends the Spaniard back to Friday's tribe to consult with the others. Before he returns, however, a ship with a mutinous crew arrives on the island. Crusoe rescues the captain and regains control of most of the mutineers. They leave the worst mutineers on the island and sail off for civilization; Crusoe apparently gives no thought to the Spaniard, who will return to the island only to find a motley collection of renegades. Defoe may, of course, simply have forgotten momentarily about the Spaniard as his narrative progressed to new adventures, but if so, this is an unfortunate lapse because it confuses the reader about character and, therefore, about Crusoe's humanity.

Another problem—this time having to do with theme—occurs at the end of the novel. After being delivered to Spain, Crusoe and another group of travelers set out to cross the Pyrenees, where they are beset by fierce wolves. They manage to escape, and Crusoe returns to England, marries, has three children, travels back to his island, and continues having adventures, which, he says, "I may perhaps give a farther account of hereafter." One might argue that the adventures after he leaves the island are anticlimactic, although some critics try to justify them on thematic grounds, the killing of the wolves thus being the extermination of Crusoe's earthly passions. The question remains whether the narrative can bear the weight of such a symbolic—indeed, allegorical—reading. The fact that the sequels to *Robinson Crusoe* are merely about external journeys—not internal spiritual states—shows, perhaps, that Defoe was not as conscious an allegorist as some critics imagine.

Given these thematic problems, it may seem odd that the novel has enjoyed the popularity it has over the centuries. In part, this may simply be due to the element of suspense involved in Crusoe's plight. On one level, the reader wonders how Crusoe is going to survive, although the minute rendering of the day-to-day activities involved in survival can become tedious. Of more interest are Crusoe's mental states: His fluctuating moods after he finds the footprint, for example, have a psychological reality about them. Further, the very traits that make Crusoe unappealing in certain situations lend the novel interest; Crusoe is a survivor, and, while one sometimes wishes he were more compassionate or humane, his will to endure is a universal one with which the reader can empathize.

Aside from the basic appeal of allowing the reader to experience vicariously Crusoe's struggles to survive, the novel also offers the reader a glimpse of Crusoe's soul. While some of Crusoe's pieties seem perfunctory, Defoe is capable of portraying the character's internal states in sophisticated ways. For example, early in his stay on the island Crusoe discovers twelve ears of barley growing, which convinces him "that God had miraculously caused this grain to grow without any help of seed sown and that it was so directed purely for my sustenance on that wild miserable place." Two paragraphs later, however, "it occurred to my thoughts that I had shook a bag of chicken's meal out in that place, and then the wonder began to cease; and I must confess, my religious thankfulness to God's Providence began to abate too." The mature Crusoe who is narrating this story can see in retrospect that "I ought to have been as thankful for so strange and unforeseen Providence as if it had been miraculous; for it was really the work of Providence as to me" that God allowed the seed to take hold and grow. Here the reader finds Defoe using a sophisticated narrative situation as the older Crusoe recounts—and comments on—the spiritual states of the young Crusoe. Indeed, one problem in the novel is determining when Crusoe's egocentric outlook simply reflects this early unregenerate state of which his mature self would presumably disapprove and when it reflects a healthy individualism in which Defoe acquiesces. Perhaps Crusoe is most appealing when he is aware of his own foibles—for example, when he prides himself on building a gigantic canoe only to find that he cannot possibly transport it to water.

COLONEL JACK

If *Robinson Crusoe* shows an uneasy balance between egocentricity and spiritual humility, materialism and religion, *The Life, Adventures and Pyracies of the Famous Captain Singleton*, more commonly known as *Captain Singleton*, displays what Everett Zimmerman calls a "soggy amalgam of the picaresque and Puritan." This problem reappears in *The History and Remarkable Life of the Truly Honourable Col Jacque, Commonly Call'd Col Jack*, known to readers simply as *Colonel Jack*. Jack's motives are often suspect. When he becomes an overseer in Virginia, for example, he finds that he cannot whip his slaves because the action hurts his arms. Instead, he tells the slaves they will be severely punished by an absentee master and then pretends to have solicited their pardon. Grateful for this mercy, the slaves then work for Jack willingly and cheerfully. While Jack describes this whole episode in words denoting charity and mercy, the reader is uneasily aware that Jack is simply playing on the slaves' ignorance. It is method rather than mercy that triumphs here.

MOLL FLANDERS *and* ROXANA

The confusion in *Captain Singleton* and *Colonel Jack* between expediency and morality can also be found in *Moll Flanders* and, to a lesser extent, in *Roxana*. What makes these latter novels enduring is the power of their central characters. Both Moll and Roxana bear many children, and although they manage to dispose of their offspring conveniently so that they are not hampered in any way, their physical fertility sets them apart from Defoe's more sterile male heroes. This fertility may, of course, be ironic—Dorothy Van Ghent calls Moll an earth mother, but only insofar as she is a "progenitrix of the wasteland"—but it adds a dimension to the characters that both Jack and Singleton lack. One also feels that Defoe allows his female characters greater depth of feeling: Each one takes husbands and lovers for whom she has no regard, but Moll's telepathic communication with her Lancashire husband and Roxana's precognitive vision of her jeweler lover's death imply that both women are involved deeply in these relationships—even though Roxana manages to use the jeweler's death as a way of rising in the world by becoming the Prince's mistress. Defoe's heroines may mourn their losses yet also use them to their advantage.

Another difference between the female and male protagonists in Defoe's novels is that neither Moll nor Roxana descends to murder, whereas Defoe's male picaros often do. Although Moll can occasionally rejoice when a criminal cohort capable of exposing her is hanged, she feels only horror when she contemplates murdering a child from whom she steals a necklace. Similarly, while Roxana may share an emotional complicity in Amy's murder of her importunate daughter, she explicitly tells Amy that she will tolerate no such crime. *Roxana* also seems to have more thematic unity than Defoe's other novels: Instead of advocating an uneasy balance between spiritual and material values, *Roxana* shows a tragic awareness that these are finally irreconcilable opposites. Roxana, although recognizing her weaknesses, cannot stop herself from indulging in them, and her keen awareness of what she calls her "secret Hell within" aligns her more with John Milton's Satan than with Defoe's earlier protagonists.

If Defoe begins to solve the thematic problems of his earlier novels in *Moll Flanders* and *Roxana*, he does so through fairly dissimilar characters. Moll equivocates and justifies her actions much more than does Roxana; when she steals the child's necklace, she reflects that "as I did the poor child no harm, I only thought I had given the parents a just reproof for their negligence in leaving the poor lamb to come home by itself, and it would teach them to take more care another time." She also shows a tendency to solve moral dilemmas by the simple expedient of maintaining two opposing moral stances simultaneously. When she meets a man at Bartholomew Fair who is intoxicated, she has sex with him and then robs him. She later reflects on his "honest, virtuous wife and innocent children" who are probably worrying about him, and she and the woman who disposes of her stolen goods both cry at the pitiable domestic scene Moll has painted. Within a few pages, however, she has found the man again and taken him as her lover, a relationship that lasts for several years.

Moll seems to see no conflicts in her attitudes. Her speech also shows her ability to rationalize moral problems, and she often uses a type of equivocation that allows her to justify her own actions. When a thief is pursued through a crowd of people, he throws his bundle of stolen goods to Moll. She feels herself free to keep them "for these things I did not steal, but they were stolen to my hand."

Contrary to the character of Moll, Roxana recognizes her failings. After her first husband leaves her in poverty, her landlord offers to become her lover. Although he has a wife from whom he is separated, he argues that he will treat Roxana in every way as his legal wife. Throughout their life together, Roxana distinguishes between their degrees of guilt: The landlord, she says, has convinced himself that their relationship is moral; she, however, knows that it is not and is thus the greater sinner.

Indeed, Roxana is portrayed in much greater psychological depth than is Moll; one measure of this is the relationship between Roxana and her maid, Amy. While Defoe's characters often have close friends or confidants—Friday in *Robinson Crusoe*, the midwife in *Moll Flanders*, Dr. Heath in *A Journal of the Plague Year*—it is only in *Roxana* that the friend appears in the novel from the beginning to the end and provides an alter ego for the main character. When Roxana is deciding whether to take the landlord as her lover, for example, Amy volunteers several times to sleep with him if Roxana refuses. Once the landlord and Roxana are living together, Roxana decides to put Amy into bed with the landlord, which she does—literally tearing off Amy's clothes and watching their sexual performance. By the next day, the landlord's lust for Amy has turned to hatred and Amy is suitably penitent. The logical question is why Roxana does this destructive deed, and the answer seems to be that, since she herself feels intense guilt at sleeping with the landlord, she wants to degrade Amy and the landlord as well.

Amy, similarly manipulative, is less passive than Roxana. At the end of the novel, Susan, one of Roxana's daughters, appears, guesses her mother's identity, and begs Roxana to acknowledge her. Amy's suggestion is that she kill Susan, who alone can reveal Roxana's past, having been, unknowingly, a maid in her mother's household when Roxana had many lovers. Roxana recoils from this idea although she admits that Amy "effected all afterwards, without my knowledge, for which I gave her my hearty Curse, tho' I could do little more; for to have fall'n upon Amy, had been to have murther'd myself." Some critics argue that Roxana actually acquiesces in Susan's murder, even though she forbids Amy to do it; her statement that to fall upon Amy would be to destroy herself does lend credence to this view. Amy, perhaps, acts out the desires that Roxana will not admit, even to herself.

In fact, both *Moll Flanders* and *Roxana* seem to hint at an irrational perverseness in their characters that explains, in part, their crimes. At one point after beginning her life as a thief, Moll actually tries to earn her living with her needle and admits that she can do so, but temptation makes her return to crime. She appears to enjoy living outside the law, no matter how much she may talk of her fears of Newgate Prison. Similarly, she once steals a horse simply because it is there; she has no way to dispose of it, but the irrational impulse in her that leads her to crime causes her to commit the theft anyway. Defoe is not given to high comedy, but the picture of Moll leading the horse through the streets, wondering how she is ever going to rid herself of it, is a memorably comic scene.

The frequent irrationality of Moll's behavior seems reiterated in the actions of Roxana; without Moll's self-justifying rationalizations, however, Roxana becomes a tragic figure who knows that her behavior is wrong but cannot stop it. About halfway through the novel, for example, she meets a Dutch merchant who helps her out of some difficulties; she has sex with him, but when he proposes marriage she refuses him on the grounds that marriage is a kind of slavery for women. Actually, she fears that he is trying to take over her fortune. When he answers this unspoken objection, promising not to touch her wealth, she is left in the uncomfortable position of having to admit that her initial reluctance was based solely on financial considerations or else continue her spirited defense of female freedom. She chooses the latter option, arguing until the merchant admits defeat. After she is left alone, Roxana regrets her decision and wishes the merchant back, arguing that no "Woman in her Senses" would ever behave as she did.

In these two novels, Defoe seems to be exploring the nature of evil, and it is seen repeatedly as an irrational drive that can deprive its victims of free choice. In fact, *Roxana* is noteworthy for the ambiguously dark atmosphere that pervades the novel, even apart from Roxana's actions. Although *Moll Flanders* touches on incest, madness, and murder, these seem to be the understandable results of understandable causes: If you do not know your mother, you may marry your brother; if your brother-husband discovers your identity, he may go mad with grief; if you steal from a child, you may contemplate murder to cover up your crime. In *Roxana*, however, many of the characters seem motivelessly malignant, obscurely evil. The midwife whom the Prince hires for Roxana seems so murderous that Roxana has him dismiss her, yet there has been no suggestion in the novel that the Prince intends Roxana harm. On the contrary, he seems delighted with her pregnancy and even spends some time with her during labor. The sexual promiscuity found in *Moll Flanders* turns to sexual perversion in *Roxana*: Roxana's final lover before she goes to live with the Quaker disgusts her "on some Accounts, which, if I cou'd suffer myself to publish them, wou'd fully justifie my Conduct; but that Part of the Story will not bear telling."

Even the Quaker is an ambiguous figure. Although strictly truthful—Roxana states several times that the woman will not tell a lie—she hardly seems above reproach: She shows a surprising adeptness at bringing together Roxana and her former lover; she knows how to disguise the smell of alcohol on one's breath; she says at one point that she is almost tempted to abandon her sober Quaker attire and wear Roxana's Turkish costume, although the costume by this time has come to be an emblem of Roxana's sinful life.

Perhaps Defoe's darkening vision is best seen through a comparison of the conclusions of *Moll Flanders* and *Roxana*. After a life of crime—through which she becomes quite wealthy—Moll is finally caught and sent to Newgate. Sentenced to die, she is instead transported, but not before she meets Jemmy, her Lancashire husband, who has been a highwayman and who also ends up in Newgate. They leave for America together, and since they have enough money to pay the captain of the ship handsomely, they are treated like gentry on their voyage. Once in America, they prosper, only returning to England at the end of the novel, presumably repentant but certainly wealthy from their life of crime.

The uneasy balance of religion and roguery in *Moll Flanders*—Moll's pieties interspersed throughout the work sometimes sound as perfunctory as Crusoe's—shifts in *Roxana*, where Defoe's character finally realizes that one cannot reconcile sin and prosperity in the easygoing synthesis that Moll seems to achieve. The novel ends with Susan's death and Amy's desertion; the final paragraph tells the reader that Roxana and her husband prospered for a while but that a "Blast from Heaven" finally destroyed Roxana's tranquillity and she ended her days miserably. The abruptness of this conclusion makes for an unsatisfactory ending, but at least it does show Defoe solving the thematic problems inherent in all his earlier novels: Roxana recognizes a higher power but is unable to obey it. Instead of having the best of two worlds—prosperity and religion—she is doomed by a just Providence that punishes her unrepentance.

If, like Defoe's heroes and heroines, one is given to keeping balance sheets, one might summarize Defoe's weaknesses and strengths easily. On a basic level, Defoe is often slipshod in his handling of narrative: At one point Moll tells the reader how many lovers she has had in her life, but Moll's list of lovers falls far short of the number she mentions in her own narrative. More serious are the thematic problems that Defoe seems to solve only in his final novel. Finally, his realism is quite crude in some places; descriptions of objects assail the reader without having any sensuous reality to them. To Defoe's credit, he is able to establish a convincing conversational tone for most of his characters, and they often have an energy that far exceeds their function as counters through whom Defoe can manipulate his episodic plots. When reading Defoe, however, one does not tend to think in terms of balance sheets. In his best works, the problems in Defoe's writings are so well masked by the vitality of his fiction as to be unnoticeable. Like all artists, Defoe has the ability to make his readers suspend disbelief.

Carole Moses

OTHER MAJOR WORKS

SHORT FICTION: *A True Relation of the Apparition of One Mrs. Veal*, 1706.

POETRY: *The True-Born Englishman: A Satyr*, 1701.

NONFICTION: *An Essay upon Projects*, 1697; *The Shortest Way with the Dissenters*, 1702; *The History of the Union of Great Britain*, 1709; *An Appeal to Honour and Justice*, 1715; *The Family Instructor, in Three Parts*, 1715; *A New Voyage Round the World by a Course Never Sailed*, 1724; *A Tour Thro' the Whole Island of Great Britain*, 1724-1727 (3 volumes); *A General History of the Robberies and Murders of the Most Notorious Pyrates*, 1724-1728 (2 volumes); *The Complete English Tradesman*, 1725-1727 (2 volumes); *The Four Years Voyages of Capt George Roberts*, 1726; *A New Family Instructor*, 1727; *Augusta Triumphans: Or, The Way to Make London the Most Flourishing City in the Universe*, 1728; *A Plan of the English Commerce*, 1728.

MISCELLANEOUS: *The Novels and Miscellaneous Works of Daniel Defoe*, 1840-1841 (20 volumes; Walter Scott, editor); *Romances and Narratives by Daniel Defoe*, 1895 (16 volumes; George Aitken, editor); *The Shakespeare Head Edition of the Novels and Selected Writings of Daniel Defoe*, 1927-1928 (14 volumes).

BIBLIOGRAPHY

Blewett, David. *Defoe's Art of Fiction: "Robinson Crusoe," "Moll Flanders," "Colonel Jack," and "Roxana."* Toronto, Ont.: University of Toronto Press, 1979. In an examination of Defoe's letters and nonfiction, Blewett finds a worldview that sees the individual as isolated in an indifferent or hostile universe. Shows how four of Defoe's novels artfully voice this outlook.

Bloom, Harold, ed. *Daniel Defoe*. New York: Chelsea House, 1987. Contains thirteen essays representing three decades of criticism. Subjects include point of view, theme, style, and characterization. Bloom's introduction, Leo Braudy's "Daniel Defoe and the Anxieties of Autobiography," and John J. Burke, Jr.'s "Observing the Observer in Historical Fictions by Defoe" are of particular interest. Includes chronology, brief bibliography, and index.

Lund, Roger D., ed. *Critical Essays on Daniel Defoe*. New York: G. K. Hall, 1997. Collection of essays discusses Defoe's domestic conduct manuals, his travel books, his treatment of slavery, his novels, and his treatment of the city. Includes an informative introduction and an index.

Novak, Maximillian E. *Daniel Defoe: Master of Fictions—His Life and Ideas*. New York: Oxford University Press, 2001. Biographical study by a leading Defoe scholar focuses on Defoe's writings. Includes analysis of *Robinson Crusoe*, *Moll Flanders*, and other novels as well as discussion of the author's works in other genres.

_____. *Realism, Myth, and History in Defoe's Fiction*. Lincoln: University of Nebraska Press, 1983. Treats various aspects of Defoe's artistry, such as the psychological realism of *Roxana*, the use of history in *A Journal of the Plague Year* and *Memoirs of a Cavalier*, and mythmaking in *Robinson Crusoe*.

Richetti, John J. *Daniel Defoe*. Boston: Twayne, 1987. Argues that examination of Defoe's fiction should be balanced by a careful study of his nonfiction. This valuable work looks at both, noting both similarities and inconsistencies. Includes chronology, biographical overview, notes, and bibliography with secondary sources briefly annotated.

_____. *Life of Daniel Defoe: A Critical Biography*. Malden, Mass.: Blackwell, 2005. Provides a thorough look at Defoe's writing within the context of his life and opinions, including analysis of his fiction and political and religious journalism. Focuses on Defoe's distinctive literary style.

_____, ed. *The Cambridge Companion to Daniel Defoe*. New York: Cambridge University Press, 2008. Collection of essays designed to introduce students to Defoe includes discussions of Defoe and criminal fiction, money and character in Defoe's fiction, Defoe as a narrative innovator, and gender issues in *Moll Flanders* and *Roxana*.

Rogers, Pat, ed. *Daniel Defoe: The Critical Heritage*. 1972. Reprint. New York: Routledge, 1995. Comprehensive collection of critical commentary on Defoe's work is essential for an understanding of such a complex figure. The editor's introduction provides an excellent overview. Includes appendixes, bibliography, and index.

Spaas, Lieve, and Brian Stimpson, eds. *"Robinson Crusoe": Myths and Metamorphoses*. New York: St. Martin's Press, 1996. Collection of essays explores many aspects of the seminal novel. Includes examinations of Crusoe's women and of the novel within the context of eighteenth century history; several essays focus on how other writers and filmmakers have adapted Defoe's novel for their own works.

Watt, Ian. *The Rise of the Novel: Studies in Defoe, Richardson, and Fielding.* 2d ed. Berkeley: University of California Press, 2001. Discusses *Robinson Crusoe, Moll Flanders,* and Defoe's contribution to the realistic novel. Relates Defoe's fiction to the social and economic conditions of his age.

West, Richard. *Daniel Defoe: The Life and Strange, Surprising Adventures.* New York: Carroll & Graf, 1998. Covers all aspects of Defoe's careers as journalist, novelist, satirist, newsman, and pamphleteer as well as tradesman, soldier, and spy. Written with considerable flair by a journalist and historian of wide-ranging experience.

DENIS DIDEROT

Born: Langres, France; October 5, 1713
Died: Paris, France; July 31, 1784
Also known as: Pantophile

PRINCIPAL LONG FICTION
   Les Bijoux indiscrets, 1748 (*The Indiscreet Toys*, 1749)
   Jacques le fataliste et son maître, 1796 (wr. c. 1771; *Jacques the Fatalist and His Master*, 1797)
   La Religieuse, 1796 (*The Nun*, 1797)
   Le Neveu de Rameau, 1805 (in German; 1821 in French; 1891 complete edition; wr. 1761-1774; *Rameau's Nephew*, 1897)

OTHER LITERARY FORMS

Although the official complete edition of the novels of Denis Diderot (DEED-uh-roh) is found in the twenty-volume *Œuvres complètes* (1875-1877), edited by Jean Assézat and Maurice Tourneax, the novels are readily available in the Classiques Garnier, edited by Henri Bénac (1962). An edition of *Œuvres complètes* (1975-1995) has been updated under the editorship of Herbert Dieckmann, Jean Fabre, and Jacques Proust. All the novels are available in English in various popular editions.

Diderot began his literary career with translations, the most important of which are *L'Histoire de Grèce* (1743), a translation of the English *Grecian History* (1739) by Temple Stanyan; *Principes de la philosophie morale: Ou, Essai de M. S.*** sur le mérite et la vertu, avec réflexions* (1745), of the earl of Shaftesbury's *An Inquiry Concerning Virtue and Merit* (1699); and *Dictionnaire universel de médecine* (1746-1748), of Robert James's *A Medical Dictionary* (1743-1745).

Diderot was a prolific essayist. His first important essay, *Pensées philosophiques* (1746; English translation, 1819), was immediately condemned for its rationalistic critique of supernatural revelation. It is available in English in *Diderot's Early Philosophical Works* (1916), translated by Margaret Jourdain. *La Promenade du sceptique* (1830; the skeptic's walk), which was written in 1747, was described by Diderot himself as a "conversation concerning religion, philosophy, and the world." *De la suffisance de la religion naturelle* (on the sufficiency of natural religion), written the same year but not published until 1770, extols natural religion. The famous *Lettre sur les aveugles* (1749; *An Essay on Blindness*, 1750; also as *Letter on the Blind* in Jourdain's book) puts forth Diderot's ideas on the supremacy of matter; this work was the cause of his imprisonment at Vincennes. It was followed in 1751 by the *Lettre sur les sourds et muets* (*Letter on the Deaf and Dumb* in Jourdain's book), which was circulated by tacit permission of the authorities and which contains important ideas on music and poetry. *Pensées sur l'interprétation de la nature*

Denis Diderot
(Library of Congress)

(1754; thoughts on the interpretation of nature) explores some implications of the scientific method.

In 1759, Diderot began his contributions to Friedrich Melchior von Grimm's *Correspondance littéraire*, a periodical that had a very limited circulation among the aristocracy abroad, reporting on the latest happenings in French arts and letters. Diderot's art criticism, contained in the famous *Les Salons* (1845, 1857), first appeared there. These annual reviews of Paris exhibitions were published from 1759 to 1781, the most famous being those of 1761, 1763 (considered the best), 1765, 1767, and 1769. Other essays during this time include the famous *Le Rêve de d'Alembert* (1830; *D'Alembert's Dream*, 1927), written in 1769, which contains scientific and philosophical ideas together with an exploration of dreams. *Entretien d'un père avec ses enfants* (1773; *Conversations Between Father and Children*, 1964) and *Paradoxe sur le comédien* (1830; *The Paradox of Acting*, 1883), written in 1773, are among other important essays. Diderot's last philosophical work was his *Essai sur Sénèque* (1778; essay on Seneca), which was revised as *Essai sur les règnes de Claude et Néron* (1782), a digressive amplification of the former. Both of these essays mix autobiographical material with an exposition of Diderot's ideas on politics and morality.

All of these works are included in the *Œuvres complètes*; they are also found in the Classiques Garnier volumes, *Œuvres philosophiques* (1956), *Œuvres esthétiques* (1959), and *Œuvres politiques* (1962). In addition to *Diderot's Early Philosophical Works*, English editions include *Diderot, Interpreter of Nature: Selected Writings* (1937), translated by Jean Stewart and Jonathan Kemp, and *Selected Writings* (1966), edited by Lester Crocker.

In 1757, Diderot began to write for the theater. Although he developed a new genre, the so-called *drame bourgeois*, he was not a successful playwright, for his plays lack dramatic qualities. *Le Fils naturel: Ou, Les Épreures de la vertu* (*Dorval: Or, The Test of Virtue*, 1767) was published in 1757 but not staged until 1771. It was followed by an essay, *Entretiens sur "Le Fils naturel"* (1757; conversations on "The Natural Son"). *Le Père de famille* (1758; English translation, 1770; also as *The Family Picture*, 1871) was staged in 1761. This play, too, was followed by an important essay, *Discours sur la poésie dramatique* (1758; English translation of chapters 1-5 in *Dramatic Essays of the Neoclassical Age*, 1950). Diderot's last play, *Est'il bon? Est'il méchant?* (pr. 1781; Is it good? Is it bad?), is considered his best.

In addition to long fiction, Diderot also wrote several short stories. They include "L'Oiseau blanc" (the white bird), written and published in 1748, and several stories written in 1772 that were published at later dates: "Les Deux Amis de Bourbonne" (1773; "Two Friends from Bourbonne," 1964), "Ceci n'est pas un conte" (1798; "This Is Not a Story," 1960), "Madame de la Carlière: Ou, Sur l'inconséquence du jugement public de nos actions particulières" (1798), and *Supplément au voyage de Bougainville* (1796; *Supplement to Bougainville's Voyage*, 1926). Several of these stories are available in English in Ralph Bowen's translation *Rameau's Nephew, and Other Works* (1964).

Diderot's voluminous correspondence is collected in sixteen volumes by George Roth (1955-1970). The most famous of these letters are the 187 extant to his mistress Sophie Volland (1755-1774). Other important letters are those to Paul Landois on determinism (1756); those to the princess of Nassau-Saarbruck (1758), translated as *Concerning the Education of a Prince* (1941); and the farewell letter to Catherine II of Russia (1774). Finally, Diderot wrote many articles in the famous *Encyclopédie: Ou, Dictionnaire raisonné des sciences, des arts, et des métiers* (1751-1772), many of which are unsigned. Some of these are available in English in the Bobbs-Merrill edition, *Encyclopedia* (1965), translated by Nelly S. Hoyt and Thomas Cassirer.

Achievements

Although Denis Diderot is one of the major novelists of the eighteenth century, it is as the editor of the *Encyclopedia* that he is most remembered. Along with Jean le Rond d'Alembert, who was to abandon the project in 1758, he began in 1746 what was intended to be a translation of Ephraim Chambers's major English reference work, *Cyclopedia* (1728). Diderot's version later became a compendium of knowledge in seventeen volumes of text and eleven volumes of plates, published from 1751 to 1772 amid countless difficulties and attacks by clergy and government. Diderot was not only the principal, and eventually sole, editor but also the author of numerous articles, many of which were unsigned in later volumes, and some mutilated by André Le Breton. It is particularly through Diderot's articles that his philosophical ideas come to light, as demonstrated in Arthur M. Wilson's masterful 1972 study and confirmed by numerous other scholars.

Diderot was above all else a *philosophe*, one of the great eighteenth century Enlightenment figures who prepared the way for modern thought. The philosophes were not philosophers in the classical sense. In fact, they criticized many such thinkers, although Diderot had great respect for Plato, to the extent of using ideas from the Socratic dialogues as the basis for many of his works, at least in the opinion of Donal O'Gorman. The philosophes, Diderot among them, believed strongly in personal freedom, as seen in *The Indiscreet Toys* and *The Nun*; in reason and progress, the whole thesis of the *Encyclopedia*; and in a more representative government. Generally they were Deists, although Diderot himself was associated with the atheist circle of Baron Paul-Henri-Dietrich d'Holbach.

Diderot as a philosophe explored the question of morals, of virtue and vice—which he named *bienfaisance* and *malfaisance*, or good-doing and evildoing. He concluded that morality as such is the result of naturalistic and materialistic causes that determine a person's conduct—hence, that traditional morality has no meaning. *Rameau's Nephew* and *Jacques the Fatalist and His Master* explore essentially the question of the modifiability of human behavior, determinism, and freedom. Diderot also attributes pleasure to natural causes, becoming one of the forerunners of "sensibility," the Romantic emphasis on feeling and the heart. His novels bear the stamp of Samuel Richardson and Laurence Sterne and anticipate the reign of Romanticism. Diderot's sensitivity to aesthetic beauty is expressed in the art criticism contained in *Les Salons*; it is also reflected in his fiction, notably in the digressions in *The Indiscreet Toys* and the musical discussions in *Rameau's Nephew*.

As a novelist, Diderot was an innovator. *The Nun* anticipates twentieth century psychological fiction, especially in its exploration of the abnormal. *Jacques the Fatalist and His Master* is, by Diderot's own description, an antinovel, a forerunner of the twentieth century New Novel, which is not really a story but rather a collaboration between author and reader. *Rameau's Nephew* is a fascinating study of the paradox of the human personality. The independence of thought that distinguishes all of Diderot's works is particularly evident in his fiction; he produced novels with few models and with rich possibilities for further development.

BIOGRAPHY

Denis Diderot was born on October 5, 1713, in Langres, France, one of the seven children of the master cutler Didier Diderot and Angélique Vigneron. The family of the future anticleric was pious and devout, and Diderot's youngest brother, Didier-Pierre, was later to become a canon at Langres, deeply alienated from the great writer. Diderot's younger sister, Angélique, died insane in a convent; her cruel fate inspired Diderot's invective against convents in *The Nun*. Although Diderot began his studies at home, he was an excellent student of the Jesuits from 1723 to 1728, receiving several prizes. He also began his study of Latin and Greek with them, and he remained devoted to the classics throughout his life. He even received the tonsure in 1726, in the hope of a benefice from his uncle's inheritance, and later passed through some periods of religious fervor.

In 1728, Diderot went to Paris, where he was to spend the rest of his long life. Very little is known about his activities during the subsequent fifteen years, other than that he received his master's degree from the University of Paris in 1732 and led a fairly dissolute, though not degenerate, life. In 1743, he fell in love with Anne-Toinette Champion, a modest lace maker, and asked his father's permission to marry her. His father not only refused but also had his son imprisoned in a monastery. Diderot escaped and married Anne-Toinette secretly. It was, however, to be a tumultuous and basically unhappy marriage, from which only Angélique, of the four children born to the Diderots, was to survive. Well educated by her father, she was to become the author of several memoirs that are very valuable to Diderot studies.

Diderot's sensual nature was soon awakened in a liaison with a certain Madame de Puisieux, about whom little is known, except that Diderot wrote his first novel, *The Indiscreet Toys*, to raise money for her. It was around this time, in the late 1740's, that Diderot became associated with d'Alembert, Étienne Bonnot de Condillac, and Jean-Jacques Rousseau. He began working on the *Encyclopedia* with them and Le Breton. Soon, Diderot and d'Alembert became coeditors, and after 1758 Diderot assumed total responsibility for the work. The production of the *Encyclopedia* was Diderot's greatest achievement and essentially his lifework. By no means a child prodigy, he had produced almost nothing in the literary field until that time, but he immediately threw himself into the new project and other philosophical works.

In 1749, Diderot found himself in prison as a result of his controversial writings, particularly his *Letter on the Blind*. Diderot's brief and not uncomfortable imprisonment was perhaps more noteworthy for Rousseau than for him. It was on his way to visit the incarcerated Diderot that Rousseau experienced his famous "illumination" that led to his *Discours sur les sciences et les arts* (1750; *The Discourse Which Carried the Praemium at the Academy of Dijon*, 1751; better known as *A Discourse on the Arts and Sciences*, 1913), which won for Rousseau the prize of the Academy of Dijon. Diderot's release did not bring an end to his clashes with the law, the harsh censorship of the day, and the criticism of the Jesuits against the *Encyclopedia*. In 1752, the first two volumes were suppressed, and Diderot's papers were confiscated. Because of the support of the honest and liberal censor Chrétien-Guillaume de Lamoignon de Malesherbes and the influence of Madame de Pompadour, Louis XV's favorite, the work continued under a "tacit permission," but its publication was fraught with difficulties. The contributors often quarreled among themselves, the most noteworthy division being that between Rousseau and d'Alembert (and ultimately Diderot), and the attacks from the outside continued.

Nevertheless, Diderot's assiduous work brought him increasing financial independence and a reputation among scholars in France and abroad. It also brought him the love and support of Sophie Volland, whom Diderot met in 1755 and continued to see at least until 1774. Their liaison was characterized by a passionate and intellectual correspondence, of which 187 letters from Diderot are extant, although none of Volland's has survived. In 1757, Diderot began to write plays, creating a new type that became known as the *drame bourgeois*, or bourgeois drama; at the same time, he continued to produce essays and carried on, almost single-handedly, the editorship of the *Encyclopedia*.

The year 1759 was a difficult one for Diderot. His father died, the privilege for printing the *Encyclopedia* was revoked, and the work was condemned by Pope Clement XIII. The difficulties of Diderot's domestic life were intensified by quarrels and jealousy between his wife and Volland. Shortly afterward, Charles Palissot de Montenoy's satiric play *Les Philosophes* (pr. 1760) greatly offended Diderot, although it became one of the sources of inspiration for his masterpiece, *Rameau's Nephew*. Not all was somber, however. Diderot's friends, Grimm, d'Holbach, and his disciple and future editor Jacques-André Naigeon, proved very faithful. Catherine the Great of Russia offered her support to Diderot, purchasing his library for fifteen thousand livres and allowing him to use it for the rest of his life. She invited him to Russia, where he eventually spent the year 1773 to 1774. He was also responsible for selling her several famous art collections and for sending the noted French sculptor Étienne-Maurice Falconet to execute the famous statue of Peter the Great. Toward the end of Diderot's stay in Russia, Catherine's enthusiasm for his ideas waned, as the times were not favorable to the types of reforms that he advocated.

Diderot's last years were filled with literary activity and interest in his newly married daughter Angélique, now Madame de Vandeul. Although his troubles with the authorities continued on a minor scale, he was honored at his native Langres, and he posed for busts by sculptors Jean-Baptiste Pigalle and Jean-Antoine Houdon. In 1783, he became seriously ill, and he died on July 31, 1784, on not unfriendly terms with the Church. He received Christian burial and was interred at the Church of Saint-Roch, where Pierre Corneille is also buried—an unusual setting for a militantly anticlerical philosophe, an avowed materialist, and a sometime atheist.

Analysis

One of Denis Diderot's shorter works of fiction is titled "This Is Not a Story." He might have said of any one of his characteristic works of long fiction, "This is not a novel." At first sight, all of his novels, with the exception of *The Nun*, look like plays. That is because Diderot's favorite method is the dialogue; even many of his philosophical works, such as *D'Alembert's Dream* and *The Paradox of Acting*, are written in this form. It is in the give-and-take of dialogue that Diderot excels, and his dramatic power, though not of first-rate quality on the stage, comes to life here. The unusually extensive use of dialogue, however, leads to a blurring of genres and a consequent disorder in all of Diderot's works. Critics such as Crocker, O'Gorman, and Francis Pruner have sought to bring order out of this chaos—much to the dismay of others, who see the disorder as the message.

As novels, all of Diderot's fictional works are weak in plot. *The Indiscreet Toys* consists of a series of licentious anecdotes. *Jacques the Fatalist and His Master* is a trip from somewhere to nowhere, with intermittent stops here and there. *Rameau's Nephew* consists of a single conversation in which the two participants discuss everything from seduction to French and Italian music. *The Nun*, which comes closest to the traditional idea of plot, does have a beginning and end but does not use any forward or backward reflection. Although it is based on memory, all is told in a kind of eternal present.

As with plot, the timelines are also weak in Diderot's novels. With the exception of *The Nun*, all of his novels are poorly marked in time and lack traditional novelistic beginnings or ends. They are also vaguely situated in space. *The Indiscreet Toys* takes place in a harem in the Congo, a rather incongruous juxtaposition lacking in credibility. *Jacques the Fatalist and His Master* is situated in France but, despite the efforts of critics to identify the towns and cities that figure in the narrative, there is very little local color to guide the reader. *Rameau's Nephew*, situated in the café du Palais Royal, and *The Nun*, at the convents of Longchamp and Arpajon, are a bit more localized, yet Diderot could have put them anywhere, for his scenery is subservient to the representation of the characters.

Of all the fictional qualities in his works, it is in the portrayal of character that Diderot excels, although his best characters are in fact caricatures. He dislikes the literary portrait and provides little, if any, physical description of his characters; the reader knows nothing of their size, facial expressions, or clothing. Their personalities are revealed by contrast with those of other characters: Jacques is played against his master, Lui against Moi, Sister Suzanne against the three superiors.

Instead of well-rounded, complex characters, Diderot creates striking types. Among the most memorable are Jacques the Fatalist and Rameau's nephew, the latter simply called Lui, or He. Jacques is a picaresque hero in the tradition of Panurge, Cacambo, and the Spanish Lazarillo de Tormes. In contrast to his dull master, who spends his time looking at his watch and sniffing tobacco, Jacques is clever, witty, independent; indeed, not unlike Pierre-Augustin Caron de Beaumarchais's Figaro, he is clearly superior to his master. Lui, vaguely modeled on Jean-François Rameau, is a parasite raised to heroic proportions, a seducer, procurer, and indolent cynic who nevertheless excels in pantomime and offers brilliant reflections on society and its morals.

Having produced such picaresque and cynical heroes, it is not surprising that Diderot expends his flair for satire in other directions. Throughout his novels, Diderot attacks the institutions of eighteenth century France. Like Voltaire, Diderot regarded the clergy and the religious—that is, those who had taken monastic orders—as his greatest enemies. Again and again, he reproached the monasteries for infringing on civil and social freedom and for imposing celibacy on their members. Diderot saw hypocrisy in his society, not only in the court but also in the social conventions that people accepted as a kind of false morality; he censures such conventions with particular force in *Rameau's Nephew*.

In the *esprit gaulois* of Renard the Fox and the fabliaux and the Rabelaisian spirit so close to nature, Diderot delights in the details of sexual passions. He sees the genital act as simply a phenomenon of nature, as a purely physical act like eating and smelling. Although he champions women's rights in *The Indiscreet Toys*, women in his novels are presented as essentially unfaithful and little more than objects of desire for men, although Amisdar looks for fidelity and devotion in a wife. The cynic Lui in *Rameau's Nephew* regrets that his beautiful wife has died, for she might have become the mistress of a wealthy *fermier-général* (tax collector). *Jacques the Fatalist and His Master* is based on the amorous exploits of both Jacques and his master, all of which are totally devoid of any spiritual attraction. By contrast, *The Nun* shows the abnormalities and excesses that result from the frustration of nature.

Diderot's novels are essentially philosophical explorations. In his materialistic system, intuition is ruled out as a cause of human behavior, and free will also becomes questionable, although Diderot was a champion of freedom and human rights. All is the result of predetermined natural causes, a doctrine given symbolic expression by Jacques's "great scroll" and his refrain that "all is written on high." His fatalism is really Diderot's determinism. Diderot, however, observed the role of chance and coincidence in life and was torn by the paradox of freedom and necessity. His two major novels, *Rameau's Nephew* and *Jacques the Fatalist and His Master*, explore this tension in a most creative way, without solving the dilemma.

Diderot is an excellent stylist. As well as a knowledge of music (so aptly related in *Rameau's Nephew*), he had an ear for harmony. His style can be witty, full of plays on words, fast-paced, with the give-and-take of quick argument. It can also be passionate, even mystical—most notably in the moment of physical desire expressed by the superior of Arpajon for Sister Suzanne and in the two pantomimes of Lui in *Rameau's Nephew*, especially the pantomime of the orchestra. In fact, the novels of Diderot reveal a marked talent for mimicry and pantomime, a talent better displayed in his fiction than in his theater.

THE INDISCREET TOYS

Despite their very readable and attractive prose, Diderot's novels, as vehicles of what was regarded as dangerous philosophical propaganda, were not likely candidates for the ordinary publisher. None of them was published in France when written. *The Indiscreet Toys* was written and published in 1748. Diderot wrote this first work of long fiction to help defray the mounting expenses he incurred in his liaison with Madame de Puisieux. Madame de Vandeul, Diderot's daughter, maintained that her father wrote the book in two weeks, to prove that such a novel could be composed very quickly, provided one had a workable idea. It sold well, with six editions in several months, and was immediately translated into English and German. Reprinted several times in Diderot's lifetime, it continues to be his most popular book.

Although the novel contains social and political allusions to the reign of Louis XV, it is by no means hostile to the king, portrayed as the Sultan Mangogul, or to his favorite, Madame de Pompadour, represented by Mirzoza. It does, however, reveal the licentious behavior of the court in the confessions made by the indiscreet jewels. The king, Mangogul, bored with his court and his harem, consults the genie Cucufa and asks for a means to discover the secrets of the women at his court. Cucufa gives him a magic ring that will make him invisible and will make the women's jewels reveal their wearers' secret passions. Throughout the thirty episodes of the book, licentious secrets entertain both the king and the reader.

While the plot lacks substance and depth, *The Indiscreet Toys* is important because it is one of the earliest works in which Diderot reveals his philosophical preoccupations. He discusses the scientific and metaphysical views of Sir Isaac Newton and René Descartes, satirizes religious practices, ventures into literary criticism (concerning the lack of naturalness on the French stage), and compares the music of Jean-Baptiste Lully and Jean-Philippe Rameau, thus anticipating *Rameau's Nephew*. He also parodies a sermon (his daughter said that he had composed and sold real sermons) and investigates dreams, a phenomenon that he was to explore later, especially in *D'Alembert's Dream*. He already extols the scientific method, and even in the most licentious scenes he shows a naturalistic and methodical bent.

THE NUN

Diderot's second novel, *The Nun*, shows a marked advance in technique over *The Indiscreet Toys*, perhaps in part as a result of Diderot's reading of Richardson. Like all of Diderot's novels, *The Nun* had a fascinating origin. Based partly on a true story and partly on a hoax, it lay dormant for twenty years before Diderot even considered publication. The idea for the novel began with a lawsuit in Paris from 1755 to 1758 in which a certain Marguerite Delamarre—whose story has been illuminated through the research of Georges May—applied for dispensation from her religious vows. Her request was refused as contrary to the authority of parents over their children. A friend of Diderot, Marquis de Croismare, had tried to support the nun. Diderot and his friends wrote a series of forged letters to Croismare, supposedly from the nun, who ostensibly had escaped from her convent. Croismare took such an interest in her that his friends were forced to "kill her off" in 1760. Croismare did not discover the hoax until 1768, but in the meantime Diderot had prepared the greater part of the manuscript, which, after revision in 1780, he offered to Grimm's successor, Jakob Heinrich Meister, for the *Correspondance littéraire*. The novel was first published by Naigeon in 1796.

The Nun is a simple, rapidly moving story featuring deep psychological analysis and great artistic restraint. It tells the story of Suzanne Simonin, whose parents force her into a convent because she is illegitimate. She at first refuses to make her vows but is forced into a second convent, where she does make her profession. Her first superior is gentle and maternal, but the second is cruel and vindictive and treats her with extreme brutality. Although Suzanne manages to receive support for a plea to be dispensed from her vows, the request is rejected, and she is sent to another convent, at Arpajon. There the discipline is lax, and the superior makes lesbian advances to Suzanne. This arouses the jealousy of the superior's former favorite, which eventually drives the superior to madness and the unsuspecting Suzanne to flight. The ending is disappointing and illogical, as Suzanne, weakened from her escape, dies.

Although Diderot has frequently been accused of immorality in *The Nun*—a film based on his book was temporarily banned in France in 1966—his intentions were, rather, to show the injustice of the enforced cloister and its dangerous effects on the subjects. His technique is masterful, for he presents a young woman who is not tempted to break her vows by the desire for marriage or a lover but who simply finds she does not have a vocation to the cloister. She is innocent, observant of the discipline in the convent, and even unaware of the significance of the advances made by the superior at Arpajon. Diderot's treatment of the physical desire expressed by the superior is artful and delicate, quite different from his open and licentious descriptions in *The Indiscreet Toys* and in *Jacques the Fatalist and His Master*. The psychological analysis of Sister Suzanne, of her jealous rival, Sister Thérèse, and of the three superiors with whom Suzanne lives is excellent, making *The Nun* a forerunner of the works of Marcel Proust and André Gide.

RAMEAU'S NEPHEW

The story of Diderot's third novel, generally acknowledged as his masterpiece, is even more fascinating than those of the two preceding ones. Evidently begun in 1761, *Rameau's Nephew* was revised by Diderot in 1762, 1766, 1767, and 1775, but—no doubt because of the allusions to his enemies, especially Palissot—was never published during his lifetime, nor did it appear in Naigeon's edition of Diderot's works, *Œuvres* (1798; 15 volumes). In 1805, a German translation by Johann Wolfgang von Goethe was published, and in 1821 the text was retranslated into French, by this time substantially altered. Several other undocumented versions appeared in the nineteenth century, and it was not until 1891 that a genuine text was published by Georges Monval from a manuscript he had located at a *bouquiniste*'s stall in Paris.

Written in the form of a dialogue, *Rameau's Nephew* was staged at the Théâtre Michodière in 1963, starring Pierre Fresnay. Whether it is a novel is debatable; Diderot called it "Satire seconde" (second satire), and its dramatic possibilities are evident. It is, however, a witty, exuberant, rapid exchange of conversation between two characters, Moi and Lui. Lui is vaguely based on Jean-François Rameau, the nephew of the great French musician Jean-Philippe Rameau, whose French severity Diderot disliked, preferring Italian spontaneity. Moi is vaguely reminiscent of Diderot, at least in some biographical details, such as the education of his daughter. Critics have advanced innumerable theories concerning the identities of the characters Moi and Lui. Some say that they are two aspects of Diderot's personality, others that Lui is the id and Moi the ego, still others that they are literally Rameau's nephew and Diderot. Perhaps the most original interpretation is that of O'Gorman, who sees the work both as a Horatian satire and as a Socratic dialogue with the figures of Apollo and Marsyas, and who also identifies Rameau's nephew with Rousseau.

Rameau's Nephew, which discusses music, anti-Rousseauesque education, the hypocrisy of society, the art of seduction, and numerous other themes, opens as a casual conversation at the café du Palais Royal during a chess game. It is also a searching inquiry into the basis of morality and a study of the paradox involved in determining the right way to live. For Diderot, morality is nonexistent, because all is based on natural phenomena and matter is the root of human behavior. Yet the existence of a cynical parasite such as Rameau's nephew, who contends that his way of life is the best, poses a problem to Diderot's materialistic system, for society cannot survive with a number of Rameau's nephews. The debate is never neatly resolved; Diderot's dialectical method in the novel has been much praised by Marxist critics, who differ from many readers in finding a clear message within the twists and turns of the dialogue.

JACQUES THE FATALIST AND HIS MASTER

Diderot continued his metaphysical speculations on the paradox of morality in his last novel, *Jacques the Fatalist and His Master*, which rivals *Rameau's Nephew* as his masterpiece. Like the two preceding novels, it was not published during his lifetime, although it was written probably around 1771 and revised during or after his stay in Russia of 1773 to 1774, as evidenced by the travel theme. Diderot gave the manuscript to the *Correspondence littéraire* before 1780, but the work was not published until 1796, by Buisson. It was inspired by a passage from Laurence Sterne's *The Life and Opinions of Tristram Shandy, Gent.* (1759-1767), which Diderot had read in English.

Constructed along the lines of Miguel de Cervantes' *Don Quixote de la Mancha* (1605, 1615), *Jacques the Fatalist and His Master* is, however, quite different in tone from the great Spanish masterpiece. It is the most disorderly of all of Diderot's "chaotic" works, with interruptions of interruptions, interference by the author (who holds dialogues with his reader), and unfinished stories left to the reader's imagination. Jacques, a sort of Figaro, accompanies his rather empty-headed master, not unlike Count Almaviva, on a trip. In order to entertain his master, Jacques relates the story of his amorous exploits, and various interruptions preclude a real end to his tale. At the end, the master also tells his story; it is not unlike Jacques's, but it lacks his sparkling wit.

Their stops at inns along the way precipitate other tales, the two most important of which are the stories of Madame de la Pommeraye and Père Hudson. Madame de la Pommeraye is resentful of her lover's unfaithfulness and decides to avenge herself. She hires a prostitute and her mother to pose as a respectable young woman accompanied by her devout widowed mother. This done, Madame de la Pommeraye arranges to have her former lover, Monsieur des Arcis, fall in love with the prostitute. The day after the marriage, Madame de la Pommeraye tells him the truth, but the revenge is thwarted because he really loves his new wife and forgives her completely. Père Hudson is a sensual and domineering superior who reforms a monastery but exempts himself from its discipline. He arranges for the two priests sent to investigate his conduct to be trapped with a young woman he has seduced, thus escaping censure himself.

Despite the adventures and interruptions, the real theme of the book is the paradox of freedom and necessity. Jacques the Fatalist is really a determinist who, like Diderot, believes that "all is written on high," that one cannot change one's destiny. The very form of the novel, however, proves that chance does indeed exist. All of this seems to rule out freedom, which, like good and evil, becomes a mere illusion.

Crocker's observations on why *Jacques the Fatalist and His Master* is a great work but not a great novel may serve to classify all of Diderot's novels. A great novel must embody human life in all of its emotional and intellectual range, in all of its intensity. It must contain a view of human life in terms of concrete problems and human suffering. By contrast, *Rameau's Nephew* and *Jacques the Fatalist and His Master* are preoccupied with abstract philosophical problems. Although these two works may be Diderot's most profound fictions, it is perhaps *The Nun* that comes closest to the ideal of the novel. Diderot himself wept over *The Nun*; its characters and their suffering were real to him, as they are to his readers.

Irma M. Kashuba

OTHER MAJOR WORKS

SHORT FICTION: "L'Oiseau blanc," 1748; "Les Deux Amis de Bourbonne," 1773 ("The Two Friends from Bourbonne," 1964); *Supplément au voyage de Bougainville*, 1796 (*Supplement to Bougainville's Voyage*, 1926); "Ceci n'est pas un conte," 1798 ("This Is Not a Story," 1960); "Madame de la Carlière: Ou, Sur l'inconséquence du jugement public de nos actions particulières," 1798; *Rameau's Nephew, and Other Works*, 1964.

PLAYS: *Le Fils naturel: Ou, Les Épreuves de la vertu*, pr., pb. 1757 (*Dorval: Or, The Test of Virtue*, 1767); *Le Père de famille*, pb. 1758 (*The Father of the Family*, 1770; also known as *The Family Picture*, 1871); *Est'il bon? Est'il méchant?*, pr. 1781.

NONFICTION: *Pensées philosophiques*, 1746 (English translation, 1819; also known as *Philosophical Thoughts*, 1916); *Lettre sur les aveugles*, 1749 (*An Essay on Blindness*, 1750; also known as *Letter on the Blind*, 1916); *Notes et commentaires*, 1749; *Lettre sur les sourds et muets*, 1751 (*Letter on the Deaf and Dumb*, 1916); *Pensées sur l'interprétation de la nature*, 1754; *Entretiens sur "Le Fils naturel,"* 1757; *Discours sur la poésie dramatique*, 1758 (English translation of chapters 1-5 in *Dramatic Essays of the Neo-classical Age*, 1950); *Les Salons*, 1759-1781 (serial; 9 volumes), 1845, 1857 (book); *Éloge de Richardson*, 1762 (*An Eulogy of Richardson*, 1893); *De la suffisance de la religion naturelle*, 1770 (wr. 1747);

Entretien d'un père avec ses enfants, 1773 (*Conversations Between Father and Children*, 1964); *Essai sur Sénèque*, 1778 (revised and expanded as *Essai sur les règnes de Claude et de Néron*, 1782); *Essais sur la peinture*, 1796 (wr. c. 1765); *Pensées détachées sur la peinture*, 1798; *Plan d'une université pour le gouvernement de Russie*, 1813-1814 (wr. c. 1775-1776); *Paradoxe sur le comédien*, 1830 (wr. 1773; *The Paradox of Acting*, 1883); *La Promenade du sceptique*, 1830 (wr. 1747); *Le Rêve de d'Alembert*, 1830 (wr. 1769; *D'Alembert's Dream*, 1927); *Diderot's Early Philosophical Works*, 1916 (includes *Letter on the Blind, Letter on the Deaf and Dumb, Philosophical Thoughts*); *Concerning the Education of a Prince*, 1941 (wr. 1758); *Correspondance*, 1955-1970 (16 volumes); *Œuvres philosophiques*, 1956; *Œuvres esthétiques*, 1959; *Œuvres politiques*, 1962.

TRANSLATIONS: *L'Histoire de Grèce*, 1743 (of Temple Stanyan's history); *Principes de la philosophie morale: Ou, Essai de M. S.*** sur le mérite et la vertu, avec réflexions*, 1745 (of the earl of Shaftesbury's essay); *Dictionnaire universel de médecine*, 1746-1748 (of Robert James's dictionary).

EDITED TEXTS: *Encyclopédie: Ou, Dictionnaire raisonné des sciences, des arts, et des métiers*, 1751-1772 (17 volumes of text, 11 volumes of plates; partial translation *Selected Essays from the Encyclopedy*, 1772; complete translation *Encyclopedia*, 1965).

MISCELLANEOUS: *Œuvres*, 1798 (15 volumes); *Œuvres complètes*, 1875-1877 (20 volumes); *Diderot, Interpreter of Nature: Selected Writings*, 1937 (includes short fiction); *Selected Writings*, 1966.

BIBLIOGRAPHY

Creech, James. *Diderot: Thresholds of Representation*. Columbus: Ohio State University Press, 1986. Presents a very clear explanation of Diderot's aesthetics that enables readers to appreciate the originality of Diderot's art criticism. Also shows how Diderot utilized these theories in representing social reality in his fiction.

Cronk, Nicholas. "Reading Expectations: The Narration of Hume in *Jacques le fataliste*." *Modern Language Review* 91 (April, 1996): 330-341. Argues that David Hume's ideas of causation and determinism influenced Diderot's philosophical voice and narrative structure. Asserts that Diderot exemplifies the compatibility of the apparently contradictory positions of "reader-freedom" and "reader-direction."

Curran, Andrew. *Sublime Disorder: Physical Monstrosity in Diderot's Universe*. Oxford, England: Voltaire Foundation, 2001. Examines Diderot's fascination with anatomical monstrosity and analyzes how he represents the physically grotesque in his novels and other works. Includes bibliography and index.

Fellows, Otis. *Diderot*. Rev. ed. Boston: Twayne, 1989. Offers an excellent short introduction to the works of Diderot. Describes very well Diderot's evolution as a writer despite the fact that censorship prevented him from publishing his major works during his lifetime. Includes a good annotated bibliography.

Furbank, Philip Nicholas. *Diderot: A Critical Biography*. New York: Alfred A. Knopf,

1992. Excellent biography of the philosopher-writer includes analysis of Diderot's works, including the novels *The Nun, Jacques the Fatalist and His Master,* and *Rameau's Nephew.*

Goodden, Angelica. *Diderot and the Body.* Oxford, England: Legenda, 2001. Examines Diderot's fiction and other works to describe his ideas about the relationship of the body to the mind, anatomy, ethical extensions of the body, sensuality, sexuality, and other concerns.

Loy, Robert J. *Diderot's Determined Fatalist.* New York: King's Crown Press, 1950. Focuses on *Jacques the Fatalist and His Master* but argues persuasively that Diderot's experimentation with various narrative techniques in this novel enables readers to understand his originality as a writer of other works of long fiction.

Rex, Walter E. *Diderot's Counterpoints: The Dynamics of Contrariety in His Major Works.* Oxford, England: Voltaire Foundation, 1998. Examines Diderot's works in relation to his era, including analysis of the novels *Rameau's Nephew* and *Jacques the Fatalist and His Master.* Includes bibliographical references and index.

Umdank, Jack, and Herbert Joseph, eds. *Diderot: Digression and Dispersion, a Bicentennial Tribute.* Lexington, Ky.: French Forum, 1984. Presents nineteen essays that cover Diderot's many activities and interests. In their diversity, the contributions mirror the editors' view that Diderot did not seek unity but rather regarded diversity as the rule of nature.

Werner, Stephen. *Socratic Satire: An Essay on Diderot and "Le Neveu de Rameau."* Birmingham, Ala.: Summa, 1987. Begins with an introduction that explores Diderot's view of satire, and subsequent chapters analyze different forms of satire as they apply to Diderot and to his conception of irony. Includes notes and substantial bibliography.

Wilson, Arthur M. *Diderot.* New York: Oxford University Press, 1972. Essential and well-researched biography includes insightful analyses of Diderot's major works. Defines Diderot's importance in the development of the French Enlightenment and the critical reception of his works since the eighteenth century. Includes notes and bibliography.

HENRY FIELDING

Born: Sharpham Park, Somersetshire, England; April 22, 1707
Died: Lisbon, Portugal; October 8, 1754

PRINCIPAL LONG FICTION
An Apology for the Life of Mrs. Shamela Andrews, 1741 (commonly known as *Shamela*)
The History of the Adventures of Joseph Andrews, and of His Friend Mr. Abraham Adams, 1742 (commonly known as *Joseph Andrews*)
The History of the Life of the Late Mr. Jonathan Wild the Great, 1743 (revised 1754; commonly known as *Jonathan Wild*)
The History of Tom Jones, a Foundling, 1749 (commonly known as *Tom Jones*)
Amelia, 1751

OTHER LITERARY FORMS

Henry Fielding's literary output, aside from his novels, can be categorized into three groups: plays, pamphlets and miscellaneous items, and journals. In addition, the publication of his three-volume *Miscellanies* (1743) by subscription brought together a number of previously published items as well as new works, including the first version of *Jonathan Wild*, and an unfinished prose work, "A Journey from This World to the Next."

Fielding's dramatic works, many presented with great success at either London's Little Theatre in the Haymarket or the Drury Lane Theatre, include ballad opera, farce, full-length comedy, and adaptations of classical and French drama. Most are overtly political in theme. Because of their contemporary subject matter, few have survived as viable stage presentations, although *The Covent Garden Tragedy* (pr., pb. 1732) was presented by the Old Vic in London in 1968. Fielding also wrote a number of prologues, epilogues, and monologues that were performed in conjunction with other dramatic pieces.

The pamphlets and miscellaneous items that are currently attributed to Fielding, excluding those for which he merely wrote introductions or epilogues, are "The Masquerade" (1728), a poem; *The Military History of Charles XII King of Sweden* (1740), a translation; "Of True Greatness" (1741), a poem; "The Opposition: A Vision" (1741), a poem; "The Vernoniad" (1741), a poem; "The Female Husband" (1746); "Ovid's Art of Love Paraphrased" (1747); "A True State of the Case of Bosavern Penlez" (1749); "An Enquiry into the Causes of the Late Increase in Robbers" (1751); "Examples of the Interposition of Providence in the Detection and Punishment of Murder" (1752); "A Proposal for Making an Effectual Provision for the Poor" (1753); "A Clear State of the Case of Elizabeth Canning" (1753); and *The Journal of a Voyage to Lisbon*, which was published posthumously (1755).

Fielding edited and made major contributions to four journals: *The Champion* (No-

Henry Fielding
(Library of Congress)

vember 15, 1739-June, 1741; the journal continued publication without Fielding until 1742); *The True Patriot* (November 5, 1745-June 17, 1746); *Jacobite's Journal* (December 5, 1747-November 5, 1748); and *The Covent-Garden Journal* (January 4-November 25, 1752).

ACHIEVEMENTS

Fielding's lasting achievements in prose fiction—in contrast to his passing fame as an essayist, dramatist, and judge—result from his development of critical theory and from his aesthetic success in the novels themselves. In the preface to *Joseph Andrews*, Fielding establishes a serious critical basis for the novel as a genre and describes in detail the elements of comic realism; in *Joseph Andrews* and *Tom Jones*, he provides full realizations of this theory. These novels define the ground rules of form that would be followed, to varying degrees, by Jane Austen, William Makepeace Thackeray, George Eliot, Thomas Hardy, James Joyce, and D. H. Lawrence, and they also speak to countless readers across many generations. Both novels, in fact, have been translated into successful films (*Tom Jones* was released in 1963; *Joseph Andrews*, in 1977).

The historical importance of the preface to *Joseph Andrews* results from both the seriousness with which it treats the formal qualities of the novel (at the time a fledgling and barely respectable genre) and the precision with which it defines the characteristics of the genre, the "comic epic-poem in prose." Fielding places *Joseph Andrews* in particular and the comic novel in general squarely in the tradition of classical literature and coherently argues its differences from the romance and the burlesque. He also provides analogies between the comic novel and the visual arts. Fielding thus leads the reader to share his conception that the comic novel is an aesthetically valid form with its roots in classical tradition and a form peculiarly suited to the attitudes and values of its own age.

With his background in theater and journalism, Fielding could move easily through a wide range of forms and rhetorical techniques in his fiction, from direct parody of Samuel Richardson in *An Apology for the Life of Mrs. Shamela Andrews* to ironic inversion of the great man's biography in *Jonathan Wild* to adaptation of classical structure (Vergil's *Aeneid*, c. 29-19 B.C.E.; English translation, 1553) in *Amelia*. The two major constants in these works are the attempt to define a good, moral life, built on benevolence and honor, and a concern for finding the best way to present that definition to the reader. Thus the moral and the technique can never be separated in Fielding's works.

Joseph Andrews and *Tom Jones* bring together these two impulses in Fielding's most organically structured, brilliantly characterized, and masterfully narrated works. These novels vividly capture the diversity of experience in the physical world and the underlying benevolence of the natural order, embodying them in a rich array of the ridiculous in human behavior. Fielding combines a positive assertion of the strength of goodness and benevolence (demonstrated by the structure and plot of the novels) with the sharp thrusts of the satirist's attack on the hypocrisy and vanity of individual characters. These elements are held together by the voice of the narrator—witty, urbane, charming—who serves as moral guide through the novels and the world. Thus beyond the comic merits of each of the individual novels lies a collective sense of universal moral good. The voice of the narrator conveys to the reader the truth of that goodness.

Although the novels were popular in his own day, Fielding's contemporaries thought of him more as playwright-turned-judge than as novelist. This may have been the result of the low esteem in which the novel as a form was held as well as of Fielding's brilliant successes in these other fields. These varied successes have in common a zest for the exploration of the breadth and variety of life—a joy in living—that finds its most articulate and permanent expression in the major novels.

Today Fielding is universally acknowledged as a major figure in the development of the novel, although there is still some debate about whether he or Richardson is the "father" of the British novel. Ian Watt, for example, has asserted that Richardson's development of "formal realism" is more significant than Fielding's comic realism. Other critics, notably Martin Battestin, have demonstrated that Fielding's broader, more humane moral vision, embodied in classical structure and expressed through a self-conscious narrator, is the germ from which the richness and variety of the British novel grows. This disagreement ultimately comes down to personal taste, and there will always be Richardson and Fielding partisans to keep the controversy alive. There is no argument, however, that of their type—the novel of comic realism—no fiction has yet surpassed *Joseph Andrews* or *Tom Jones*.

BIOGRAPHY

Henry Fielding was born April 22, 1707, in Sharpham Park, Somersetshire, to Edmund and Sarah Fielding. His father, an adventurer, gambler, and swaggerer, was a sharp contrast to the quiet, conservative, traditional gentry of his mother's family, the Goulds. In 1710, the family moved to Dorset, where Fielding and his younger brother and three sisters (including the future novelist Sarah Fielding) would spend most of their childhood on a small estate and farm given to Mrs. Fielding by her father, Sir Henry Gould.

The death of Fielding's mother in April, 1718, ended this idyllic life. Litigation over the estate created a series of family battles that raged for several decades. In 1719, Fielding was sent to Eton College, partly because the Goulds wanted him influenced as little as possible by his father, who had resumed his "wild" life in London, and partly because Fielding disliked his father's new Catholic wife. Remaining at Eton until 1724 or 1725, Fielding made many friends, including George Lyttleton and William Pitt. At Eton he began his study of classical literature, which became a profound influence on his literary career.

Few details are known of Fielding's life during the several years after Eton. He spent a good deal of time with the Goulds in Salisbury, but he also led a hectic, boisterous life in London, spending much time at the theater, where the popular masquerades and burlesques influenced him greatly. His visits to the theater stimulated him to try his own hand at comedy, and in February, 1728, *Love in Several Masques*, based on his own romantic adventures of the previous year, was performed at Drury Lane. In March, 1728, Fielding enrolled in the Faculty of Letters at the University of Leyden (Netherlands), where he pursued his interest in the classics. In August, 1729, at the age of twenty-two, he returned to London without completing his degree.

It is clear from his literary output in the 1730's that Fielding was intensely involved in theatrical life. From 1730 through 1737 he authored at least nineteen different dramatic works (as well as presenting revivals and new productions of revised works), most with political themes, at both the Little Theatre in the Haymarket and the Drury Lane. In addition to writing ballad opera, full-length comedies, translations, and parodies, Fielding was also producing, revising the plays of other writers, and managing theater business. He also formed a new, important friendship with the artist William Hogarth.

His theatrical career came to an abrupt halt (although a few more plays appeared in the 1740's) with the passage of the Licensing Act of 1737 which resulted in the closing of many theaters. Fielding's political satire offended Prime Minister Sir Robert Walpole and had been part of the motivation for the government's desire to control and censor the theaters.

In addition to this theatrical activity with its political commentary, Fielding found time in the years 1733-1734 to court and marry Charlotte Cradock of Salisbury. Charlotte's mother died in 1735, leaving the entire estate to the Fieldings and alleviating many of the financial problems caused by the legal disputes over the estate in Dorset. The couple moved from London to East Stour the same year, although Fielding regularly visited London, because he was manager, artistic director, and controller in chief of the Little Theatre. The first of their three children, Charlotte, was born April 17, 1736.

Fielding's relentless energy (and desire to add to his income) compelled him to begin a new career in late 1737, whereupon he began to study law at the Middle Temple. He became a barrister on June 20, 1740, and spent the next several years in the Western Circuit. During this service he became friends with Ralph Allen of Bath. He remained active in the practice of justice, as attorney and magistrate, until he left England in 1754.

Fielding continued to involve himself in political controversy, even while studying law. He edited, under pseudonyms, *The Champion*, an opposition newspaper issued three times a week, directed against Prime Minister Walpole (a favorite subject of Fielding's satire). Later he would edit *The True Patriot* in support of the government during the threat of the Jacobite Rising, *Jacobite's Journal*, and *The Covent-Garden Journal*.

From theater to law to journalism—Fielding had already charged through three careers when the first installment of Richardson's *Pamela: Or, Virtue Rewarded* appeared on November 6, 1740. Deeply disturbed by the artificiality of the novel's epistolary technique, and appalled by its perversion of moral values, Fielding quickly responded with *An Apology for the Life of Mrs. Shamela Andrews*, often referred to as *Shamela*, an "antidote" to *Pamela*. Although published anonymously, Fielding's authorship was apparent and created ill feelings between the two authors that would last most of their lives.

The success of *Shamela* encouraged Fielding to try his hand at a more sustained satire, which eventually grew into *Joseph Andrews*. In 1743 he published, by subscription, the *Miscellanies*, a collection of previously published works, and two new ones: an unfinished story, "A Journey from This World to the Next," and the first version of *Jonathan Wild*.

Although the mid-1740's brought Fielding fame, success, and money, his personal life was beset with pain. He suffered continually from gout, and his wife died in November, 1744. In the following year he became involved in the propaganda battles over the Jacobite Rising. On November 27, 1747, he married his wife's former maid, Mary Daniel, and some sense of peace and order was restored to his private life. They would have five children.

While forming new personal ties and continuing strong involvement in political issues, Fielding was preparing his masterwork, *Tom Jones*. He also took oath as justice of the peace for Westminster and Middlesex, London, in 1748, and he opened an employment agency and estate brokerage with his brother in 1749. His last novel, *Amelia*, was not well received, disappointing those readers who were expecting another *Tom Jones*.

The early 1750's saw Fielding's health continue to decline, although he remained active in his judgeship, producing a number of pamphlets on various legal questions. In June of 1754, his friends convinced him to sail to Lisbon, Portugal, where the climate might improve his health. He died there on October 8, 1754, and is buried in the British Cemetery outside Lisbon. *The Journal of a Voyage to Lisbon*, his last work, was published one year after his death.

Analysis

Analysis and criticism of Henry Fielding's fiction have traditionally centered on the moral values in the novels, the aesthetic structure in which they are placed, and the relationship between the two. In this view, Fielding as moralist takes precedence over Fielding as artist, since the aesthetic structure is determined by the moral. Each of the novels is judged by the extent to which it finds the appropriate form for its moral vision. The relative failure of *Amelia*, for example, may be Fielding's lack of faith in his own moral vision. The happy ending, promulgated by the deus ex machina of the good magistrate, is hardly consistent with the dire effects of urban moral decay that have been at work upon the Booths throughout the novel. Fielding's own moral development and changes in outlook also need to be considered in this view. The reader must examine the sources of Fielding's moral vision in the latitudinarian sermons of the day, as well as the changes in his attitudes as he examined eighteenth century urban life in greater detail, and as he moved in literature from *Joseph Andrews* to *Amelia*, and in life from the theater to the bench of justice.

As is clear from the preface to *Joseph Andrews*, however, Fielding was equally interested in the aesthetics of his fiction. Indeed, each of the novels, even from the first parody, *Shamela*, conveys not only a moral message but a literary experiment to find the strongest method for expressing that message to the largest reading public. This concern is evident in the basic plot structure, characterization, language, and role of the narrator. Each novel attempts to reach the widest audience possible with its moral thesis. Although each differs in the way in which Fielding attempts this, they all have in common the sense that the *how* of the story is as important as the *what*. The novels are experiments in the methods of moral education—for the reader as well as for the characters.

This concern for the best artistic way to teach a moral lesson was hardly new with Fielding. His classical education and interests, as well as the immediate human response gained from theater audiences during his playwriting days, surely led him to see that fiction must delight as well as instruct. Fielding's novels are both exemplars of this goal (in their emphasis on incidents of plot and broad range of characterization) and serious discussions of the method by which to achieve it (primarily through structure and through narrative commentary).

The direct stimulation for Fielding's career as novelist was the publication of Samuel

Richardson's *Pamela*, a novel that disturbed Fielding both by its artistic ineptitude and by its moral vacuousness. Fielding was as concerned with the public reaction to *Pamela* as he was with its author's methods. That the reading public could be so easily misled by *Pamela*'s morals disturbed Fielding deeply, and the success of that novel led him to ponder what better ways were available for reaching the public with his own moral thesis. His response to *Pamela* was both moral (he revealed the true state of Pamela/Shamela's values) and aesthetic (he exposed the artificiality of "writing to the moment").

Sermons and homilies, while effective in church (and certainly sources of Fielding's moral philosophy), were not the stuff of prose fiction; neither was the epistolary presentation of "virtue rewarded" of *Pamela* (or the "objectively" amoral tone of Daniel Defoe's *The Fortunes and Misfortunes of the Famous Moll Flanders, Written from Her Own Memorandums*, 1722). Fielding sought a literary method for combining moral vision and literary pleasure that would be appropriate to the rapidly urbanizing and secular society of the mid-eighteenth century. To find that method he ranged through direct parody, irony, satire, author-narrator intrusion, and moral exemplum. Even those works, such as *Jonathan Wild* and *Amelia*, which are not entirely successful, live because of the vitality of Fielding's experimental methods. In *Joseph Andrews* and *Tom Jones*, he found the way to reach his audience most effectively.

Fielding's informing moral values, embodied in the central characters of the novels (Joseph Andrews, Parson Adams, Tom Jones, Squire Allworthy, Mr. Harrison) can be summarized, as Martin Battestin has ably done, as Charity, Prudence, and Providence. Fielding held an optimistic faith in the perfectability of humanity and the potential for the betterment of society, based on the essential goodness of human nature. These three values must work together. In the novels, the hero's worth is determined by the way in which he interacts with other people (charity), within the limits of social institutions designed to provide order (prudence). His reward is a life full of God's provision (Providence). God's Providence has created a world of abundance and plenitude; man's prudence and charity can guarantee its survival and growth. Both Joseph Andrews and Tom Jones learn the proper combination of prudence and charity. They learn to use their innate inclination toward goodness within a social system that ensures order. To succeed, however, they must overcome obstacles provided by the characters who, through vanity and hypocrisy, distort God's Providence. Thus Fielding's moral vision, while optimistic, is hardly blind to the realities of the world. *Jonathan Wild*, with its basic rhetorical distinction between "good" and "great," and *Amelia*, with its narrative structured around the ill effects of doing good, most strongly reflect Fielding's doubts about the practicality of his beliefs.

These ideas can be easily schematized, but the scheme belies the human complexity through which they are expressed in the novels. Tom Jones is no paragon of virtue, but he must learn, at great physical pain and spiritual risk, how to combine charity and prudence. Even Squire Allworthy is, as Sheldon Sacks has observed, a "fallible" paragon. These ideas do not come from a single source, but are derived from a combination of sources, rooted in Fielding's classical education; the political, religious, and literary movements of his own time; and his own experience as dramatist, journalist, and magistrate.

Fielding's familiarity with the classics, begun at Eton and continued at the University of Leyden, is revealed in many ways: through language (the use of epic simile and epic conventions in *Joseph Andrews*), through plot (the symmetry of design in *Tom Jones*), through theme (the importance of moderation in all the novels), and through structure (the relationship of *Amelia* to Vergil's *Aeneid*). The preface to *Joseph Andrews* makes explicit how much Fielding saw in common between his own work and classical literature. His belief in the benevolent order of the world, especially illustrated by country living, such as at Squire Allworthy's estate (Paradise Hall), is deeply rooted in the pastoral tradition of classical literature. These classical elements are combined with the beliefs of the latitudinarian homilists of the seventeenth and eighteenth centuries, who stressed the perfectibility of humankind in the world through good deeds (charity) and good heart (benevolence).

While Fielding's thematic concerns may be rooted in classical and Christian thought, his literary technique has sources that are more complex, deriving from his education, his own experience in the theater, and the influence of Richardson's *Pamela*. It is difficult to separate each of these sources, for the novels work them into unified and original statements. Indeed, *Joseph Andrews*, the novel most closely related to classical sources, is also deeply imbued with the sense of latitudinarian thought in its criticism of the clergy, and satire of Richardson in its plot and moral vision.

The London in which Fielding spent most of his life was a world of literary and political ferment, an age of factionalism in the arts, with the Tory wits (Jonathan Swift, Alexander Pope, John Gay, John Arbuthnot) allied against Colley Cibber, the poet laureate and self-proclaimed literary spokesman for the British Isles. Swift's *Gulliver's Travels* (1726) and Gay's *The Beggar's Opera* (1728) had recently appeared; both were influential in forming Fielding's literary methods—the first with its emphasis on sharp political satire, the second with the creation of a new literary form, the ballad opera. The ballad opera set new lyrics, expressing contemporary political and social satire, to well-known music. Fielding was to find his greatest theatrical success in this genre and was to carry it over to his fiction, especially *Jonathan Wild*, with its emphasis on London low life and its excesses of language.

It was a time, also, of great political controversy, with the ongoing conflicts between the Tories and Jacobites about the questions of religion and succession. Prime Minister Walpole's politics of expediency were a ripe subject for satire. Fielding's career as journalist began as a direct response to political issues, and significant portions of *Joseph Andrews* and *Tom Jones*, as well as *Jonathan Wild*, deal with political issues.

These various sources, influences, and beliefs are molded into coherent works of art through Fielding's narrative technique. It is through the role of the narrator that he most clearly and successfully experiments in the methods of teaching a moral lesson. Starting with the voice of direct literary parody in *Shamela* and moving through the varied structures and voices of the other novels, Fielding's art leads in many directions, but it always leads to his ultimate concern for finding the best way to teach the clearest moral lesson. In *Tom Jones* he finds the most appropriate method to demonstrate that the world is a beautiful place if people practice charity and prudence.

SHAMELA

The key to understanding how *Shamela* expresses Fielding's concern with both the moral thesis and the aesthetic form of fiction is contained in the introductory letters between Parsons Tickletext and Oliver. Oliver is dismayed at Tickletext's exuberant praise of *Pamela* and at the novel's public reception and popularity. The clergy, in particular, have been citing it as a work worthy to be read with the Scriptures. He contends that the text of *Shamela*, which he encloses, reveals the "true" story of Pamela's adventures and puts them in their proper moral perspective. By reading Oliver's version, Tickletext will correct his own misconceptions; by reading *Shamela* (under the guidance of the prefatory letters), the public will laugh at *Pamela* and perceive the perversity of its moral thesis.

Shamela began, of course, simply as a parody of Richardson's novel, and, in abbreviated form, carries through the narrative of the attempted seduction of the young serving girl by the squire, and her attempts to assert her virtue through chastity or marriage. Fielding makes direct hits at Richardson's weakest points: His two main targets are the epistolary technique of "writing to the moment" and the moral thesis of "virtue rewarded" by pounds and pence (and marriage).

Fielding parodies the epistolary technique by carrying it to its most illogical extreme: Richardson's technical failure is not the choice of epistolary form, but his insistence on its adherence to external reality. Shamela writes her letters at the very same moment she is being attacked in bed by Squire Booby. While feigning sleep she writes: "You see I write in the present tense." The inconsistency of Pamela's shift from letters to journal form when she is abducted is shown through Fielding's retention of the letter form throughout the story, no matter what the obstacles for sending and receiving them. He also compounds the criticism of Richardson by including a number of correspondents in addition to Shamela (her mother, Henrietta Maria Honora Andrews, Mrs. Jewkes, Parson Williams) and including various complications, such as letters within letters within letters.

Fielding retains the essential characters and key scenes from *Pamela*, such as Mr. B's hiding in the closet before the attempted seduction, Pamela's attempted suicide at the pond, and Parson Williams's interference. For each character and scene Fielding adopts Richardson's penchant for minute descriptive detail and intense character response to the event; he also parodies the method and seriousness of the original by revealing the motives of the characters.

The revealing of motives is also Fielding's primary way of attacking the prurience of Richardson's presentation as well as the moral thesis behind it. He debunks the punctilio (decorum) of the central character. Shamela's false modesty ("I thought once of making a little fortune by my person. I now intend to make a great one by my virtue") mocks Pamela's pride in her chastity; the main difference between them is Shamela's recognition and acceptance of the mercenary motives behind her behavior and Pamela's blindness to her own motivation. Richardson never examines the reliability of Pamela's motivations, although he describes her thoughts in detail. Fielding allows Shamela to glory in both her ability to dupe the eager Squire Booby and her mercenary motives for doing so. The reader may, as Parson Oliver wants Tickletext to do, easily condemn Shamela for a villain but never for a hypocrite.

Fielding also attacks Richardson's refusal to describe the sexual attributes of his characters or to admit the intensity of their sexual desires, particularly in the case of Pamela herself. Pamela always hints and suggests—and, Fielding claims, wallows in her suggestiveness. Fielding not only describes the sexual aspects directly, but exaggerates and reduces them to a comic level, hardly to be taken sensually or seriously. *Shamela* quickly, fully, and ruthlessly annihilates the moral thesis of "virtue rewarded" through this direct exaggeration. Fielding does not, however, in his role as parodist, suggest an alternative to *Pamela*'s moral thesis; he is content, for the time, with exposing its flaws.

This first foray into fiction served for Fielding as a testing ground for some of the rhetorical techniques he used in later works, especially the emphasis on satiric inversion. These inversions appear in his reversal of sexual roles in *Joseph Andrews*, the reversal of rhetoric in the "good" and "great" in *Jonathan Wild*, and the reversal of goodness of motive and evil of effect in *Amelia*. Fielding's concern to find a rhetorical method for presenting a moral thesis was confined in *Shamela* to the limited aims and goals of parody. He had such success with the method (after all, he had his apprenticeship in the satiric comedy of the theater), that he began his next novel on the same model.

JOSEPH ANDREWS

Like *Shamela*, *Joseph Andrews* began as a parody of *Pamela*. In his second novel, Fielding reverses the gender of the central character and traces Joseph's attempts to retain his chastity and virtue while being pursued by Lady Booby. This method of inversion creates new possibilities, not only for satirizing Richardson's work but for commenting on the sexual morality of the time in a more positive way than in *Shamela*. The most cursory reading reveals how quickly Fielding grew tired of parody and how *Joseph Andrews* moved beyond its inspiration and its forerunner. Even the choice of direct narration rather than epistolary form indicates Fielding's unwillingness to tie himself to his model.

Most readers agree that the entrance of Parson Adams, Joseph's guide, companion, and partner in misery, turns the novel from simple parody into complex fiction. Adams takes center stage as both comic butt, preserving Joseph's role as hero, and moral guide, preserving Joseph's role as innocent.

Adams's contribution is also part of Fielding's conscious search for the best way to convey his moral thesis. The narrative refers continually to sermons, given in the pulpit or being carried by Adams to be published in London. These sermons are generally ineffectual or contradicted by the behavior of the clergy who pronounce them. Just as experience and the moral example of Adams's life are better teachers for Joseph than sermons—what could be a more effective lesson than the way he is treated by the coach passengers after he is robbed, beaten, and stripped?—so literary example has more power for Fielding and the reader. Adams's constant companion, his copy of Aeschylus, is further testament to Fielding's growing faith in his exemplary power of literature as moral guide. In *Joseph Andrews*, narrative art takes precedence over both parody and sermon.

Fielding's concern for method as well as meaning is given its most formal discussion in the preface. The historical importance of this document results from both the seriousness with which it treats the formal qualities of the novel and the precision with which it defines the characteristics of the genre, the "comic epic-poem in prose." The seriousness is established through the careful logic and organization of the argument and through the parallels drawn between the new genre and classical literature (the lost comic epic supposedly written by Homer) and modern painting (Michelangelo da Caravaggio and William Hogarth).

Fielding differentiates the "comic epic-poem in prose" from contemporary romances such as *Pamela*. The new form is more extended and comprehensive in action, contains a much larger variety of incidents, and treats a greater variety of characters. Unlike the serious romance, the new form is less solemn in subject matter, treats characters of lower rank, and presents the ludicrous rather than the sublime. The comic, opposed to the burlesque, arises solely from the observation of nature, and has its source in the discovery of the "ridiculous" in human nature. The ridiculous always springs from the affectations of vanity and hypocrisy.

Within the novel itself, the narrator will continue the discussion of literary issues in the introductory chapters to each of the first three of four books: "of writing lives in general," "of divisions in authors," and "in praise of biography." These discussions, although sometimes more facetious than serious, do carry through the direction of the opening sentence of the novel: "Examples work more forcibly on the mind than precepts." Additionally, this narrative commentary allows Fielding to assume the role of reader's companion and guide that he develops more fully in *Tom Jones*.

While the preface takes its cue from classical tradition, it is misleading to assume that *Joseph Andrews* is merely an updating of classical technique and ideas. Even more than *Shamela*, this novel brings together Fielding's dissatisfaction with Richardson's moral thesis and his support of latitudinarian attitudes toward benevolence and charity. Here, too, Fielding begins his definition of the "good" man in modern Christian terms. Joseph redefines the place of chastity and honor in male sexuality; Parson Adams exemplifies the benevolence all people should display; Mrs. Tow-wowse, Trulliber, and Peter Pounce, among others, illustrate the vanity and hypocrisy of the world.

The structure of the novel is episodic, combining the earthly journey and escapades of the hero with suggestions of the Christian pilgrimage in John Bunyan's *The Pilgrim's Progress* (1678, 1684). Fielding was still experimenting with form and felt at liberty to digress from his structure with interpolated tales or to depend on coincidence to bring the novel to its conclusion. The immediate moral effect sometimes seems more important than the consistency of rhetorical structure. These are, however, minor lapses in Fielding's progression toward unifying moral thesis and aesthetic structure.

JONATHAN WILD

In *Jonathan Wild*, Fielding seems to have abandoned temporarily the progression from the moral statement of parody and sermon to the aesthetic statement of literary example. *Jonathan Wild* was first published in the year immediately following *Joseph Andrews* (revised in 1754), and there is evidence to indicate that the work was actually written before *Joseph Andrews*. This is a reasonable assumption, since *Jonathan Wild* is more didactic in its method and more negative in its moral vision. It looks back toward *Shamela* rather than ahead to *Tom Jones*.

Jonathan Wild is less a novel, even as Fielding discusses the form in the preface to *Joseph Andrews*, than a polemic. Critic Northrop Frye's term "anatomy" may be the most appropriate label for the work. Like other anatomies—Sir Thomas More's *De Optimo Reipublicae Statu, deque Nova Insula Utopia* (*Utopia*, 1551), Swift's *Gulliver's Travels*, and Samuel Johnson's *Rasselas, Prince of Abyssinia* (1759)—it emphasizes ideas over narrative. It is more moral fable than novel, and more fiction than historical biography, altering history to fit the moral vision.

More important, it was Fielding's experiment in moving the moral lesson of the tale away from the narrative (with its emphasis on incident and character) and into the rhetoric of the narrator (with its emphasis on language). Fielding attempted to use language as the primary carrier of his moral thesis. Although this experiment failed—manipulation of language, alone, would not do—it gave him the confidence to develop the role of the narrative voice in its proper perspective in *Tom Jones*.

Fielding freely adapted the facts of Wild's life, which were well known to the general public. He chose those incidents from Wild's criminal career and punishment that would serve his moral purpose, and he added his own fictional characters, the victims of Wild's "greatness," especially the Heartfrees. Within the structure of the inverted biography of the "great" man, Fielding satirizes the basic concepts of middle-class society. He differentiates between "greatness" and "goodness," terms often used synonymously in the eighteenth century. The success of the novel depends on the reader's acceptance and understanding of this rhetorical inversion.

"Goodness," characterized by the Heartfrees, reiterates the ideals of behavior emphasized in *Joseph Andrews:* benevolence, honor, honesty, and charity, felt through the heart. "Greatness," personified in Wild, results in cunning and courage, characteristics of the will. The action of the novel revolves around the ironic reversal of these terms. Although

Wild's actions speak for themselves, the ironic voice of the narrator constantly directs the reader's response.

Parts of *Jonathan Wild* are brilliantly satiric, but the work as a whole does not speak to modern readers. Fielding abandoned the anatomy form after this experiment, recognizing that the voice of the narrator alone cannot carry the moral thesis of a novel in a convincing way. In *Jonathan Wild*, he carried to an extreme the role of the narrator as moral guide that he experimented with in *Joseph Andrews*. In *Tom Jones*, he found the precise balance: the moral voice of the narrator controlling the reader's reaction through language and the literary examples of plot and character.

TOM JONES

In *Tom Jones*, Fielding moved beyond the limited aims of each of his previous works into a more comprehensive moral and aesthetic vision. No longer bound by the need to attack Richardson or by the attempt to define a specific fictional form, such as the moral fable or the "comic epic-poem in prose," Fielding dramatized the positive values of the good man in a carefully structured narrative held together by the guiding voice of the narrator. This narrator unifies, in a consistent pattern, Fielding's concern for both the truthfulness of his moral vision and the best way to reach the widest audience.

The structure of *Tom Jones*, like that of *Joseph Andrews*, is based on the secularization of the spiritual pilgrimage. Tom must journey from his equivocal position as foundling on the country estate of Squire Allworthy (Paradise Hall) to moral independence in the hellish city of London. He must learn to understand and control his life. When he learns this lesson, he will return to the country to enjoy the plenitude of paradise regained that Providence allows him. He must temper his natural, impetuous charity with the prudence that comes from recognition of his own role in the larger social structure. In precise terms, he must learn to control his animal appetites in order to win the love of Sophia Western and the approval of Allworthy. This lesson is rewarded not only by his gaining these two goals, but by his gaining the knowledge of his parentage and his rightful place in society. He is no longer a "foundling."

Unlike the episodic journey of *Joseph Andrews*, *Tom Jones* adapts the classical symmetry of the epic in a more conscious and precise way. The novel is divided into eighteen books. Some of the books, such as 1 and 4, cover long periods of time and are presented in summary form, with the narrator clearly present; others cover only a few days or hours, with the narrator conspicuously absent and the presentation primarily scenic. The length of each book is determined by the importance of the subject, not the length of time covered.

The books are arranged in a symmetrical pattern. The first half of the novel takes Tom from his mysterious birth to his adventures in the Inn at Upton; the second half takes him from Upton to London and the discovery of his parentage. Books 1 through 6 are set in Somerset at Squire Allworthy's estate and culminate with Tom's affair with Molly. Books

7 through 12 are set on the road to Upton, at the Inn, and on the road from Upton to London; the two central books detail the adventures at the Inn and Tom's affair with Mrs. Waters. Books 13 through 18 take Tom to London and begin with his affair with Lady Bellaston.

Within this pattern, Fielding demonstrates his moral thesis, the education of a "good man," in a number of ways: through the narrative (Tom's behavior continually lowers his moral worth in society); through characters (the contrasting pairs of Tom and Blifil, Allworthy and Western, Square and Thwackum, Molly and Lady Bellaston); and through the voice of the narrator.

Fielding extends the role of the narrator in *Tom Jones*, as teller of the tale, as moral guide, and as literary commentator and critic. Each of these voices was heard in *Joseph Andrews*, but here they come together in a unique narrative persona. Adopting the role of the stagecoach traveler, the narrator speaks directly to his fellow passengers, the readers. He is free to digress and comment whenever he feels appropriate, and there is, therefore, no need for the long interpolated tales such as appeared in *Joseph Andrews*.

To remind his readers that the purpose of fiction is aesthetic as well as moral, the narrator often comments on literary topics: "Of the Serious in Writing, and for What Purpose it is introduced"; "A wonderful long chapter concerning the Marvelous"; "Containing Instructions very necessary to be perused by modern Critics." Taken together, these passages provide a guide to Fielding's literary theory as complete as the preface to *Joseph Andrews*.

Although in *Tom Jones* Fielding still schematically associates characters with particular moral values, the range of characters is wider than in his previous novels. Even a minor character, such as Black George, has a life beyond his moral purpose as representative of hypocrisy and self-servingness.

Most important, *Tom Jones* demonstrates Fielding's skill in combining his moral vision with aesthetic form in a way that is most pleasurable to the reader. The reader learns how to live the good Christian life because Tom learns that lesson. Far more effective than parody, sermon, or moral exemplum, the combination of narrative voice and literary example of plot and character is Fielding's greatest legacy to the novel.

Lawrence F. Laban

Other major works

PLAYS: *Love in Several Masques*, pr., pb. 1728; *The Author's Farce, and the Pleasures of the Town*, pr., pb. 1730; *Rape upon Rape: Or, Justice Caught in His Own Trap*, pr., pb. 1730 (also known as *The Coffee-House Politician*); *The Temple Beau*, pr., pb. 1730; *Tom Thumb: A Tragedy*, pr., pb. 1730 (revised as *The Tragedy of Tragedies: Or, The Life and Death of Tom Thumb the Great*, pr., pb. 1731); *The Letter-Writers: Or, A New Way to Keep a Wife at Home*, pr., pb. 1731; *The Welsh Opera: Or, The Grey Mare the Better Horse*, pr., pb. 1731 (revised as *The Grub-Street Opera*, pb. 1731); *The Covent Garden Tragedy*, pr., pb. 1732; *The Lottery*, pr., pb. 1732; *The Mock Doctor: Or, The Dumb Lady Cur'd*, pr., pb. 1732 (adaptation of Molière's *Le Medecin malgré lui*); *The Modern Husband*, pr., pb. 1732 (five acts); *The Old Debauchees*, pr., pb. 1732; *The Miser*, pr., pb. 1733 (adaptation of Molière's *L'Avare*); *Don Quixote in England*, pr., pb. 1734; *The Intriguing Chambermaid*, pr., pb. 1734 (adaptation of Jean-François Regnard's *Le Retour imprévu*); *An Old Man Taught Wisdom: Or, The Virgin Unmask'd*, pr., pb. 1735; *The Universal Gallant: Or, The Different Husbands*, pr., pb. 1735 (five acts); *Pasquin: Or, A Dramatic Satire on the Times*, pr., pb. 1736; *Tumble-Down Dick: Or, Phaeton in the Suds*, pr., pb. 1736; *Eurydice Hiss'd: Or, A Word to the Wise*, pr., pb. 1737; *Eurydice: Or, The Devil's Henpeck'd*, pr. 1737 (one act); *The Historical Register for the Year 1736*, pr., pb. 1737 (three acts); *Miss Lucy in Town*, pr., pb. 1742 (one act); *The Wedding-Day*, pr., pb. 1743 (five acts; also known as *The Virgin Unmask'd*); *The Fathers: Or, The Good-Natured Man*, pr., pb. 1778 (revised for posthumous production by David Garrick).

NONFICTION: *The Journal of a Voyage to Lisbon*, 1755.

TRANSLATION: *The Military History of Charles XII King of Sweden*, 1740.

MISCELLANEOUS: *Miscellanies*, 1743 (3 volumes).

BIBLIOGRAPHY

Battestin, Martin C. *A Henry Fielding Companion*. Westport, Conn.: Greenwood Press, 2000. Comprehensive reference work covers the life and writings of Fielding in a thorough fashion. Includes sections on where Fielding lived, his family, and significant historical figures and literary influences, in addition to material on Fielding's works, themes, and characters. Includes bibliography and index.

Battestin, Martin C., with Ruthe R. Battestin. *Henry Fielding: A Life*. New York: Routledge, 1989. The *Sunday Times* of London voted this work one of the four best biographies of the year. Based on fourteen years' research, this detailed biography provides a definitive story of Fielding. Includes a useful bibliography of Fielding's writings.

Bertelsen, Lance. *Henry Fielding at Work: Magistrate, Businessman, Writer*. New York: Palgrave, 2000. Presents analysis of Fielding in his roles as writer, magistrate, and businessman, discussing how his various work experiences affected the form and content of his writing. Includes bibliography and index.

Dircks, Richard J. *Henry Fielding*. Boston: Twayne, 1983. Provides a useful introduction to Fielding, integrating his central ideas and vision of life as they are experienced in his works as a novelist, dramatist, journalist, and pamphleteer. Focuses on Fielding's major works. Includes an excellent bibliography and a chronology.

Mace, Nancy A. *Henry Fielding's Novels and the Classical Tradition*. Newark: University of Delaware Press, 1996. Examines the classical influence on Fielding's novels and other writings, discussing his knowledge of classical literature and his use of classical allusions and quotations.

Pagliaro, Harold E. *Henry Fielding: A Literary Life*. New York: St. Martin's Press, 1998. Excellent work presents an interesting account of Fielding's life and writings, with one chapter devoted to his novels and other prose fiction. Includes bibliographical references and index.

Paulson, Ronald. *The Life of Henry Fielding: A Critical Biography*. Malden, Mass.: Blackwell, 2000. Examines how Fielding's literary works—novels, plays, and essays—all contained autobiographical elements. Each chapter begins with an annotated chronology of the events of Fielding's life in the period covered within the chapter. Includes bibliography and index.

Rawson, Claude, ed. *The Cambridge Companion to Henry Fielding*. New York: Cambridge University Press, 2007. Collection of essays, commissioned for this volume, includes an examination of Fielding's life and discussion of his major novels, his style, his theatrical career, and his journalism work.

Rivero, Albert J., ed. *Critical Essays on Henry Fielding*. New York: G. K. Hall, 1998. Interesting collection of essays about Fielding that were published originally in the 1980's and 1990's, including discussions of the novels *Joseph Andrews*, *Tom Jones*, *Amelia*, and *Jonathan Wild*. Includes bibliographical references and index.

Watt, Ian. *The Rise of the Novel: Studies in Defoe, Richardson, and Fielding*. 2d American ed. Berkeley: University of California Press, 2001. Focuses on three novelists—Fielding, Daniel Defoe, and Samuel Richardson—in tracing the social conditions, public attitudes, and literary practices in eighteenth century England that contributed to the emergence of the novel as an important literary genre. Includes a chapter titled "Fielding and the Epic Theory of the Novel" as well as a chapter analyzing *Tom Jones*.

NIKOLAI GOGOL

Born: Sorochintsy, Ukraine, Russian Empire (now in Ukraine); March 31, 1809
Died: Moscow, Russia; March 4, 1852
Also known as: Nikolai Vasilyevich Gogol

PRINCIPAL LONG FICTION
Myortvye dushi, 1842, 1855 (2 parts; *Dead Souls*, 1887)
Taras Bulba, 1842 (revision of his 1835 short story; English translation, 1886)

OTHER LITERARY FORMS

Nikolai Gogol (GAW-guhl) authored many short stories, most of which are part of his "Ukrainian cycle" or his later "Petersburg cycle." He also wrote many plays, including *Revizor* (pr., pb. 1836; *The Inspector General*, 1890) and *Zhenit'ba* (pr., pb. 1842; *Marriage: A Quite Incredible Incident*, 1926), as well as a great deal of nonfiction, much of it collected in *Arabeski* (1835; *Arabesques*, 1982) and *Vybrannye mesta iz perepiski s druzyami* (1847; *Selected Passages from Correspondence with Friends*, 1969). Gogol's *Polnoe sobranie sochinenii* (1940-1952; collected works), which includes unfinished works and drafts as well as his voluminous correspondence, fills fourteen volumes. All of Gogol's finished works, but not his drafts or correspondence, are available in English translation.

ACHIEVEMENTS

Nikolai Gogol's first collection of short stories, *Vechera na khutore bliz Dikanki* (1831, 1832; *Evenings on a Farm near Dikanka*, 1926), made him famous, and his second collection, *Mirgorod* (1835; English translation, 1928), highlighted by the story "Taras Bulba," established his reputation as Russia's leading prose writer. While Gogol's early stories, set in the Ukraine, are for the most part conventionally Romantic, his later Petersburg cycle of short stories, among which "Zapiski sumasshedshego" ("Diary of a Madman") and "Shinel" ("The Overcoat") are two of the best known, marks the beginning of Russian critical realism. Gogol's comedic plays are classics and are as popular on the stage (and screen) today as they were in Gogol's lifetime.

Gogol's novel *Dead Souls* is rivaled only by Leo Tolstoy's *Voyna i mir* (1865-1869; *War and Peace*, 1886) as the greatest prose work of Russian literature. Russian prose fiction is routinely divided into two schools: the Pushkinian, which is objective, matter-of-fact, and sparing in its use of verbal devices; and the Gogolian, which is artful, ornamental, and exuberant in its use of ambiguity, irony, pathos, and a variety of figures and tropes usually associated with poetry. Tolstoy and Ivan Turgenev belong to the Pushkinian school; Fyodor Dostoevski, to the Gogolian. In his historical, critical, and moral essays, but especially in *Selected Passages from Correspondence with Friends*, Gogol established

Nikolai Gogol
(Library of Congress)

many of the principles of Russian conservative thought, anticipating the ideas of such writers as Dostoevski and Apollon Grigoryev.

BIOGRAPHY

Nikolai Vasilyevich Gogol, the son of a country squire, was born and educated in the Ukraine. Russian was to him a foreign language, which he mastered while attending secondary school in Nezhin, also in the Ukraine. After his graduation in 1828, Gogol went to St. Petersburg, where he joined the civil service. His first literary effort, "Hans Küchelgarten" (1829), a sentimental idyll in blank verse, was a failure, but his prose fiction immediately attracted attention. After the success of *Evenings on a Farm near Dikanka*, Gogol decided to devote himself entirely to his literary career. He briefly taught medieval history at St. Petersburg University (1834-1835) and thereafter lived the life of a freelance writer and journalist, frequently supported by wealthy patrons. The opening of his play *The Inspector General* at the Aleksandrinsky Theater in St. Petersburg on April 19, 1836, attended and applauded by Czar Nicholas I, was a huge success, but it also elicited vehement attacks by the reactionary press, enraged by Gogol's spirited satire of corruption and stupidity in the provincial administration, and Gogol decided to go abroad to escape the controversy.

From 1836 to 1848, Gogol lived abroad, mostly in Rome, returning to Russia for brief periods only. The year 1842 marked the high point of Gogol's career with the appearance of the first part of *Dead Souls* and the publication of a four-volume set of collected works, which contained some previously unpublished pieces, in particular the great short story "The Overcoat." After 1842, Gogol continued to work on part 2 of *Dead Souls*, but he was becoming increasingly preoccupied with questions of religion and morality. His book *Selected Passages from Correspondence with Friends*, actually a collection of essays in which Gogol defends traditional religious and moral values as well as the social status quo (including the institution of serfdom), caused a storm of protest, as liberals felt that it was flagrantly and evilly reactionary, while even many conservatives considered it to be unctuous and self-righteous.

Sorely hurt by the unfavorable reception of his book, Gogol almost entirely withdrew from literature. He returned to Russia for good in 1848 and spent the rest of his life in religious exercise and meditation. Shortly before his death, caused by excessive fasting and utter exhaustion, Gogol burned the final version of part 2 of *Dead Souls*. An earlier version was later discovered and published in 1855.

Analysis

The cover of the first edition of *Dead Souls*, designed by Nikolai Gogol himself, reads as follows: "*The Adventures of Chichikov or Dead Souls*. A Poem by N. Gogol. 1842." "The Adventures of Chichikov" is in the smallest print, "Dead Souls" is more than twice that size, and "A Poem" is twice again the size of "Dead Souls." The word "or" is barely legible. The fact that "The Adventures of Chichikov" was inserted at the insistence of the censor, who felt that "Dead Souls" alone smacked of blasphemy, accounts for one-half of this typographical irregularity. The fact that "A Poem" (Russian *poema*, which usually designates an epic poem in verse) dominates the cover of a prose work that at first glance is anything but "poetic" also had its reasons, as will be seen.

Dead Souls

The plot structure of *Dead Souls* is simple. Chichikov, a middle-aged gentleman of decent appearance and pleasing manners, travels through the Russian provinces on what seems a mysterious quest: He buys up "dead souls," meaning serfs who have died since the last census but are still listed on the tax rolls until the next census. Along the way, he meets various types of Russian landowners: the sugary and insipid Manilov; the widow Korobochka, ignorant and superstitious but an efficient manager of her farm; the dashing Nozdryov, a braggart, liar, and cardsharp; the brutish but shrewd Sobakevich; and the sordid miser Plyushkin. Having returned to the nearby provincial capital to obtain legal title to his four-hundred-odd "souls," Chichikov soon comes under a cloud of suspicion and quickly leaves town. Only at this stage does the reader learn about Chichikov's past and the secret of the dead souls. A civil service official, Chichikov had twice reached the threshold of prosperity through cleverly devised depredations of the state treasury, but each time he had been foiled at the last moment. After his second fiasco, he had been allowed to resign with only a small sum saved from the clutches of his auditors. Undaunted, he had conceived yet another scheme: He would buy up a substantial number of "dead souls," mortgage them at the highest rate available, and disappear with the cash.

The plot of part 1 takes the story only this far. In what is extant of part 2, Chichikov is seen not only trying to buy more dead souls but also getting involved in other nefarious schemes. It also develops, however, that Chichikov is not happy with his sordid and insecure existence and that he dreams of an honest and virtuous life. He would be willing to mend his ways if he could only find a proper mentor who would give him the right start. There is reason to believe that Gogol planned to describe Chichikov's regeneration and return to the path of righteousness in part 3. The whole plot thus follows the pattern of a picaresque novel, and many details of *Dead Souls* are, in fact, compatible with this genre, which was well established in Russian literature even before Gogol's day.

Actually, part 1 of *Dead Souls* is many things in addition to a picaresque novel: a humorous novel after the fashion of Charles Dickens's *Pickwick Papers* (1836-1837, serial; 1837, book), with which it was immediately compared by the critics; a social satire attacking the corruption and inefficiency of the imperial administration and the crudity and mental torpor of the landed gentry; a moral sermon in the form of grotesque character sketches; and, above all, an epic of Russia's abjection and hoped-for redemption. The characters of part 2, while copies, in a way, of those encountered in part 1, have redeeming traits and strike the reader as human beings rather than as caricatures. The landowner Tentetnikov, in particular, is clearly a prototype of Oblomov, the hero of Ivan Goncharov's immortal novel of that title (1859; English translation, 1915), and, altogether, part 2 of *Dead Souls* is a big step in the direction of the Russian realist novel of the 1850's and 1860's. The following observations apply to part 1, unless otherwise indicated.

The structure of *Dead Souls* is dominated by the road, as the work begins with a description of Chichikov's arrival at an inn of an unidentified provincial capital and ends with him back on the road, with several intervening episodes in which the hero is seen on his way to his next encounter with a potential purveyor of dead souls. Chichikov's tippling coachman, Selifan, and his three-horse carriage (*troika*) are often foregrounded in Gogol's narrative, and one of the three horses, the lazy and stubborn piebald, has become one of the best-known "characters" in all of Russian fiction. The celebrated *troika* passage concludes part 1. Vladimir Nabokov has written that critic Andrey Bely saw "the whole first volume of *Dead Souls* as a closed circle whirling on its axle and blurring the spokes, with the theme of the wheel cropping up at each new revolution on round Chichikov's part."

When Chichikov is not on the road, the narrative becomes a mirror, as each new character is reflected in Chichikov's mind with the assistance of the omniscient narrator's observations and elucidations. One contemporary critic said that reading *Dead Souls* was like walking down a hotel corridor, opening one door after another—and staring at another human monster each time.

The road and the mirror by no means exhaust Gogol's narrative attitudes. *Dead Souls* features some philosophical discussions on a variety of topics; many short narrative vignettes, such as when Chichikov dreamily imagines what some of his freshly acquired dead souls may have been like in life; an inserted novella, *The Tale of Captain Kopeikin*, told by the local postmaster, who suspects that Chichikov is in fact the legendary outlaw Captain Kopeikin; repeated apostrophes to the reader, discussing the work itself and the course to be taken in continuing it; and, last but not least, Gogol's much-debated lyric digressions. Altogether, while there is some dialogue in *Dead Souls*, the narrator's voice dominates throughout. In fact, the narrative may be described as the free flow of the narrator's stream of consciousness, drifting from observation to observation, image to image, and thought to thought. It is often propelled by purely verbal associations. A common instance of the latter is the so-called realized metaphor, such as when a vendor of hot mead, whose large red face is likened to a copper samovar, is referred to as "the samovar"; when Chichikov, threatened with bodily harm by an enraged Nozdryov and likened to a fortress under siege, suddenly becomes "the fortress"; or when the bearlike Sobakevich is casually identified as a "fair sized bear" in the role of landowner. It is also verbal legerdemain that eventually turns Sobakevich's whole estate into an extension of its owner: "Every object, every chair in Sobakevich's house seemed to proclaim: 'I, too, am Sobakevich!'"

Hyperbole is another device characteristic of Gogol's style. Throughout *Dead Souls*, grotesque distortions and exaggerations are presented as a matter of course—for example, when the scratching of the clerks' pens at the office where Chichikov seals his purchase of dead souls is likened to "the sound of several carts loaded with brushweed and driven through a forest piled with dead leaves a yard deep." Often the hyperbole is ironic, such as when the attire of local ladies is reported to be "of such fashionable pastel shades that one could not even give their names, to such a degree had the refinement of taste attained!"

A sure sign of the author's own point of view surfaces in frequent literary allusions and several passages in which Gogol digresses to discuss the theory of fiction—for example, the famous disquisition, introducing chapter 7, on the distinction between the writer who idealizes life and the writer who chooses to deal with real life. Gogol, who fancies himself to be a realist, wryly observes that "the judgment of his time does not recognize that much spiritual depth is required to throw light upon a picture taken from a despised stratum of life, and to exalt it into a pearl of creative art" but feels "destined by some wondrous power to go hand in hand with his heroes, to contemplate life in its entirety, life rushing past in all its enormity, amid laughter perceptible to the world and through tears that are unperceived by and unknown to it!" The phrases "to exalt it into a pearl of creative art" and "amid laughter perceptible to the world and through tears that are unperceived by and unknown to it" have become common Russian usage, along with many others in *Dead Souls*.

Dead Souls is studded with many outright digressions. It must be kept in mind, however, that the mid-nineteenth century novel was routinely used as a catchall for miscellaneous didactic, philosophical, critical, scholarly, and lyric pieces that were often only superficially, if at all, integrated into the texture of the larger work. Still, the number and nature of digressions in *Dead Souls* are exceptional even by the standards of a *roman feuilleton* of the 1840's. As described by Victor Erlich, two basic types of digressions are found in *Dead Souls:* "the lateral darts and the upward flights." The former are excursions into a great variety of aspects of Russian life, keenly observed, sharply focused, and always lively and colorful. For example, having observed that Sobakevich's head looks quite like a pumpkin, Gogol, in one of his many "Homeric similes," veers off into a village idyll about a peasant lad strumming a balalaika made from a pumpkin to win the heart of a "snowy-breasted and snowy-necked Maiden."

Gogol's upward flights are of a quite different order. They permit his imagination to escape the prosaic reality of Chichikov's experience and allow him to become a poet who takes a lofty view of Russia and its destiny. In several of these passages, Gogol's imagination becomes quite literally airborne. One of them, at the conclusion of chapter 5, begins with a lofty aerial panorama: "Even as an incomputable host of churches, of monasteries, with cupolas, bulbous domes, and crosses, is scattered all over holy and devout Russia, so does an incomputable multitude of tribes, generations, peoples swarm, flaunt their motley and scurry across the face of the earth." It ends in a rousing paean to "the Russian word which, like no other in the world, would burst out so, from out the very heart, which would seethe so and quiver and flutter so much like a living thing."

Early in chapter 11, Gogol produces another marvelous panoramic vision of Russia, apostrophized in the famous passage, "Russia, Russia! I behold thee—from my alien, beautiful, far-off vantage point I behold thee." (Gogol wrote most of *Dead Souls* while living in Italy.) The conclusion of this, the final chapter of part 1, then brings the most famous lines of prose in all of Russian literature, the *troika* passage in which a speeding three-horse carriage is elevated to a symbol of Russia's historical destiny. The intensity and plenitude of life and emotion in these and other airborne lyric passages stand in stark contrast to the drab world that is otherwise dominant in *Dead Souls*. These lyric digressions were challenged as incongruous and unnecessary even by some contemporary critics who, as do many critics today, failed to realize that Gogol's is a dual vision of manic-depressive intensity.

As a *poema* (epic poem), *Dead Souls* is a work that Gogol perceived as the poetic expression of an important religious-philosophical conception—that is, something on the order of Dante's *La divina commedia* (c. 1320; *The Divine Comedy*, 1802) or John Milton's *Paradise Lost* (1667, 1674). Incidentally, there is one rather inconsequential allusion to Dante in chapter 7, where one reads that a collegiate registrar "served our friends even as Virgil at one time had served Dante, and guided them to the Presence."

Immediately after the appearance of *Dead Souls*, critics were split into two camps: those who, like Konstantin Aksakov, greeted the work as the Russian national epic, found numerous Homeric traits in it, and perceived it as a true incarnation of the Russian spirit in all of its depth and plenitude, and those who, like Nikolai Alekseevich Polevoi and Osip Ivanovich Senkovsky, saw it as merely an entertaining, though rather banal and in places pretentious, humorous novel. The latter group—which included even the great critic Vissarion Belinsky, who otherwise felt that *Dead Souls* was a perfect quintessence of Russian life—found Gogol's attempts at philosophizing and solemn pathos merely pompous and false. There has never been agreement in this matter. Nevertheless, several passages in part 1, the whole drift of part 2, and a number of quite unequivocal statements made by Gogol in his correspondence (in *Selected Passages from Correspondence with Friends* and in his posthumous "Author's Confession") all suggest that Gogol did indeed perceive *Dead Souls* as a *Divine Comedy* of the Russian soul, with part 1 its *Inferno*, part 2 its *Purgatory*, and part 3 its *Paradise*.

How, then, is part 1 in fact an *Inferno*, a Russian Hell? It is set in a Hades of dead souls, of humans who lead a shadowy phantom existence bereft of any real meaning or direction. Thus, it must be understood that in the Romantic philosophy of Gogol's time, the "normal" existence of a European philistine was routinely called "illusory," "unreal," and even "ghostly," while the ideal quest of the artist or philosopher was considered "substantial," "real," and "truly alive." As Andrey Bely demonstrated most convincingly, all of part 1 is dominated by what he calls "the figure of fiction." Whatever is said or believed to be true is from beginning to end a fiction, as unreal as Chichikov's financial transactions. For example, when the good people of N. begin to suspect that something is wrong with Chichikov, some of them believe that he plans to abduct the Governor's daughter, others conjecture that he is really Captain Kopeikin, a highway robber of legendary fame, and some actually suspect that he is Napoleon escaped from his island exile, but nobody investigates his motive for buying dead souls. As Bely also demonstrated, even time and space in *Dead Souls* are fictitious: The text will not even allow one to determine the season of the year; Chichikov's itinerary, if methodically checked, is physically impossible; and so on. Behind the figure of fiction, there looms large the message that all earthly experience and wisdom are in fact illusory, as Gogol makes explicit in a philosophical digression found in chapter 10.

In this shadowy world of fiction there exist two kinds of dead souls. There are the dead serfs who are sold and mortgaged and who, in the process, acquire a real semblance of life. Mrs. Korobochka, as soon as she has understood that Chichikov is willing to pay her some money for her dead serfs, is afraid that he may underpay her and somewhat timidly suggests that "maybe I'll find some use for them in my own household." Sobakevich, who haggles about the price of each dead soul, insists on eloquently describing their skills and virtues, as though it really mattered. Chichikov himself firmly rejects an offer by the local authorities to provide him with a police escort for the souls he has purchased, asserting that "his peasants are all of eminently quiet disposition." The same night, however, when he returns home from a party thrown by the local police chief to honor the new owner of four hundred souls, he actually orders Selifan "to gather all the resettled peasants, so he can personally make a roll call of them." Selifan and Petrushka, Chichikov's lackey, barely manage to get their master to bed.

The humanitarian message behind all of this is obvious: How could a person who finds the buying and selling of dead souls "fantastic" and "absurd" have the effrontery to find the same business transactions involving living souls perfectly normal? This message applies not only to Russia in the age of serfdom (which ended only in 1861—that is, at about the same time formal slavery ended in the United States) but also to any situation in which human beings are reduced to their social or economic function.

The other dead souls are the landowners and government officials whom we meet in *Dead Souls*. As the critic Vasily Rozanov observed, the peculiar thing about Gogolian characters is that they have no souls; they have habits and appetites but no deeper human emotions or ideal strivings. This inevitably deprives them of their humanity and renders them two-dimensional personifications of their vices—caricatures. Sobakevich is a very shrewd talking bear. Nozdryov is so utterly worthless that he appears to be a mere appendage of his extraordinarily handsome, thick, and pitch-black sideburns, thinned out a bit from time to time, when their owner is caught cheating at cards and suffers a whisker pulling. Plyushkin's stony miserliness has deprived him of all feeling and has turned him, a rich landowner, into a beggar and an outcast of society. *Dead Souls* has many such caricatures, which have been likened to Brueghelian grotesque paintings. This analogy applies to the following passage in chapter 11, for example: "The clerks in the Treasury were especially distinguished for their unprepossessing and unsightly appearance. Some had faces for all the world like badly baked bread: one cheek would be all puffed out to one side, the chin slanting off to the other, the upper lip blown up into a big blister that, to top it all off, had burst."

As early as 1842, the critic Stepan Shevyrev suggested that *Dead Souls* represented a mad world, thus following an ancient literary and cultural tradition (which today is often referred to as that of the "carnival"). The massive absurdities, non sequiturs, and simply plain foolishness throughout the whole text could, for Gogol and for many of his readers, have only one message: That which poses for "real life" is in fact nothing but a ludicrous farce. The basic course of Gogol's imagination is that of a descent into a world of ridiculous, banal, and vile "nonbeing," from which it will from time to time rise to the heights of noble and inspired "being."

Taras Bulba

While *Dead Souls* is unquestionably Gogol's masterpiece, his only other work of long fiction, *Taras Bulba*, is not without interest. The 1835 version of this work is a historical novella; the 1842 version, almost twice as long and thus novel-sized, has many digressions and is at once more realistic and more gothic but also more patriotic, moralizing, and bigoted. The plot is essentially the same in both versions.

Taras Bulba is a Ukrainian Cossack leader, so proud of his two fine sons recently back from school in Kiev that he foments war against the hated Poles, so that Ostap and Andriy can prove their manhood in battle. The Cossacks are initially successful, and the Poles are driven back to the fortress city of Dubno. The Cossacks lay siege to it, and the city seems ready to fall when Andriy is lured to the city by a messenger from a beautiful Polish maiden with whom he had fallen in love as a student in Kiev. Blinded by her promises of love, Andriy turns traitor. The Cossacks' fortunes now take a turn for the worse. They are pressed hard by a Polish relief force. On the battlefield, Taras meets Andriy (now a Polish officer), orders him to dismount, and shoots him. The Cossacks, however, are defeated, and Ostap is taken prisoner. Old Taras makes his way to Warsaw, hoping to save him, but can only witness his son's execution. Having returned to the Ukraine, Taras becomes one of the leaders of yet another Cossack uprising against the king of Poland. When peace is made, Taras alone refuses to honor it. He continues to wreak havoc on the Poles all over the Ukraine but is finally captured by superior Polish forces. He dies at the stake, prophesying the coming of a Russian czar against whom no power on earth will stand.

There is little historical verity in *Taras Bulba*. Different details found in the text point to the fifteenth, sixteenth, and seventeenth centuries as the time of its action. It is thus an epic synthesis of the struggle of the Orthodox Ukraine to retain its independence from Catholic Poland. The battle scenes are patterned on those in the works of Vergil and Homer, and there are many conventional epic traits throughout, such as scores of brief scenes of single combat, catalogs of warriors' names, extended Homeric similes, orations, and, of course, the final solemn prophecy. Taras Bulba is a tragic hero who expiates his hubris with the loss of his sons and his own terrible death.

The earlier version of *Taras Bulba* serves mostly the glorification of the wild, carefree life at the Cossack army camp. In the later version, this truly inspired hymn to male freedom is obscured by a message of Russian nationalism, Orthodox bigotry, and nostalgia for a glorious past that never was. The novel features almost incessant baiting of Poles and Jews. Gogol's view of the war is a wholly unrealistic and romantic one: The reader is told of "the enchanting music of bullets and swords" and so on. From a literary viewpoint, *Taras Bulba* is a peculiar mixture of the historical novel in the manner of Sir Walter Scott and the gothic tale. The narrator stations himself above his hero, gently faulting him on some of his uncivilized traits, such as the excessive stock Taras puts in his drinking prowess or his maltreatment of his long-suffering wife. Rather often, however, the narrator descends to the manner of the folktale. His language swings wildly from coarse humor and naturalistic grotesque to solemn oratory and lyric digressions. Scenes of unspeakable atrocities are reported with relish, but some wonderful poems in prose are also presented, such as the well-known description of the Ukrainian steppe in the second chapter.

Altogether, *Taras Bulba* contains some brilliant writing but also some glaring faults. It immediately became a classic, and soon enough a school text, inasmuch as its jingoism met with the approval of the czar—and eventually of Soviet school administrators. Several film versions, Russian as well as Western, have been produced.

Although Gogol's production of fiction was quite small by nineteenth century standards, both his novels and his short stories have had extraordinary influence on the development of Russian prose—an influence that was still potent at the end of the twentieth century, as witnessed by the works of Andrei Sinyavsky and other writers of the Third Emigration.

Victor Terras

OTHER MAJOR WORKS

SHORT FICTION: *Vechera na khutore bliz Dikanki*, 1831, 1832 (2 volumes; *Evenings on a Farm near Dikanka*, 1926); *Arabeski*, 1835 (*Arabesques*, 1982); *Mirgorod*, 1835 (English translation, 1928); *The Complete Tales of Nikolai Gogol*, 1985 (2 volumes; Leonard J. Kent, editor).

PLAYS: *Revizor*, pr., pb. 1836 (*The Inspector General*, 1890); *Utro delovogo cheloveka*, pb. 1836 (revision of *Vladimir tretey stepeni*; *An Official's Morning*, 1926); *Igroki*, pb. 1842 (*The Gamblers*, 1926); *Lakeyskaya*, pb. 1842 (revision of *Vladimir tretey stepeni*; *The Servants' Hall*, 1926); *Otryvok*, pb. 1842 (revision of *Vladimir tretey stepeni*; *A Fragment*, 1926); *Tyazhba*, pb. 1842 (revision of *Vladimir tretey stepeni*; *The Lawsuit*, 1926); *Vladimir tretey stepeni*, pb. 1842 (wr. 1832); *Zhenit'ba*, pr., pb. 1842 (wr. 1835; *Marriage: A Quite Incredible Incident*, 1926); *The Government Inspector, and Other Plays*, 1926.

POETRY: *Hanz Kuechelgarten*, 1829.

NONFICTION: *Vybrannye mesta iz perepiski s druzyami*, 1847 (*Selected Passages from Correspondence with Friends*, 1969); *Letters of Nikolai Gogol*, 1967.

MISCELLANEOUS: *The Collected Works*, 1922-1927 (6 volumes); *Polnoe sobranie sochinenii*, 1940-1952 (14 volumes); *The Collected Tales and Plays of Nikolai Gogol*, 1964.

BIBLIOGRAPHY

Bojanowska, Edyta M. *Nikolai Gogol: Between Ukrainian and Russian Nationalism.* Cambridge, Mass.: Harvard University Press, 2007. Analyzes Gogol's life and works in terms of his conflicted national identity. Gogol was born in Ukraine when it was a part of the Russian empire; Bojanowska describes how he was engaged with questions of Ukrainian nationalism and how his works presented a bleak and ironic portrayal of Russia and Russian themes.

Erlich, Victor. *Gogol.* New Haven, Conn.: Yale University Press, 1969. Provides an accessible and evenhanded discussion of Gogol for nonspecialists. Focuses on Gogol's oeuvre, dealing with much of the "myth" about the author, and supplies interesting background to the making of Gogol's works.

Fanger, Donald L. *The Creation of Nikolai Gogol.* Cambridge, Mass.: Belknap Press of Harvard University Press, 1979. Digs deeply into background material and includes discussion of Gogol's works both published and unpublished in an effort to reveal the genius of Gogol's creative power. Worthwhile in many respects, particularly for the wealth of details provided about Gogol's life and milieu. Includes endnotes and index.

Gippius, V. V. *Gogol*. Translated by Robert Maguire. Ann Arbor, Mich.: Ardis, 1981. Originally written in 1924, this famous monograph supplies not only the view of a fellow countryman but also a vast, informed, and intellectual analysis of both the literary tradition in which Gogol wrote and his innovation and contribution to that tradition. Vastly interesting and easily accessible. Includes notes and a detailed list of Gogol's works.

Luckyj, George Stephen Nestor. *The Anguish of Mykola Hohol a.k.a. Nikolai Gogol*. Toronto, Ont.: Canadian Scholars' Press, 1998. Explores Gogol's life and discusses how it affected his work. Includes bibliographical references and index.

Maguire, Robert A. *Exploring Gogol*. Stanford, Calif.: Stanford University Press, 1994. One of the most comprehensive studies of Gogol's ideas and entire writing career available in English. Includes chronology, detailed notes, and extensive bibliography.

_____, ed. *Gogol from the Twentieth Century: Eleven Essays*. Princeton, N.J.: Princeton University Press, 1974. Collection of essays represents some of the most famous and influential opinions on Gogol in the twentieth century. Following a lengthy introduction by the editor and translator, the contributors address and elucidate some of the most problematic aspects of Gogol's stylistics, thematics, and other compositional elements. Includes bibliography and index.

Setchkarev, Vsevolod. *Gogol: His Life and Works*. Translated by Robert Kramer. New York: New York University Press, 1965. Standard work on Gogol is still often recommended in undergraduate courses. Concentrates on both the biography and the works, seen individually and as an artistic system. Very straightforward and easily readable.

Spieker, Sven, ed. *Gogol: Exploring Absence—Negativity in Nineteenth Century Russian Literature*. Bloomington, Ind.: Slavica, 1999. Collection of essays focuses on the negativity in *Dead Souls* and Gogol's other works and in the works of other Russian writers. Includes bibliography and index.

Troyat, Henri. *Divided Soul*. Translated by Nancy Amphoux. Garden City, N.Y.: Doubleday, 1973. Provides perhaps the most information on Gogol's life available in English in a single volume. Demonstrates masterfully how Gogol's life and work are inextricably intertwined and does not neglect the important role that "God's will" played in Gogol's life, as the thread that lends the greatest cohesion to the diverse developments in his creative journey. Includes some interesting illustrations as well as bibliography, notes, and index.

Weiner, Adam. "The Evils of *Dead Souls*." In *By Authors Possessed: The Demonic Novel in Russia*. Evanston, Ill.: Northwestern University Press, 1998. Chapter focusing on *Dead Souls* is included in a wider analysis of nineteenth and twentieth century Russian "demonic novels," defined as novels in which the protagonists are incarnated with the evil presence of the Devil.

HANS JAKOB CHRISTOFFEL VON GRIMMELSHAUSEN

Born: Gelnhausen (now in Germany); March 17, 1621(?)
Died: Renchen (now in Germany); August 17, 1676
Also known as: Hans Johann Jakob Christoffel von Grimmelshausen; Samuel Greifnson von Hirschfeld

PRINCIPAL LONG FICTION

Der keusche Joseph, 1666
Der abenteuerliche Simplicissimus, 1669 (*The Adventurous Simplicissimus*, 1912)
Die Continuatio, 1669 (*The Continuation*, 1965; selections)
Dietwald und Amelinde, 1670
Lebensbeschreibung der Ertzbetrügerin und Landstörtzerin Courasche, 1670 (*Courage: The Adventuress*, 1964; also as *The Life of Courage: The Notorious Thief, Whore, and Vagabond*, 2001)
Der seltsame Springinsfeld, 1670 (*The Singular Life Story of Heedless Hopalong*, 1981; also known as *Tearaway*, 2003)
Proximus und Lympida, 1672
Das wunderbarliche Vogelsnest I, 1672
Das wunderbarliche Vogelsnest II, 1675 (*The False Messiah*, 1964)

OTHER LITERARY FORMS

Almost everything that Hans Jakob Christoffel von Grimmelshausen (GRIHM-uhls-how-zuhn) wrote falls into the category of narrative fiction. One exception is a series of annual almanacs published between 1671 and 1675. In addition to this series, Grimmelshausen produced a special type of almanac titled *Des Abenteuerlichen Simplicissimi Ewig-währender Calender* (1671; the adventurous Simplicissimus's perpetual calendar). None of the almanacs constitutes a work of major importance, but they remain of interest to literary scholars because they contain a vast amount of information pertaining to the popular culture of the Baroque era. In *Des Abenteuerlichen Simplicissimi Ewig-währender Calender*, moreover, there is an extensive dialogue between an astrologer and the protagonist of *The Adventurous Simplicissimus* that sheds light on certain aspects of the novel's structure.

One may also find Grimmelshausen's views on a variety of mundane and spiritual matters in the twenty discussions in the two volumes of *Der satyrische Pilgram* (1666, 1667; the satiric pilgrim). Although Grimmelshausen wrote but few poems, most of which appear within the context of his novels, his poetry is of a high order, and selections from it are frequently included in anthologies of German verse.

Achievements

Hans Jakob Christoffel von Grimmelshausen's *The Adventurous Simplicissimus* is undoubtedly the greatest German novel of the seventeenth century. The work proved to be an immediate popular success, albeit not a critical one, when it was published in 1669, and Grimmelshausen extended the story by issuing a separately bound continuation in the same year. *The Continuation* was eventually incorporated into later printings of *The Adventurous Simplicissimus*, where it now supplements the five books into which the original novel was divided. Public demand, moreover, led Grimmelshausen to write a number of other sequels over the next few years. Of these continuations, *Courage, The Singular Life Story of Heedless Hopalong*, and the two sections of *Das wunderbarliche Vogelsnest* are particularly important. *The Adventurous Simplicissimus* and its sequels are today referred to collectively as the Simplician cycle. What distinguishes these writings from the standard German fiction of that era is that they give the reader a vivid and realistic picture of the devastation caused by the Thirty Years' War and the demoralization of the country in its aftermath. The only other novelist to write anything in a similar vein was Johann Michael Moscherosch, whose *Wunderliche und warhafftige Gesichte Philanders von Sittewald* (1643; the strange and true visions of Philander von Sittewald) contains, as one of its four parts, a section titled "Soldaten Leben" (soldier's life) that foreshadows *The Adventurous Simplicissimus* in presenting a graphic account of the disasters of war.

The literary establishment in Germany during the Baroque period favored the more aristocratic genres, such as the heroic-gallant and historical-political novels, and condemned *The Adventurous Simplicissimus* for its crudity. Eager for critical acclaim, Grimmelshausen attempted to write in the style of courtly literature and produced a pair of tedious novels, *Dietwald und Amelinde* and *Proximus und Lympida*, that embodied this alien aesthetic. These works are, however, of little interest to the modern reader; only the Simplician cycle has survived the test of time. Much of the literary distinction of *The Adventurous Simplicissimus* stems from the ingenious way that Grimmelshausen adapted the form of the picaresque novel to make it serve as a vehicle for religious content. Some critics even go as far as to refer to the novel as antipicaresque. Unlike the usual picaresque novel, there is genuine character development in *The Adventurous Simplicissimus*. Many literary historians, for this reason, regard Grimmelshausen's masterwork as a forerunner of both the bildungsroman (the novel of education) and the *Entwicklungsroman* (the novel of development).

Biography

The author of *The Adventurous Simplicissimus* could trace his descent back to a line of landed nobility that had established itself in Thuringia during the Middle Ages. In the course of the sixteenth century, however, the family gradually became impoverished, to the point that the author's paternal grandfather, Melchior Christoffel, was forced to take up the occupation of baker and innkeeper in Gelnhausen, a predominantly Lutheran town located in Hesse not far from Hanau, and even stopped using his noble surname. It was in Gelnhausen that Hans Johann Jakob Christoffel von Grimmelshausen was born.

On the basis of autobiographical remarks to be found in one of Grimmelshausen's almanacs, the year of his birth appears to be either 1621 or 1622, although subsequent scholarship places the date at or near March 17, 1621. His father, Johannes Christoffel, died a few years later, and his mother, Gertraud, soon moved from Gelnhausen to nearby Frankfurt in order to remarry, leaving her six-year-old son in the care of her father-in-law. The relationship between Melchior and his grandson was full of affection, and the character of the kindly grandfather was later depicted in fictional form in the person of the elderly hermit who plays a key role in the early part of *The Adventurous Simplicissimus*.

For six or seven years, young Grimmelshausen attended the only school in Gelnhausen, receiving, in addition to a thorough indoctrination into the Lutheran faith, extensive instruction in both music and Latin. In 1634, when he was about thirteen years of age, Gelnhausen was sacked by Croatian soldiers serving in the Imperial army. Many of the town's inhabitants, including Grimmelshausen, sought refuge in the city of Hanau for protection by the Swedish garrison stationed there. A month or so later, Grimmelshausen was captured by Croatian soldiers as he was playing outside the walls of Hanau. His period of captivity under the Croatians was relatively brief; he soon fell into the hands of Protestant units composed of Hessians and was pressed into their service.

What happened to Grimmelshausen while he was with the Hessians is uncertain, but in 1636, at age fifteen, he found himself part of a cavalry unit in the Imperial army that was besieging the Protestant fortress of Magdeburg. He continued to serve as both a light cavalryman and a musketeer in various Catholic armies for the next few years, eventually receiving an appointment as regimental secretary to Count Hans Reinhard von Schauenburg, the commander of the imperial stronghold of Offenburg (a city near the Rhine River to the east of Strasbourg). In 1648, the year in which the Peace of Westphalia was signed, Grimmelshausen left his post with Schauenburg and served with the Bavarian army in some of the final campaigns of the war. He was discharged from military service the following year at about the age of twenty-eight, after having spent some fifteen years at war.

On August 30, 1649, Grimmelshausen married Katharina Henninger, the daughter of an officer who had served in Schauenburg's regiment. That the wedding ceremony was performed by a priest is proof of the bridegroom's formal membership in the Roman Catholic Church at the time of his marriage. Precisely when his conversion to Catholicism occurred, however, remains an unresolved issue. The marital union turned out to be a happy one, and Katharina was to have ten children over the next two decades. A week after the wedding ceremony, Grimmelshausen assumed the duties of a steward on the estate of Count Schauenburg outside the village of Gaisbach near Oberkirch. He left the employ of Schauenburg in 1660 and from 1662 to 1665 worked in a similar position at the summer residence of a Strasbourg physician. After a brief period as the proprietor of an inn in Gelnhausen called The Silver Star, Grimmelshausen accepted an appointment from the bishop of Strasbourg to serve as *Schultheiss* (mayor) in the Black Forest village of Renchen. He continued to occupy that office for the remaining nine years of his life. His last three years proved to be quite trying for him, owing to the warfare between French and Imperial forces that had engulfed the area. At one point in this conflict, he was obliged to resume military service for a time. Grimmelshausen died in Renchen on August 17, 1676, survived by his wife and six of their children.

Grimmelshausen's literary career did not begin until he was nearly forty years old. In 1659, he published a German-language version of a French translation of Francis Godwin's *The Man in the Moon: Or, A Discourse of a Voyage Thither by Domingo Gonsales, the Speedy Messenger* (1638). The next year, Grimmelshausen published two satiric dream visions of his own, but his first significant works—*Der satyrische Pilgram I* and *Der keusche Joseph* (the chaste Joseph)—appeared later. It was, however, only after he became mayor of Renchen that Grimmelshausen became truly productive. In addition to publishing *The Adventurous Simplicissimus* and its sequels while at Renchen, he tried his hand at writing aristocratic fiction such as *Dietwald und Amelinde* and *Proximus und Lympida*. Except for these two heroic-gallant novels, which were published under his own name, Grimmelshausen made it a practice to conceal his authorship of fictional works by using pseudonyms that were anagrams of his full name. *The Adventurous Simplicissimus*, for example, was published under the pseudonym Samuel Greifnson von Hirschfeld. He also used eight other pseudonyms. It was not, in fact, until the middle of the nineteenth century, when interest in Baroque literature revived, that German literary scholars were able to establish the identity of the author of *The Adventurous Simplicissimus*.

Analysis

In keeping with the traditional form of the picaresque novel, Hans Jakob Christoffel von Grimmelshausen's *The Adventurous Simplicissimus* is written from the first-person point of view, and the events it relates are presented as autobiography. The protagonist narrates his life history from boyhood to early manhood against the background of the Thirty Years' War and its aftermath. The contents of the novel are highly episodic and often anecdotal in character. Even though supernatural incidents occur with some frequency, most of the narrative is realistic in tone. There is, in fact, much gross physical detail depicting the sexual escapades of the hero as well as the act of brutality committed by combatants serving on both sides of this savage conflict.

Like many other creative spirits of the Baroque era, the author of the Simplician cycle was preoccupied with opposition and contradiction. *The Adventurous Simplicissimus* is frequently described as contrapuntal in its contrast of dualities such as innocence and experience, civilian and military, Catholic and Protestant, and spiritual and mundane. Another prominent feature of the novel is its allegorical character. Although far less didactic than John Bunyan's *The Pilgrim's Progress* (1678, 1684), *The Adventurous Simplicissimus* is likewise an account of the journey of a human soul through the perils of a sinful world in a quest for salvation.

Of the various autobiographical parallels in *The Adventurous Simplicissimus*, the protagonist's conversion to Roman Catholicism is certainly the most controversial. Many scholars suspect that Grimmelshausen's own adherence to this creed was purely a matter of expediency. There is clearly much evidence in the novel to corroborate this opinion. At one point midway through the third book, Simplicius Simplicissimus informs a Protestant clergyman with whom he is debating the merits of competing Christian denominations that the doctrinal differences that separate these sects have nothing to do with the essence of Christianity. When Simplicius does finally convert to Catholicism, moreover, it is out of fear of the Devil rather than from any conviction in the absolute truth of Catholic theology.

In all likelihood, however, Grimmelshausen's impatience with doctrinal disputes manifests itself most emphatically in the visionary exhortations of the madman who believed himself to be the great god Jupiter. In one of the opening chapters of the third book, "Jupiter" prophesies that Germany will one day play host to a national leader who will unify Europe under German hegemony and convene a church council to resolve all theological differences. After that, the prophet goes on to declare, anyone who continues to foster religious dissension will do so only on pain of death. In the light of twentieth century historical experience, the idealism that inspired this utopian vision has too much in common with the goals of the Third Reich to elicit any degree of sympathy from modern readers of *The Adventurous Simplicissimus*.

Grimmelshausen's ardent desire to see religious unity restored to his homeland was a direct response to the horrendous suffering that he witnessed during the course of the Thirty Years' War. This conflict, which lasted from 1618 to 1648, had its origin in the tensions between Catholic and Protestant rulers within the Holy Roman Empire of the German nation. Although the kingdom of Bohemia was traditionally part of the domain of the Habsburg emperors in Vienna, the Bohemian nobility struck a blow for religious freedom by choosing a German prince of the Calvinist faith as their king. Imperial forces soon reestablished Habsburg control over Bohemia, but their subsequent attempt to extend Catholic domination over other areas in Germany provoked a Protestant reaction on both a national and an international level. Before long, Denmark and Sweden sent in troops to aid the beleaguered Protestant states within Germany.

The emperor's chief German ally was Bavaria, but he was also able to draw upon forces from satellite areas such as Croatia. France, despite its formal allegiance to Catholicism, consistently supported the Protestant cause out of fear that a Habsburg victory would pose a threat to its national interests and eventually intervened militarily in order to ensure continued sectarian division among the German states. The religious character of the conflict was thus diluted by political considerations. The German nobility, for its part, was likewise motivated by dynastic and property concerns. Grimmelshausen's own bitterness toward his country's rulers finds full expression in the assertion made by the prophet Jupiter, in which the promised German hero is described as depriving the nobility of its hereditary privileges altogether and instituting a parliamentary government whose membership will be composed of the two wisest men summoned from each town in all of Germany.

THE ADVENTUROUS SIMPLICISSIMUS

Grimmelshausen's masterwork begins with a motif that later was popular among the Romantics: The child who comes to be known as Simplicius Simplicissimus is described as having been reared in total isolation from society on a farm in a forest region known as the Spessart. His putative parents are indifferent to his education, and he therefore grows up as a simpleton who spends most of his time tending to the needs of livestock. His greatest joy is to play the bagpipes, the sound of which, he is told, will scare off the wolves that might attack the sheep under his care.

At the age of ten, the boy is forced to flee for safety into a nearby forest in order to escape from a band of marauding soldiers who were plundering the farmstead and who were sure to abduct him if he fell into their hands. To his good fortune, a hermit living in the forest befriends him. It is this hermit who names him Simplicius and attempts to educate him. Among other things, the hermit teaches him to read and write; he also succeeds in transforming the boy into a pious Christian. This tutelage comes to an abrupt end after two years, upon the death of the hermit. Utterly distraught, Simplicius wanders about aimlessly until he is captured by a group of soldiers and taken to the city of Hanau, which at that time was a Protestant stronghold under the control of Swedish forces.

The governor of the fortress is James Ramsay, a Scottish soldier of fortune in the service of the Swedish crown and the sole historical personage to appear in Grimmelshausen's novel. It is soon determined that the hermit who had come to the boy's aid was Ramsay's brother-in-law, an entirely fictional character whose surname is reported to be Sternfels von Fuchshaim and who at one time held the military rank of captain. This nobleman, already sickened by the war, decided to renounce the world altogether after his pregnant wife, Susanna, disappeared amid the turmoil of battle. Much later in the novel, Simplicius, during a visit to a spa near Strasbourg, encounters the peasant who reared him as a child and learns from him that the hermit and Susanna were his true parents. The peasant and his wife had assisted Susanna in the process of childbirth and had decided to adopt the baby after the mother died as a consequence of the dire circumstances surrounding the delivery. Ramsay, of course, has no knowledge of the fact that Simplicius is his nephew, but he takes an immediate liking to the boy and decides to make him his page. This partiality toward Simplicius, the reader is led to believe, may stem from the striking resemblance that the youth bears to his mother, the governor's sister.

Shortly after Simplicius becomes a page, a commissioner representing the Swedish war council comes to inspect the garrison of Hanau. The boy is therefore required to have a family name in order to answer properly during the roll call, and it is the governor himself who proposes that he be called Simplicius Simplicissimus because of his extreme innocence. Totally unfamiliar with the ways of the world, Simplicius is continually appalled by the un-Christian behavior of the men whom he encounters in the garrison. He proves to be so inept as a page, moreover, that the governor finally decides to make him a court jester. A scheme is thereupon concocted to derange the boy's mind in order to render him an even better buffoon than he already is. A clergyman who was a friend of the hermit discovers the plot and forewarns Simplicius of the ordeal that lies ahead. The next night, Simplicius is abducted by four men dressed like devils and is subjected to several unnerving experiences calculated to deprive him of his reason. Following the clergyman's advice, he feigns madness and allows himself to be cast in the role of fool.

Despite the indignity of having to wear a costume that makes him resemble a calf, Simplicius finds the life of a court jester much to his liking; he not only is well fed but also is able to express his unconventional thoughts quite freely. Misfortune, however, soon strikes again. A raiding party composed of Croatian soldiers who were part of the Imperial army captures Simplicius during one of his frequent strolls outside the walls of the fortress and compels him to become a stableboy for their cavalry troop.

Highly dissatisfied with his new masters, Simplicius escapes from the Croatian cavalry unit at the first opportunity and takes to stealing food from peasant homesteads in order to survive. While in a forest, he comes upon a large knapsack containing some provisions and a purse within which is a large sum of gold coins. After consuming the food, he conceals the gold coins by cleverly sewing them into his clothing. Shortly thereafter, he comes upon a witches' Sabbath being held in a wooded area and is obliged to participate. By invoking the Lord's name, however, he manages to cause the entire gathering to disappear and finds himself flying through the air immediately. When he finally descends, Simplicius discovers that he has been supernaturally transported to an open field near Magdeburg, a city that at that time was under siege by Imperial forces.

The colonel in charge of the Imperial camp to which Simplicius is eventually taken decides to keep him on as a fool after hearing the boy's story. Simplicius is, however, provided with a tutor named Ulrich Herzbruder to further his education. The tutor's son, who bears the same name as his father, becomes a steadfast friend of Simplicius. The younger Herzbruder wishes to become the colonel's secretary, a position already held by a villainous character named Olivier. In order to eliminate this threat to his position, Olivier plants evidence to make it appear that the tutor's son has stolen a valuable object from the colonel. The younger Herzbruder, now in total disgrace, would like to be able to purchase an honorable discharge from the Imperial army, and Simplicius comes to the rescue by providing his friend with the necessary sum. A short while after his son's departure, the elder Herzbruder is senselessly killed by an officer who has taken offense at a prophecy concerning his fate that was made by the clairvoyant tutor.

As Simplicius matures, he advances in rank from stableboy to dragoon and finally to elite cavalryman. Simplicius becomes part of a group of horsemen whose task it is to obtain supplies by foraging through the countryside around the Westphalian city of Soest.

Military units of that day customarily lived off the land while campaigning. Dressed in the distinctive green attire of a hunter, Simplicius achieves great renown for his courage and resourcefulness and soon acquires the title of Huntsman of Soest. Simplicius considers the rich to be fair game, but he takes great pains never to exploit the poor. It is during this phase of his military career that Simplicius encounters the madman who believes himself to be Jupiter.

Another major episode that occurs at this point involves the entrapment of a villain who, dressed in a habit similar to the one worn by Simplicius, seeks to trade on his reputation as the Huntsman of Soest and has been perpetrating great crimes on the civilian populace under that disguise. The imposter is eventually captured, but when Simplicius sees how terrified the man is, he decides to spare his life. Simplicius's companions, however, insist on forcing the man to perform a degrading act involving animals and scratch up his face before releasing him. Even though there is a bright moon on this particular night, Simplicius inexplicably fails to recognize the culprit as his erstwhile companion, Olivier. Not until he encounters Olivier years later does Simplicius become aware of the identity of the imposter.

While conducting raids, Simplicius usually manages to divert much of the looted treasure to his personal coffer in the hope that this wealth might someday help him achieve his ambition to rise to the rank of officer and perhaps even to be made a member of the nobility itself. After some time, he takes this treasure to Cologne and leaves it with a merchant for safekeeping. Returning from Cologne, Simplicius is captured by Swedish forces and taken to their headquarters in Lippstadt. When the commander learns that his prisoner is the renowned Huntsman of Soest, he proposes to make him an officer in his own battalion. The offer is respectfully declined, but the captive is nevertheless granted complete freedom to move inside and outside the city after pledging not to attempt to escape. During the next six months, Simplicius devotes much time to improving his mastery of firearms and fencing, as well as to reading historical works, heroic fiction, and manuals of love. He also womanizes on a grand scale and is soon the father-to-be of several offspring. His courtship of a retired officer's daughter, however, is a case of true love. When her father catches them in bed together—although a physical union has not been consummated and the entire incident appears to have been calculated to force Simplicius into marriage—Simplicius agrees to marry the girl.

Despite the coercive character of the marriage, Simplicius is so pleased with his new situation that he agrees to become an officer in the Swedish army, and he is permitted to go to Cologne for the purpose of retrieving his fortune. The lovers, however, are destined never to see each other again. Only after the passage of many years is Simplicius able to return to the region and inquire about the fate of his bride of one month. He then learns that his wife died soon after giving birth to a male child and that the boy has been adopted by his sister-in-law and her husband. Simplicius, whose physical appearance has so altered over the years that he is not even recognized, deems it not in the best interests of the child to disrupt this arrangement and therefore decides not to reveal his identity as the child's father.

The journey from Lippstadt to Cologne proves uneventful, but once in the city, Simplicius discovers that he is unable to retrieve his treasure. The merchant to whom he entrusted his money has declared himself bankrupt and left the country. A local attorney, however, volunteers to help Simplicius recover the money. Because the legal process promises to be a protracted one, Simplicius, in order to earn enough wages to meet his living expenses, agrees to drive two noblemen to Paris in the attorney's coach. As soon as the party arrives at its destination, the coach and horses are confiscated by the authorities to settle an outstanding debt owed by the attorney, and Simplicius thus finds himself stranded in the French capital. Forced to live by hook or crook, he eventually becomes a prostitute.

Known locally as Monsieur Beau Alman, Simplicius is in great demand among wellborn Parisian ladies and soon accumulates sufficient funds to enable him to return to Germany. On the way back, he suffers from an attack of smallpox that leaves his face permanently disfigured. He is, moreover, robbed of all of his money while undergoing treatment for the affliction and can find no other means of paying for his traveling expenses than to become an itinerant medicine man. Soon after he arrives in his homeland, Simplicius encounters a freebooter who turns out to be Olivier, the nemesis of the younger Herzbruder. Despite his antipathy for Olivier, he enters into a partnership with him and agrees to participate in acts of brigandage. On one of their expeditions, they are attacked by a group of six soldiers. Olivier is slain in the encounter after he kills two of them, and Simplicius is left to dispatch the other four on his own. In this way, the prophecy of the elder Herzbruder, to the effect that Simplicius would avenge the death of Olivier, is fulfilled.

Simplicius soon meets the younger Herzbruder himself and decides to accompany his good friend on a pilgrimage to the shrine of Our Lady of Einsiedeln in Switzerland. There he witnesses an exorcism and becomes so frightened of the Devil that he immediately converts to the Catholic faith. Returning to Germany, Simplicius succeeds, with the assistance of Herzbruder, in obtaining a commission as captain in the Imperial forces. His service in this new rank is, however, a brief one. His company's first engagement with the enemy ends in defeat, and Herzbruder's testicles are shot off as well. Simplicius gives up his commission in order to take care of Herzbruder, who by now is also paralyzed from the waist down. The two friends settle down at a spa near Strasbourg, and while Herzbruder is undergoing treatment, Simplicius visits Cologne and then goes on to Lippstadt.

There he learns of his wife's death and, deeply saddened by the news, returns to the spa in time to witness Herzbruder's death. Before long he runs into his foster father, Melchior, whom he recognizes by the enormous wart in the middle of his forehead, and learns the true identity of his parents. His baptismal name, moreover, proves to have been Melchior Sternfels von Fuchsheim. (This is another anagram of the author's own name.) Simplicius decides to marry a woman that he previously met at the spa, and to make her happy he buys the farm where she was born as their new homestead. His wife, who among other serious shortcomings is guilty of infidelity, gives birth to a baby that looks exactly like one of the hired hands. Both his wife and the child die soon after, from alcohol-related causes.

A widower once again, Simplicius has his foster parents move in with him and turns the management of his estate over to them. In this way, he is free to devote his time to study and meditation. Some local peasants tell him about an unusual body of water called the Mummelsee, located atop one of the highest mountains in the region. His curiosity whetted, Simplicius goes to the lake and makes contact with the water sprites that inhabit it. Their prince takes him on a journey to the center of the earth through the waters of the bottomless lake and endeavors to instruct him in religion and philosophy. After being given a tour of the subterranean realm, Simplicius is returned to the earth's surface, and he once again consecrates himself to his studies.

Swedish forces, however, overrun the region, and their colonel offers to make him a lieutenant colonel under his command. Simplicius accepts and accompanies the colonel to Livonia for the purpose of recruiting a new regiment. The project fails, and the two men go on to Moscow in the hope of obtaining high military positions in the Russian army. After many adventures in Russia and Asia, Simplicius returns to Germany to find that the war has ended; he decides to renounce the world by becoming a hermit and living in a high mountain range that is part of the Black Forest.

Much of what Simplicius learns about life in the course of the novel is foreshadowed in a dream that he has shortly after the death of his hermit mentor. He dreams that all of the trees in the forest in which he dwells are magically transformed into hierarchical symbols of society. At the top of each tree sits a cavalier and below him are branches consisting of groups of soldiers neatly divided according to rank. There is a constant effort among these individuals to rise to higher branches where they would be able to receive greater exposure to rain and sunshine. The roots of the trees are made up of common people—craftsmen and peasants whose labors support the entire social order. At one point in the dream, the forest merges into a single tree on top of which sits the war god, Mars.

In the course of the novel, Simplicius plays several roles in this hierarchy, but at every level the motive forces are lust, greed, and social ambition. Having spent his boyhood in a state of extreme innocence, Simplicius must experience the full measure of the busyness of society before he can bring himself to renounce worldly vanities for a life of piety. When he informs his foster father of his intention to join a community of Hungarian Anabaptists whose simple lifestyle he has come to admire, Melchior cautions Simplicius to remember that there are no honest men. Simplicius thereupon makes his decision to forgo human companionship entirely and to commune with God in the solitude of the forests.

The novel ends with a lengthy adieu to the world that is taken verbatim from a German translation of a work by the Spanish moralist Antonio de Guevara. Grimmelshausen lays the ground for a continuation of Simplicius's story by having his protagonist remark: "Whether I will be able to persevere to the end, as my blessed father did, remains to be seen."

THE CONTINUATION

The Continuation (or book 6 of *The Adventurous Simplicissimus*) begins with Simplicius reporting how his ardor for the life of an anchorite gradually diminished after a few months. He therefore sets out on a pilgrimage to the holy places at Loretto and Rome. After unexpectedly coming into possession of some gold coins, Simplicius persuades himself to go on to Jerusalem as well, but he is captured by robbers in Egypt while en route to Palestine. These robbers exhibit him as a wild man until he is rescued by a party of Europeans. The Middle East has in the meantime become engulfed in war, and Simplicius therefore decides to return to Europe in a large Portuguese galleon via the Cape of Good Hope. Somewhere in the vicinity of Madagascar, the vessel is wrecked in a storm, and only Simplicius and the ship's carpenter manage to reach the shores of a nearby island.

The island proves to be uninhabited but bountiful. Before long, an Abyssinian woman drifts ashore in a box and volunteers to become their cook. She promptly connives with the carpenter to kill Simplicius. The Lord causes her to disappear, however, when Simplicius makes the sign of the cross over his food and asks for divine blessing. The two men are then reconciled, but the carpenter dies an early death as a consequence of his addiction to palm wine. Simplicius resumes the contemplative life of a hermit and finally attains peace of mind. When a Dutch sea captain stops at the island and offers to take Simplicius back to Europe, the offer is declined. Before the captain departs, Simplicius presents him with some palm fronds on which he has recorded his life story; the sea captain later publishes these writings. The memoirs of Simplicius thus come to a formal end.

The Continuation is, for the most part, a worthy supplement to the five books of the original edition of *The Adventurous Simplicissimus*. The effect of the narrative is to intensify the inner struggle experienced by the protagonist in his quest to achieve spiritual salvation. The episode on the island was, incidentally, in no way inspired by Daniel Defoe's *Robinson Crusoe* (1719), a work that first made its appearance fifty years later. An earlier English prototype for Grimmelshausen's "Robinsonade" may, however, be found in the widely translated novel by Henry Nevil titled *The Isle of Pines* (1618).

COURAGE

The next two sequels to *The Adventurous Simplicissimus* are *Courage* and *The Singular Life Story of Heedless Hopalong*. Both Courage and Springinsfeld are characters who make brief appearances in *The Adventurous Simplicissimus*. Although Grimmelshausen never referred to her by a specific name in the earlier work, Courage turns out to be one of the women of easy virtue with whom Simplicius slept with at the spa in the Black Forest when he was caring for the younger Herzbruder. After Simplicius had married for the second time, Courage left a baby at his doorstep, along with a written message identifying Simplicius as the father of her illegitimate child. In *Courage*, she confesses that the child was not hers at all but that of her maid, who had exchanged sexual favors with an unknown gentleman for a modest sum of money. It is clear that Courage made her allegation against

Simplicius out of pure spite for his having jilted her and that her sole intent was to cause problems for her former lover, both with the authorities and with his wife.

Courage's own story begins in 1620, in Bohemia, when she is a thirteen-year-old girl named Libuschka, and ends fifty years later, when she is part of a Gypsy band whose chieftain is her husband. Over this time span, she manages to marry five army officers and a musketeer, as well as to engage in sex for pleasure and profit with a multitude of other men. She acquires the nickname Courage after inadvertently using this term in reference to her genitalia. Modern readers have become familiar with this captivating character through Bertolt Brecht's chronicle play *Mutter Courage und ihre Kinder* (1939; *Mother Courage and Her Children*, 1941). Brecht, however, uses the nickname in its literal sense, to convey the notion of his character's personal tenacity in overcoming adversity.

The episode in Grimmelshausen's novel that serves as the point of departure for Brecht's play occurs when Courage becomes a camp follower who peddles provisions to soldiers. To assist her, Courage enlists the services of a callow youth who is madly in love with her; she promptly calls him Springinsfeld. Best translated as "jump-into-the-field," the name is derived from the opening words of the first command given to him by Courage and is intended to remind him of his subordinate position in both their commercial and their sexual relationships. Under Courage's tutelage, Springinsfeld develops into an accomplished rogue in his own right, but she decides to rid herself of his company after he takes to assaulting her in his sleep, even though he is deeply apologetic once awake. It is after his separation from Courage that Springinsfeld joins Simplicius and his band of marauders in the forests of Soest. Later in life, he encounters an unemployed secretary in the guest room of an inn, to whom he dictates his autobiography. It is this purported narrative that Grimmelshausen published under the title of *The Singular Life Story of Heedless Hopalong*.

THE SINGULAR LIFE STORY OF HEEDLESS HOPALONG

One item of information contained in *The Singular Life Story of Heedless Hopalong* pertains to the identity of the man who fathered the baby boy whom Courage's maid has borne out of wedlock. It comes to light that the unknown gentleman who has made her pregnant is Simplicius himself. By placing this child at his doorstep, Courage has unintentionally done him a great favor, because he would otherwise never have had the pleasure of rearing a child of his own. Her malicious attempt to spite Simplicius, therefore, brings forth the opposite effect. In the final chapters of *The Singular Life Story of Heedless Hopalong*, a magical bird's nest that has the power to render a person invisible comes into the possession of the protagonist and his young wife. The nest soon passes into the hands of a young soldier, who happens to kill Springinsfeld's wife while attempting to arrest her for a series of thefts committed while her spouse was away on military duty. Springinsfeld likewise meets with misfortune, losing a leg in battle. Upon his return from the wars, the penniless widower is granted permission to spend his remaining years on Simplicius's farmstead.

DER WUNDERBARLICHE VOGELSNEST

The further adventures of the young soldier who killed Springinsfeld's wife are related in part 1 of *Das wunderbarliche Vogelsnest* (the magical bird's nest). His ownership of the nest provides him with an unparalleled opportunity to pry into private affairs and to discover the evil that lies behind humankind's facade of civility. The situation is thus remarkably similar to the one depicted in Alain-René Lesage's *Le Diable boiteux* (1707; *The Devil upon Two Sticks*, 1708). Possession of the nest changes hands for a third time after the young soldier attempts to destroy the object that he has come to regard as an instrument of Satan. The new owner is a young merchant whose experiences are described in part 2. Neither part of *Das wunderbarliche Vogelsnest* appears to have any direct connection with the other works in the Simplician cycle. However, in his preface to part 2, which was translated into English as *The False Messiah* (1964), Grimmelshausen insists that both are essential components of the total saga. Regardless of their relationship to the rest of the opus, the two parts of *Der wunderbarliche Vogelsnest* succeed in enlarging our picture of life in seventeenth century Germany. Grimmelshausen, it should never be forgotten, was the only German writer of that century who fully appreciated the literary value of the contemporary scene.

Victor Anthony Rudowski

OTHER MAJOR WORKS

NONFICTION: *Der satyrische Pilgram I*, 1666; *Der satyrische Pilgram II*, 1667; *Des Abenteuerlichen Simplicissimi Ewig-währender Calender*, 1671; *Der Bart-Krieg*, 1673; *Der teutsche Michael*, 1673.

BIBLIOGRAPHY

Anderson, Susan C. *Grass and Grimmelshausen: Günter Grass's "Das Treffen in Telgte" and Rezeptionstheorie*. Columbia, S.C.: Camden House, 1987. A critical study that looks at Grimmelshausen in relation to one of Germany's most famous modern novelists—Günter Grass. Anderson analyzes how Grass's novel *The Meeting in Telgte* was influenced by Grimmelshausen's characters Simplex and Courage.

Aylett, R. P. T. *The Nature of Realism in Grimmelshausen's "Simplicissimus" Cycle of Novels*. Las Vegas, Nev.: Peter Lang, 1982. Aylett reevaluates the novel cycle, analyzing its characters, Grimmelshausen's use of time and space, the integration of real and fictional history, and other common features of the novels. Includes a bibliography.

Bertsch, Janet. "Grimmelshausen's *Der abentheurliche Simplicissimus Teutsch* and *Der seltzame Springinsfeld*." In *Storytelling in the Works of Bunyan, Grimmelshausen, Defoe, and Schnabel*. Rochester, N.Y.: Camden House, 2004. Bertsch examines Grimmelshausen's novels and works by John Bunyan, Daniel Defoe, and J. G. Schnabel. These works were written between 1660 and 1740, a period of transition between intense religiosity and a growing secularization. Bertsch demonstrates how these authors' works reflect this societal change.

Hayens, Kenneth C. *Grimmelshausen*. New York: Oxford University Press, 1932. Remains the only full-length English-language biography of Grimmelshausen.

Horwich, Cara M. *Survival in "Simplicissimus" and "Mutter Courage."* New York: Peter Lang, 1997. A comparison of *Simplicissimus* and Bertolt Brecht's play *Mother Courage and Her Children*, which was based on Grimmelshausen's work. Horwich maintains that the novel and play share a concern with human survival in a dangerous world.

Knight, K. G. "Grimmelshausen's *Simplicissimus*—A Popular Baroque Novel." In *Periods in German Literature*, edited by J. M. Ritchie. Vol. 25. London: O. Wolff, 1970. The Simplicissimus novels are analyzed and compared to other German picaresque novels written in the seventeenth century. Includes bibliographies.

Menhennet, Alan. *Grimmelshausen the Storyteller: A Study of the "Simplician" Novels*. Columbia, S.C.: Camden House, 1997. A detailed examination of Grimmelshausen's novels, in which Menhennet focuses on their common elements. Argues that the novels should not be considered separate books but instead part of a coherent cycle. He also demonstrates how the cycle integrates religious and moral concerns with a more secular curiousness and sense of humor.

Negus, Kenneth. *Grimmelshausen*. New York: Twayne, 1974. Negus recounts the details of Grimmelshausen's life and analyzes all of his fiction—the minor novels as well as the Simplician cycle. Includes a bibliography.

Otto, Karl F., Jr., ed. *A Companion to the Works of Grimmelshausen*. Rochester, N.Y.: Camden House, 2003. A collection of essays analyzing Grimmelshausen's works. The essays examine topics such as Grimmelhausen and the picaresque novel, allegorical and astronomical elements in his works, gender identity in the Simplician cycle, and the non-Simplician novels.

FRANZ KAFKA

Born: Prague, Bohemia, Austro-Hungarian Empire (now in Czech Republic); July 3, 1883
Died: Kierling, Klosterneuburg, near Vienna, Austria; June 3, 1924

PRINCIPAL LONG FICTION
Der Prozess, 1925 (*The Trial*, 1937)
Das Schloss, 1926 (*The Castle*, 1930)
Amerika, 1927 (*America*, 1938; better known as *Amerika*, 1946)

OTHER LITERARY FORMS

In addition to long fiction, Franz Kafka (KAHF-kah) wrote numerous stories, the most famous of which are *Die Verwandlung* (1915; *The Metamorphosis*, 1936), *Ein Hungerkünstler: Vier Geschichten* (1924; *A Hunger Artist*, 1948), and *The Penal Colony: Stories and Short Pieces* (1948). He also left behind extensive diaries and letters.

ACHIEVEMENTS

What W. H. Auden wrote of Sigmund Freud—that he had become less a person than a climate of opinion—is equally true of Franz Kafka. He is the twentieth century prophet of alienation, his name a household synonym for "angst." His stories—visionary, hallucinatory, yet very controlled artistically—have exerted their powerful influence over modern fiction. Few would dispute the assertion that he is one of the major literary figures of the twentieth century. None of this, however, could have been anticipated of a writer who was not widely known at the time of his death.

Kafka's genius was difficult for him to harness: The fact is that he never completed any of his three novels. Before dying, he left instructions with Max Brod, his friend and executor, to destroy his manuscripts. Reasoning that Kafka was not committed to their destruction as much as he was ambivalent over their fate—could not he have destroyed them had he really wished to do so?—Brod preserved the manuscripts, arranged to have them printed, wrote a biography of his friend, and generously championed his cause. Thus, *The Trial* and *The Castle*, books which so remarkably capture Kafka's paradoxical vision of human existence, came to light.

BIOGRAPHY

Despite the strange occurrences that animate Franz Kafka's fiction, the events of his life are colorless and mundane. Like Emily Dickinson or Henry David Thoreau, however, Kafka could, by sheer imagination, transform the most ordinary life into fascinating reading. Tirelessly, he penned his impressions of his life, recording the nuances of his thoughts and actions in ethical and ontological terms.

Kafka was born on July 3, 1883, in Prague, Bohemia, into a bourgeois German-Jewish family. The Czechs of Kafka's day felt oppressed by the Austrian-Germans and in turn oppressed the Jews, so from his earliest days Kafka was accustomed to the pain of a threefold prejudice—as non-Austrian, as non-Czech, and as a Jew. Franz was the oldest child, the sole surviving son in a family that was later to include three girls. The father, Herrmann Kafka, struggled to achieve financial security for his family, and he succeeded, but the ordeal coarsened him; he became autocratic and irascible. Money and status were his chief passions, and he directed his considerable energy to their acquisition. Nevertheless, he had a zest for life that left its imprint on his son, who could admire though never attain it. Kafka's mother, on the other hand, came from a family of rabbis, scholars, and physicians, and from her Kafka probably inherited his sensitive nature and dreamy tendencies.

As Kafka was heir to divergent traditions in his family, so, too, the city of Prague offered him contrasting traditions. On one hand, Prague, influenced by Austria, looked westward, toward rationalism and the Enlightenment; on the other hand, it gazed eastward, toward Russia with its semimystical fervor. In his Jewish studies, too, Kafka discovered similar tensions: the casuistic flavor of the Talmud straining against the impassioned piety of the mystics. These elements ultimately recombine themselves in Kafka's fiction.

Photographs of Kafka reveal him as dark and slender, respectable in appearance, with an intense and boyish face, delicate and sensitive. He spent his school years in Prague—first at a German elementary school and later at a *gymnasium*; he ultimately graduated from the German Karl-Ferdinand University. For two weeks, he specialized in chemistry but found it uncongenial; soon after, he succumbed to pressure from his friends and family, especially his father, and commenced the study of law. Unhappy, he described it as "living in an intellectual sense, on sawdust, which had, moreover, already been chewed for me in thousands of other people's mouths."

Kafka, however, needed some means to support himself, and the legal profession was an eminently respectable career—especially appealing to Jews. Though he never cared for the practice of law, a major consideration was the hope of winning his father's long-withheld approval. In this, he never succeeded; here was a struggle that allowed neither victory nor retreat.

Much has been written on the subject of Kafka and his father. Are not the fathers in his fiction oversize presences that visit judgment and wrath on their sons? Are not his protagonists accused persons, judged guilty of some undefined transgression against an all-powerful and implacable force that hounds the hero and destroys him? In story after story, in all of his novels, one finds Kafka returning, irresistibly, obsessively, to the theme of the judging father in an effort to exorcise this demon—in vain. Kafka's friend and biographer, Brod, first reported and later released an amazing document penned by the twenty-six-year-old Kafka, the *Brief an den Vater* (1952, wr. 1919; *Letter to His Father*, 1954). The manuscript was given to Kafka's mother for delivery to her spouse. More than one hundred pages long, the document minutely scrutinizes the son's pained relations with his father. Its tone—mingling abjectness and defiance—can be heard in Kafka's fiction as well, where it expresses his protagonists' attitudes toward their parents. One can only speculate how Herrmann Kafka might have responded to the missive: Kafka's mother never delivered the letter.

Completing his studies, Kafka gained legal experience in a district, then in a criminal court, where he observed at first hand the workings of the law, which he later fictionalized in *The Trial*. Soon after, he secured a position with the Workers' Accident Insurance Office, where he remained a respected and admired figure until illness forced his retirement in 1922. There he gained intimate knowledge of the operations of a bureaucracy, which he transferred to his novel *The Castle*.

Though Kafka never married, he did seek romance and the consolation of women. In 1912, he began courting a woman he had met at Brod's house, Felice Bauer. (Her initials are echoed both in *The Trial*, in the name of Fraulein Burstner, and in *The Castle*'s Frieda.) Curiously, Kafka avoided contact with her, although he maintained a voluminous correspondence with her, sometimes writing as many as three letters a day. He feared that marriage would infringe both on his privacy and on his writing, and for three years the relationship waxed and waned; Kafka's ambivalence denied him the domestic peace he so desperately sought. In 1917, soon after their second engagement, Kafka discovered that he had tuberculosis, and once again he and his fiancé were disengaged. After several years of battling this disease, Kafka succumbed in June of 1924.

Though Kafka's life was marked by suffering, both intimates and casual acquaintances testify to the sweetness of his disposition, to his sympathy for others, to his unfailing humor and quiet courage. Brod's biography takes pains to overcome the impression that his friend's character was morbid; indeed, Kafka had a gift for finding wry humor both in his life and in the most dreadful predicaments of his characters. He had a gift for whimsy as well; Brod relates that once, when Kafka was about twenty years old, he came to visit Brod and inadvertently awakened Brod's father, who was napping on the sofa. "Please look upon me as a dream," murmured Kafka as he glided by.

Analysis

The name Franz Kafka conjures up images of a world without a center, of people alienated both from society and from themselves. Kafka lived at the threshold of the modern technological world, and his stories are prophetic of the bewilderment and anxiety that typify modern frustrations and darkest moods: humans increasingly out of touch with their essential nature or, when confronted by totalitarian oppression, out of touch with society. When Eugene O'Neill's hairy ape laments that "I ain't in heaven, and I ain't on oith, but takin' the woist from both woilds," he captured something of the spirit, if not the flavor, of Kafka's tragic vision. For Kafka, humanity has only glimmerings of its formerly blessed state yet desperately attempts to recover it.

With the story *Das Urteil* (1913, 1916; *The Sentence*, 1928; also as *The Judgment*,

1945), Kafka created the kind of fiction that characterizes his maturity, combining the unreality of dream states with images of startling vividness. In this early story, as in *The Trial* and *The Castle*, the protagonist faces a judgment on himself, a fate in which the horrible and the absurd intertwine. In Kafka's fiction, every interpretation begets an alternative— one that may contradict its predecessor. This is partly a result of narrative technique: In limiting the narrative to the protagonist's point of view, Kafka ensures that the reader will share his character's bewilderment without benefit of an omniscient author.

In terms of literary form, Kafka's stories most closely resemble the parable: simple yet enigmatic. His work may be read for its historical and social import as the reflections of a German Jew living in Czech Prague, a city under Austrian influence. Neither Austrian nor Czech but Jewish, he was an outsider. His work may be viewed psychologically, as an anxious son's efforts to deal with an accusing father. (Note that all the novels' protagonists bear the author's initial, *K*.) Finally, his work may be read for its religious content, as Everyman's craving to reconcile the demands of the physical with the yearnings of the spiritual.

Characteristically, Kafka's protagonist is a man going about his normal domestic business when a violent and inexplicable eruption warns him that his life has gone astray. Often he awakens one morning to discover that some incomprehensible change has occurred. In *The Trial*, the protagonist discovers men in his room, mysterious functionaries who announce that he has been arrested on charges they will not explain. In the novella *The Metamorphosis*, Gregor Samsa arises, or attempts to do so, only to discover that during the night he has been transformed into a giant dung beetle. No explanation is forthcoming. Is this a judgment on Gregor from above or from within, or is it caused by some force whose will is unknown and unknowable? Is the transformation a necessary but painful path to enlightenment or a punishment? One reads on, hoping for an explanation, a hint of rational purpose in such mysterious happenings; one watches fascinated as others respond to the protagonist's dilemma; one searches for clues in their responses; and one is disarmed at every turn by paradox piled upon paradox, an infinite regression of possibilities that welcome analysis but will never yield to it. Ultimately, the Kafka protagonist perishes or disappears, but whether he is enlightened remains obscure.

AMERIKA

In 1911, Kafka began a novel that Brod later published as *Amerika*. The first chapter was released during Kafka's lifetime as *Der Heizer* (1913; the stoker), but his journals refer to this chapter as "The Man Who Was Lost Sight Of." The most naturalistic of Kafka's novels, *Amerika* relates the story of an innocent youth, not yet sixteen years old, who is forced to leave home for an indiscretion: He was seduced by an older woman, who conceived a child. Like most of Kafka's fictional parents, Karl Rossmann's, too, harshly judge their loving son, who, despite their punishment of him, yearns to be reunited with them.

Rossmann's first intimation of what the new Eden of America will be like occurs when he sees the Statue of Liberty, holding aloft not a torch but a sword (justice? wrath? expulsion from Eden?). This is not the America of Emma Lazarus's poem "The New Colossus" (1883) but rather a capitalistic/ technological society replete with Mark Twain-like rogues—Robinson and Delemarche—and tycoons à la Frank Norris and Theodore Dreiser.

At first, Rossmann seems blessed: His uncle Jacob, a politician and an industrialist, discovers him aboard a ship and takes the lad under his wing. Rossmann quickly perceives, however, that this highly industrialized state called America degrades all those who come in contact with it—workers, rulers, and politicians. Through the familiar device of the picaresque novel, the hero undergoes a series of adventures loosely strung together—adventures among the rich and poor, insiders and outcasts. Rossmann himself is an innocent, hopelessly entangled in a fallen world, and this is the major problem of the work. Unlike the protagonists of the later novels, Rossmann is not part of the world he observes, merely its victim. The reader can pity Rossmann, impressed with Kafka's diagnosis of a world grown increasingly bureaucratic, but one is not astonished and mesmerized, as readers of the later two novels are. The nightmare in *Amerika* is someone else's nightmare, not the reader's. When Rossmann is vilified and loses his job at the Hotel Occidental for his momentary lapse from duty, the reader is too keenly aware of the injustice, too eager to protest on his behalf.

Compare this, for example, to Kafka's well-known short story *The Metamorphosis*, in which Gregor is transformed into a giant insect. At first, one shares the protagonist's shock—how could such a thing happen, and what does it mean?—but this is quickly succeeded by a more pressing question: How does Gregor know that he is an insect? Not through his senses, for he does not need to look at himself; rather he seems to have intuited the transformation, perhaps invited it. Whether the metamorphosis is a judgment, an injustice, or a signpost to salvation, Gregor's fate, unlike Rossmann's, is part of his character.

Still, in *Amerika* many of Kafka's familiar themes are developed, however embryonically. The theme of justice is manifest in the opening chapter, when Rossmann unsuccessfully attempts to aid the confused stoker in airing his grievances. As in many scenes that follow, Rossmann will be forced to leave those he cares about without succeeding in accomplishing his aims. His departure from the ship with his Uncle Jacob marks the climax of his good fortune. (Indeed, most of Kafka's fiction climaxes in the opening chapter, with the rest of the story exploring the consequences of what proves to be an irreversible judgment.) For ingratitude, Rossmann is promptly disinherited by his uncle, a capitalist and exploiter with overtones of Yahweh (the sort of paradox in which Kafka delighted). The sword that the Statue of Liberty holds aloft adds to the impression that Rossmann is being expelled from his American Eden.

Like the stoker, Rossmann will have difficulties with authority. Soon after departing from his uncle, he is employed at the Hotel Occidental in Rameses—in other words, a symbol of civilization, whether Western or Eastern. Under the patronage of the "Manageress," Rossmann does well at his menial job of elevator operator, but one evening he is caught in a minor infraction. As in the case of the stoker, his efforts to obtain justice—his attempt to justify himself, to minimize his error, to benefit from the help of the Manageress—come to naught, and he is dismissed. The author here creates the kind of nightmarish scene that has become known as Kafkaesque, one in which everything that can go wrong does. The accused cannot stand before authority and state with certainty that he is truly innocent, while the officials on whom his fate depends are blasé, bored, indifferent to petitions, sometimes mocking and malicious.

Leaving the hotel in disgrace (he is even suspected by the police, though no charges have been filed against him), Rossmann is forced once more into the company of the scoundrels Delemarche and Robinson, who have taken up with the former singer Brunelda, a gross embodiment of sensuality who enslaves all three in her love nest. Usually in Kafka's works, the artist points the way to transcendence, but this singer has given up her art to satisfy her lusts. In a memorable scene, she presses her huge body against Rossmann, literally pinning him to the balcony railing while they watch a political demonstration on the streets. The scene reveals humans given over to their appetites: On the balcony, Brunelda pursues carnality; on the streets, the crowd pursues drunkenness. Though this scene is vividly delineated, it reminds the reader once again of the problem Kafka faces here: What has his protagonist to do with the gross bodily appetites which indeed appall him?

At the beginning of the uncompleted final chapter, Rossmann finds himself at the nature theater of Oklahoma. What the author intended here may be inferred from Brod's report that Kafka wished to end the book on a note of reconciliation. Had Kafka realized these intentions, this work would have been unique in his fiction for its promise of hope and transcendence. The extant fragment, however, suggests that Kafka was deviating from his announced plan. The paradoxes continue: The welcoming angels blowing their horns are not angels, or even good musicians, and they are elevated above common humanity with the aid of ladders that can be seen through their gowns. Rossmann does get a job, but again it is a lowly one, far from a profession. At the novel's end, he is on a train, presumably heading westward—to a promising future or, as the title suggests, simply to vanish.

THE TRIAL

"Someone must have denounced Joseph K., for without having done anything wrong he was arrested one morning." Thus begins Kafka's second novel, *The Trial*. What are the charges? K. never learns, though he encounters several functionaries of the court, attends preliminary hearings, and hires a lawyer to defend him. This might have been the opening of a novel of political repression, but one quickly discovers that the law here, unlike its operation in Arthur Koestler's *Darkness at Noon* (1940), for example, does not represent the state judiciary system but a shadow court, one that is paradoxically both loftier and seedier. When Kafka speaks of the law, he means what the Chinese philosopher Laozi (Laotzu) called The Way—that style of living that conduces to right conduct and enlightenment. Kafka's protagonists (and his readers) grope for truth along a path circumscribed by darkness.

Has K. really done nothing "wrong"? He is certainly innocent of civil or criminal wrongdoing. A respected bank official, his conduct has been apparently irreproachable. Yet he is under arrest—a curious form of arrest, in which he is not "prevented from leading [his] ordinary life." Curiously, the "criminal" must not only defend himself but also discover his crime. Critics diverge in their efforts to understand the nature of the charge against him. According to Brod, K. is unable to love; according to another commentator, his mediocrity condemns him. A third argues that his crime lies in his suppression of his guilt. For yet another, K. is one who refuses to act in accordance with his knowledge of good and evil because he lacks the strength for such action. No easy answer emerges. Whether humanity is indeed guilty or is falsely accused by a divinity unable or unwilling to help it comprehend its own essence is never revealed. What is clear is that K. feels guilty even while defending his innocence.

What sort of man is K.? Like most Kafka protagonists, he is a bachelor, uncommitted to others. He dwells in a rooming house, ignoring both his cousin, who lives in town, and his mother, who lodges in the country. His friends are mainly business associates; his lover, a woman visited once a week. No doubt, Kafka, in his diaries, often expressed contempt for such an existence ("My monotonous, empty, mad bachelor's life"), but is this K.'s crime? If so, he could easily have been informed of that by any number of the officials he encounters. Moreover, K. seems to be living a life similar to that of most of the officials of the court. Can the priest denounce him for bachelorhood? The Examining Magistrate or the painter Titorelli for womanizing? The Magistrates for vanity? Lawyer Huld for placing his profession before his personal life? Rather, Joseph K. is a flawed human being, flawed in some fundamental spiritual way, one who lacks self-confidence. The best clue to understanding his situation is the guilt he only halfway acknowledges. He is told, "Our officials never go hunting for guilt in the populace, but, as the Law decrees, are attracted by guilt, and must then send out us warders." The implication is that K. himself lured the warders to him in the interests of self-realization and self-extermination—the two are synonymous in Kafka's fiction.

Joseph K., respectable, even dignified in the world's eyes, experiences a number of humiliations, each of which will signify the hopelessness of his position. Arrested in his own bedroom by intruders who offer to sell his clothing (they confiscate his underwear), observed by a couple across the courtyard as well as by his landlady and three of his subordinates at the bank, K. finds his privacy, self-respect, and professional competence shredded. He has indeed awakened to a nightmare.

What authority has this court? It is independent of the civil judiciary system; K. is notified that his first hearing is to be held on a Sunday, in a shabby part of town. In fact, he discovers, he is being tried in an attic; most of the attics in the city, he learns, house divisions of this omnipresent bureaucracy. Very likely, Kafka is suggesting that most people are under indictment. The hearing is alternately comic and maddening. At the outset, the judge mistakes the chief clerk of a bank for a house painter. Have they arrested the wrong man? Are they incompetent, or are they simply ignorant underlings blindly administering a form of justice they themselves do not comprehend?

K.'s efforts to denounce these outrageous proceedings, however, reveal that he does not grasp the nature or gravity of his situation. However clownish these officials may appear (the Examining Magistrate browses over obscene drawings throughout the hearing), their power should not be underestimated. K.'s speech mocking the court proceedings does not reveal confident self-sufficiency but swaggering ignorance. "I merely wanted to point out" remarked the Examining Magistrate afterward, "that today . . . you have deprived yourself of the advantage an interrogation usually confers on an accused man." Unfortunately, this and all the other bits of information about the court that K. receives, whether valid or invalid (and how is he to distinguish between them?), are equally useless to him.

Of K.'s plight the philosopher Martin Buber remarked that, though men and women have been appointed to this world, they are forever caught in the thick vapors of a mist of absurdity. Is divinity unwilling to reveal itself? Possibly. "The highest court . . . is quite inaccessible to you, to me, and to all of us," K. is told. It is equally possible, though, that it reveals itself every moment but that people either blind themselves or are simply ill-equipped to internalize the message. Near the novel's conclusion, the priest shrieks out to him, "Can't you even see two inches in front of your nose?" K. both can and cannot: Indeed, the tragedy of human relations with divinity is the near-impossibility of communication between them.

K. can never get beyond dealing with underlings; humans lack the spiritual strength and the understanding necessary for their quest. In the often excerpted passage of the doorkeeper of the Law, the priest suggests that the petitioner might have merely stepped through the first door of justice had he the temerity and the wisdom. Presumably, the same applies to K., but all of his efforts to assert himself—to demonstrate that he is innocent or that the Law is in error—come to naught. Even the women from whom he has sought comfort have misled him. He has made many errors, and now, the priest informs him, his guilt is all but proved.

Earlier, K. had met another functionary of the court, the painter Titorelli. The name itself is a pseudonym, an amalgam of the names of famous Italian artists. In reality, he is a hack court painter, as degenerate as another artist, Brunelda, in Kafka's *Amerika*. Efforts that artists once dedicated to the glory of God, during an age of worship, Titorelli now dedicates to cynical aggrandizement of petty officials. From the painter, K. learns of the three possible directions for his case: definite acquittal, ostensible acquittal, and indefinite postponement. Even this, however, may be merely a joke: Definite acquittals do not occur. "I have never heard of one case," avers the artist. Ostensible acquittal grants provisional freedom, which may last for years or only for an hour, followed by re-arrest. Postponement seems to be the tactic another accused man, Mr. Block, has resolved to follow, but such an approach would deny K. an opportunity to face his creator and accuser; it would reduce him to the status of a beggar, more a cringing beast than a man. Are the courts merely playing with people? Possibly: Titorelli's drawing of Justice makes her look "exactly like the Goddess of the Hunt in full cry."

Exactly one year after K.'s arrest, when K. is thirty-one years old (Kafka's age at the time the novel was written), two men come for him. Garbed in black, K. is prepared for his executioners. Somber as this scene is, however, it has comically grotesque elements. "Tenth rate old actors they send for me," he muses. "Perhaps they are tenors." Joseph K. is led through the streets; at times he even does the leading, indicating acceptance of his fate. The final scene is richly textured and enigmatic. His executioners require that he lie down on the ground and intimate that he is to reach for the knife and execute himself. Wordlessly, K. refuses. Is this further evidence of his rebellious nature or his own judgment of the shameful justice rendered by the court? He is stabbed and dies "like a dog, it was as if the shame should survive him." As one critic has asked, whose shame, that of the man or of the court? On this ambiguous and troubling note, Kafka's unfinished novel ceases.

THE CASTLE

Sometime in 1922, less than two years before his death, Kafka began his final novel, the longest and most thematically complex of his narratives. In *The Castle*, Kafka's settings grow even sparer than those of his earlier works, reinforcing the parablelike nature of the tale. *The Castle* is the story of K., a land surveyor, who leaves his village to live and work near the castle. Unlike Joseph K., who is summoned to trial, K. seeks out the castle of his own volition: He wishes to be the castle's land surveyor. Unable to enter the castle, he attempts to secure an interview with the Court Official in charge of land surveyors, Klamm. Like the petitioner who has come to the Law in *The Trial*, K. finds his way barred. No matter what he attempts, he is no nearer the castle at the novel's end than he was on the first day. His quest wears him out, and though Kafka never concluded this novel, he did make it clear that K. was to die, exhausted by his efforts.

Again, Kafka's enigmatic art has kindled various interpretations. Brod interprets the castle theologically, as the attempt to secure Divine Law and Divine Grace. Others assert that Kafka's novels describe human efforts to overcome limitations as physical beings to grapple with the spiritual self in a vain effort to unify the two sides. Another group perceives this novel as a denunciation of the bureaucracy that ruled Kafka's country. All sides can adduce strong arguments—more testimony to the paradoxical and allegorical nature of Kafka's art.

K. is an outsider, an Everyman attempting to find a meaningful life in a world that has lost its spiritual moorings. In doing so, he looks toward the castle, but whether the castle is even occupied, whether it has corporeal existence or is the inward world the narrator yearns to reach, must remain a mystery: At the novel's opening, K. stands "for a long time gazing into the apparent emptiness above him." This emptiness echoes and amplifies the spirit of T. S. Eliot's *The Waste Land* (1922) and Oswald Spengler's *Der Untergang des Abendlandes* (1918-1922; *The Decline of the West*, 1926-1928). The never seen owner of the castle is named Count Westwest.

Like many of Kafka's protagonists, K. is aroused from a deep sleep to face an identity crisis. He claims at the inn where he is staying that he has been summoned by the castle, but a telephone call to the castle brings a hasty denial; then, before K. can be ejected from the inn, another call reverses the first judgment. The issue of K.'s status is further complicated when he observes that the castle "was accepting battle with a smile." The castle accepts the intruder's invasion but its smile is not easily decipherable. Much suggests that it is mocking. The assistants assigned to him are childish and troublesome, very likely dispatched as spies. The messages he receives are so ambiguous in language, so ill-informed regarding his activities, that he despairs after receiving them, despite the fact that he wants nothing more than to be acknowledged. One official, Bürgel, even informs him that the present moment holds the key to his hopes, implying that if he were to present his petition at once, it would be accepted. Alas, K. has fallen asleep.

As in *The Trial*, the protagonist's efforts to justify himself before officialdom prove fruitless. His superior, Klamm, is perceived by K. through a peephole, but all attempts to speak to him are rebuffed. To K.'s request for an interview comes the reply "Never. Under no conditions!" Resolutely, K. determines to intercept Klamm at his carriage, but the official will not venture forth. Stalemated, K. feels he

> had won a freedom such as hardly anybody else had ever succeeded in winning, as if nobody could . . . drive him away . . . [but] at the same time there was nothing more senseless, nothing more hopeless, than this freedom.

K. cannot be driven away, but he will never be recognized.

By means of subplots, mainly involving the family of K.'s messenger, Kafka reinforces his theme that humans are alienated from their society, their inner self, their God. The reader who is familiar with the Aristotelian formula of a protagonist who successfully completes an action will be disarmed by Kafka's novel, in which developments serve only to clarify the impossibility of a successful completion of the goal.

Like Joseph K. of *The Trial*, K. discovers some respite in women. Frieda (peace), the mistress of Klamm, represents domestic pleasure, the highest Earth has to offer. Although she agrees to leave Klamm for K., his Faustian spirit is not satisfied. Forsaking the sensual and domestic comforts, K. continually leaves Frieda in pursuit of his goal, transcendence of the merely mundane, while maintaining that he does so in part for her. This paradoxical attitude probably mirrors Kafka's own relationship with Felice Bauer. Kafka was torn between committing himself to his fiancé and freeing himself for his art, an ambivalence reflected in K.'s inconsistent behavior with Frieda. After losing her, K. remarks that though he "would be happy if she were to come back to me . . . I should at once begin to neglect her all over again. This is how it is." Thus, the reader sees why K. can never know peace, why he is doomed to wear himself out.

In addition to Frieda, K. is intimate with Olga, Barnabas's sister. Like K., she is desperate to reach the castle to redress a wrong done to her family by one of its officials. Olga's sister, Amalia, has been grossly propositioned by one of the castle officials. Her family has worn itself out, as K. is doing, in a fruitless attempt to justify themselves before the authorities, to gain access to the Law; even the villagers find the authorities inaccessible. From K.'s perspective, the authorities seem impersonal, aloof. In ruling, they are attentive to trivial detail but bureaucratically indifferent to human considerations.

Though Kafka did not complete *The Castle*, his intended ending was communicated to Brod. Around K.'s

> deathbed the community assembles and from the castle comes this decision: that K. has no claim to live in the castle by right—yet taking certain auxiliary circumstances into account, it is permitted him to live and work there.

With remarkable prescience, Kafka had sketched his own epitaph. Consider the treatment accorded his memory: Czech authorities placed signs in five languages to mark his grave, yet for more than twenty years they forbade sale of his works.

Stan Sulkes

OTHER MAJOR WORKS

SHORT FICTION: *Betrachtung*, 1913 (*Meditation*, 1948); *Das Urteil*, 1913, 1916 (*The Sentence*, 1928; also known as *The Judgment*, 1945); *Die Verwandlung*, 1915 (*The Metamorphosis*, 1936); "In der Strafkolonie," 1919 ("In the Penal Colony," 1941); *Ein Hungerkünstler: Vier Geschichten*, 1924 (*A Hunger Artist*, 1948); *Beim Bau der Chinesischen Mauer: Ungedruckte Erzählungen und Prosa aus dem Nachlass*, 1931 (*The Great Wall of China, and Other Pieces*, 1933); *Erzählungen*, 1946 (*The Complete Stories*, 1971); *The Penal Colony: Stories and Short Pieces*, 1948; *Selected Short Stories*, 1952.

NONFICTION: *The Diaries of Franz Kafka*, 1948-1949; *Tagebücher, 1910-1923*, 1951; *Brief an den Vater*, 1952 (wr. 1919; *Letter to His Father*, 1954); *Briefe an Milena*, 1952 (*Letters to Milena*, 1953); *Briefe, 1902-1924*, 1958; *Briefe an Felice*, 1967 (*Letters to Felice*, 1974); *Briefe an Ottla und die Familie*, 1974 (*Letters to Ottla and the Family*, 1982); *I Am a Memory Come Alive: Autobiographical Writings*, 1974 (Nahum N. Glatzer, editor); *Franz Kafka: The Office Writings*, 2009.

MISCELLANEOUS: *Hochzeitsvorbereitungen auf dem Lande und andere Prosa aus dem Nachlass*, 1953 (*Dearest Father: Stories, and Other Writings*, 1954; also known as *Wedding Preparations in the Country, and Other Posthumous Prose Writings*, 1954).

Bibliography

Anderson, Mark, ed. *Reading Kafka: Prague, Politics, and the Fin de Siecle*. New York: Schocken Books, 1989. Collection of essays presents a good sampling from the enormous body of contemporary scholarship, in both English and German, on Kafka's writings.

Bloom, Harold, ed. *Franz Kafka*. New York: Chelsea House, 2005. Essays in this collection provide good, readable general introductions to several contemporary approaches to Kafka's work.

Gray, Richard T., Ruth V. Gross, Rolf J. Goebel, and Clayton Koelb. *A Franz Kafka Encyclopedia*. Westport, Conn.: Greenwood Press, 2005. Comprehensive volume contains alphabetized entries that discuss all aspects of Kafka's life and work, including characters, places, and events.

Gray, Ronald. *Franz Kafka*. New York: Cambridge University Press, 1973. Concise study by a renowned Kafka scholar. Still one of the best overviews of his work available in English.

Hayman, Ronald. *K: A Biography of Kafka*. New ed. London: Phoenix, 2001. Presents a solid and readable account of Kafka's life, intended for the general reader. Includes a chronology and an extensive bibliography. First published 1981.

Karl, Frederick. *Franz Kafka: Representative Man—Prague, Germans, Jews, and the Crisis of Modernism*. New York: Ticknor & Fields, 1991. Massive study is perhaps the most comprehensive attempt to place Kafka within the context of his own time and to study his writings as central to the modernist movement in twentieth century literature.

Pawel, Ernst. *The Nightmare of Reason: A Life of Franz Kafka*. New York: Farrar, Straus and Giroux, 1984. Revisionist work places Kafka in historical context and attempts to dispel the myths of the author as a helpless neurasthenic clerk. Describes him as an effective executive who was in many ways typical of his age and class.

Preese, Julian, ed. *Cambridge Companion to Kafka*. New York: Cambridge University Press, 2002. Collection of essays presents various approaches to Kafka's work. Part of Cambridge's respected companion series.

Robertson, Ritchie. *Kafka: Judaism, Politics, and Literature*. Oxford, England: Clarendon Press, 1985. Discusses a wide variety of Kafka's works in the context of his politics and his interest in Judaism.

ALAIN-RENÉ LESAGE

Born: Sarzeau, Brittany, France; May 8, 1668
Died: Boulogne, France; November 17, 1747
Also known as: Alain-René Le Sage

PRINCIPAL LONG FICTION
Le Diable boiteux, 1707 (*The Devil upon Two Sticks*, 1708, 1726)
Histoire de Gil Blas de Santillane, 1715-1735 (4 volumes; *The History of Gil Blas of Santillane*, 1716, 1735; better known as *Gil Blas*, 1749, 1962)
Histoire de Don Guzman d'Alfarache, 1732 (*The Pleasant Adventures of Gusman of Alfarache*, 1812)
Les Aventures de M. Robert Chevalier dit de Beauchêne, 1732 (*The Adventures of Robert Chevalier*, 1745)
Histoire d'Estévanille Gonzalès, 1734 (*The Comical History of Estévanille Gonzalez*, 1735; also known as *The History of Vanillo Gonzales, Surnamed the Merry Bachelor*, 1821-1824)
Le Bachelier de Salamanque, 1736 (*The Bachelor of Salamanca*, 1737-1739)

OTHER LITERARY FORMS

In addition to being a novelist, Alain-René Lesage (leh-SAHZH) was a playwright. While he was with the Comédie-Française, he penned two major plays: *Crispin, rival de son maître*, pr., pb. 1707 (*Crispin, Rival of His Master*, 1766) and *Turcaret: Comédie en cinq actes*, pr., pb. 1709 (English translation, 1923). After these plays were written, Lesage quarreled with the company and commenced writing pieces, both singly and in collaboration with others, for the Théâtre de la Foire. The pieces written for the Théâtre de la Foire were chiefly farces, interspersed with lyrics sung to popular songs of the day, and were categorized as *comédies à vaudevilles*. The ten-volume *Le Théâtre de la Foire: Ou, L'Opéra comique* (pr. 1712-1738) includes many of these theatrical pieces. Lesage also wrote short fiction, such as the two-volume *La Valise trouvée* (1740).

ACHIEVEMENTS

The novelistic work of Alain-René Lesage has been called a parenthesis in the history of French letters, and such a formula, though in need of technical improvements (it should be said that Lesage's work is between parentheses), is neither cruel nor inaccurate. Both the provenance of his sources for *Gil Blas* and the subsequent picaresque tales, and that for *The Devil upon Two Sticks* were Spanish, and the subsequent impact of Lesage's work has been felt not so much in France as in England, in the persons of his translator Tobias Smollett and of Henry Fielding, whose *The History of Tom Jones, a Foundling* (1749) carries faint echoes of Lesage's world. In truth, Lesage's novels seem to constitute rather a halfway house for Spanish techniques making their way to England. Since scholars in any literature prefer to study authors who can connect with other trends and larger movements within that literature, Lesage has come to be a writer of whom characteristically only one work is read, and that not to the end.

Part of the difficulty of assessing Lesage's achievement is a matter of simple authorship questions. First, Voltaire, no Lesage partisan in any case, accused him of lifting *Gil Blas* in its entirety from the Spaniard Vicente Martínez de Espinel's *Marcos de Obregón* (1618). This splenetic assertion proved easy to refute. A more serious, because more detailed, charge was leveled by the Padre de Isla, who argued that *Gil Blas* was little more than a translation from some Spanish original. Though more detailed, the charge proved equally baseless: Despite the reality that Lesage collected picaresque manuscripts and had begun his career as a translator of Spanish, this putative manuscript from which Lesage was supposed to have plucked his story was precisely that—putative, never proved to exist. Given that de Isla's plagiarism accusations came out at the very time—in Restoration France of the early nineteenth century—when Lesage's literary reputation was nearing its zenith, the matter had all the makings of an international incident.

In 1818, the French Academy commissioned the Count François de Neufchâteau to probe the charges, and his famous "Examen" of that year gave Lesage a clean bill of health. Nevertheless, a cloud has always hung over this novelist's claim to originality, in part because he himself freely admitted his liberal borrowings from Spanish originals for such books as *The Devil upon Two Sticks* and for plays with plots taken from the likes of the Spanish playwright Pedro Calderón de la Barca. As a result, the question of what Lesage merely inherited and passed on, as opposed to what he actually invented and contributed, remains murkier even than such questions usually are.

It is undeniable, however, that Lesage's techniques and witty, cynical style did leave their mark on the eighteenth century English novel. *The Adventures of Roderick Random* (1748) and *The Adventures of Peregrine Pickle: In Which Are Included Memoirs of a Lady of Quality* (1751), by Smollett—the very titles proclaim their picaresque heritage—clearly owe to Lesage, despite their occasional tone of indignation; indeed, Smollett's preface to *Roderick Random* pays explicit tribute to Lesage. Fielding also, as mentioned, seems to have drawn from him in some substantial measure. The French, by contrast, moved quickly to resume the psychologistic course set by Madame de La Fayette and to develop, with Marivaux, Jean-Jacques Rousseau, and others, the epistolary novel of sensibility. Even in Great Britain, the influence of Lesage's kind of narrative was cut short by Samuel Richardson's *Pamela* (1740-1741), a book that inaugurated a trend toward novelistic psychology similar to that in France.

In another cross-cultural irony, it may well be that Richardson had more influence on later eighteenth century French novelists than their own countryman. Still, the unexpected resurgence of Lesage's hero in Victor Hugo's early nineteenth century play *Ruy Blas* (1838; English translation, 1890) kept Lesage popular and read throughout that century;

even after the interest in Lesage had crested, around the time of the July Monarchy in 1830, he was cited frequently as an alternative to the increasingly prevalent "socially aware" novel in France written by people such as Eugène Sue. This is especially odd considering the heavy amount of social satire in Lesage and the similarities in technique between, for example, Sue's *Les mystères de Paris* (1842-1843; *The Mysteries of Paris*, 1896) and Lesage's *The Devil upon Two Sticks*. The thing to bear in mind is that, for all of these historical pitfalls of influence on other novelists, Lesage's influence on many readers has not wavered.

Biography

Alain-René Lesage was born in Sarzeau, on the peninsula of Rhuys in the north of France. His father, Claude Le Sage, was a combined notary, advocate, and registrar of the royal court of Rhuys, which was a legal district. Both parents died when Lesage was very young, and his patrimony was thieved and squandered by guardians. He studied with the Jesuits until he was eighteen years old; he was called to the Paris bar in 1692. Anything beyond these few facts about his early years is conjecture. In August, 1694, Lesage married Marie Élisabeth Huyard; though beautiful, she had little dowry, and his practice was failing as well.

On the advice of Danchet, an old classmate, Lesage turned to literature, beginning as a translator. His first effort, a French translation of the *Epistles* of Aristaenetus in 1695, met with a thud of indifference. (Even the otherwise tolerant commentator George Saintsbury wondered why Lesage bothered.) Soon, however, Lesage found a patron in the Abbé de Lyonne, who, in addition to giving him six hundred livres annually, advised Lesage to forget translating the classics and to turn his efforts to Spanish literature instead.

Plays by Francisco de Rojas Zorilla, Lope de Vega Carpio, and other Spaniards were Lesage's main prey as translator. Lesage's adaptations of their works, *Le Traître puni* and *Le Point d'honneur* (from Rojas) and *Don Félix de Mendoce* (from Vega) were all acted or published around the turn of the eighteenth century. In 1704, Lesage brought out the French version of Alonso Fernández de Avellaneda's sequel to Miguel de Cervantes' *Don Quixote de la Mancha* (1605, 1615)—Saintsbury did not appreciate this choice, either—and in 1707 adapted Calderón's *Peor está que estaba* (1630) as *Don César Ursin*. *Neck or Nothing*, however, was the farce that gained for him, at the age of thirty-eight, his first real fame; then, in this annus mirabilis, *The Devil upon Two Sticks* was published and went through many editions until Lesage altered it and improved it, rendering it in its present form. In spite or perhaps because of Lesage's growing popularity, the actors were displeased with him, rejecting a small play he had written in 1707 called "Les Étrennes"; the rejection proved to be a fortunate one for Lesage, who recast the play as *Turcaret*, creating what is now thought to be his theatrical masterpiece, as well as one of France's best stage comedies.

When, in 1715, the first two volumes of *Gil Blas* appeared, they were, curiously, less popular than *The Devil upon Two Sticks* had been. Nevertheless, Lesage worked hard on the third volume, which came out in 1724, and he brought out the fourth and final volume in 1735. (He had been paid for this last volume, according to legend, almost a decade before the book actually appeared.) During this same period, Lesage was continuing to write light theatrical pieces, although no longer for the Comédie-Française. In the year in which he published the first two volumes of *Gil Blas*, he went to work for the Théâtre de la Foire, which consisted of comic opera in booths for festival occasions. There are varying reports on the quantity of his output, but it was unquestionably considerable: as many as a hundred pieces, both alone and with others, from individual songs to musical comedies, as one would now term them.

The 1720's and 1730's also saw the publication of much prose fiction by Lesage, including *The Pleasant Adventures of Gusman of Alfarache*, *The Bachelor of Salamanca*, *The Comical History of Estévanille Gonzalez*, and *The Adventures of Robert Chevalier*. Both the originality and the quality of these productions is much debated, but the energy of output cannot be disputed. In addition, he also produced minor pieces such as *La Valise trouvée*, which was a collection of imaginary letters bearing some resemblance to Montesquieu's later satire *Lettres persanes* (1721; *Persian Letters*, 1722), and *Une journée des parques* (1735; *A Day of the Fates*, 1922), a short piece that is often compared to the Latin poetry of Lucian. Lesage continued working more or less steadily through the age of seventy. When his oldest son became an actor, Lesage disowned him; one cannot help recalling the acid portraiture the author so often devotes to the performers in *Gil Blas*. The second of Lesage's sons became a canon at Boulogne and was amply appointed as well; in 1740, Lesage and his wife both went to his home to spend their declining years with him. Lesage died at Boulogne on November 17, 1747.

Little is known anecdotally of Lesage, except that he had a very independent cast of mind, one ill accorded with the assumed need on the part of writers of that time to please their patrons. For example, when the duchess of Bouillon objected to Lesage's tardy arrival at her house to read from *Turcaret*, despite his claim that the delay was unavoidable, he simply walked out, never to return. He held himself aloof, by and large, from royal patronage and from salon and coterie approval—or perhaps it simply was not offered him. In either case, his situation as a writer, in this respect, was almost unique among the great names of both seventeenth and eighteenth century French letters. It is amusing to wonder how many modern-day scholars and creative-writing teachers in the realm of fiction would survive professionally for as long a time as Lesage did if fortune were to consign them to a similar independence.

Analysis

Although Alain-René Lesage wrote several novels, only two of his endeavors in long fiction are read at all widely today: *The Devil upon Two Sticks* and *Gil Blas*. The first novel, a brief tour de force, is sometimes seen, by critic Frederick C. Green, for example, as a sort of "practice run" for the greater feat of the later novel.

The Devil upon Two Sticks had as its admitted inspiration *El diablo cojuelo* (1641), by the Spanish author Luis Vélez de Guevara; this pattern of adaptation was followed throughout Lesage's career and occasioned much subsequent comment through the years, especially by Spaniards—a circumstance that, on reflection, is not surprising. (Saintsbury, however, claims the debt to Guevara to be "exaggeration.") After all, even the French have long since conceded Lesage to be more in the Spanish tradition of picaresque than the more introspective French lineage, extending from Madame de La Fayette through Marivaux to Stendhal. In this case, Lesage's recasting of his Spanish original allows him to do what he most revels in doing: exposing a cross section of his society. The framing conceit of this novel is that Asmodeus, the bottle imp of the title, reveals for the benefit of Don Cléophas, his liberator from the bottle, all the rich variety of life in the city of Madrid, allowing voyeurism on a grand scale.

THE DEVIL UPON TWO STICKS

The core idea of the narrative of *The Devil upon Two Sticks*—the unroofing of Madrid's houses for Cléophas's amusement—is unmistakably Guevara's. The elaboration of the conceit, however, is Lesage's: from the exposure of a lunatic asylum in the process to the revelation of the innards of a prison. Even the secrets of the dream lives of several people are served up for scrutiny—likewise Lesage's own freewheeling invention. Even though Cléophas is present at these encounters, and despite the fact that at one point the bottle imp assumes Cléophas's form in order to rescue from a fire the beautiful woman who will in gratitude become Cléophas's bride—for all that, the two major figures are primarily the mere frames for this *roman de mœurs*, this collection of scenes and brief anecdotes.

Nicolas Boileau's reportedly intense loathing of the book—to the point of declaring that "such a book and such a critic . . . should never pass a night under the same roof"—seems now to be a bit overstated, at the least. Yet, it must be acknowledged as well that such a book, by modern standards, is scarcely a novel at all. Lesage inflates Guevara's development of his idea to roughly twice its original length, knowing a popular gimmick when he sees one, no doubt; the recapture of the bottle imp by the magician, closing off the narrative, is arbitrary enough that it could have come a hundred pages earlier or later, so many tales taken up or excised, as in a scrapbook.

It is not for the architectonics, however, that a reader would go to *The Devil upon Two Sticks*—or to Lesage in general, for that matter; it is rather for his dry, ironic, and lapidary style and for the keen satirist's eye he turns on his character types (one hesitates to call them, in the modern sense of the term, "characters") in their various walks of life. This early narrative effort of Lesage has put more than one reader in mind of the *Caractères de Théophaste traduits du grec* (1688-1694), by Jean de La Bruyère, that "prince of observers," as Green has called him. Depth psychology was not a demonstrable part of Lesage's equipment, but clearness of eye and apprehension of detail—all that one calls the novelist's ability to observe human nature—are manifest even in this text, manifest with an ease and lightness conspicuously absent from, say, the epistolary novelists of sensibility of the latter eighteenth century in France.

GIL BLAS

What in a two-hundred-page trifle may look like ease and lightness, however, can easily, in an eight-hundred-page novel in four volumes, come to resemble superficiality. That novel is *Gil Blas*, and it represents in many respects an advance over the earlier work. Whereas *The Devil upon Two Sticks* had been essentially a portrait gallery, a flimsy narrative excuse to peer into various styles of life of the time, the later work became a somewhat more purposive whole, one with more of a dramatic forward thrust. In *Gil Blas*, the reader will find the sort of inspection of social types that always distinguishes a novel of manners, but more attempt is made to tie the various anatomies to the fortunes of the hero and to retain him as the unifying lens through which the events are viewed. Gil Blas not only witnesses these moments as a spectator or voyeur but also participates in them, and what transpires in these worlds is often material to his success or failure. As the novel proceeds, moreover, Gil Blas attains ever-increasing prominence, eventually making his way into the court—not once, but twice, in fact.

As in *The Devil upon Two Sticks*, however, the main purpose is less to involve the reader viscerally with the fortunes of the hero than to display various aspects of society, usually to satiric purpose or effect. The setting and time of the novel are presented as early seventeenth century Spain; but the thinly disguised targets and the points made about them are clearly early eighteenth century French, even Breton. Critics of the novel have subsequently uncovered the likes of Madame de Lambert and Madame de Tencin (both of whom kept famous salons in Lesage's day) under fictional cloaks; Martin Turnell has even argued, though without stated evidence, that most of the inserted stories of lesser characters are actually autobiographical on the part of the author. Given the space these framed tales consume in the narrative, this would mean that roughly one-third of the complete novel consists of veiled autobiography. Certainly, the material having to do with the stage seems too close to Lesage not to have been wrung from bitter experience, even from what little can be ascertained about the author's life. The sarcastic condescension with which the acting troupe in book 3 treats its starving author, and the repeated inability of the performers throughout the book to account for or to predict their audience's taste, have the ring of astringent authenticity.

Indeed, to the extent that the novel has any moral at all, the proliferation of ruses, false identities, and theatrical metaphorics suggests that "All the world's a stage" would be a likely candidate. Initially sent on his way from Oviedo to Salamanca by his generous uncle, Gil Blas is soon waylaid, quite literally, from his original itinerary, which was to become a student. Instead, the highwaymen under Captain Rolando capture him and initiate him in fraud and deception. Realizing, after a thwarted attempt to escape, that he must accommodate to his captors, Gil ingratiates himself with the gang in order later to take advantage of their complacency; he must join them to beat them, and eventually he does escape the gang whose loyal member he pretended to be. This opening narrative sequence of the novel is really only the extreme form of his tactic, and his strategy, throughout his adventures. Lacking his own resources, Gil adopts with great facility the role favored by whichever patron is shoring him up at the moment.

Scruple plays scarcely any part in Gil's undertakings. Although it is largely left to supernumeraries such as Don Raphael and Ambrose de Lamela to don costumes of disguise, Gil himself wears disguises on occasion, and he unquestionably rivals Don Raphael and Ambrose, in a subtler way, at dissimulating the right character for his master of the day. In book 2, serving as apprentice to Doctor Sangrado, Valladolid's infamous practitioner of the bloodletting cure, Gil is quite happy to apply the identical method during a village epidemic, with predictably fatal results that he blandly recites for the reader's information.

By contrast, there are few instances in which Gil is totally candid with an employer; one of them occurs in book 7, where Gil has entered the service of an archbishop. Significantly, this candor seems to have resulted from his patron's insistence on candor; more significantly, and ironically, Gil's obedience is fatal to his tenure under the Archbishop. He has been enjoined by the Archbishop to be brutally frank in critiquing his master's sermons. Soon thereafter, the Archbishop, recently recovered from a stroke, delivers a sermon that betrays with painful clarity exactly how limited the recovery has been; Gil Blas, having previously been urged to be honest under pain of losing his job, tells the Archbishop, with immense tact, that there has been a slight falling off in the quality of the most recent sermon. (He is thereupon relieved of his post.)

What moral can be drawn from this famous moment in the novel—assuming any moral can be judiciously drawn from the insouciant Lesage—is that honesty is scarcely, if ever, the best policy, if the goal of policy is to prosper and succeed. The loot that the highwaymen take by force of violence is bettered by Gil, who amasses his fortune, even acquiring an estate and a title, by flattery, discretion, and, above all, intrigue and deceit. It has been said that volumes 3 and 4 satirize the reigns of Louis XIV and the regency in France, rather than those of Philip III and Philip IV of Spain. Regardless of the extent of intended allusion to his own time, Lesage's view of life at court is certainly a dim one. Gil is oddly suited to it by dint of a peculiar talent, first revealed in book 4.

At that point, Gil is in the service of a woman named Aurora de Guzman. He manages to convince her to dress herself as a man in order to find out about, and ultimately win, a man she desires, Don Lewis Pacheco. Not the initiator himself, Gil with his usual tact is the go-between, or facilitator, of this romance. His talents as a diplomat in this area become particularly useful at court later, while under the wing of the duke of Lerma. Gil is requested to act as the procurer for the heir apparent to the Spanish throne. Yet the king himself does not approve of his son's activities, and he puts Gil into prison for promoting them, once his spies discover the prince accompanying Gil into a house of ill fame.

This signal turn of events in book 9 makes clear several points. First, this incident, as with the Archbishop's sermon, shows Gil's pliable eagerness to please his masters. Second, both incidents indicate that while disobedience to superiors almost invariably gets one into trouble, obedience does not by any means necessarily save one from trouble. What makes this second twist of fate different from the first, however, is that in the nature of court life, it is not merely one master who must be pleased but numerous masters simultaneously. What delights one superior—in this case, a trip to the local house of prostitution (itself an interesting figure for life at court)—may not delight others, yet more superior.

There is perhaps a fourth lesson here as well, though it is an ironic aftershock of this particular sequence of events, occurring as it does in the eleventh and final book. Once Gil is rehabilitated and returns to court as the underling of the now prime minister, the count of Olivarez, he becomes a pimp yet again, this time joining forces with his actor friend Laura to coax her daughter, Lucretia, into the king's bed. As it turns out, Lucretia dies almost instantly of grief upon contact with the lustful monarch, whereupon Laura enters a convent in penitential sorrow and Gil once more feels impelled to leave, only this time it is he who resigns first. That he voluntarily quits may be the only evidence that Gil learned anything from his earlier role as procurer; other than that, he ignores any conceivable lesson the first disaster may have held for him.

This fact is important, and not only because it accounts in part for the feeling of repetition some of those commentators who have already soldiered through volume 3 sense when they encounter volume 4. It is important, too, as an index of what a picaresque novel such as *Gil Blas* is not—and decidedly not. It is not a story with a gathering message, a unified character as one now conceives of it, or even, finally, much of a plot. As mentioned, it does mark a greater narrative unity than did *The Devil upon Two Sticks*. Finally, however, the hero of this tale, much as he progresses in rank and wealth, does not exactly develop as the nineteenth century novelistic characters such as Stendhal's Julien Sorel—of whom Gil is sometimes, perhaps tendentiously, seen as the prototype—may be said to do. He remembers the characters who continually reappear in the novel: Captain Rolando, Laura the actress, Don Raphael, and Don Alphonso all pop in and out in good picaresque fashion, as does Gil's servant Scipio, who gets in a great deal of travel toward the book's end. It may even be that Gil acquires manipulative skills as he moves up the hierarchy. The kind of education one associates with the fuller characters of the later French novel—the kind called "wisdom"—is not, however, forthcoming. No doubt the irony that Gil never arrives at his studies is meant to argue that he becomes a student of life, but he shows little evidence of maturing very much in that school, either.

Lesage ends the book as flat and superficial as at the outset. The reader, as one would expect with a *roman de mœurs* or satire, does learn a fair amount about the great world. For all the recurrent interest in veiled motive and social gamesmanship, lovers of Henry James, for example, had best look elsewhere for psychological subtlety. Even in the case of the narrator himself, it is as actors rather than as mentalities that Lesage's people engage interest.

Along with the lack of introspection goes the thin sense of time passing. So many of the characters in what is now termed "novels" move through a time of which they have only a limited amount. The decisions of Isabel Archer in James's *The Portrait of a Lady* (1881), of Charles Dickens's David Copperfield, or of Leo Tolstoy's Anna Karenina are lent weight by the escalating pressure of mortality. In contrast, Gil seems neither to age nor to accumulate a determining history: As in the American clean-slate fantasy, everything can seemingly be razed and built anew each day. (Such weightless skipping from incident to incident leads one to wonder whether Lesage bothered with an outline.) This curiously atemporal ambience allows for, among other things, the frequent coincidences that keep this narrative from shutting down.

To take a notorious example, the first chapter of book 11 narrates the death, in rapid succession, of Gil Blas's wife and child at the estate at Lirias, where he still resides, followed immediately by the news that Philip III, who had imprisoned Gil, has died, and that the duke of Lerma has been removed from his post, with the count of Olivarez—friendly, like the new king, to Gil and his patron Alphonso—replacing him. All three deaths, in this felicitous conjunction, allow Gil to return to court life for another "go." In a nineteenth or twentieth century novel, such a coincidence would obtrude garishly in the reader's mind; here, Gil's experiences have so little causal shape to them, and are so helter-skelter and random in their eruptions and cessations, that one scarcely notices the fortuity in this particular outbreak of deaths.

Beyond the matter of coincidence, however, the entire way death is treated in the novel is probably symptomatic of this lack of accumulating time, this atemporality. The deaths of Gil's parents may be taken as emblematic. In yet another notable coincidence, in book 10, Gil, though not generally given to nostalgia, suddenly decides to make a sentimental journey back to Oviedo, arriving just in time for his father to die. This chapter of grievous loss becomes—typical of Lesage—one of the novel's funniest.

With his new wealth, Gil decides to have an opulent funeral for his father, so as to "instil into the conceptions of the bystanders a high sense of my generous nature." Instead, the townspeople, driven to rage by a luxurious show of pompous mourning by a son content to have left his father to die poor, stage a vicious riot at the funeral and run Gil ignominiously out of town. It is a hilarious bit, no question; one feels not the slightest sympathy for the self-important hero, yet that is part of the foreignness of the form of picaresque for the modern reader. It is not as if the death of a parent would necessarily teach the title character any great truths, but here it is as externally observed, as much the excuse for risible hijinks as anything else in Lesage's Spain. The mother—who refuses to accompany Gil back, incidentally—is dispatched with even greater brevity. In a few sentences, Gil receives word that the simple serving woman has died, feels a moment's remorse, and then reflects with his usual sang-froid that she had never been very affectionate toward him, so why should he brood. These deaths put neither title character nor reader in mind of his or her own mortality; in fact, but for the most conventional sort of shorthand, the events have no affective weight whatsoever.

This very lightness is part of the novel's refreshing appeal. Thomas Pynchon has spoken of the way the "elitism and cruelty often found in college humor arises from" a certain sense of "one's own Exemption, not only from time and death, but somehow from the demands of life as well." It is, in a loose sense of the word, an aristocratic kind of wit, and much as Lesage was no more aristocratic than Gil (Anatole France once said of him, "He worked for his living," meaning, at least in part, that he was bourgeois), there is still in his narrative flow a "breeziness," a sense of the unreflective "open air," as Green remarks, which conveys the lighthearted—and sometimes seemingly coldhearted—wit of the aristocrat, of one who feels exempt from death, from having to work for a living, even from living itself.

It should not surprise that the high-water mark of the novel's prestige in the eyes of French critics was during the Bourbon Restoration, roughly from the early 1810's to the late 1820's. That bourgeois era, so desperately desirous of appearing aristocratic, had reason to admire this bourgeois novel that had succeeded so well in simulating an aristocratic worldview. Lesage, in this respect, could well be an even better chameleon than Gil.

The aristocratic narrative is the scion of a literary estate, prodigally spewing forth plot turns, inset stories, and unrelated characters. (It is interesting that Saintsbury compares Lesage to a man with rich forebears—here presumably the Spanish picaresque writers—"whose property he now enjoys.") The later novels of sensibility, both of France and of England, have less abundance with which to make free, and they work more on the model of capital accumulation, like good bourgeois. They start with modest properties—a few characters, a clutch of related incidents—and create a dramatic structure that in the course of reading gradually accumulates meaning and emotional impact, just as a well-managed factory or home gradually accrues value.

This is definitely not the case with Lesage's work, as Vivienne Mylne argues very convincingly. Although the novel can be said to have a narrative structure that, at least abstractly, looks dramatic and purposive—coming to a sort of climax about two-thirds of the way, and so forth—the reading of it conveys little or none of the accumulated impact or meaning the narrative incidents could have. Given the offhand style of Lesage, it is even difficult at times to register who are the crucial characters. (Don Alphonso, for example, gets short shrift when one considers his sponsorship of Gil Blas at central moments.) The obvious rejoinder to this complaint, if that is what it is, would be that modern novel readers, on the lookout for the author who carefully husbands resources and cultivates properties—that is, a novelist with "unity" of plot, steady development of character, gradual clarification of theme—should cheerfully accept a different style of narrative, one that at first may look like squandering the literary patrimony but that has its own joys as well.

Indeed, it does. The best things about Lesage, as Mylne acknowledges, are not his novels, or even his volumes, but his chapters—which are often shaped quite well dramatically, as in the marvelously irrelevant interpolated tale in book 4, chapter 4—and, above all, his sentences. It is in these epigrammatic, La Rochefoucauld-like moments that the reader glimpses Lesage's truest gift.

When Laura announces that she has chosen an actor's life because the standard of virtue in such circles is so low that she can see as many men as she likes and that as long as they do not overlap she will be thought virtuous; or when Gil at court avoids doing a favor for his friend Navarro, so instrumental in his first gaining his present position, and then snubs poor Navarro because it would "not have been at all the thing," given his current prominence, to "keep company with a certain description of people"—when the reader hits upon passages such as these, he or she sees the wit that is Lesage's best letter of introduction to any reader. The reader begins to see why Stendhal preferred Lesage to the novelists of sensibility, arguing that it is harder to provoke laughter than sympathy. As Lesage himself remarks, however (in the person of Gil), "Great wits . . . have short memories."

Perhaps the reader who wants to approach Lesage's works in the most appropriate spirit could best do so not by starting at page one and reading religiously to the end, but by leafing through the table of contents and turning to chapters that appear most promising; by trying the various inset stories and finishing only the intriguing ones; or even by opening the novel more or less at random and reading from the first chapter one encounters. The delight is not in the onward rush of narrative suspense and excitement or in the building up of psychological meaning or emotional impact; it is in the brief snapshots, the satiric glimpses into social mores and oddities, the elegantly treacherous turns of phrase.

In sum, Lesage's books are long, his art fleeting. His best impact is made in miniature, not *en gros*, and in this regard, he may well be seen as a precursor of Honoré de Balzac, another master of the feuilleton-like sketch. Lesage's brilliance is fitful and shines to best advantage in occasional snatches. That he should be read there is no question; that he should be read as a great anecdotist more than as a great novelist per se is scarcely less certain.

Mark Conroy

Other major works

short fiction: *Une Journée des parques*, 1735 (*A Day of the Fates*, 1922); *La Valise trouvée*, 1740 (2 volumes).

plays: *Crispin, rival de son maître*, pr., pb. 1707 (*Crispin, Rival of His Master*, 1766); *Turcaret: Comédie en cinq actes*, pr., pb. 1709 (English translation, 1923); *Le Théâtre de la Foire: Ou, L'Opéra comique*, pr. 1712-1738 (10 volumes; with d'Orneval, Louis Fuzilier, and others).

miscellaneous: *Œuvres de Lesage*, 1821 (12 volumes); *Bibliothèque amusante*, 1865 (4 volumes; includes *Le Diable boiteux, Histoire de Gil Blas de Santillane, Histoire de Don Guzman d'Alfarache*, and *Histoire d'Estévanille Gonzalès*).

Bibliography

Alter, Robert. *Rogue's Progress: Studies in the Picaresque Novel*. Cambridge, Mass.: Harvard University Press, 1964. Alter's examination of picaresque literature includes a study of Lesage's novels. Includes a bibliography.

Bjornson, Richard. *The Picaresque Hero in European Literature*. Madison: University of Wisconsin Press, 1977. Bjornson examines Lesage's novels in the context of the European picaresque novel. Includes a bibliography and an index.

Fellows, Otis. "Alain-René Lesage." In *European Writers: The Age of Reason and the Enlightenment*, edited by William T. H. Jackson. New York: Charles Scribner's Sons, 1984. The entry on Lesage in this historical study provides a concise overview of his life and writings.

Green, Frederick C. *Literary Ideas in Eighteenth Century France and England*. New York: Frederick Ungar, 1966. A revised edition of Green's 1935 *Minuet: A Critical Survey of French and English Literary Ideas in the Eighteenth Century*. Includes a study of Lesage's novels.

Magruder, James. Introduction to *Three French Comedies*, edited by C. B. Coleman. New Haven, Conn.: Yale University Press, 1996. In the introduction to this collection, which contains a translation of *Turcaret*, Magruder describes both the work and Lesage.

Mylne, Vivienne. "Le Sage and Conventions." In *The Eighteenth Century French Novel: Techniques of Illusion*. 2d ed. New York: Cambridge University Press, 1981. This study of French literature contains a chapter on Lesage's novels. Includes a bibliography.

Rivers, Kenneth T., ed. *A Survey of French Literature*. Vol. 3, *The Eighteenth Century*. 3d ed. Newburyport, Mass.: Focus/R. Pullins, 2005. A French-language anthology that contains an English-language introduction to trends in eighteenth century French literature and a short biography of Lesage in English.

JOAQUIM MARIA MACHADO DE ASSIS

Born: Rio de Janeiro, Brazil; June 21, 1839
Died: Rio de Janeiro, Brazil; September 29, 1908
Also known as: Bruxo do Cosme Velho

PRINCIPAL LONG FICTION
Resurreicão, 1872
A mão e a luva, 1874 (*The Hand and the Glove*, 1970)
Helena, 1876 (English translation, 1984)
Iaiá Garcia, 1878 (*Yayá Garcia*, 1977)
Memórias póstumas de Brás Cubas, 1881 (*The Posthumous Memoirs of Brás Cubas*, 1951; better known as *Epitaph of a Small Winner*, 1952)
Quincas Borba, 1891 (*Philosopher or Dog?*, 1954; also known as *The Heritage of Quincas Borba*, 1954)
Dom Casmurro, 1899 (English translation, 1953)
Esaú e Jacob, 1904 (*Esau and Jacob*, 1965)
Memorial de Ayres, 1908 (*Counselor Ayres' Memorial*, 1972)

OTHER LITERARY FORMS

Although Joaquim Maria Machado de Assis (muh-SHAH-dew dee ah-SEES) is best known for his novels, especially in the non-Portuguese-speaking world, he did not begin writing in this genre until comparatively late in life. He started with poetry at the age of fifteen and the short story at eighteen. During the first fifteen years of his writing career, Machado de Assis produced some six thousand lines of poetry, nineteen plays and opera librettos, twenty-four short stories, almost two hundred newspaper columns and articles, and a number of translations, chiefly from French and Spanish into Portuguese. Most of this work appeared in periodicals, but ten volumes were published in book form as well. Machado de Assis continued to work in other literary forms after he began to write novels.

ACHIEVEMENTS

Joaquim Maria Machado de Assis is so singular a figure in Brazilian literature, one who lends himself so little to inclusion in any school, that in any history of Brazilian literature he must be discussed in a separate chapter. He was a contemporary of the second generation of Romantics, who influenced him in his formative years, but during the succeeding generations of late Romantics, Parnassians, and Symbolists, he developed along highly personal lines. In addition, he merits special consideration because of his unquestionable supremacy in Brazilian letters, a supremacy that he exercised during his lifetime and that would continue to grow.

Machado de Assis's talent could not be contained by any one form or genre. His

Ocidentais (Occidentals), first published in the *Revista brasileira* in 1879 and 1880, contains poems that in perfection of form were not to be surpassed by the Parnassians and whose thought sums up the bitter, disillusioned philosophy that seems to characterize Machado de Assis's prose work from 1881. Collections of short works such as *Papéis avulsos* (1882; miscellaneous papers), *Histórias sem data* (1884; undated stories), and *Várias histórias* (1896; various stories) include some of Machado de Assis's finest writing, among which are "Missa do galo" ("Midnight Mass") and "O alienista" ("The Psychiatrist").

Another important facet of Machado de Assis's oeuvre is the series of *crônicas* (columns) and articles of literary criticism that he wrote for the press over a period of some forty years. Collected, these pieces fill seven volumes; among them are some of the author's finest pages, such as those he wrote on "*o velho senado*" (the old senate). His critical essays and journalistic columns not only give intimate glimpses into Machado de Assis's life and his times but also serve as footnotes and marginalia to his fictional works.

Machado de Assis's first four novels, all written between 1872 and 1878, are marked by the spirit and devices of Romanticism. Their interest resides less in the observation of manners than in the analysis of a moral situation in which there is a clash of wills. In *Epitaph of a Small Winner*, his fifth novel, Machado de Assis introduced several devices that were to become characteristic of his novels thereafter: short chapters and short sentences; a humorous, skeptical, and ironic tone; and an intentionally disconnected narrative in which psychological analysis is effected through omissions, alternate assertions, and reservations. The reader sees the steady emergence of an intellect, of a conception of the art of writing and the role of the artist in human progress. Each of Machado de Assis's four novels that followed *Epitaph of a Small Winner* is a masterpiece as well—each in its own way, despite a similarity of manner. Outside Brazil or Portugal, critics who stumbled across Machado de Assis's novels only in Portuguese, or perhaps translated into a language other than English, did not hesitate to place their author among the world's greatest. Some expressed surprise that so subtle a genius could have sprung from the "jungles" of Latin America. Machado de Assis is by no means a wild jungle flower; however, his roots reach deep into Brazilian culture—and deeper still, into more than two millennia of Western culture.

Although shy and retiring, Machado de Assis was greatly interested in literary society and attended many meetings of various groups throughout his life. He was a member of the society that met at the offices of the *Revista brasileira*, which did not exclude Portugal. For his many years of hard work in the Brazilian Academy of Letters as well as his devotion to numerous duties in the service of his country and native city, not to mention his prodigious literary production, the Chamber of Deputies voted to give him a state funeral with civil and military honors. This was the first time in the history of Brazil that a man of letters was buried in the manner of a hero.

Biography

Joaquim Maria Machado de Assis was born on June 21, 1839, and was baptized on November 13, 1839, in the Senhora do Livramento (Our Lady of Deliverance) Chapel of the Church of Saint Rita in Rio de Janeiro. His father, Francisco Joze de Assis, was a native of Rio de Janeiro, and his mother, Maria Leopoldina Machado de Assis, came from São Miguel in the Azores. She was Portuguese, then, and not black, as had been reported prior to the discovery of the baptismal record. Other parish registries later revealed that the author's father was a mulatto born of freed slaves from Rio de Janeiro. The registries revealed other facts about the Assis family, including those given on the death certificates of Machado de Assis's younger sister, who died of measles at the age of four, and of his mother, who died of tuberculosis at thirty-four.

Patriarchal estates such as the one to which the Assis family was attached offered a better chance of education for former slaves and their offspring and for poor immigrants from Portugal than was possible in Rio de Janeiro itself. Humble by today's standards, the family's condition seems to have been good for the times. They were artisans, including Maria Leopoldina, who probably had black help for her heavy household chores; moreover, they were relatively literate and on their way up the social scale. Undoubtedly, they enjoyed a degree of intimacy, if not equality, with the proprietress's family. Machado de Assis's formal schooling, if any, was slight; however, in addition to what he was taught at home, he may well have been tutored by a loving godmother until her death (of measles, three months after that of Machado de Assis's sister) and thereafter by priests attached to the estate or to churches where the youngster served, perhaps as an altar boy, perhaps as a sacristan. There can be no question that Machado de Assis was largely self-taught, but without the basic learning acquired in the extended family situation, he could never have succeeded in his heroic task.

Machado de Assis's youth, from the time he left home at about fifteen until he married at thirty, was relatively normal in some respects, most extraordinary in others. In order to earn his living, never better than a precarious one, he tried a number of occupations, all of them connected in some way with the printed word. At first probably a clerk in a book or stationery shop, he became a typesetter, a proofreader, and eventually an editor and a staff writer. He entered the field of journalism enthusiastically, expecting to be able to live, more or less well, by his pen; he soon discovered how poorly remunerated this profession was. Not until 1867 would Machado de Assis achieve some measure of economic security in the bureaucracy of government service, where he worked first on the *Diário oficial* and, from 1874, as a functionary in the Ministry of Agriculture.

Machado de Assis was an astonishingly prolific writer. Although much of his work was published in periodicals and newspapers and was far from lucrative, he continued his frenetic production of such work even during the years in which he was producing his great and successful novels, at the same time that he was all but submerged in the bureaucratic paperwork of government service. Apart from his literary work, Machado de Assis participated in numerous other artistic and social endeavors. His considerable interest in and contribution to opera and theater in Rio de Janeiro and São Paulo, both in original works and in translations or adaptations, are evidenced by his work for the Conservatório Dramático Brasileiro, where for some years he served as censor, passing judgment on the moral and political propriety of manuscripts submitted to the conservatory and giving his literary opinions as well. During this period, Machado de Assis was assiduous in his attendance at the theater and at musical events in Rio de Janeiro, becoming personally or professionally acquainted with many artists and contributing numerous reviews to the periodicals of that city at the time. As though all of this activity were not enough, Machado de Assis held various positions in a number of literary societies and often contributed and even recited poems, his own or others'—despite his supposed timidity and severe stammering—and created short plays for special meetings and benefits. Machado de Assis's significant participation in the cultural life of Rio de Janeiro was recognized in 1867, when he was decorated with the Order of the Rose by Emperor Dom Pedro II.

Among Machado de Assis's many acquaintances before 1869 was a Portuguese poet, Faustino Xavier de Novaes, who, like others of his family, went to Brazil to seek his fortune. Beset by financial and marital problems, Faustino eventually suffered a severe nervous breakdown with serious physical manifestations. After his parents' death in Oporto, his youngest sister, Carolina, was sent to assist in caring for Faustino. Almost five years older than Machado de Assis, Carolina was intelligent, sensitive, and affectionate, and she and Machado de Assis fell in love. Her suffering, which Machado de Assis mentions as one of the reasons for his love, may have been caused by an earlier love affair and possibly influenced her departure for Portugal. Very little is known of the courtship of Machado de Assis and Carolina except for one letter and a substantial fragment of a second, written to "Carola" by her "Machadinho" during the de Novaeses' stay in Petrópolis, in which there is evidence of their great concern and love for each other.

She chided him for not confiding in her. In response, Machado de Assis told her briefly of his earlier loves. The first was Corinna, who did not requite his love, and consequently there is nothing more to say (although in the tradition of such matters, Machado de Assis had published some 385 verses to Corinna). The second, who remains nameless but was possibly an actress and married, loved him in return and was the greater love. The situation was a painful one, however, and Machado de Assis was persuaded to break off the affair. Carolina was the one true love of his life. Despite a probable infidelity on the part of her husband—an "infidelity of the senses"—she was to be so always.

Against the wishes of some of her family, they were married November 12, 1869, a short time after the death of Faustino. In spite of some sorrow, it would seem that their marriage was a very happy one. In the style of the day, Carolina remained in the shadow of her husband, who was himself reserved and, in spite of fame, did not seek public acclaim. As has been mentioned, except for rare references to her in his correspondence, mostly very conventional in nature, Machado de Assis never wrote directly of his wife. Some of the feminine characters in the author's novels may well have Carolina's qualities, and a few of his poems were inspired by her, especially one sonnet, "A Carolina," published after her death. Her literary influence on him, grossly exaggerated by some critics, was at best very slight.

Once Machado de Assis was established as comptroller in the Ministry of Agriculture—later the Ministry of Transportation, as promotions and the evolution of ministries led him into related positions—and he and Carolina were settled in a chalet-style house on the Rua Cosme Velho in the city, they had no serious financial worries. Their great sorrow was to be childless. In addition, there were problems of health, first those of Machado de Assis, who for a time had an extremely serious eye ailment and later suffered from increasingly frequent and grave attacks of epilepsy, then Carolina's growing fragility and a tumor that eventually caused her death. Nothing, however, kept Machado de Assis from his literary production, which, if it did not bring him wealth, was a source of many satisfactions and gave him fame.

Machado de Assis was motivated in his activities by love for those who were close to him (especially promising young writers in need of encouragement), by deep interest in humanity and culture, and certainly by a desire to leave something lasting of himself, his thought, and his art. Posterity perhaps assumed greater importance for him than for other artists, because he had no children. Further, his works were not fully understood or appreciated in his day, often bringing him no more than a *succès d'estime*, and so posterity was probably all the more important to him.

Everything that Machado de Assis represents is embodied in the Brazilian Academy of Letters. When at last in 1905 its membership honored him, he was presented with the oak branch from the tree growing over Torquato Tasso's tomb that Joaquim Nabuco, the famous statesman and man of letters who was a friend of Machado de Assis and a member of the Academy, had sent from Italy for such a symbolic ceremony. Machado de Assis treasured the branch and other mementos, leaving them to be housed in the Academy after his death, brought about by a variety of as yet poorly defined causes on September 29, 1908.

Analysis

The first four novels by Joaquim Maria Machado de Assis constitute his apprenticeship as a novelist, during which he refined the vision and the skills that came to focus in *Epitaph of a Small Winner* and the powerful novels that followed. In his famous criticism (1878) of José Maria Eça de Queiróz's *O Primo Basílio* (1878; *Dragon's Teeth*, 1889; better known as *Cousin Bazilio*, 1953), Machado de Assis states that the aim of the novel should be to describe action derived from the passions and ideas of its characters. He refers to William Shakespeare's *Othello, the Moor of Venice* (pr. 1604), in which the natures of Othello, Iago, and Desdemona are the chief ingredients of the action, not the handkerchief. Machado de Assis thus favors the tenets of realism and opposes naturalism as too often superficial and therefore artificial, not to mention tasteless.

Machado de Assis's persistent concern with character—his references to *Othello* and his creation of the figure of Felix in *Resurreicão*—leads one to think that he was interested above all in tragedy. Felix, torn between a sincere desire for love and cynical doubt regarding his and others' sincerity, is a tragic figure surrounded by characters drawn too much either from life or from less noble forms of literature. The whole, therefore, falls short of being tragic. In *The Hand and the Glove*, there is a clash between two strong-willed characters, developed in a structure of Romantic comedy. Some significant details are reminiscent of Shakespeare's *All's Well That Ends Well* (pr. c. 1602-1603) as well as the triumph rather than the defeat of love in the conclusion.

Helena, which also contains reminiscences of *All's Well That Ends Well*, is not a Romantic comedy; its main characters are fully developed. Unfortunately, their passions and consequent frustrations stem from a case of Rio de Janeiro etiquette largely regarding the status of women. The substance is so slight as to lack any claim to the universality required for genuine tragedy. The reader experiences both comic and tragic emotions, but at times he or she is incredulous and even impatient with what proves to be a melodramatic situation and conclusion. In *Yayá Garcia*, Machado de Assis uses classical allusions and symbolism to a high degree and elaborates on the class, family, and personal pride of women as never before. Above all, there is the theme of love thwarted by society, whose interference is caused by the evils of self-love. Ultimately it is love that triumphs in *Yayá Garcia*, both in the main plot and principal characters and in the figure of the ex-slave, Raymundo, a symbol of Brazilian civilization as opposed to that of Europe. In future novels, Machado de Assis was to stress the passions of individuals in their struggle to be true to themselves, which, for the author, meant to love. Social problems would reappear only whenever love became subordinate to vanity.

Epitaph of a Small Winner

In *Epitaph of a Small Winner*, for the first time in Machado de Assis's works, the main character is a man. Never again was a woman to be his principal subject. Self-love is the theme, and with it the several forms of evil and death to which vanity gives rise. Brás Cubas, the narrator of these memoirs, is dead, not only at the time of publication but also at the time of composition. Brás Cubas writes to pass time in eternity, still preoccupied with his fellows and in a detached mood much like the one that was his throughout life. Despite its seemingly misanthropic theme and its deep pessimism, the novel can be interpreted as profoundly comic.

There are many literary allusions and influences in *Epitaph of a Small Winner*. Very early in the novel, the reader is made aware of the importance of the picaresque genre, especially Charles Dickens's *Pickwick Papers* (1836-1837, serial; 1837, book), Laurence Sterne's *The Life and Opinions of Tristram Shandy, Gent.* (1759-1767), and Alain-René Lesage's *Histoire de Gil Blas de Santillane* (1715-1735; *The History of Gil Blas of Santillane*, 1716, 1735; better known as *Gil Blas*, 1749, 1962). The picaresque novel is comic in its parody, satire, and irony; at the same time, it may be very serious in its portrayal of manners, with philosophical implications, as is Miguel de Cervantes' *Don Quixote de la Mancha* (1605, 1615).

The traditional picaresque novel has one main character, usually male, who, whatever the circumstances of his birth, finds himself in the criminal or low class of society, rising after many adventures of all sorts to marry and settle down to lead a respectable if somewhat parasitic life. The life of the picaro is customarily traced in minute detail, from his origins through his childhood, adolescence, and early maturity and into middle age. Machado de Assis parodies his predecessors by having Brás Cubas begin his narrative after death and move backward through a series of regressions to his funeral and last illness. Contrary to the practice of his predecessors, however, Machado de Assis's is most economical and dramatic. Brás sees Virgília, his former mistress, when he is on his deathbed, not as she is, but as she was when they were lovers, and in his delirium he is taken back in time to his birth.

Brás has the proper genealogy for a picaro. The Cubas family is well-to-do—their wealth is based on the efforts of the founder of the family in Brazil, who was originally a mender of *cubas* (vats or barrels)—and Brás's father named his son after a famous early Brazilian patriot in the hope of associating his relatively humble family with the more distinguished one. The name of Brás further suggests Brazil, and there are numerous references and overtones to suggest that Brás may be taken as a kind of epic figure for Brazilians. Brás's upbringing is typical for the son of such a family in the Rio de Janeiro of the early nineteenth century. Spoiled by his parents and debauched by one uncle, he is little influenced by the ineffectual religious education of his other uncle. When Brás takes up with Marcella, a high-priced girl who promptly sets about depleting the Cubas fortune, his father has him abducted and sent off to the University of Coimbra. Typically, Brás forgets Marcella even before the ship reaches Portugal.

Although he claims to be inclined to melancholy, Brás never experiences serious emotion for very long. Like Jacques in Shakespeare's *As You Like It* (pr. c. 1599-1600), he leads a frivolous, empty life. Awareness of his apathy gives Brás the overtones of a tragic figure, but he does not struggle in the manner of an epic or tragic hero. Rather, he uses his great intelligence to observe, analyze, and write of his defects, which are also those of his fellows. He is thus primarily the comic author of a kind of comedy, human if not divine. The reader is occasionally led to expect more emotion of Brás, to no avail. During his long affair with Virgília, for example, she conceives a child by him but soon miscarries. He does not have time to feel emotion for mother or child. When Virgília at last passes out of his life, Brás, then in his forties, decides that it is time to marry. Alas, the lovely young Eulália dies of yellow fever before the wedding. Again there is no opportunity for very serious involvement.

Whether as the hero of a serious genre or of the picaresque, Brás must consider himself a failure. He lists his many defeats, including his one bid for fame, the invention of his medicinal plaster, which, instead of curing his melancholy, caused his death. When finally he balances the good against the evil in his life, Brás finds the only credit to be that, having had no child, he has bequeathed the legacy of human wretchedness to no one.

Despite the apparent pessimism of this last remark, often applied to Machado de Assis himself, Brás has the spirit if not the luck of a true picaro, both in his tour of life and in his tomb. Although he stresses pessimism and death, Brás is a most carefree corpse, and his tomb seems cozy enough. *Epitaph of a Small Winner* is a comedy of human vanity, of which almost all the characters are guilty, to the virtual exclusion of any other flaw. Vanity gives rise to ambition, which is the source of much that is good as well as evil. The point is that good, generous actions have the same source as vicious ones. Indeed, the latter are merely exaggerations of the former; as such, vice and virtue are one and the same.

"Humanitism"—the mad philosophy of Quincas (a nickname for Joaquim, Machado de Assis's given name) Borba, a secondary character in this novel—is a complete expression of egotism. In the elaboration of humanitism, Machado de Assis was no doubt satirizing many "isms" (and perhaps even himself as something of a philosopher). As he had previously criticized the determinism of naturalism in literature, Machado de Assis was now criticizing above all the positivism of Auguste Comte that had taken root as a religion in Brazil. Although Brás Cubas is sane and Quincas Borba insane, there is considerable similarity between their philosophies. Brás's determinism, expressed in his theory of "rolling balls," when projected in the action of the novel suggests that a combination of human will and chance governs life. The "pessimism" of Machado de Assis's work is thus relieved by a certain moral tone. Like much comedy, it has a moral purpose. Moreover, its author and its hero are not to be confused. If at times they bear some resemblance to each other—as posterity and the critics (to whom the novelist alluded as "worms") have not always understood—it must be understood that Machado de Assis often poked fun at himself, as he causes Brás to poke fun at himself and life in all of its aspects. Brás's true cure for melancholy is not his medicinal plaster but his book.

Dom Casmurro

Machado de Assis's seventh novel, *Dom Casmurro*, both incorporates elements of its predecessors and is a more nearly perfect work of art than any of them. Especially impressive is Machado de Assis's progress in the use of symbolism. The narrator and chief character, Bento Santiago, explains early his nickname and the title of the work, but only partially. *Dom*, an honorary term applied only to the highest nobility and clergy, was given to him to ridicule his aristocratic pretensions. *Casmurro* meant "stubborn" in Machado de Assis's day, but was added to the *Dom* by an angry neighbor to signify "morose and withdrawn." This meaning has since found its way into Portuguese dictionaries; however, both meanings of the word characterize Santiago, his obstinacy making him morose and withdrawn.

Like other of Machado de Assis's characters, Santiago is two men in one. In his case, the combination comprises Othello and Iago, creating an almost purely tragic figure and one to bring about tragedy for others. Santiago is born into a family of wealth and rank, and he is handsome, well educated, and quite intelligent. Moreover, the narrator creates a semidivine aura for himself by telling the reader that his safe birth was considered miraculous by his mother and the family priest, and that in thanksgiving he was named Bento (blessed) and destined for the seminary. Santiago tells the reader directly that he is an Othello with a guilty Desdemona. Indirectly, because he likes to confide in his reader, he reveals that he is Iago as well, innately evil and determined to find an object for his jealousy.

Machado de Assis intrudes not at all. The reader must therefore be attentive to discover the real Santiago as, often with considerable wit, he narrates his life, describes the members of his family and his acquaintances, and above all paints a wonderful portrait of his lovely Capitu as a girl, young woman, and wife. Bento and Capitu conspire to persuade his mother to break her vow to make a priest of him, a vow that she does not wish to keep in any case. It is easy to see how Capitu captivates Bento, especially as he cleverly includes details that encourage the careless reader to accept the eventual adultery of which he accuses her. The real culprit, one learns, is Santiago, a man who refused to love and to be loved.

Again, the action in *Dom Casmurro* stems from the characters' passions, from a clash of opposing wills. Both are found in the principal character, the will to love and the will to deny that love. He is not without feelings of guilt, however, and must project that guilt onto others, especially Capitu. Again, the theme is self-love, evil, and death (albeit a living death) versus love, good, and life. Santiago suggests that it is Capitu and Escobar, her supposed lover, who murdered his love; even if they were guilty of adultery, however, the tragic jealousy was in him even before his wife and best friend met. At the end, Santiago, made to love, faces a terrible life without love. Any victory on the part of Capitu or the other characters pales before the tragedy of the dominant figure of the narrator.

COUNSELOR AYRES' MEMORIAL

Counselor Ayres' Memorial is a sequel to *Esau and Jacob*, an allegorical work the characters of which are largely abstractions. Ayres, the narrator of both novels, becomes a real human being in the sequel at the same time that he embodies Machado de Assis's customary theme. His heart desires love, and in order to attain it he must undergo the emotional evolution that others of the author's protagonists have failed to accomplish. An intimate diary aptly replaces the somewhat self-conscious narrative of *Esau and Jacob*.

The action of *Counselor Ayres' Memorial* takes place during 1888 and 1889, although the characters are so universal as to be of any period. Old Ayres and his sister, the faithful widow Rita, are the only characters taken from *Esau and Jacob*, but they are very different emotionally if not physically. In addition, there is the loving middle-aged couple Aguiar and Carmo—he a self-made banker but an honest and kindly man, she a homebody who, though childless, is a motherly type. These and other atypical characters reflect changing times in Brazil as well as a mellower attitude on the part of Machado de Assis favoring social and economic progress. Political change had been initiated under the empire, was continued through the period of emancipation, and brought about Dom Pedro II's abdication. A new nationalism prevailed during the Republic, and Brazilians loved their country as never before.

With most of Brazilian society, Ayres has been under foreign influence, particularly English. As the name suggests, he has been much like the stereotype of the cold, dry, rational, and detached Englishman. Not only has he preferred foreign authors and foreign women, but he has also traveled in Europe and, as a diplomat, has lived most of his life abroad. In early 1888, however, Ayres is glad to come home to Brazil. Among the first entries in his diary, Ayres reports a visit paid by him and his sister Rita to the cemetery, a symbol of nonexistent or dead love, where he notices a beautiful young woman in black.

As Rita tells him of the romantic and tragic love of Fidélia and Eduardo, Ayres compares them to Romeo and Juliet. Their story is similar to a point, but the outcome is quite different, for they are not English, but Portuguese. With Portuguese stubbornness on all sides, they were permitted to marry but were disowned by their fathers. After less than a year of happiness, Eduardo died, and Fidélia has been faithfully tending his grave for more than two years. Ayres is still cynical enough to remark that she may remarry, with which Rita, of course, disagrees, but says that, as her brother is a very well preserved sixty-two, he can try to woo Fidélia.

Ayres persists in his fondness for English literature, so that, when he meets Fidélia at the home of Aguiar and Carmo, he recalls the first line of a love sonnet by Percy Bysshe Shelley that he has been unable to translate into Portuguese with the passionate conclusion of the original. Now begins a new kind of odyssey, during the course of which Ayres composes his poem with the desired conclusion, as Bento Santiago could not. Unlike the latter, Ayres is successful in conquering coldness and achieving resurrection through love. He learns to love not only from Shelley but also from the happily married Aguiar and Carmo; behind them are Machado de Assis and his Carolina.

Unlike Rita, who gives her love for her dead husband to everyone around her, Ayres has never loved. He married for convenience and, when his wife died, buried her in Europe and forgot about her. None of the women with whom he has had affairs abroad means anything to him. He has never been a father and has no regrets in this matter. Yet in Europe he experienced nostalgia for home and for the warmth of Rio de Janeiro and his native language. His heart, it seems, was not entirely dead. When Ayres comes to know Fidélia, he first experiences sexual attraction, then appreciation of her beauty, later admiration for her intellectual and spiritual qualities, and finally a disinterested love for her happiness that includes everyone who made or could make her happy.

Much of the transformation in Ayres and similar ones in other characters are brought about by Aguiar and Carmo, not only in love with each other for twenty-five years but also full of love for all people and animals around them. Under Carmo's maternal love, Fidélia's heart comes alive again, at first symbolically when she resumes playing the piano, then more concretely when she falls in love with Tristão. Another of Carmo and Aguiar's foster children, Tristão has a cold heart, too, when he arrives from Portugal on an English ship. He, like most of the other characters, has fallen under Aguiar's spell, however, and comes to replace Eduardo for Fidélia.

The several resurrections developed in *Counselor Ayres' Memorial* are mutually influential, but the one that affects Ayres most is Fidélia's. Her return to love is his as well. The old habits die hard, however, and the cynical old diplomat is intermittently beset by doubts regarding the other's sincerity. It is only his own sincere love for Fidélia that makes him recognize that she loves Tristão just as sincerely. Eduardo continues to be remembered and loved, but life has its rights, the same as death. Fidélia's love for Tristão must therefore be understood as a continuation of her love for Eduardo. Ayres understands many seemingly contradictory things that escaped him as a skeptic. His new faith gives him a father's love for Fidélia, Tristão, and all children. Indeed, under the influence of love he has become like a child himself. With his attainment of the ideal of love, Ayres completes his sonnet and his odyssey.

Richard A. Mazzara
Updated by Stephen M. Hart

OTHER MAJOR WORKS

SHORT FICTION: *Contos fluminenses*, 1870; *Histórias da meia-noite*, 1873; *Papéis avulsos*, 1882; *Histórias sem data*, 1884; *Várias histórias*, 1896; *Histórias românticas*, 1937; *The Psychiatrist, and Other Stories*, 1963; *What Went on at the Baroness'*, 1963; *The Devil's Church, and Other Stories*, 1977.

PLAYS: *Desencantos*, pb. 1861; *Quase ministro*, pb. 1864; *Os deuses de casaca*, pb. 1866; *Tu só, tu, puro amor*, pb. 1880; *Teatro*, pb. 1910.

POETRY: *Crisálidas*, 1864; *Falenas*, 1870; *Americanas*, 1875; *Poesias completas*, 1901.

NONFICTION: *Páginas recolhidas (contos ensaios, crônicas)*, 1899; *Relíquias de Casa Velha (contos crônicas, comêdias)*, 1906; *A semana*, 1910; *Crítica*, 1910; *Crítica por Machado de Assis*, 1924; *Crítica literária*, 1937; *Crítica teatral*, 1937; *Correspondência*, 1938.

MISCELLANEOUS: *Outras relíquias*, 1908; *Obra completa*, 1959.

BIBLIOGRAPHY

Caldwell, Helen. *The Brazilian Othello of Machado de Assis*. Berkeley: University of California Press, 1960. Focuses on Machado de Assis's masterpiece, *Dom Casmurro*, and shows how Machado apparently used a modified version of Othello's plot structure. Also discusses numerous other examples of the influence William Shakespeare had on

Machado de Assis's work. Caldwell was the first critic to argue that the novel's heroine, Capitu, was not necessarily guilty of adultery, as generations of readers had assumed.

_____. *Machado de Assis: The Brazilian Master and His Novels*. Berkeley: University of California Press, 1970. Presents a concise survey of Machado de Assis's nine novels and his various narrative techniques. Includes discussions of his primary themes, a useful bibliography, and some comments on his plays, poems, and short stories.

Dixon, Paul. *Retired Dreams: "Dom Casmurro," Myth, and Modernity*. West Lafayette, Ind.: Purdue University Press, 1989. Critical discussion of *Dom Casmurro* enables readers to understand how Machado de Assis cultivated a radically new style of writing that featured ambiguity as the most "realistic" aspect of language and conceived of language as a system of tropes only arbitrarily connected to physical reality. Suggests that Machado de Assis was critical of his society's patriarchal codes and that, as evidenced in the relationship between the novel's two major characters, Bento and Capitu, he implies the virtues inherent in a more matriarchal approach to sociopolitical organization.

Fitz, Earl E. *Machado de Assis*. Boston: Twayne, 1989. First English-language book to examine all aspects of Machado de Assis's literary life—his novels, short stories, poetry, theater, critical theory, translations, and nonfiction. Includes sections on his life, his place in Brazilian and world literature, his style, and his themes. Features an annotated bibliography and argues that Machado de Assis—largely because of his ideas about the connections among language, meaning, and reality—is best appreciated as a modernist.

Gledson, John. *The Deceptive Realism of Machado de Assis: A Dissenting Interpretation of "Dom Casmurro."* Liverpool, England: Francis Cairns, 1984. Focuses on *Dom Casmurro* in arguing against the interpretation of Machado de Assis either as a modernist or as a precursor of the New Novel in Latin America. Asserts that the author should be regarded instead as a master (if unique) realist and as a subtle and artful stylist whose work accurately reflects the prevailing social and political tensions of his time.

Graham, Richard, ed. *Machado de Assis: Reflections on a Brazilian Master Writer*. Austin: University of Texas Press, 1999. Collection of four essays includes two that examine the novel *Dom Casmurro* and two that discuss the political dialogues in and English translations of Machado de Assis's works.

Kristal, Efraín, and José Luiz Passos. "Machado de Assis and the Question of Brazilian National Identity." In *Brazil in the Making: Facets of National Identity*, edited by Carmen Nava and Ludwig Lauerhass, Jr. Lanham, Md.: Rowman & Littlefield, 2006. Discussion of Machado de Assis's impact on Brazilian identity is included in a collection of essays examining the unique character of the country and the identity of its citizens.

Neto, José Raimundo Maia. *Machado de Assis, the Brazilian Pyrrhonian*. West Lafayette, Ind.: Purdue University Press, 1994. Part 1 of this study explores the first phase of Machado de Assis's career, from 1861 until 1878, during which he went from writing essays to writing stories and, eventually, his first novels. Part 2 concentrates on his second phase, 1879-1908, with separate chapters on *Epitaph of a Small Winner, Dom Casmurro*, and later fiction. Includes detailed notes and bibliography.

Nunes, Maria Luisa. *The Craft of an Absolute Winner: Characterization and Narratology in the Novels of Machado de Assis*. Westport, Conn.: Greenwood Press, 1983. Excellent study addresses Machado de Assis's novelistic techniques, his skill at characterization, and his primary themes. Offers good summaries of his novels and shows both how they compare to one another and how their author grew in sophistication and skill. Argues that the essence of Machado de Assis's genius, like that of all truly great writers, lies in his singular ability to create powerful and compelling characters.

Peixoto, Marta. "*Dom Casmurro* by Machado de Assis." In *The Cambridge Companion to the Latin American Novel*, edited by Efraín Kristal. New York: Cambridge University Press, 2005. Analysis of *Dom Casmurro* is included in a comprehensive historical survey that traces the development of the Latin American novel. Includes bibliography and chronology.

Schwarz, Roberto. *A Master on the Periphery of Capitalism: Machado de Assis*. Translated by John Gledson. Durham, N.C.: Duke University Press, 2001. Schwarz, a Brazilian literary theorist, applies a Marxist interpretation to his literary and cultural analysis of *Epitaph of a Small Winner*, discussing the novel's style and structure as well as its views of nineteenth century Brazilian society.

FREDERIC PROKOSCH

Born: Madison, Wisconsin; May 17, 1908
Died: Plan de Grasse, France; June 2, 1989

PRINCIPAL LONG FICTION
The Asiatics, 1935
The Seven Who Fled, 1937
Night of the Poor, 1939
The Skies of Europe, 1941
The Conspirators, 1943
Age of Thunder, 1945
The Idols of the Cave, 1946
Storm and Echo, 1948
Nine Days to Mukalla, 1953
A Tale for Midnight, 1955
A Ballad of Love, 1960
The Seven Sisters, 1962
The Dark Dancer, 1964
The Wreck of the Cassandra, 1966
The Missolonghi Manuscript, 1968
America, My Wilderness, 1972

OTHER LITERARY FORMS

Frederic Prokosch (proh-KAWSH) published five books of poetry. Some of his poems enjoyed a transitory popularity and appeared in anthologies, notably those of Oscar Williams. In addition, he translated the love sonnets of Louise Labé in 1947, some of the poetry of Friedrich Hölderlin in 1943, and Euripides' *Medea* (431 B.C.E.) in 1947.

Many of the poems in Prokosch's first collection, *The Assassins* (1936), celebrate places and journeys and aspire to create an exotic mood. The collection also contains one of his most anthologized poems, "The Dolls," where Prokosch writes at his musical best of the sweet, crescent-eyed shapes that, reaching into the poet's "secret night," become the "furies" of his sleep. Dylan Thomas later parodied this poem, giving to his own poem the title "The Molls."

Prokosch's second volume of poems, *The Carnival* (1938), depends less on the dazzling imagery of geography and more on the ordinary things of life and was an attempt, according to the author, to convey the darkness of the prewar decade, as in "Fable," where the "rippled snow is tracked with blood,/ And my love lies cold in the burning wood." The volume contains a long, autobiographical "Ode" that describes the phases of Prokosch's first thirty years of life and his various discoveries (of fairy tales, his body, the past, Asia).

Frederic Prokosch
(Library of Congress)

His "Nocturne," beginning "Close my darling both your eyes,/ Let your arm lie still at last," shares similarities with W. H. Auden's well-known poem "Lay your sleeping head, my love,/ Human on my faithless arm."

The poems contained in *Death at Sea* (1940) concern the plight of the individual in a chaotic world. In "The Festival," for example, a pair of lovers who are apparently homosexual note the "coming tempest" and follow "Silent the paths of longing and regret/ Which all our learning taught us to despise"; the poem is set against a backdrop of earrings trembling in the dark and fairies huddling by a bridge.

Reviewers were not kind to Prokosch the poet, and time itself has been still less kind. Although he assembled an anthology, *Chosen Poems*, in 1944, it was not until 1983 that he published his next volume of verse, *The Sea*, a collection of sonnets that once again reflects Prokosch's fascination with geography. Finally, in 1983, Prokosch published his memoirs, *Voices*, a series of vignettes in which many of the literary giants of the twentieth century appear in a decidedly unheroic light.

Achievements

Frederic Prokosch is said to have created the novel of geography, a distillate of the reflective travelogue. More than half of his sixteen novels fall into this category, and even those that do not are dominated in some way by the theme of geography and involve cosmopolitan, travel-loving characters. With the publication of his first novel, *The Asiatics*, in 1935, a book highlighted by Asian scenes and attitudes when other American novelists were writing realistic novels set in their own country, Prokosch achieved instant fame and maintained a high reputation for approximately the next ten years. William Butler Yeats was deeply struck by Prokosch's poetic gifts, and André Gide, Thomas Mann, and Albert Camus all praised his works during his stellar decade. Even his later works were praised by W. Somerset Maugham, Thornton Wilder, and Marianne Moore.

The Asiatics, which was translated into seventeen foreign languages and was even more popular in Europe than in the United States, would remain in print for more than fifty years. *The Seven Who Fled* won the Harper Novel Prize, awarded by a panel of judges consisting of Wilder, Sinclair Lewis, and Louis Bromfield. In 1944, Warner Bros. released a film adaptation of *The Conspirators* starring Hedy Lamarr and Paul Henreid.

Radcliffe Squires observed that Prokosch's recurring theme—the death-defying search for truth in travel—began to seem irrelevant to a postwar generation looking for stability in suburbia. Subsequently, his novels were not so much condemned by the critics as they were ignored. Nevertheless, no complete discussion of twentieth century literature can afford to gloss over the fictional subgenre—the novel of geography—pioneered by the wunderkind Prokosch.

Biography

Frederic Prokosch was born in Madison, Wisconsin, on May 17, 1908, the middle child of three children born to Eduard and Mathilde Depprich Prokosch. His father, who had left Austria to escape a duel, was professor of Germanic philology at the University of Wisconsin, and his mother was an accomplished pianist. In 1913, Eduard Prokosch assumed a position at the University of Texas at Austin, which he lost six years later as a result of the anti-German hysteria that followed World War I.

Prokosch was sent in 1914 to spend a year in Europe, visiting his grandfather in Austria and attending private schools there and in Munich. His Austrian-Slavic-Germanic ancestry and his early acquaintance with European culture encouraged Prokosch's cosmopolitan spirit and love for geography. As a child, he developed an interest in fairy tales, and this he credits for his fascination as a novelist with picaresque and allegorical characters who strive inexorably for fulfillment.

In 1920, the family moved to Bryn Mawr, where Prokosch attended high school; in 1922, he entered Haverford College. In college, he became an athlete, particularly in tennis and squash, which he continued to play for years to come; he won the national squash championship of France in 1939 and that of Sweden in 1944. An avid lepidopterist, in later years he became as dexterous wielding his butterfly net as he had been with a racket.

After receiving his first master's degree from Haverford in 1928, Prokosch proceeded to earn a second one from King's College, Cambridge, in 1930. Two years later, he earned his doctorate at Yale. While a doctoral student, Prokosch taught English (from 1931 to 1933), continuing as a research fellow in 1934. The following year, *The Asiatics* appeared, and he returned to England, later visiting Africa and Asia. In 1936 and 1937, he was teaching at New York University, but when in 1937 he received both a Guggenheim Fellowship and the Harper Novel Prize of seventy-five hundred dollars, he abandoned teaching altogether. He was then at the apogee of his renown as a writer, and he could write from Prague in 1937 that one of his main interests was "trying to avoid the vulgarizations of money and publicity." Ironically, the vagaries of the reading public would facilitate this goal considerably in coming years.

After the fall of France, Prokosch spent two years in Lisbon, which served as the setting for *The Conspirators*. When the United States entered World War II, Prokosch returned home to enter government service in the Office of War Information and then spent two years (1943 to 1944) as an attache in the American Legation in Stockholm, Sweden. After the war, he went to Rome (1947 to 1953), where, on a Fulbright scholarship (1951 to 1952), he researched in the Vatican Library the material for his first attempt at a historical novel, *A Tale for Midnight*, about the Renaissance Cenci family.

The 1960's found Prokosch living in Paris; he finally settled in Grasse in the south of France. He continued his writing—now largely ignored by critics—and indulged his interest in rare books. Between 1968 and 1970, he printed and bound a series of elegant gift books, each containing a single poem by a well-known modern writer; these books' imprints dated the printing between 1933 and 1940, making them collectors' items. Eventually, Nicolas Barker exposed these "self-forgeries" and Prokosch admitted to the books' late date. Prokosch died in June, 1989, in Plan de Grasse, France.

Analysis

Frederic Prokosch was a lover of travel and even of maps themselves. In *America, My Wilderness*, he defines the place-name as a "talisman that guides us through the terror of anonymity," and his novelist's fascination with place-names is, at its best, lyrical and evocative, at its worst, pedantic and tedious. It follows that such a lover of the places of this world would be a proponent of internationalism, and in most of his novels written after 1940, Prokosch urged his American readers to abandon their isolationism and to nurture links and bonds with the other peoples of the world.

All of Prokosch's fiction is an attempt in some way to probe the spiritual malaise characteristic of the twentieth century. In his novels of the 1930's, there is an abiding, non-Western fatalism. A sense of impending doom for the world saturates *The Asiatics* as the natives philosophize to the young American traveler about the resignation implicit in the Asian personality. This doom is counterbalanced by the lyrical nature of the writing and by the luxuriance of detail, however, and the beguiling, unutterable beauty of life strains to prevail even in these prewar novels. When the fear and foreboding of the 1930's was eventually replaced by worldwide optimism after the war, the tenor of Prokosch's novels changed in tune with the times. In *Storm and Echo*, the emphasis is on Africa as a new continent rather than on Asia as a dying one, and the hint of a positive note in the destiny of humankind is unmistakable.

THE ASIATICS

In the picaresque narrative of *The Asiatics*, the nameless young American hero crosses the entire Asian continent from Lebanon to China. The character of the hero is elusive and vague, and many of the secondary characters with whom he forms friendships—friendships that are sometimes intense but always temporary—seem to take on more life than he. The hero is jailed in Turkey and suffers a plane crash in Iran, but always keeps his mind open and unbiased in order to soak up all the aphorisms proffered him both by the Asians and by the Western travelers whom he encounters. There is a chillingly prophetic mood to the novel; Asia is old and tired and waiting for death. When the hero enters a snowy-domed *dagoba* in Kandy and begins to converse with an old monk, it is of the coming of the twenty-fifth Buddha and of the accompanying dissolution of the world into Nirvana that they speak. The novel never ceases to analyze and emphasize the decadence and resignation of the enigma that is Asia.

THE SEVEN WHO FLED

In *The Seven Who Fled*, Prokosch weaves an allegory around a group of seven travelers, each representing a country in Europe (England, France, Spain, Germany, Austria, Belgium, and Russia), set adrift in the hostile vastness of Chinese Turkestan. After their caravan reaches Aqsu from Kashgar, the two German-speaking geologists are put into prison by local authorities; two others are kept as hostages; the Frenchman de la Scaze falls prey to a fever. Only the Englishman Layeville and de la Scaze's beautiful Spanish wife are free to proceed; the former joins a caravan to Tibet, and the latter continues eastward on a caravan in the company of Dr. Liu, a wealthy Chinese merchant. Much of the first half of the book details the disintegration and eventual death of Layeville in the icy summits of Tibet. In his relationship with the barbaric and tantalizing Tansang, his Turgot guide whose powerful face combines the strengths of "a young man, a woman and a child," Layeville feels the possibility of a renewal of his spirit, but he loses his last chance when Tansang dies.

Like Layeville and Tansang, the hostages back in Aqsu, the Russian Serafimov (an inarticulate bear of a man) and the Belgian thief Goupilliere, form an uneasy pair. When Serafimov is rejected by the Russian prostitute Madame Tastin while his companion Goupilliere is accepted, Serafimov consummates his hatred for the Belgian by murdering him. The two geologists, the German Wildenbruch (who worships heroism and ambition) and the blond, angelic Austrian Von Wald, escape from prison together and travel to Shanghai, where the tubercular Wildenbruch departs for home and Von Wald decides to remain. The last pair, the most mismatched of all, are Paul and Olivia de la Scaze. Olivia, who abandons her husband in Aqsu, comes under the complete control of Dr. Liu and ends up joining a house of prostitution in Shanghai. Paul recovers from his fever, eventually catches cholera from a dancing girl, and dies.

Although the seven characters do not correspond exactly to the seven cardinal sins of medieval theology, each sin is very much in evidence. Certainly sloth is implied in the flight of the seven from the responsibilities of their European lives to the distractions of adventure abroad. Lust is evident in Layeville's reminiscences of homosexuality, in Olivia's eventual choice of occupation, and in Serafimov's obsession with Madame Tastin. Wildenbruch feels envy for the innocence of Von Wald, and only Von Wald seems relatively immune to the ravages of the deadly sins.

NINE DAYS TO MUKALLA

Nine Days to Mukalla is the story of four plane-crash survivors who make their way from an island in the Indian Ocean to Mukalla in Arabia (now Saudi Arabia, Yemen, and the Persian Gulf states), where they will be able to get a boat for Aden and return to civilization. The novel employs the rich, evocative style that characterizes Prokosch's best work and allegorizes the contrasting sensibilities of the four victims lost in a mysterious Arabia, which, in its capacity to distill good and evil, "reveals the human skeleton."

The group is composed of two Englishwomen, Miss Todd and Sylvia Howard; and two Americans, an archaeologist, Dr. Moss, and David Gilbert, who is the only survivor by the end of the novel. David, described by Miss Todd as not quite a typical American, seems symbolic of a new, postwar, cosmopolitan America. Miss Todd, although she dies early in the narrative, possesses such great vitality that her spirit persists throughout the novel. It is the gift of her jewelry to David that enables him to reach Mukalla successfully. Dr. Moss is Miss Todd's foil, and just as the party's Bedouin guide thinks of Miss Todd as their good spirit, Moss is viewed by him as their bad spirit. He steals some of Miss Todd's jewels, abandons the party in his own interest, and is finally murdered in the desert. The primness of Sylvia Howard, the sketchiest of the four characters, is broken down in the Arabian desert, and before she dies of exhaustion when she actually reaches Mukalla, she asks David to make love to her.

THE SEVEN SISTERS

The Seven Sisters is Prokosch's first novel in which an American setting (Bishop's Neck, Maryland) is handled as powerfully as the foreign settings are in his earlier works. Each of the seven Nightingale sisters has a story, and the story of each sheds light on the character of Peter, an orphan who lives with the family. Peter is another of Prokosch's searching artists, but this time, untypically for Prokosch, his search ends in a kind of maturity. Five of the seven sisters, after frantic struggles, gradually achieve a kind of maturity as well.

The death of one of the sisters, young Elizabeth, who succumbs to a snakebite while still innocent, signals the real start of the action of the novel, suggesting a world divested of its innocence. The oldest sister, the repressed Augusta, marries a neighboring aristocrat, recognizes that the marriage is a mistake, and returns to her parents' home. Daphne leaves home dressed as a boy, falls in with a lesbian, meets a runaway New Yorker named Pancho, loses him to another man and to death, rejects the lesbian, and returns home. The elfin and visionary Grace never leaves home, but follows the advice of a ouija board, becomes pregnant, and goes to a cave, where she dies in the act of childbirth.

Consuelo, Barbara, and Freya, in the company of Peter and their mother, go to Europe. Consuelo links up with a Hungarian refugee. Blond, beautiful Barbara marries a wealthy, aging Italian prince, falls in love with his handsome nephew, and ends up, after losing both, praying for forgiveness for her vanity and pride. Freya gives up her career as a painter and goes to Brazil as a social worker, where she perishes in the jungle. It is the character of Peter that acts as the cohesive force in the novel; it is with him that the novel begins and ends.

THE SKIES OF EUROPE

The Skies of Europe is Prokosch's first realistic novel and covers the events that led up to World War II. Philip, a young American journalist, loves Saskia, a failed artist who does not love him. The novel abounds in characters who are unsuccessful artists and neglected poets; one such unnamed character seems intended to represent Adolf Hitler. *The Skies of Europe* has affinities with a later novel, *A Ballad of Love*, Prokosch's most nearly autobiographical novel, his "portrait of the artist as a young man." It is, moreover, a portrait of a defeated artist. The hero, Henry, is a poet who grows up in Austria, Texas, and Wisconsin and becomes involved in a disastrous love affair similar to those in *The Skies of Europe* and *The Idols of the Cave*.

STORM AND ECHO

Storm and Echo follows the pattern of Prokosch's first two novels, and the landscape of Africa is even more brilliantly painted than that of Asia in his earlier novels. There is a Conradian power in this tale of an American's search for a mysterious friend who has gone off to Mount Nagala. Central Africa is typically fraught with dangers of all kinds, but the friend is found (albeit as a corpse impaled upon a rock), and the protagonist emerges victorious over his own death wish.

THE WRECK OF THE CASSANDRA

The Wreck of the Cassandra is similar to *Nine Days to Mukalla* but lacks the latter's allegorical sweep. Here, nine survivors of a shipwreck somewhere between Hong Kong and

Australia reach a large island and settle down idyllically for a short time before the spirit of the island distills their personalities into various shades of good and evil. The presence of hostile natives adds to the tensions in the group, they confront one another violently, and some of their number are lost before their inevitable rescue.

WORLD WAR II NOVELS

Three of Prokosch's novels are set against the backdrop of World War II. *Night of the Poor*, the title of which was taken from a painting by Diego Rivera, is perhaps the author's weakest novel and amounts to little more than a conventional travelogue. It is the first of Prokosch's novels that has an American setting, and American place-names are savored and enumerated to such an extent that they tax the reader's patience. The plot chronicles the travels of Tom on his way to Texas after the death of an uncle in Wisconsin, and the gamut of depravity and inhumanity that he encounters on the way.

Thirty-three years later, Prokosch would rework the same idea in *America, My Wilderness*, dressing it up with generous amounts of Surrealism and modernistic bizarrerie. After the murder of his uncle in the Midwest, a half-black outcast named Pancho Krauss wanders from the Atlantic to the Pacific, savoring the "slow transition of one landscape into another."

Prokosch is destined to be remembered, if not as a great novelist, as a pioneer of the novel of geography and as an internationalist. He focused on the exotica of faraway lands but always called his fellow Americans to abandon their parochialism and recognize the underlying unity of humankind.

Jack Shreve

OTHER MAJOR WORKS

POETRY: *The Carnival: Poems*, 1938; *Death at Sea: Poems*, 1940; *Chosen Poems*, 1944; *The Sea*, 1983.

NONFICTION: *Voices: A Memoir*, 1983.

TRANSLATIONS: *Some Poems of Friedrich Hölderlin*, 1943; *Love Sonnets of Louise Labé*, 1947; *Medea*, 1947 (in *Greek Plays in Modern Translation*, Dudley Fitts, editor).

BIBLIOGRAPHY

Austen, Roger. *Playing the Game: The Homosexual Novel in America*. Indianapolis, Ind.: Bobbs-Merrill, 1977. Contains a useful discussion of Prokosch and his works, situating him in the context of twentieth century American literature about homosexuality. Includes a bibliography and an index.

Carpenter, Richard C. "The Novels of Frederic Prokosch." *College English* 18 (1957): 261-267. Provides much insight into the development of Prokosch's novelistic style. An appreciative essay by a sympathetic critic of Prokosch.

Iyer, Pico. "The Perfect Traveler." *The New York Review of Books*, November 18, 2004.

This portrait of Prokosch focuses on *The Asiatics*, describing how Prokosch came to write the novel and examining its plot and its critical and popular reception. Iyer, a noted writer of place-related works, situates *The Asiatics* within the context of Prokosch's life and literary career.

Squires, Radcliffe. *Frederic Prokosch*. New York: Twayne, 1964. Presents Prokosch's works in a chronological format and is useful as a critical introduction. Squires focuses on the timeless qualities of "interplay of emotion and intellect" in Prokosch's work but acknowledges that his writing was a "casualty" of World War II, which changed the values of the reading public. A selected bibliography is provided.

SALMAN RUSHDIE

Born: Bombay (now Mumbai), India; June 19, 1947
Also known as: Ahmed Salman Rushdie

PRINCIPAL LONG FICTION
Grimus, 1975
Midnight's Children, 1981
Shame, 1983
The Satanic Verses, 1988
Haroun and the Sea of Stories, 1990 (fable)
The Moor's Last Sigh, 1995
The Ground Beneath Her Feet, 1999
Fury, 2001
Shalimar the Clown, 2005
The Enchantress of Florence, 2008

OTHER LITERARY FORMS

In addition to his novels, Salman Rushdie (ROOSH-dee) has produced short stories and works of nonfiction. *The Jaguar Smile: A Nicaraguan Journey* (1987) is a book of travel and political observations written following Rushdie's visit to Nicaragua in July, 1986, as a guest of the Sandinista Association of Cultural Workers. Among his short stories, the best known is "The Prophet's Hair," which appeared originally in the *London Review of Books* in 1981 and has been reprinted in *The Penguin Book of Modern British Short Stories* (1987). A fable in the style of *The Arabian Nights' Entertainments*, *Haroun and the Sea of Stories* was published in 1990, and the collection of short stories *East, West: Stories* (1994) includes "The Prophet's Hair" and the dazzling "At the Auction of the Ruby Slippers." The essays in Rushdie's *Step Across This Line: Collected Nonfiction, 1992-2002* (2002) deal with a variety of subjects, including popular culture, politics, and soccer.

ACHIEVEMENTS

Although furor and indignation have followed the publication of a number of Salman Rushdie's novels, the works have also received critical praise and rave reviews. *Midnight's Children* won the James Tait Black Memorial Prize, the English Speaking Union Literature Award, and the Booker Prize; it has been translated into twelve languages. Although *Shame* was banned in Pakistan, as *Midnight's Children* had been in India, it too received critical plaudits for its seriocomic portrait of Pakistani life. No writer since English satirist Jonathan Swift has aroused as much ire from so many sources, notwithstanding the notoriety of *The Satanic Verses*, which won the Whitbread Award as best novel of 1988.

On February 14, 1989, the Ayatollah Ruhollah Khomeini, the fundamentalist spiritual leader of Iran, issued a fatwa (a proclamation concerning a matter of Muslim faith) that called for Rushdie's death as an enemy of Islam and sanctioned similar reprisals against those who published or distributed *The Satanic Verses*. Rushdie became a Knight of the British Empire in 2007. Ironically, this royal honor served to rekindle the hatred and many of the threats that haunted him following publication of *The Satanic Verses*.

Rushdie's novels, actually modern picaresques, explore the tragicomic results of lost identity; they portray in exuberant, highly inventive, satirical style what the author considers to be the consequences of living in cultures that have become mixed, distorted, and diluted through combinations of expediency, political ineptitude, and exploitative religion.

BIOGRAPHY

Ahmed Salman Rushdie was born in Bombay (now Mumbai), India, on June 19, 1947, less than two months before the end of the British Raj. His father, Anis Ahmed Rushdie, and his mother, Negin Butt Rushdie, were Muslims with ties to the region that would become Pakistan. The family did not at first join the Muslim exodus to Pakistan that began after partition in September, 1947. Even so, they became increasingly aware of their minority status as Muslims in a predominantly Hindu state.

Although the Rushdies were nominally Muslim, they also identified with India and with Great Britain. Rushdie's father had been educated in England, at Cambridge University, and had determined to rear his son and three daughters to appreciate their multicultural background. As a result, Rushdie had, from boyhood, access to a variety of works in his father's library. It became a recurring argument between father and son, however, that the boy did not make adequate use of this wealth of books. His private reading during boyhood was generally limited to an English translation of the fifteenth century collection of stories known as *The Arabian Nights' Entertainments* (or *The Thousand and One Nights*). His mother, considered "keeper of the family stories," regaled young Rushdie and his sisters with a wealth of anecdotes on their family history; he remembered them all and would later adapt many of them in his writings.

Rushdie was sent to the Cathedral and John Connon School, a British-administered primary school with Anglican affiliation located in Bombay. As his sister Sameen has recalled, "He mopped up all the prizes," was not very adapt at games, read extensively in both serious and popular literature, and loved both American B films and Hindu hit films. In 1961, at the age of thirteen, he was sent to the prestigious Rugby public school in England. At Rugby, however, although the masters were generally fair-minded, Rushdie felt alienated from his classmates, the "old boys" from British established families, who subjected him to cruel pranks. Rushdie compensated for the pranks and racial taunts by excelling at debates, appearing in theatrical productions, and thriving in academic areas, winning the Queen's Medal for history and securing (but refusing) a scholarship at Balliol College, Oxford.

In 1964, the Rushdie family had emigrated to Karachi, Pakistan, and while Rushdie was not enthusiastic about returning to England, he had been offered a scholarship at his father's university, King's College, Cambridge, and amid the India-Pakistan war in 1965, his father literally pushed him onto an airplane bound for the United Kingdom. Rushdie's attitude toward his father was often argumentative, and there was a serious rupture in their relationship when he entered Cambridge. Shortly before the elder Rushdie's death in 1987, there was a rapprochement between the two men.

At Cambridge, Rushdie decided to read for a degree in history, and he eventually attained a 2.2 (that is, "second-rate") degree, but he thrived in the social atmosphere of the mid-1960's. "It was a very good time to be at Cambridge," he has stated. "I ceased to be a conservative snob under the influence of the Vietnam War and dope." He continued his involvement in theater, and upon his graduation in 1968, he attempted to work in the entertainment industry in Pakistan. He found that censorship was inescapable there, however, and returned to London, where he worked in amateur theatricals and supported himself as a copywriter at the J. Walter Thompson advertising agency. He had already begun to think of himself as a writer, however, and he completed a never-published novel in 1971, "The Book of the Pir," which he has described as "post-Joycean and sub-Joycean."

Grimus was Rushdie's first published novel, written while he was still working irregularly in advertising to earn an income. It was a commercial failure and never was published in the United States, but it was favorably reviewed in London's *The Times Literary Supplement* (January 21, 1975), and it attracted notice and the beginnings of an audience for Rushdie. It took several short stories and five years before Rushdie produced his next novel, *Midnight's Children*. This work won rave reviews on both sides of the Atlantic, but it also offended a great many people, among them the family of Indira Gandhi, then prime minister of India. Rushdie made a public apology for the cutting satirical references to her and specific members of her family in the novel, but he made no changes in subsequent editions. The affair was exacerbated by the fact that Rushdie's accusations coincided with the Indian army's assault on the Golden Temple of the Sikh Muslims. The assassination of Mrs. Gandhi in 1984 brought a tragic end to this series of events.

Having offended large numbers of Indians with *Midnight's Children*, Rushdie published *Shame*, his portrayal of the blood feuds that led to the deposing and execution of Pakistan's prime minister Zulfikar Ali Bhutto by his former protégé, Mohammad Zia-ul-Haq. The same pattern followed publication of this novel, but this time Rushdie had offended the Pakistanis, India's enemies. Again Rushdie had great commercial success and received critical plaudits, but *Shame*, which Rushdie has called *Midnight's Children's* "antisequel," was denied publication in Pakistan just as *Midnight's Children* had been banned in India.

By 1985, Rushdie was sought after by every major publisher. Viking Penguin offered him an advance of $850,000 for rights to his work then in progress, leading to a rancorous break with Liz Calder, an old friend trying to establish her own publishing firm. Everyone in publishing circles knew that the new book would cause a sensation, but no one, not even Rushdie, could have known that *The Satanic Verses* would make him a marked man.

After February 14, 1989, with the Khomeini decree of death, Rushdie's life came to resemble the plots of his novels. The threat of assassination forced him to close his London home and go into hiding. Viking Penguin received thousands of threatening letters. Bookstores that did not remove *The Satanic Verses* from their shelves were threatened with bombings. Riots related to the book broke out in Bombay; at least five people were killed and dozens injured in Islamabad, Pakistan; and two Muslim leaders were killed in Brussels, Belgium, after they expressed opposition to censoring the book. Two bookstores in Berkeley, California, were firebombed, and a bomb blast in London, which killed the terrorist who had placed the bomb, was attributed to the anti-Rushdie campaign. Rushdie's Japanese translator was murdered, his Italian translator was wounded in a knife attack, and his Norwegian publisher was almost killed in a shooting.

Although some members of the British political establishment expressed a personal distaste for Rushdie, and authors such as John le Carré and Roald Dahl (who called him a "dangerous opportunist") claimed that Rushdie deserved his predicament, Scotland Yard was assigned the task of protecting him.

The fatwa on Rushdie's life inevitably continued as the bane of his existence. Writers such as William Styron, Milan Kundera, and Norman Mailer called upon the governments of democratic nations to exert pressure on Iran, and, without making his position public, horror writer Stephen King insisted that any bookstore chain that gave in to threats and removed Rushdie's books from its shelves would have to remove King's as well. In 1990, Rushdie issued a statement that he had "converted" to Islam to show "people who viewed me as some kind of enemy that I wasn't one," but he realized that he had acted out of "despair and disorientation" and "made strenuous steps to get out of the false position."

When Rushdie made a secret trip to the United States in 1992, President George H. W. Bush's administration avoided contact with him, but in 1993 he was able to arrange a brief meeting in the White House with President Bill Clinton. The British government of Prime Minister John Major was more supportive, albeit discreetly, than its predecessor. In the third year of his concealment, Rushdie began to write again, remarking "If I can't write, then, in a way, the attack has been successful." His fable *Haroun and the Sea of Stories*, written as a means of speaking to his son, whom he could not contact while in hiding, was published in 1990, and a collection of short fiction, *East, West*, was released in 1994. After five years of labor, *The Moor's Last Sigh* was published in 1995.

The fatwa and life in hiding ended Rushdie's marriage to his second wife, the American novelist Marianne Wiggins; they divorced in 1993 (his first marriage, to Clarissa Luard, with whom he had a son, ended in divorce in 1985). His third marriage, to Elizabeth West, produced one son and ended in divorce in 2004. Rushdie's *The Enchantress of Florence* was written even as his fourth marriage, to actor Padma Lakshmi, was unraveling (they divorced in 2007) and contains, amid much else, a meditation on an ideal wife conjured in dream.

During the mid-1990's, Rushdie appeared in public more often, unannounced but usually greeted with considerable enthusiasm, and was active in encouraging international resistance to the fatwa. In 1998, some more moderate members of the Iranian government moved toward a withdrawal of the fatwa, but Rushdie's safety was still not entirely guaranteed, and he remained cautious in terms of his movements into the early years of the twenty-first century.

Analysis

Many Western readers, ignorant of Islam and Hinduism, the 1947 partition of the Indian subcontinent and the creation of Pakistan, the India-Pakistan war of 1965, and the Pakistani civil war of 1974, may tend to read Salman Rushdie's novels as bizarre entertainments. This is unfortunate, since each is a picaresque allegory into which the author has inserted details from his own life in order to prove that myth is history, today is yesterday, and the life of one person is integral to the history of nations. Rushdie masks events here and there and relentlessly mixes Persian and Hindu myths, but the hiatus in logic that this method creates is merely to prove his contention that an Anglo-Indian-Pakistani is a person with a hole in the body, a vital place in which there is a haunting void.

Midnight's Children

Midnight's Children is Rushdie's allegorical picaresque on the history of the modern state of India. Its narrator, Saleem Sinai, is one of those whose birth coincided with the hour and day India achieved independence: midnight, August 15, 1947. He and many others, including Jawaharlal Nehru, India's first prime minister, considered these "midnight's children" singled out, privileged by the hopeful hour at which they began their lives. Saleem discovers that he does indeed have special powers; he can, in his mind, summon all the other children born during the midnight hour of August 15, 1947, and, when a boy, he does so nightly, establishing the "Midnight Children's Conference," a forum he hopes will augur well for organizing the leaders of the new state.

Saleem's family is prosperous; they reside in one of Bombay's more affluent sections on an estate of homes once owned by an Englishman, William Methwold, who left India on the very day the Raj ended. Through a bizarre series of events (an accident at school that reveals that his blood type corresponds to neither parent and the subsequent confession of Mary Pereira, a nurse who had worked at the hospital at which Saleem was born), Saleem's family discovers that Mary had intentionally switched children, giving the Sinais a child of one of Bombay's poorest families. Only Saleem, through his telepathic powers, knows that the Sinais's real son, reared as a street urchin named Shiva, is actually an illegitimate child of the Englishman Methwold. Though the Sinais make no attempt to locate their own boy and do accept Saleem as their own, Saleem recognizes Shiva as his nemesis and realizes that Shiva may well destroy him.

Each of the children of midnight has some special talent or ability by virtue of time and date of birth: Saleem's telepathic skills, Shiva's extraordinarily strong knees (which he uses to kill the Indian street entertainer he believes is his father), and the abilities of Parvati-the-witch, who seeks to use her talents only for good. All the children become caught up in the political machinations that follow upon India's independence and the creation of Pakistan. Saleem's family, aware that they are part of India's unwanted Muslim minority, immigrate to Pakistan. This event, plus the fact that Saleem no longer wishes to have any contact with Shiva, the rightful heir of the Sinais, ends Saleem's nightly summoning of the Midnight Children's Conference. Once in Pakistan, Saleem discovers that his telepathic powers do not work. He tries, instead, to develop his exceptional power of smell, utilizing his huge nose to smell danger, injustice, unhappiness, poverty, and other elements of Pakistani life.

Saleem and his family become caught up in Pakistan's 1965 war with India. Saleem's former countrymen become his enemies, and all of his family are killed in the war, except his sister, who has taken the name Jamila Singer and has become famous as a singer of patriotic songs. When the east wing of Pakistan secedes in 1973 and declares itself the independent state of Bangladesh, Saleem enlists in Pakistan's canine patrol, the Cutia, performing the function of a dog to sniff out traitors. Pakistan's devastating loss in the war leaves Saleem without a country. Ultimately, it is Parvati-the-witch who uses her magic to make him disappear and return him to India.

Saleem marries Parvati but is unable to consummate the marriage. Whenever he tries to do so, he sees the decaying face of Jamila, the woman who had been reared as his sister. Saleem had loved Jamila, but he also had come to recognize that their nominal brother-sister relationship would not allow her to be his. Out of frustration, Parvati takes Shiva, now a major in India's army, as her lover. She gives birth to his child, named Aadam, whom Saleem acknowledges as his own son.

Shiva, the destroyer, supervises the slum clearance project that not only eliminates the Bombay quarter in which the magicians had lived but also kills Parvati and many of her magician colleagues who had refused to leave their homes. Saleem is one of those arrested and brought to Benares, the town of the widows. Here he is imprisoned, forced by Shiva to name and identify the skills of the children of midnight; he is released only after he has been forcibly sterilized. Oddly, those arrested as a result of Saleem's information do not blame him; they, too, are sterilized.

Much more happens in *Midnight's Children*. The novel is structured as a family history that reaches back to Saleem's grandparents and describes the political circumstances in India after World War I, through World War II and the end of the Raj, to the war with Pakistan and the Pakistani civil war. It is also highly mythic. Sinai, the surname of the narrator, masks the name of the Arabian philosopher Avicenna (980-1037), who saw the emanations of God's presence in the cosmos as a series of triads of mind, body, and soul. The triads appear in the three generations of Sinais who appear in the novel, but the three religions of India—Hinduism, Islam, and Christianity—which also appear, do nothing to reverse the downward course of India's fortunes after 1947. Sin is the ancient moon god of Hadhramut, who acting at a distance can influence the tides of the world. He is represented by the letter *S* and is as sinuous as the snake. Appropriately, Saleem discovers his son Aadam in the care of a master snake charmer, Picture Singh. Sinai is both the place of revelation, of commandments and the golden calf, and the desert of barrenness and infertility that is Rushdie's view of modern India.

Saleem's nose resembles the trunk of the elephant deity, Kali, who is the god of literature, and the huge ears of Saleem's son Aadam carry the motif into India's future. Shiva is the Hindu god of destruction and reproduction, a member of the trinity that includes Brama and Vishnu. The closing chapters of the novel find Saleem the manager of a Bombay pickle factory owned by his former nurse, Mary Pereira, the woman who had originally exchanged him for the true son of the Sinais, underscoring the motif of absurd continuity, pickled history, and Saleem's huge nose, which is called a cucumber as often as it is an elephant's trunk.

The most savage satire of the book is reserved for Indira Gandhi, daughter of Nehru and, until her 1984 assassination, prime minister of India. Rushdie repeatedly cites a famous newspaper photograph in which her hair is white on one side and black on the other to symbolize her hypocrisy. He ridicules Sanjay Gandhi, her son, now also dead, as the mastermind of India's slum clearance and birth-control plans. Specific members of Gandhi's cabinet appear in the novel with appendages to their titles, such as "Minister for Railroads and Bribery." Gandhi's campaign slogan "Indira is India, and India is Indira," which Rushdie often quotes in these contexts, thus becomes a dire prophecy. It is little wonder that distribution of *Midnight's Children*, published during India's state of national emergency, was prohibited in India. The novel also made Rushdie persona non grata in the country of his birth.

SHAME

Rushdie has called *Shame* his "antisequel" to *Midnight's Children*. It has picaresque and seriocomic elements that resemble those of the earlier novel, but its characters are Pakistanis, members of the power elite that had its historical counterpart in the circle of deposed prime minister Zulfikar Ali Bhutto and Bhutto's protégé, the man who engineered the coup and Bhutto's trial and execution, Mohammad Zia-ul-Haq. *Shame* created as much consternation in Pakistan as *Midnight's Children* had in India, with precisely the same result: The novel was banned in Pakistan, and Rushdie was considered subversive.

The title of *Shame* derives from the Urdu word *Sharam*, and it contains an encyclopedia of nuance the English barely suggests: embarrassment, discomfiture, indecency, immodesty, and the sense of unfulfilled promise. Rushdie thus explores in this work themes that are similar to those of his first novel. All the characters experience shame in one or another of these forms as well as some its converse, shamelessness.

Shame also maintains the highly mythic, literary tone of *Midnight's Children*. Its unprepossessing hero, evocatively named Omar Khayyám Shakil, is a paunchy doctor of great promise with the name of the Persian poet known for the twelfth century *Rubáiyát*, the erotic lyric poems imitated in English by Edward FitzGerald in 1859. Rushdie's Omar is born in a crumbling house called Nishapur (also the town of the historical poet's birth), once the mansion of an Englishman, Colonel Arthur Greenfield, in a Pakistani backwater identified only as "Q," but perhaps Quetta.

The circumstances of Omar's birth are ambiguous. He has three mothers: Chhunni, Munnee, and Bunny Shakil. These three sisters all consider him their son, and none discloses which of them actually gave him birth, nor will they disclose the name of his father, though the reader learns that he is an Englishman. Omar's situation is thus a metaphor of the mixed cultural legacy Rushdie often describes. Indeed, Rushdie has often spoken of himself as a man with three mothers: India, Pakistan, and England. The house in which Omar is reared is a labyrinth, a relic of the British Raj; its corridors lead to rooms unoccupied for generations, and Omar, who in his early boyhood is prohibited from leaving the house at any time, is frightened out of his wits when he ventures too far and sees that the water-seeking roots of a tree have punctured the house's outer walls. All of this is Rushdie's metaphorical description of the state of mind of a person with mixed and hostile origins: alienated, loveless, relentlessly, fearfully traversing the labyrinth of the mind, and feeling shame. Omar's only glimpse of the world outside Nishapur is through his telescope, appropriately, given that the poet for whom he was named was also an astronomer.

The novel is filled with a wealth of characters whose backgrounds are similarly symbolic and complex. Rushdie draws them together both through family relationships and through their individually shameful actions as well as their capacity to feel shame. For example, Bilquìs Kemal Hyder is a woman reared in Bombay, India, by her father, Mahound "the Woman" Kemal, owner of a motion-picture theater. The epithet regularly applied to her father is simultaneously an indication of his motherly solicitude for his daughter and a jibe at his having lost his masculinity by assuming the burden of child rearing. After her father dies in a terrorist bomb blast that also destroys his theater, Bilquìs is rescued by Raza "Razor Guts" Hyder, Rushdie's version of Zia, an ambitious young military officer who takes her as his bride and returns to the family home in Karachi, Pakistan, the country created by partition of the Indian subcontinent. Thrust into an uncompromisingly Muslim environment, she finds herself shamed when she is unable to bear Hyder a son. Of their two daughters, Sufiya Zinobia Hyder and Naveed "Good News" Hyder, the first is perpetually childlike, the result of a mistreated case of meningitis. Bilquìs and Hyder's second daughter, "Good News," atones for her mother's relative infertility by bearing twenty-seven children.

The focus of *Shame* is the rise to power of Omar's companion in dissipation, Iskander "Isky" Harappa, based on Zulfikar Ali Bhutto. Isky gives up drinking and womanizing in middle age, adopts the veneer of a devout Muslim, and seizes power after the loss of Pakistan's east wing. For a time he remains popular, assisted by his beautiful unmarried daughter, Arjumand "Virgin Ironpants" Harappa, Rushdie's satiric depiction of Benazir Bhutto, who would later become prime minister of Pakistan. Isky's wife, Rani Humayun Hyder, remains out of the limelight on the family's isolated estate, where she weaves shawls that document all of her husband's acts of shame—a twist on the Penelope motif of Homer's *Odyssey* (c. 725 B.C.E.; English translation, 1614). By the time Isky is hanged in a military coup, Rani has completed eighteen of these shawls. (Rushdie enumerates the details of each in an angry excursus modeled on a Homeric epic catalog.)

When Hyder seizes power, he encourages the trial and conviction of Isky Harappa. After a curious combination of circumstances causes Harappa's death, Hyder orders the corpse hanged, ostensibly carrying out the court's sentence of execution. Hyder's increasing concern is, however, the deviant behavior of his daughter, Sufiya Zinobia. Though well past twenty, she has the mental age of less than ten. Hyder accepts Omar Shakil's offer to marry her, made out of shame for his past womanizing and platonic love for the young woman whose life he had saved. Sufiya Zinobia is, however, aware that some act about which she knows nothing regularly accompanies marriage. She twice escapes from the Hyder house, where she is literally imprisoned (recalling Shakil's own imprisonment in youth), allows herself to be raped at random by street-walking men, then decapitates the men who have raped her. The villagers who discover these decapitated corpses create the legend of a wild white panther to explain the murders, but Hyder knows that his daughter is the killer and fears that she will eventually decapitate him.

When Hyder's downfall appears imminent, he, his wife Bilquìs, and Shakil escape to the closed mansion of Shakil's youth, and Shakil's three mothers give them sanctuary. Shakil quickly realizes, however, that the three old women plan to kill Hyder in reprisal for his having ordered the death of their younger son, Babar Shakil, for his terrorist involvements. This they do, though not before the accidental death of Bilquìs. Shakil dies soon thereafter, shot by Talvar Ulhaq, Hyder's son-in-law and former state police chief. The pantherlike figure of Sufiya Zinobia observes the carnage, with Harappa's daughter Arjumand hovering as a vision of a future of "a new cycle of shamelessness."

Rushdie's point, developed through these and other complexities of plot, is that shame and shamelessness develop through religious and political failure; the images of Islam and Pakistan that he invokes are filled with parricide and cruelty, but never genuine and simple love. That those who destroy one another are related by family as well as national ties merely compounds the tragedy and the shame. Rushdie's Pakistan is presented as "a failure of the dreaming mind."

THE SATANIC VERSES

The Satanic Verses is Rushdie's strongest indictment of politicized religion, mixed cultural identity, and insensitive, arbitrary officialdom. Its tone is allegorical, picaresque, satiric, and irreverent. Those who know details concerning the founding of Islam, British politics, and contemporary London will recognize the objections made to the book; those unaware of these particulars will likely be puzzled by the novel's character and chronological shifts and may even wonder why the work has caused such consternation.

The novel begins with an explosion, a passenger airplane destroyed by a terrorist bomb as it flies over the English Channel. Only two passengers survive: Gibreel Farishta and Saladin Chamcha, two actors of Indian origin. Miraculously, they float to earth unharmed. Farishta, whose first name is the Indian form of that of the angel Gabriel, has made his reputation playing Krishna, Gautama Buddha, Hanuman, and other Indian deities in films known as theologicals. Chamcha, a complete Anglophile, has achieved fame by doing commercial voice-overs in England, though his face is unknown to his admiring audience. With this as background, Rushdie establishes the figure of the angel Gibreel (in Islam associated with bringing Allah's call to the Prophet Muhammad) and the apparently diabolical Chamcha, who has traded his ethnic identity for a pseudo-British veneer.

When they land, Chamcha discovers that he has grown horns under his very English bowler, as well as cloven hooves and a huge phallus—this despite his mild demeanor, elegant manners, and proper British appearance. Farishta (whose surname means "sweet") finds that he has a halo, despite his being an unconscionable womanizer. His very trip to England was a pursuit of Alleluia Cone, the British "ice queen" of Polish refugee parents. Cone is an internationally famous mountain climber who has conquered Mount Everest. Rushdie thus mixes the imagery of good and evil, angel and demon; this is an exponential motif of the entire novel. It follows that the British police arrest Chamcha as an illegal immigrant and brutalize him terribly. Farishta, however, because of his angelic appearance, remains free, having charmed the police and having refused to identify Chamcha.

The narrative then abruptly shifts to introduce Mahound, a blasphemous name for Muhammad, the founder of Islam. Edmund Spenser used the name Mahound in *The Faerie Queene* (1590, 1596) to represent a heathen idol reserved for oaths sworn by the wicked. Rushdie's Mahound profanely re-creates Muhammad's call from Allah through the angel Gabriel. Mahound, like Muhammad, is a businessman; he climbs Mount Cone and looks down on the city of sand that Rushdie calls Jahilia, a fictive town that corresponds to Mecca. Mahound's pursuit of his destiny on Mount Cone corresponds to Gibreel's pursuit of mountain climber Alleluia Cone; his dream-filled sleeps as he awaits the angel Gibreel resemble the trancelike seizures, ever increasing in severity, of Gibreel Farishta.

Mahound's companions are described as the scum of Jahilia (Muhammad's companions were former slaves), and Rushdie puckishly names one of them Salman. They have the habit, dangerous in a city built entirely of sand, of constantly washing themselves (a parody of Muslim ritual purification). The twelve whores of Jahilia (which means "ignorance" or "darkness"), reminiscent of Muhammad's twelve wives and known as Mothers of the Believers, reside in a brothel called the Curtain. Translated as *hejab*, this can be associated with the curtainlike veil worn by pious Muslim women.

Abu Simbel, the name of the village flooded in the 1960's when Egypt constructed the Aswan High Dam, is the name given here to the ruler of Jahilia, a city also endangered by water. Because he recognizes Mahound as a threat to his power, Abu Simbel offers him a deal. If Mahound's Allah will accept a mere 3 of Jahilia's 360 deities into the new monotheistic religion, he will recognize it and give Mahound a seat on the ruling council. It will not be much of a compromise, Abu Simbel insists, since Mahound's religion already recognizes Gibreel as the voice of Allah and Shaitan (Satan) as the spirit the Qur'an records would not bow before Adam.

Mahound decides to compromise. He climbs Cone Mountain, consults with his Gibreel, then returns to Jahilia to announce the new verses: "Have you thought upon Lat and Uzza, and Manat, the third, the other? . . . They are the exalted birds, and their intercession is desired indeed." These are the so-called Satan-inspired inclusions of the goddesses of motherhood (Lat), beauty and love (Uzza), and fate (Manat) as daughters of Allah, which the Qur'an rejects as heresy. Mahound later publicly recants this heretical insertion and flees to Yathrib (the ancient name for Medina), corresponding to the historical account of the *hegira*, Muhammad's flight from Mecca to Medina. Gibreel reappears to announce: "It was me both times, baba, me first and second also me." One can draw implications that Islam was founded by rationalizing good and evil, that its founder was both a sincere mystic and a power-hungry entrepreneur, and that Gibreel, an actor who specializes in impersonating deities, had given at least one bravura performance that changed history.

Rushdie goes on to recount a masked sardonic version of the holy war to establish Islam, continuing to blur the distinction between ancient and modern times. A bearded, turbaned imam in exile in London (which he considers Sodom) is in exile from his homeland, called Desh. When a revolution begins in Desh and overthrows the corrupt empress, named Ayesha (ironically also the name of Muhammad's favorite wife), Gibreel (perhaps the angel, perhaps the actor Farishta, perhaps one and the same) flies the imam to Desh on his back in time to see the carnage. This episode can be interpreted as the recall to Iran of the Ayatollah Khomeini, who was in exile near Paris until the overthrow of the shah. When the revolution succeeds, Ayesha metamorphoses into the mother goddess, Al-Lat, she whom Mahound had falsely named a daughter of Allah in the satanic verses.

In a parallel sequence, an epileptic peasant girl, also named Ayesha, arouses the lust of a landowner named Mirza Saeed, whose wife is dying of breast cancer. As Moses led the Israelites out of Egypt, so Ayesha, who declares that her husband the archangel Gibreel has told her to do so, leads the entire village, including Saeed's wife, on a pilgrimage by foot to Mecca. She declares that the Arabian Sea will open to admit them (recalling the parting of the Red Sea in Exodus); butterflies mark their privileged status, and they are Ayesha's only food (recalling the manna of the Israelites). All that the unbelievers see as they watch the pilgrims is their disappearance into the Arabian Sea. The implication remains that Ayesha parts the sea for those who believe; to everyone else, the entire enterprise ends as a cult suicide. This motif emphasizes the novel's focus on migration, which Rushdie has claimed is its central subject.

Much more happens in *The Satanic Verses*. London, called "Ellowen Deeowen" by Farishta, is beset by ethnic antagonisms. Its police and most whites are brutal racists; its Indians are rogues or displaced mystics. Still, nothing in Rushdie's novel is what it appears to be, and that is his point. Empires and religions alike arise from a combination of noble and sordid motives. It is impossible to admire or hate anything unreservedly; there is evil even in that which appears absolutely good, and, conversely, one can explain evil in terms of good gone awry. Such relativism is hardly new, but the notoriety *The Satanic Verses* has received has obscured the author's point. What is clear is that *The Satanic Verses* is the logical sequel to ideas Rushdie began to develop in *Midnight's Children* and *Shame*, as well as an allegory that strains narrative and religious sensibilities to the breaking point.

THE MOOR'S LAST SIGH

As a kind of permanent immigrant, a man who can neither return to a home country (India) nor feel really at home in any other land, Rushdie has, as Henry Louis Gates, Jr., has noted, presented a "vision of migrancy as the very condition of cultural modernity." A crucial aspect of this aesthetic position, however, has been an intense examination of the various homelands that formed—and continued to inform—the intellectual, spiritual, and political components of Rushdie's psychological being. Whereas *Midnight's Children* and *Shame* focus on India and Pakistan at specific, contemporary moments in their postcolonial history, *The Moor's Last Sigh* is an attempt to account for and understand the origins and evolution of the complex cultural matrix that Rushdie refers to as "Mother India." Its narrative combines the overall structure of the classic nineteenth century novel, projecting the epic sweep of history, with an episodic linkage of individual incidents and characters akin to the picaresque; it is also similar to Eastern story cycles.

The Moor of the title is Moraes Zogoiby, son of Aurora Da Gama, whose lineage is Indian Muslim, and Abraham Zogoiby, whose ancestors include Muslim and Jewish exiles who were banished from Spain in 1492. Through the course of the novel, Moraes tells the story of his family from the mid-nineteenth century to the present (the 1990's), where he, the lone survivor, has returned to Spain to continue a frustrating quest for his mother's legacy: the Moorish paintings that may reveal the essential truth and meaning of his life.

This intricate, swirling mix of history, myth, legend, personal feuds, ethnic rivalries, and disappointed love is the story of a man trying to make some sense of his life as well as the story of his fascinating, driven family. It is also the saga of a country with a long past, an interim as a semisubjugated colonial entity, and a turbulent, troubled present. While much of the narrative is written with the kind of vivid, detailed realism that is one of the marks of Rushdie's style—an abundance of descriptive images and evocative details—frequent infusions of mystic moments, almost hallucinatory states of being, apparent intrusions of the supernatural, and other features of Magical Realism contribute to a larger dimension than a historic record. This is especially apparent in the presentation of Aurora

Zogoiby as a symbol for India itself, an equivalent to the *Mother India* (the name of a film released in 1957, the year of Moraes's birth) that represents all of the clashing, tempestuous qualities exerting an immense emotional pull on its inhabitants. It is also apparent in Moraes's (meaning Rushdie's) exhilarated response to and evocation of the city of Bombay, an urban masculine complement to the more pastoral, and historically traditional, feminine motherland.

Moraes states early in the novel that his account is one of regret, "a last sigh for a lost world," and the world that he re-creates or reimagines is a rich fusion of cultures, a hybrid set in sharp contrast to what Rushdie calls "the fundamentalist, totalized explanation of the world" that he has challenged throughout his work. The novel begins in the region of Cochin, where the West (Europe) and the East (India) met and mingled for the first time. It was the central site of the pepper crop, and among other extended metaphors that are threaded through the novel, spice—the source of the Da Gama family wealth—stands for passionate love. The shift from commerce in the spice trade to the contemporary economics of currency and technology underscores the separation of the human from its most significant strengths and is one of the primary causes of the downward course that the Da Gama line takes.

For Rushdie, love begins as an irresistible rush of physical feeling that overwhelms the senses but then is complicated by circumstances of family, ambition, and cultural forces beyond individual control. While Moraes maintains that "defeated love would still be love," Rushdie has observed that "the central story of Aurora and Abraham in the book is a story of what happens when love dies." Moraes struggles to fill the "dreadful vortex" of its absence, and though his life in retrospect reveals his failure in all the realms where love matters (nation, parents, partner), his efforts to understand love's power and to use it in accordance with a set of human values redeem his failure.

The loss of Moraes's family foundation due to love's blindness and treachery is balanced by the restoring capacity of the love for a place and by the invigorating experience of artistic consciousness as a means of illumination. *The Moor's Last Sigh* is a paen to a special place, the vanishing (perhaps never existent) India of Rushdie's heart's core, the "romantic myth of a plural, hybrid nation," which he lovingly describes in Aurora's paintings.

A sense of loss permeates the narrative, as Moraes's three sisters, his treacherous lover Uma Sarasvati (possibly based on Marianne Wiggins), many acquaintances, and various semiadversaries die prematurely. Adding to this loss are his estrangement from his parents and his separation from the places he has known as home. As a compensation of sorts, India continues to glow in Moraes's mind, rendered indelibly in Rushdie's verbal paintings. It is the unifying concept for what Rushdie calls "the four anchors of the soul," which he lists as "place, language, people, customs." The sheer size of the India that Rushdie constructs, in addition to a palimpsest of its layers, makes it an elusive, almost chimerical country. *The Moor's Last Sigh*, laced with loss, disappointment, frustration, and anger, is not a pessimistic vision of existence, because even when place, peoples, and customs are removed, language remains, and Moraes—who exhibits all of the verbal virtuosity that is a feature of Rushdie's style—utilizes the powers of language in the service of truth, to his last breath.

THE ENCHANTRESS OF FLORENCE

The Enchantress of Florence is an ambitious work; though presented as a novel, it more closely resembles medieval romance. It is concerned with the storytelling process more than with telling a sustained story. Frame tales appear within frame tales, and the result is a work that resembles the fifteenth century collection of stories *The Arabian Nights' Entertainments* (also known as *The Thousand and One Nights*) or perhaps John Barth's *Chimera* (1972), his own resetting of the Scheherazade tales.

The central figure of *The Enchantress of Florence* is Akbar the Great, the liberal Mughal emperor of the sixteenth century, a historical figure. Akbar represents toleration of religion, no doubt an attractive symbol for Rushdie, given the precarious circumstances under which he has lived since publication of *The Satanic Verses*. Akbar sees the world in which he lives dissolving into hatred and violence. Though something of a philosopher king, he seems paralyzed by his inability to trust any of those around him, even his closest advisers.

A mysterious traveler from the West suddenly appears at Akbar's court. He too has a basis in history, though his identifications are several. The stranger is variously Agostino Vespucci (cousin of the explorer Amerigo Vespucci), though he also calls himself "Uccello." The immediate reference appears to be to Paolo Uccello, born Paolo di Dono (1397-1475), a Renaissance painter known for his application of mathematical principles to his art in conveying perfect perspective. It is also true, however, that this relatively common Italian surname, meaning "bird," implies someone wise but crafty and possibly untrustworthy. Vespucci-Uccello has a third identity, perhaps the most significant, that of Mogor dell'Amore, the "Mughal of Love." Vespucci-Uccello-Mogor dell'Amore claims kinship with Akbar and quickly becomes his closest adviser, though even Akbar is aware of the seductive quality of his new adviser's tale telling.

The Enchantress of Florence is a verbal arabesque with an enormous number of characters. Many of these are historical figures fictionalized and reworked, such as the Medicis and Niccolò Machiavelli. There is also a variation on the Pygmalion myth. Despite his extensive harem, Akbar is able to conjure up only one, Jodha, who is perfect, and he has done this through a dream. Jodha's opposite is Qara Köz ("Black Eyes") whose androgynous sensuality fills Rushdie's romance. Rushdie channels this sensuality into aesthetics, however, for this is his abiding concern.

Robert J. Forman
Updated by Leon Lewis

OTHER MAJOR WORKS

SHORT FICTION: *East, West: Stories*, 1994; "The Firebird's Nest," 1997; "Vina Divina," 1999.

PLAY: *Midnight's Children*, pr., pb. 2003 (adaptation of his novel; with Simon Reade and Tim Supple).

NONFICTION: *The Jaguar Smile: A Nicaraguan Journey*, 1987; *Imaginary Homelands: Essays and Criticism, 1981-1991*, 1991; *The Wizard of Oz: A Short Text About Magic*, 1992; *Conversations with Salman Rushdie*, 2000 (Michael Reder, editor); *Step Across This Line: Collected Nonfiction, 1992-2002*, 2002.

BIBLIOGRAPHY

Appignanesi, Lisa, and Sara Maitland, eds. *The Rushdie File*. Syracuse, N.Y.: Syracuse University Press, 1990. Collection of essays surveys critical reaction to *The Satanic Verses*. Includes the text of the Khomeini fatwa.

Cundy, Catherine. *Salman Rushdie*. Manchester, England: Manchester University Press, 1996. Provides a good, readable introductory overview of Rushdie's fiction.

Dascalu, Cristina Emanuela. *Imaginary Homelands of Writers in Exile: Salman Rushdie, Bharati Mukherjee, and V. S. Naipaul*. Youngstown, N.Y.: Cambria Press, 2007. Examines how exile, voluntary and involuntary, has affected the work of these three quite different writers.

Goonetilleke, D. C. R. A. *Salman Rushdie*. New York: St. Martin's Press, 1998. Focuses on Rushdie's long fiction, examining the author's technique, autobiographical and historical elements in his work, and his position as a writer between cultures, among other topics.

Gurnah, Abdulrazak. *The Cambridge Companion to Salman Rushdie*. New York: Cambridge University Press, 2007. Provides a comprehensive introduction to Rushdie's work for the general reader.

Hamilton, Ian. "The First Life of Salman Rushdie." *The New Yorker*, December 25, 1995. Excellent, illuminating presentation of Rushdie's life before the fatwa, written with Rushdie's assistance and including accounts from interviews with many of Rushdie's friends and peers.

Hassumani, Sabrina. *Salman Rushdie: A Postmodern Reading of His Major Works*. Madison, N.J.: Fairleigh Dickinson University Press, 2002. Presents close readings of Rushdie's five major novels from *Midnight's Children* through *The Moor's Last Sigh*.

Pipes, Daniel. *The Rushdie Affair: The Novel, the Ayatollah, and the West*. New York: Birch Lane Press, 1990. Recounts the controversy attending publication of *The Satanic Verses*, but examines the question from the Muslim point of view. Suggests that valid arguments against publication of the novel were lost in the wake of the Khomeini fatwa that decreed Rushdie's death, in effect giving credence to the stereotype of Muslims held by many Westerners.

Rushdie, Salman. *Salman Rushdie Interviews: A Sourcebook of His Ideas*. Edited by Pradyumna S. Chauhan. Westport, Conn.: Greenwood Press, 2001. Handy selection of Rushdie's many interviews provides insight into his thinking, writing, and life experience.

Taneja, G. R., and R. K. Dhawan, eds. *The Novels of Salman Rushdie*. New Delhi: Indian Society for Commonwealth Studies, 1992. Wide-ranging compilation of essays by contributors from the Indian subcontinent covers all of Rushdie's writing through 1992 except *The Satanic Verses*. Provides a perspective beyond the criticism of Anglo-American authors.

WILLIAM SAROYAN

Born: Fresno, California; August 31, 1908
Died: Fresno, California; May 18, 1981
Also known as: William Stonehill Saroyan

PRINCIPAL LONG FICTION
My Name Is Aram, 1940
The Human Comedy, 1943
The Adventures of Wesley Jackson, 1946
Rock Wagram, 1951
Tracy's Tiger, 1951
The Laughing Matter, 1953 (reprinted as *The Secret Story*, 1954)
Mama I Love You, 1956
Papa You're Crazy, 1957
Boys and Girls Together, 1963
One Day in the Afternoon of the World, 1964

OTHER LITERARY FORMS

Despite his many novels, William Saroyan (suh-ROY-ehn) is more famous for his work in the short story, the drama, and autobiography. Each of these areas received emphasis at different stages in his career. In the 1930's, he made a spectacular literary debut with an avalanche of brilliant, exuberant, and unorthodox short stories. Major early collections were *The Daring Young Man on the Flying Trapeze, and Other Stories* (1934), *Inhale and Exhale* (1936), *Three Times Three* (1936), and *Love, Here Is My Hat, and Other Short Romances* (1938). *My Name Is Aram*, a group of stories detailing the experiences of Aram Garoghlanian growing up in a small California town, marks the culmination of his short-story artistry. Most of Saroyan's plays and his productions on Broadway were concentrated in the years between 1939 and 1942. *My Heart's in the Highlands* was produced by the Group Theatre in April, 1939. His second major production, *The Time of Your Life* (pr., pb. 1939), was awarded both the Pulitzer Prize and the New York Drama Critics' Circle Award and is still considered Saroyan's best play. *Hello Out There* (pr. 1941), a one-act play, is also regarded as a fine drama.

In 1951, Saroyan and Ross Bagdasarian published a popular song, "Come On-a My House." Saroyan also wrote several television plays, including an adaptation of *The Time of Your Life*. Starting with *The Bicycle Rider in Beverly Hills* (1952), Saroyan composed extensive memoirs, including *Here Comes, There Goes, You Know Who* (1961), *Not Dying* (1963), *Days of Life and Death and Escape to the Moon* (1970), *Places Where I've Done Time* (1972), *Sons Come and Go, Mothers Hang in Forever* (1976), *Chance Meetings* (1978), and *Obituaries* (1979).

Achievements

By the age of twenty, William Saroyan had already decided his role in life was to be that of a professional writer, and throughout his remaining fifty years he dedicated himself to that vocation, publishing voluminously in all literary forms, with the exception of poetry. The sheer bulk of his work and his admission that much of it was done merely to earn money have worked against him. Further, his frequent arguments with his critics and his increasingly difficult personality left him with few strong critical advocates.

Saroyan's lasting literary achievement is in the area of the short story, where he expanded the genre by linking narrative form to the essay and infusing his work with a highly individual vision of poetic intensity. Many of his stories feature a character modeled on Saroyan, a writer-persona who, though often obsessed with his own ideas and feelings, is vitally alive to the world of his immediate experience. Several of the most successful stories concern childhood experiences in an ethnic, small-town environment modeled on Saroyan's Fresno. Saroyan impressed his early readers with his rediscovery of the wondrous in the texture of ordinary American life. *The Saroyan Special: Selected Stories* (1948) is a collection of his best stories. *My Name Is Aram* delineates with some beautiful character portraits Saroyan's sense of the poetic interplay of values in the ethnic community.

Saroyan's plays oppose the vitality of personality and individual dreams to the force of social institutions and the threats of war. In their sense of improvised movement, his plays were a deliberate challenge to the strictly plotted productions of the commercial theater.

Starting in the mid-1940's, Saroyan turned his attention to longer fiction, writing over the next two decades a series of novels concerned with marriage and divorce. Apparently inspired by his own experiences, the books become increasingly skeptical about romantic love and reflect Saroyan's growing cynicism about the man-woman relationship while retaining his fondness for the charm of childhood.

Saroyan's longer fiction grows gradually out of those short stories concerned with growing up in a small town. *My Name Is Aram*, a story collection moving toward novelistic unity, leads directly to *The Human Comedy*, where Saroyan finally succeeds in making a novel out of his childhood material. While *The Adventures of Wesley Jackson* must be regarded as a failed attempt to write in the picaresque mode, *Rock Wagram* is a surprisingly mature handling of the thematic scope provided by the novel form. Whereas *The Adventures of Wesley Jackson* presents marriage as an idyllic goal for the solitary man, *Rock Wagram* focuses on the crushing effect of the title character's failed marriage. Several shorter book-length works—*Tracy's Tiger, Mama I Love You,* and *Papa You're Crazy*—seem more tied to Saroyan's earlier material in their confinement to the perspectives of childhood and youth and, for the most part, are limited in theme and story situations.

Saroyan's other novels—*The Laughing Matter, Boys and Girls Together,* and *One Day in the Afternoon of the World*—are deliberate forays into social areas where relationships are often intense and events are somber in their finality. Like *Rock Wagram*, each of these books centers on a male's struggle with marriage, death, and divorce. The last novel, *One Day in the Afternoon of the World*, features a character who at last seems to have acquired the wisdom to deal with such personal crises. Though his longer fictions are professionally wrought, Saroyan's achievements in the novel form are limited.

The mood of the later novels is picked up and carried to greater extremes in Saroyan's memoirs, a series whose loose formats encourage the author to reveal, often in free associations, his deep anxiety about his relationship to his society. Saroyan's memoirs, generally his weakest works, become increasingly preoccupied with death, the significance of his literary achievements, and with his struggle to ward off a bitterness that he occasionally admits but wants to deny.

Biography

So much of the work of William Stonehill Saroyan—especially his fiction—is drawn from the circumstances of his life that it has a biographical dimension. He was born in 1908, in Fresno, California, the city where he died on May 18, 1981. The child of Armenian immigrants, he faced his first hardship when, at his father's death in 1911, he was placed for four years in the Fred Finch orphanage in Oakland. During these years, his mother worked in San Francisco as a maid, finally gathering the money to move back to a house in Fresno with her four children. Here Saroyan lived from age seven to seventeen, learning Armenian, acquiring an irreverence for the town's chief social institutions—the church and the school—and working as a newspaper boy and as a telegraph messenger to help support the family.

At age fifteen, Saroyan left school permanently to work at his Uncle Aram's vineyards. In 1926, he left Fresno, first to go to Los Angeles, then, after a brief time in the National Guard, to move to San Francisco, where he tried a number of jobs, eventually becoming at age nineteen the manager of a Postal Telegraph branch office. In 1928, determined to make his fortune as a writer, he made his first trip to New York. He returned to San Francisco the following year, somewhat discouraged by his lack of success. In the early 1930's, however, he began to write story after story, culminating with his decision in January, 1934, to write one story a day for the whole month. That year, *Story* published "The Daring Young Man on the Flying Trapeze," and suddenly Saroyan stories were appearing in many of the top periodicals. His first book of stories was published that year, and the following year he had enough money to make an ethnic return, a trip to Soviet Armenia.

Except for a few months in 1936 spent working on motion pictures at the Paramount lot, Saroyan spent the majority of the 1930's in San Francisco. By 1939, he had shifted his activities to drama, writing and producing plays on Broadway. After *The Time of Your Life* won both the New York Drama Critics' Circle Award for the best play of 1939 to 1940 and the Pulitzer Prize, Saroyan made headlines by rejecting the Pulitzer on the grounds that he was opposed to prizes in the arts and to patronage. More controversy followed when he wrote *The Human Comedy* as a screenplay for Metro-Goldwyn-Mayer, then argued about directing the film and tried to buy his work back for twenty thousand dollars, more than he was paid for it. At that time he also was, in a letter to *The New York Times*, publicly denouncing the Broadway theater.

Even though he had pacificist sympathies, Saroyan was inducted into the U.S. Army in October, 1942, and served until 1945. His most traumatic experience in the 1940's, however, was his marriage to Carol Marcus, which lasted from 1943 to 1949 and which was resumed briefly from 1951 to 1953, before a final divorce. The couple had two children, Aram and Lucy.

In the 1950's, Saroyan began to write more long fiction, much of it dealing with marital difficulties. In addition, in 1951, he was the coauthor of a hit song, "Come On-a My House," and in the late 1950's, he began writing television plays. From 1952 to 1959, he lived in a Malibu beach house, an environment that encouraged him to work very steadily. During this time, he lived a less public existence and, feeling monetary pressure because of his gambling and his huge income tax debt, he increasingly developed a reputation as a difficult personality.

In 1960, after some travel about the world, he settled in a modest apartment at 74 Rue Taitbout, Paris. The following year he was briefly a writer-in-residence at Purdue University in Indiana. By 1962, he had arranged to buy two adjacent houses in Fresno and thereafter alternated living between Fresno and Paris. He spent most of the last fifteen years of his life working on various volumes of memoirs. Five days before his death he called the Associated Press to give this statement: "Everybody has got to die, but I have always believed an exception would be made in my case. Now what?" After much success (much money earned by writing, much money lost by gambling), international travel, controversy, fame, and obscurity, Saroyan died of cancer in his hometown in 1981.

Analysis

William Saroyan's work habits were a major determinant (for better or worse) of his unique literary effects. He regarded writing as work, something that required disciplined effort, but also as an activity whose chief characteristic was the free play of the mind. As he explained his practice, Saroyan would often give himself assignments, a story or a chapter a day (or so many hours of writing), but would seldom work from a detailed organizational plan. Uncomfortable with mulling over possible styles, attitudes, narrative directions, he would often prefer to plunge into writing, fueled by coffee and cigarettes, hoping that whatever got down on paper would inspire the story to "take off on its own." Whatever relationships would be worked out would be those of deep structure, drawn from his inner being rather than from rhetoric.

At times Saroyan would begin with a "theory" or abstract idea. (For example, the theory stated at the end of "War" is that hatred and ugliness exist in the heart of everyone.) The act of writing itself was to clarify and refine the idea for the writer. In "Myself upon the Earth," the writer's own situation, his dead father, and his attitudes toward the world begin to weave into the free connections that substitute for a conventional plot. Thematically, the apparently undisciplined becomes the true discipline as the dedication expressed in an attitude toward life—toward humanity—is transformed through the narration into a dedication to art.

There are obvious difficulties with this method of composition. "The Man with His Heart in the Highlands" begins in the course of its improvisation to split in two; when Saroyan puts it into the form of a full-length play, the theme of the importance of acceptance in forming the new American community is finally seen as a basic articulation in the material. Saroyan also acknowledged revision as an important stage in the writing process, but much of his work suffers from a lack of objectivity, the ability to see his own work clearly and revise it accordingly.

While the act of writing was for Saroyan both a kind of thinking and a performance, the materials of his art were usually the materials of his life. Much in the manner of Thomas Wolfe (an early influence), Saroyan's fiction was often drawn directly from his experience. A letter to Calouste Gulbenkian (in *Letters from 74 Rue Taitbout*, 1969) shows how Saroyan drew in detail on his external experience and his frame of mind for most of the content of "The Assyrian." Writing, he came to believe, was connected with "noticing" life and with the sense that life itself was theatrical. Although Saroyan acknowledged that the process of writing had to discover form in its materials and that the writer had to be transformed into a character framed by his art, the sense of witnessed scene and character in his best work lends a necessary solidity to his creative exuberance.

The favorite writer-personas in Saroyan's early fiction were poet-philosophers in the manner of Walt Whitman, American wise guys (the young grown suddenly smarter about the ways of the world than their elders), or combinations of the two. His later long fiction featured the writer as a veteran of life, sometimes bitter but with his own philosophical resignation, a mode of stoic humility about what he might be able to accomplish. Saroyan's typical themes—the advocacy of love and a condemnation of war and violence—are less important than the way in which he plays the narrator (usually a writer) against the narrator's circumstances. In the most deep-seated manifestation of this paradigm—the ethnic boy responding to his American environment—Saroyan associates the ethnic self in the ethnic community with naturalness, lack of self-consciousness, true being, and dignity of person. The American environment, while it promises opportunity with its training and its competitive games, also has institutions that seem to specialize in modes of restriction, punishment, and prejudice.

The ethnic boy responds to his environment with a complex involvement and detachment. On one hand, he is willing, even eager, to be assimilated; on the other hand, however, he is always aware of a kind of existence that has no adequately defined relationship to the American world of conventional social fact. The ethnic's psychological relationship to the world recalls Whitman's democratic paradox of people being intensely individual and at the same time like everyone else. In Saroyan's fiction, there is at times an emphasis on the individual's alienation—as when the protagonist in "The Daring Young Man on the Flying Trapeze" feels "somehow he had ventured upon the wrong earth" and the central character in "1,2,3,4,5,6,7,8" feels the room he is living in is not a part of him and wants a home, "a place in which to return to himself." Invariably, however, the ethnic family and its small-town environment expand quite naturally for Saroyan into a version of the democratic family of people.

This sense of communal home, however, is not easily preserved—as Saroyan's novels with their marital catastrophes and lonely protagonists repeatedly demonstrate. From the beginning, the fate of Saroyan's ethnicity was complicated by the fact that his deepest allegiance was to a national community that no longer existed. In an early story, "Seventy Thousand Assyrians," the Assyrian states, "I was born in the old country, but I want to get over it . . . everything is washed up over there." Though Saroyan could be sympathetic to such practicality, he tried to achieve, often with a deliberate naïveté, a poetic point of view that would embrace both existence in the old community of family values (which was a basic part of his being) and existence in the practical new world (which offered the only opportunity for becoming).

From the perspective of Saroyan's writer-persona, the world outside is continually new, funny, sometimes strange, often wonderful, a place of innocent relationships and suspended judgments. A recurring situation in his work has someone who is apprehended for theft trying to explain that he is not guilty because his value system is different from that of his accusers. On one hand, Saroyan believes in an attitude of joyful acceptance: Here he sees man "on the threshold of an order of himself which must find human reality a very simple unavoidable majesty and joy, with all its complications and failures." On the other hand, he imagines, like Whitman, a more somber mystic vision based on "the joyous sameness of life and death." In this mysterious crucible, life is fate, perhaps only glimpsed fully when "drawing to the edge of full death every person is restored to innocence—to have lived was not his fault." Saroyan's basic impulse is to preserve, recapture, and restore the innocence that the world has lost that state of being that sees experience only as a fantastic fate that serves ultimately to redeem the primal self.

My Name Is Aram

Like Sherwood Anderson's *Winesburg, Ohio* (1919) and William Faulkner's *The Unvanquished* (1938), *My Name Is Aram* is a book that falls midway between short-story collection and novel. The stories are separate and distinct, but they all concern the small-town experiences of the same boy, Aram, with his Armenian relatives. There is little sense of sequence but rather an accumulated manifestation of the potential wisdom in this world. Saroyan emphasizes the preservation of innocence, the warding off of the absolute element in the values of the adult culture. Aram and his friends turn social rituals into human games, and in the course of their experiences demonstrate that the many social failures in these stories have really two constituents, the innocent immediacy of the experience (its essential value) and the cultural "truths" and judgments applied to it. Through vital participation in their world, Aram and his friends begin to negotiate its preconceived ideas.

THE HUMAN COMEDY

The setting, the characters, and the young man's perspective that predominate in *The Human Comedy* all have their sources in Saroyan short stories. The background is World War II, and the California small town has accordingly become "the home front." In the book's basic drama, the innocence in this environment—its vulnerable children, young people, and women and its emotional closeness—must come to terms with death and its finalities.

Within the context of the small-town milieu, the novel focuses primarily on the Macauley family and most often on Homer Macauley, a fourteen-year-old telegraph messenger boy. As Homer delivers telegrams announcing the deaths of soldiers, he finds himself getting caught up psychologically in the shock of the family reactions. On his first such delivery, to Rosa Sandoval, the woman responds with an eerie, calm hysteria in which she confuses Homer with her dead son and begins to think of both as little boys. Feeling at first both compassion and an urge to flee, Homer gradually arrives at an awareness of the meaning of death. With the help of his mother (whose husband has recently died), he fights through feelings of loneliness and isolation toward the idea that death and change afford perspectives for redeeming the values of innocence, love, and life itself.

The ideal of the community dominates the book. The novel implies in its moments of crisis and healing—Homer becoming briefly transformed into the son of another woman; Tobey taking the place of the dead Marcus in the Macauley family—that humankind is a single family. Though the fact of death and the awareness of death are constant threats to the individual, the book, as the allusions to Homer's *Odyssey* (c. 725 B.C.E.; English translation, 1614) imply, is about to return home, the coming back from the ugly realities of the outside world to the love and security that humankind can provide.

The book seems intent on assuring its readers that despite economic tribulations, the discontent of restless desire, the anxiety connected with competition, and the confining tendency of its institutions, the community is an active, positive force. A working out in the rhythms of experience of the differences between people—age, sex, degrees of formality—invariably shows positive contrasts. The many relationships Homer has with older people are all thematically active ingredients for dramatizing the closeness of the community. *The Human Comedy* insists—perhaps too facilely at times—on the capacity of the American community to regulate the experience of life and the encounter with death.

THE ADVENTURES OF WESLEY JACKSON

The Adventures of Wesley Jackson may be Saroyan's worst novel. It is marred by two closely related problems, an uncertain grasp of form and a confusion about its issues.

Saroyan's indiscriminate use of his own military experience takes the novel hopelessly out of control. Evidently attempting to give himself ample latitude with the novel form, Saroyan chose to employ the picaresque form, referring in his comments on the novel to Mark Twain's *Adventures of Huckleberry Finn* (1884). Unfortunately, Wesley is much too introverted to be an effective picaro of any kind. He is intended to be a nonconformist, but, except for a few anti-Army establishment opinions, his personal idealism and prosaic earnestness only serve to make him seem as remote from the realities of Army life as from the realities of war. Lacking a feeling for the actual operations of the Army, the book meanders haphazardly from the bureaucratic to the personal, from one location to another, from family concerns to writing ambitions, succeeding finally in giving the impression of an Army journal rather than a picaresque novel.

At times the book develops an antiwar theme; at times the theme seems to be the pettiness of the Army bureaucracy. No one theme, however, is developed consistently. Wesley's self-absorbed narration does provide some shaping by turning the officers into bad fathers (cruel figures of authority), the women into sympathetic (though vague) images, and his fellow soldiers into boys, sometimes naughty but basically innocent. In sporadic, almost desultory, fashion the first part of the book features Wesley's search for his father, the essentially good man who has been displaced and ignored by organized society. The last part of the book becomes concerned with Wesley's search for a son (actually a search for a woman to bear him a son). Were Wesley's narration less limited, less egotistical, these thematic threads might have made firmer connections.

Rock Wagram

The split structure of *Rock Wagram*—approximately half the novel taking place in September, 1942, and half in February, 1950—emphasizes the drive of Rock Wagram (pronounced vah-GRAM) to be married to Ann Ford and his resultant puzzled desperation when that marriage fails. The chronological gap, by omitting the marriage and Rock's military experience, accents the negative quality of this part of his life. Yet by leaving out the specific difficulties that are so much a part of his later depression, the novel makes Rock's psychology a problematic frame for understanding events instead of using the events of the past to put his psychology in an understandable perspective. At times, the failure of the marriage seems explained by Ann's frivolous, lying character. At other times, the failure seems to grow out of Rock's ethnic assumption that people must become involved in a family existence.

Rock Wagram explores the tensions between people as individuals and people as social animals. In his motion-picture career, Rock has become successful as an individual star, but his acquaintance with Ann Ford kindles his memories of certain values from his Armenian background, particularly the notion that a man is not complete until he had founded his own family, been husband to his wife, father to his children. Unhappily for him, Ann turns out to be like so many other characters whose departures from their true natures disturb him; her lies signify to him that she is refusing to be herself, hoping for something better. Earlier Rock has met a series of males rebelling against their heritage: Paul Key, the Hollywood producer who hates being a Jew; Sam Schwartz, Paul's nephew, who devotes himself to becoming the image of success; and Craig Adams, the completely assimilated Armenian. Although these men are denying both their heritage and their own individuality, they are better adapted to the world of casual social relationships than he, and the book raises doubts about the possibilities of a deeply authentic existence.

Rock chooses to see his life—and the life of humans—as involving continual adjustment to a Shavian life force, a power that, once he begins to perceive it through his Armenian ethnic environment, becomes his ultimate guide to true being. To get in tune with this force, he tries to be uninhibited in his social relationships, to go with the flow of events, to pay attention to his circumstances and to the people he is with, and to be, as he puts it, "a good witness" to his own experience and to his world.

Part of Rock's effort to live in terms of true being is a half-conscious cultivation of strategies toward death. His reaction to the death of his brother Haig is rage; at the death of his friend Paul Key, he affects a Hemingwayesque stoicism; and to his mother's death, he responds by plunging deeply and intensely into his subjective nature. In spite of all attempts to come to terms with the reality of death, he seems at last depressed, left with a sense of being part not only of a dying culture but also of a dying world. As he goes back to acting at the end of the narrative, his feeling for his art is one of obligation rather than enthusiasm for an individualized expression of himself. Yet, as the humor in his last statement indicates, he is finally not without hope in probing his lonely situation for its satisfactions.

THE LAUGHING MATTER

The laughter of *The Laughing Matter* is that of black comedy. From the time Swan Nazarenus announces to her husband that she is pregnant with another man's child, *The Laughing Matter* moves powerfully but erratically toward what seems an almost self-indulgently gruesome ending. The story line is captive to the emotional tensions and explosions of Evan Nazarenus as he attempts to sort out a future direction for himself, Swan, and their two children, Red and Eva. As he resorts successively to drink, violence, a return to family harmony, an abortion, and more violence, the problem-pregnancy tends to be obscured by his confusing attempts at solution. Since his personality is never clarified in the characterization, and since he often gives the impression of running aimlessly about the countryside, Evan becomes progressively less sympathetic in his shifting relationship to people and events.

The accompaniment to the mad rhapsody of his behavior is more carefully controlled. The children are innocent victims, becoming increasingly aware that something is wrong and even acting out some of the tensions themselves. The Walzes, a neighbor couple, have their own fights, and Evan's brother, Dade, who has, after years of domestic turbulence, lost his family entirely, conveniently defines one possible outcome.

Complicating the question of what to do is the issue of who is to blame. In one scene between Evan and Dade, the two brothers—who often speak in an old-country tongue—review their ethnic fate as heads of families, Evan wondering what they as males have done wrong. Evan debates whether he ought to be more feminine, more kindly, or strive to retain his masculine pride in the face of what may be an essential challenge to his person. His solution, the abortion, is less an act of harsh morality (as he later views it) than the result of a desire to begin again, to regain a kind of innocence by reversing events.

The ironies and the deaths pile up so rapidly at the conclusion that they achieve only a blurred effect. The fact that so much violence results from simple ignorance begins to make the characters comic rather than tragic, and this may have been the prompting behind Saroyan's title. When Evan accuses the wrong man as the adulterer (pushing the poor lonely man toward suicide), and when he shoots and kills his brother Dade under the mistaken notion that they have been responsible for Swan's death from abortion, Evan seems more the incompetent than the grief-stricken victim. His own death in an auto accident may have been meant to suggest that the whole chain of events was merely a series of accidents, but this must be weighed against the remarks of the doctor who explains to Dade that Swan committed suicide and that she had evidently had a strong death wish for several years. For all its masculine madness, this book begins and ends by pointing an accusing finger at the woman.

BOYS AND GIRLS TOGETHER

Boys and Girls Together is a realistic study of a husband-wife relationship that moves with an understated satire toward black humor. The husband, Dick, is a writer who finds that his current domestic relationship has made it impossible for him to work, thus heaping financial strain upon his already turbulent marriage to Daisy. In the course of their sporadic fighting, the couple discovers greater and greater depths of incompatibility. Dick comes to the conclusion that she is ignorant, trivial, and selfish; Daisy accuses him of being egotistical and immature. Were it not for the two children (Johnny, age five, and Rosey, age two and a half), the writer, who is a family man, would undoubtedly leave.

As this account of a few days in their lives demonstrates, what keeps the marriage together is their socializing with other couples. The slight story line follows the meeting of Dick and Daisy with two other couples for a few days of fun in San Francisco. Though only casual friends, all the couples have common characteristics: In each instance, the husband has achieved prominence in the arts; in each case, the husband is many years older than the wife and the difference in age seems part of the strain on the marriage. Before all six can get together, the oldest husband, Leander, dies of a heart attack, an episode witnessed by Oscar Bard (the actor) and his wife, and by Leander's wife Lucretia. Dick and Daisy arrive soon after the attack and seem generally ineffective in preventing the scene from sliding from seriousness to farce. Dick eventually begins to act as satiric observer, commenting on Oscar's egotistical discomfort and on Lucretia's performance as grieving widow.

The scene has its climax in Oscar's long speech on the difficulties of their kind of marriage. While he begins by pointing out realistically that the women they have married are not for them, he finally comes to the conclusion that it is sexual attraction that gives the necessary life to all partners in such marriages and that makes them continue to put up with each other. Dick does not disagree. Soon the survivors are planning a trip to Reno as another distraction from the harsh realities around them. Earlier, Dick had resented it when his wife teased him about being a fool for sex. In the last part of the novel, his understated satiric vision outlines them all as characters in a sexual farce.

If all of Saroyan's writing can be regarded as his attempt to understand and define his position in the world, his long fiction must be seen as his deliberate recognition of the crueler circumstances in that world—death, the failure of love, divorce, the recalcitrant details of life itself. His own marital troubles undoubtedly inspired the novels of the 1950's and 1960's with their fragmented families, and while the intently masculine perspective in these books reveals a serious but virtually unexamined reverence for love and marriage, it also demonstrates the author's own very personal irritation with wives.

In nearly all of Saroyan's novels, the formal problem tends to be the male protagonist's varied reactions to his situation. In *Rock Wagram* and *The Laughing Matter,* Saroyan is successful in focusing these reactions by means of intense emotional pressures, but his confusion about final blame for the marital breakdown makes a fictional closure difficult. With *Papa You're Crazy* and *Mama I Love You,* he moves to the detachment of the child's point of view but is still uncertain about the extent to which the world's facts ought to—and must—impinge on the individual family member. (To what degree, for example, does the particular existence of the parent doom or mold the life of the child?) In *Boys and Girls Together* and *One Day in the Afternoon of the World,* Saroyan gets mixed results from mining the attitudes of his male protagonists for a perspective that would be both a consistent and legitimate interpretation of their marital situations. In Saroyan's long fiction, as well as in his other writing, both his strengths and his weaknesses derive from his insistent emotional presence.

Walter Shear

Other major works

SHORT FICTION: *The Daring Young Man on the Flying Trapeze, and Other Stories,* 1934; *Inhale and Exhale,* 1936; *Three Times Three,* 1936; *The Gay and Melancholy Flux: Short Stories,* 1937; *Little Children,* 1937; *Love, Here Is My Hat, and Other Short Romances,* 1938; *The Trouble with Tigers,* 1938; *Peace, It's Wonderful,* 1939; *Three Fragments and a Story,* 1939; *The Insurance Salesman, and Other Stories,* 1941; *Saroyan's Fables,* 1941; *Forty-eight Saroyan Stories,* 1942; *Dear Baby,* 1944; *Some Day I'll Be a Millionaire: Thirty-four More Great Stories,* 1944; *The Saroyan Special: Selected Stories,* 1948; *The Fiscal Hoboes,* 1949; *The Assyrian, and Other Stories,* 1950; *The Whole Voyald, and Other Stories,* 1956; *William Saroyan Reader,* 1958; *Love,* 1959; *After Thirty*

Years: The Daring Young Man on the Flying Trapeze, 1964; *Best Stories of William Saroyan,* 1964; *The Tooth and My Father,* 1974; *The Man with the Heart in the Highlands, and Other Early Stories,* 1989.

PLAYS: *The Hungerers: A Short Play,* pb. 1939; *My Heart's in the Highlands,* pr., pb. 1939; *The Time of Your Life,* pr., pb. 1939; *The Beautiful People,* pr. 1940; *The Great American Goof,* pr. 1940; *Love's Old Sweet Song,* pr., pb. 1940; *The Ping-Pong Game,* pb. 1940 (one act); *Subway Circus,* pb. 1940; *Three Plays: My Heart's in the Highlands, The Time of Your Life, Love's Old Sweet Song,* 1940; *Across the Board on Tomorrow Morning,* pr., pb. 1941; *Hello Out There,* pr. 1941 (one act); *Jim Dandy,* pr., pb. 1941; *Three Plays: The Beautiful People, Sweeney in the Trees, Across the Board on Tomorrow Morning,* 1941; *Razzle Dazzle,* 1942 (collection); *Talking to You,* pr., pb. 1942; *Get Away Old Man,* pr. 1943; *Sam Ego's House,* pr. 1947; *A Decent Birth, a Happy Funeral,* pb. 1949; *Don't Go Away Mad,* pr., pb. 1949; *The Slaughter of the Innocents,* pb. 1952; *The Cave Dwellers,* pr. 1957; *Once Around the Block,* pb. 1959; *Sam the Highest Jumper of Them All: Or, The London Comedy,* pr. 1960; *Settled Out of Court,* pr. 1960; *The Dogs: Or, The Paris Comedy, and Two Other Plays,* 1969; *An Armenian Trilogy,* 1986 (includes *Armenians, Bitlis,* and *Haratch*); *Warsaw Visitor and Tales from the Vienna Streets: The Last Two Plays of William Saroyan,* 1991.

SCREENPLAY: *The Human Comedy,* 1943.

NONFICTION: *Harlem as Seen by Hirschfield,* 1941; *Hilltop Russians in San Francisco,* 1941; *Why Abstract?,* 1945 (with Henry Miller and Hilaire Hiler); *The Twin Adventures: The Adventures of William Saroyan,* 1950; *The Bicycle Rider in Beverly Hills,* 1952; *Here Comes, There Goes, You Know Who,* 1961; *A Note on Hilaire Hiler,* 1962; *Not Dying,* 1963; *Short Drive, Sweet Chariot,* 1966; *Look at Us,* 1967; *I Used to Believe I Had Forever: Now I'm Not So Sure,* 1968; *Letters from 74 Rue Taitbout,* 1969; *Days of Life and Death and Escape to the Moon,* 1970; *Places Where I've Done Time,* 1972; *Sons Come and Go, Mothers Hang in Forever,* 1976; *Chance Meetings,* 1978; *Obituaries,* 1979; *Births,* 1983.

CHILDREN'S LITERATURE: *Me,* 1963; *The Circus,* 1986; *Horsey Gorsey and the Frog,* 1968.

MISCELLANEOUS: *My Name Is Saroyan,* 1983 (stories, verse, play fragments, and memoirs); *The New Saroyan Reader,* 1984 (Brian Darwent, editor).

BIBLIOGRAPHY

Balakian, Nona. *The World of William Saroyan.* Lewisburg, Pa.: Bucknell University Press, 1998. Balakian, formerly a staff writer for *The New York Times Book Review,* knew Saroyan personally in his last years, and her observations of him color her assessment of his later works. She viewed it as her mission to resurrect his reputation and restore him to his place among the finest of twentieth century American writers. Her book traces Saroyan's evolution from ethnic writer to master of the short story, to playwright, and finally to existentialist.

Floan, Howard R. *William Saroyan*. New York: Twayne, 1966. Floan's study remains one of the best extensive critical monographs on Saroyan's work. It focuses on Saroyan's early literature, glossing over the post-World War II period as less productive and durable. Contains a valuable annotated bibliography through 1964.

Foster, Edward Halsey. *William Saroyan*. Boise, Idaho: Boise State University Press, 1984. A condensed but helpful survey stressing Saroyan's unique voice. This work draws parallels between his work and that of the Beat generation. Includes bibliography.

Haslam, Gerald W. "William Saroyan." In *A Literary History of the American West*, edited by Thomas J. Lyon et al. Fort Worth: Texas Christian University Press, 1987. A good introduction to Saroyan's life and work. Haslam focuses on the writer's post-World War II decline in popularity and its cause. Includes a select bibliography.

———. "William Saroyan and San Francisco: Emergence of a Genius (Self-Proclaimed)." In *San Francisco in Fiction: Essays in a Regional Literature*, edited by David Fine and Paul Skenazy. Albuquerque: University of New Mexico Press, 1995. Haslam's discussion of the influence of San Francisco on Saroyan's work is included in this collection of essays that examine the relationship between the "real" city and its fictional depiction.

Keyishian, Harry, ed. *Critical Essays on William Saroyan*. New York: G. K. Hall, 1995. A collection of essays on Saroyan, from early reviews to critical articles. Some of the essays discuss Saroyan in California, the writer and his critics, and Saroyan's study of ethnicity.

Lee, Lawrence, and Barry Gifford. *Saroyan: A Biography*. New York: Harper & Row, 1984. Lee and Gifford's study is rich with anecdotes and segments of interviews with Saroyan's family, friends, and associates. Supplemented by a chronology and a bibliography.

Leggett, John. *A Daring Young Man: A Biography of William Saroyan*. New York: Alfred A. Knopf, 2002. Leggett relies heavily on Saroyan's journals to produce a sustained look at the author that is neither admiring nor forgiving. Includes a bibliography and an index.

TOBIAS SMOLLETT

Born: Dalquhurn (now Renton), Scotland; March 19, 1721 (baptized)
Died: Antignano (now in Italy); September 17, 1771
Also known as: Tobias George Smollett

PRINCIPAL LONG FICTION
  The Adventures of Roderick Random, 1748
  The Adventures of Peregrine Pickle: In Which Are Included Memoirs of a Lady of Quality, 1751
  The Adventures of Ferdinand, Count Fathom, 1753
  The Adventures of Sir Launcelot Greaves, 1760-1761
  The Expedition of Humphry Clinker, 1771

OTHER LITERARY FORMS

Tobias Smollett combined his medical practice with an active and varied career as a man of letters. His earliest, though unsuccessful, effort was as a playwright with *The Regicide: Or, James the First of Scotland, a Tragedy* (pb. 1749), published by subscription a full ten years after fruitless attempts at having it staged in London. Two other disappointments followed with his inability to secure a production for *Alceste* (pb. 1748-1749), a combination of opera, tragedy, and masque, and with the rejection of his first comedy, *The Absent Man* (wr. 1751), which was never produced or published. Both of these works have now been lost. His only success on the stage came finally with *The Reprisal: Or, The Tars of Old England* (pr. 1757), a comedy; this farce was produced by David Garrick at the Theatre Royal, Drury Lane.

Smollett's deep moral energy surfaced in two early verse satires, "Advice: A Satire" (1746) and its sequel, "Reproof: A Satire" (1747); these rather weak poems were printed together in 1748. Smollett's poetry includes a number of odes and lyrics, but his best poem remains "The Tears of Scotland." Written in 1746, it celebrates the unwavering independence of the Scots, who had been crushed by English troops at the Battle of Culloden.

As Smollett's literary career grew, his hackwork for publishers increased with translations. His most popular work among these projects was *A Complete History of England* (1757-1758) and its sequel, *Continuation of the Complete History of England* (1760-1765). He took great pride in his achievements as a historian and as a historical editor of *A Compendium of Authentic and Entertaining Voyages* (1756). A diversity of interests from medicine to politics prompted the writing of numerous pamphlets and essays. *An Essay on the External Use of Water* (1752) was a farsighted proposal for the improvement of public hygiene at Bath that caused a furor among the resort's staff and patrons.

Though his health was rapidly deteriorating from overwork, Smollett completed a thirty-five-volume edition of *The Works of M. de Voltaire* (1761-1774). In the hope that a warm climate would improve his health, he traveled to France and Italy, and on returning to England he published *Travels Through France and Italy* (1766). His didactic observations instructed his readers to accept England, for all its faults, as the best nation for securing happiness on Earth. His last nonfiction works were *The Present State of All Nations* (1768-1769) and the political satire *The History and Adventures of an Atom* (1749, 1769). Editor Lewis M. Knapp offers the best modern edition of the *Letters of Tobias Smollett* (1970).

Achievements

Tobias Smollett cannot be said to have added dignity to the art of the novel in the manner of Henry Fielding's imitation of the epic, nor can it be argued that he gave form to the genre as did Samuel Richardson, yet the eighteenth century novel cannot be discussed without giving full attention to Smollett's stylistic virtuosity and satiric intent.

Smollett successfully challenged Richardson's and Fielding's substantial popular reputation by providing "familiar scenes in an uncommon and amusing point of view." In *The Adventures of Roderick Random* (commonly known as *Roderick Random*), his first novel, he displayed a thorough understanding of the distinction between the novel and the romance, of which Samuel Johnson would speak in *The Rambler* essays (1750-1752). Borrowing from Latin comedy and Elizabethan drama, Smollett created caricatures of human beings with the dexterity of William Hogarth and Thomas Rowlandson. Though his characters lack the psychological depth of those of Richardson, they possess breathtaking energy and evocative power.

Only in the late twentieth century did Smollett's role in the development of the English novel become fully appreciated. Criticism of that time emphasized the wrongheadedness of viewing Smollett's satiric energy as a deviation from Fielding's epic ambitions for the novel. Instead, Smollett is seen at the beginning of another tradition. Sir Walter Scott and Charles Dickens both valued Smollett's work; Dickens acknowledged his debt to Smollett's picaresque realism and comic characterization in *Pickwick Papers* (1836-1837, serial; 1837, book). Among modern novelists, the savage comedy of writers as various as Evelyn Waugh and Joseph Heller is in Smollett's tradition rather than that of Fielding or Richardson.

Smollett's works continue to provoke critical inquiry. The Oxford English Novels series has published all five of his novels, and the University of Delaware has published its *Bicentennial Edition of the Works of Tobias Smollett*, with *The Expedition of Humphry Clinker* (commonly known as *Humphry Clinker*) appearing in 1979.

Biography

Tobias George Smollett was born at Dalquhurn, Dumbartonshire, in western Scotland, and baptized on March 19, 1721. He was the son of Archibald Smollett, a lawyer, who suffered from ill health, and Barbara Cunningham Smollett, a woman of taste and elegance but no fortune. Smollett's grandfather, of whom the boy was especially proud, had been knighted by King William in 1698 and had become an influential member of the landed gentry as a local Whig statesman. When Smollett's father died only two years after his son's birth, the family suffered from lack of money.

Smollett's education, for all of his family's financial deterioration, was of superior quality though erratic. He entered Dumbarton Grammar School in 1728, remaining for five years, and received the traditional grounding in the classics. His matriculation to Glasgow University (though officially unrecorded) was interrupted when he became a Glasgow surgeon's apprentice while still attending university medical lectures. In the fall of 1739, Smollett was released from his apprenticeship to go to London; now eighteen, he had some reputation as a writer of earthy satires and doggerel. While traveling to London, Smollett carried the manuscript of a tragedy, *The Regicide*, which, he soon realized, would provide no entrée for him with the London theater managers. He is described at this time as "attractive, entertaining as a *raconteur*, and blessed with self-assurance." His future as a London man of letters uncertain, Smollett received advice from a number of Scottish physicians suggesting he continue practicing medicine. On March 10, 1740, he received a medical warrant from the navy board and embarked on the HMS *Chichester* as a surgeon's second mate.

The author's naval experience, material used later for *Roderick Random*, began during the outbreak of war with Spain and continued through the bloody Carthagena, West Indies, expedition of 1741. Smollett returned to England in 1742 but was drawn back to Jamaica, where he resided until 1744. While living on the island, he met Anne Lassells, the daughter of an established family of planters; they married in 1743.

Smollett, on the advice of his wife's family, returned to London alone, where he set up a practice as a surgeon on Downing Street in May, 1744. Having never lost hope of a literary career, he worked on improving his fluency in Spanish and then began translating Miguel de Cervantes' *Don Quixote de la Mancha* (1605, 1615); his translation was published in 1755. The years from 1747 to 1750 were marked by considerable literary activity, numerous changes in residence, various trips abroad, a widening circle of acquaintances, and the birth of his only child, Elizabeth, in 1747.

In January, 1748, *Roderick Random* was published; this was followed by the impressive translations of Alain Le Sage and Cervantes, and in 1749, *The Regicide* was printed. The success of *Roderick Random* was instantaneous and prolonged, with sixty-five hundred copies sold in twenty-two months; it was to rival the popularity of Fielding's *Joseph Andrews* (1742). The success of *Roderick Random*, which was written in less than six months, became a kind of revenge on the theater managers of London. During this period, Smollett made plans to produce *Alceste*, his opera (George Frideric Handel was contracted for the music), but this effort was to fail; only a lyric from this work survives. Furthermore, Smollett's failure at drama was a continuing source of frustration throughout his career.

In June, 1750, Smollett purchased his medical degree from Marischal College, Aberdeen, and in the same month moved his family to Chelsea, a fashionable London suburb. It became an ideal home for him, where both his medical practice and his writing flourished; he remained there for thirteen years until forced abroad by his health in 1763. It was in Chelsea that he wrote *The Adventures of Peregrine Pickle* (commonly known as *Peregrine Pickle*), a work of nearly 330,000 words composed at top speed in anticipation of a trip to Paris. On February 25, 1751, his second novel was published to laudatory reviews and wide popularity.

Smollett's involvement with various periodicals began during the 1750's, first as a book reviewer for the *Monthly Review* and later as editor and proprietor of the *Critical Review*. Smollett joined Oliver Goldsmith in launching the *British Magazine* (the *Monthly Repository* beginning in 1760), remaining as coeditor until 1763. With a final venture, Smollett gained public notoriety and untold enemies by agreeing to write the *Briton*, a political effort in support of Lord Bute's ministry. Of Smollett's various journalistic efforts, only the work in the *Critical Review* is exceptional; as a literary periodical, it remains one of the most significant of the last half of the eighteenth century.

In the early 1750's, Smollett was driving himself to escape debt. Publishing a medical paper, *An Essay on the External Use of Water*, brought him little money, and in February, 1753, his third novel, *The Adventures of Ferdinand, Count Fathom* (commonly known as *Ferdinand, Count Fathom*), was published with poor financial results. The book attracted few readers, and Smollett was forced to borrow money and to supplement his medical fees with further hackwork. The years of hack writing began in earnest with *A Complete History of England*, a translation of Voltaire's writings, a geographical reference work, and several digests of travel.

The period from 1756 to 1763 destroyed Smollett's health, but his reputation as a critic and a successful writer became unquestioned. Unfortunately, this frantic production hardly kept him from debtor's prison. Returning to the novel in the *British Magazine*, Smollett published "the first considerable English novel ever to be published serially"— *The Adventures of Sir Launcelot Greaves* (commonly known as *Sir Launcelot Greaves*). In monthly installments from January, 1760, to December, 1761, the novel gave the sixpenny periodical substantial popularity.

In the middle of this literary hard labor, Smollett was imprisoned for three months, having been convicted of libeling an Admiral Knowles in an article in the *Critical Review*. On his release in early 1761, Smollett continued fulfilling his contracts with certain booksellers but also traveled extensively, possibly to Dublin, even though troubled by asthma and tuberculosis. In addition to these difficulties, his spirit was nearly broken by the illness and death of his daughter in April, 1763. This final shock caused him to cut all his London ties and move his family to the Continent, hoping to calm his wife and cure his ailments in the mild climate of the south of France and Italy. He spent two years abroad, returning to England in July, 1765; the literary result of his tour was *Travels Through France and Italy*.

Though ill health plagued him, he sought for the third time a consulship but was rejected; in 1768 he left England for the last time.

Arriving in Pisa, Italy, Smollett visited with friends at the university, finally settling at his country villa in Antignano, near Leghorn, in the spring of 1770, where he completed his masterpiece, *Humphry Clinker*. Immediately following its publication, he received the rave notices of friends and critics concerning the novel, but he had little time to enjoy the praise. On September 17, 1771, he died from an acute intestinal infection and was buried at the English cemetery at Leghorn.

Analysis

Tobias Smollett not only is a great comic novelist but also a morally exhilarating one—a serious satirist of the brutality, squalor, and hideous corruption of humankind. His definite moral purposes are firmly grounded in the archetypal topic of all novelists—people's unceasing battle for survival in the war between the forces of good and evil. Smollett insists that people defy "the selfishness, envy, malice, and base indifference of mankind"; in such a struggle, the hero will ultimately prevail and will be rewarded for his (or her) fortitude.

Roderick Random

The principal theme of Smollett's first novel, *Roderick Random*, is the arbitrariness of success and failure in a world dominated by injustice and dishonesty. Smollett's decision to use realistic detail as a guise for his satire produces a lively and inventive work; moreover, the hero, Roderick, is not a mere picaro nor a passive fool but an intent satiric observer "who recognizes, reacts, and rebukes." The novel is organized in a three-part structure. The initial stage reveals Roderick's numerous trials as a young man; he loses his innocence during the years of poverty in Scotland, of failure in London, and of brutal experience in the Navy. The middle of the narrative embodies "the lessons of adversity" as the hero declines into near collapse. In a final brief section, Roderick recovers his physical and moral equilibrium and promotes the simple human values of friendship, love, and trust as the only viable bases for a satisfying existence.

Roderick's problem is both to gain knowledge of the world and to assimilate that knowledge. M. A. Goldberg, in *Smollett and the Scottish School* (1959), finds that "at first his responses are dictated by his indignation, by passions . . . eventually, he learns . . . to govern the emotions with reason." The struggle between these two forces is central to an understanding of eighteenth century England and its literature. In Smollett's first novel, good sense seems a sufficient defense against the sordid viciousness of the world. Good sense, however, can only be achieved, or learned, when the hero can control his pride and passionate nature, which are inextricably linked. Equilibrium, an orderly existence, arises paradoxically from the ashes of his random adventures. This understanding develops as the hero pursues the happiness he thinks he deserves but can never fully attain; as a good empiricist, Roderick gathers knowledge from each reversal, finally achieving a "tranquillity of love" with the prudent Narcissa.

In *Roderick Random*, the hero's search for happiness differs significantly from the quest of the traditional picaro. While gaining an education and suffering the rebukes of others, Roderick remains good and effectual, unlike Don Quixote, who is powerless against cruelty. Roderick's youthful ferocity contributes to the practicality of the satire. Smollett's approach to correcting the ills of society is to allow no attack or insult to go unavenged. A thorough whipping of a bully or the verbal punishment of a pedant lifts the book beyond the picaresque and advances it past the formal verse satire. The center of the satiric discussion implicates the surroundings and not the hero, thus permitting Smollett to offer a long list of evil, self-centered figures who provide an excellent contrast to the goodness and charity of the ill-served protagonist. Only his faithful servant, Strap; his uncle, Tom Bowling; and the maid, Narcissa, join him in opposing his neglectful grandfather, the scoundrel Vicar Shuffle, the tyrannical Captain Oakum, the dandiacal Captain Whiffle, and the rapacious Lord Strutwell.

The last section of the novel provides the hero with the riches of his long quest: family, wealth, and love. The moral of the adventures follows as Roderick's recently discovered father "blesses God for the adversity I had undergone," affirming that his son's intellectual, moral, and physical abilities had been improved "for all the duties and enjoyments of life, much better than any education which affluence could bestow." The felicity of this final chapter provides a conventional ending, but the crucial point is that Roderick, having completed a rigorous education in the distinctions between appearance and reality, is now deserving of these rewards.

PEREGRINE PICKLE

The protagonist of Smollett's long second novel, *Peregrine Pickle*, reminds one of Roderick in every aspect, except that Peregrine is an Englishman, not a Scot. The supporting players are improved; among the novel's outstanding comic creations are Commodore Hawser Trunnion and the spinster, Grizzle Pickle. Often described as the best picaresque novel in English, *Peregrine Pickle* satirizes the upper classes of mid-eighteenth century England. Rufus Putney argues in "The Plan of *Peregrine Pickle*" (1945) that Smollett

> meant to write a satire on the affectations and meannesses, the follies and vices that flourished among the upper classes in order that his readers might learn with Peregrine the emptiness of titles, the sordidness of avarice, the triviality of wealth and honors, and the folly of misguided ambition.

The novel begins by sketching Peregrine's social and emotional background and introducing other principal characters. Following this introductory section, Smollett's protagonist describes his adolescence and education at Winchester and Oxford, where he becomes addicted to coarse practical jokes and to satisfying his overbearing pride. Here the hero meets Emilia, a beautiful orphan with whom he falls in love; because of his capricious nature, however, he cannot remain long with her. Having become alienated from his parents, Peregrine departs on the Grand Tour with the best wishes of his guardian, Trunnion.

Peregrine returns from France an unprincipled, arrogant rogue whose every action supports his vanity. After numerous incidents including the death of Trunnion and his replacement with the eccentric Cadwallader Crabtree as Peregrine's mentor, the hero tests the virtue of Emilia and is rebuffed. The remainder of the novel observes the long distress, the eventual imprisonment, and the final rehabilitation of the protagonist, who by now is convinced of the fraud and folly of the world. As Putney mentions, only after matriculating to the "school of adversity," which reduces his pride and vanity, can Peregrine hope to achieve wealth, marry his true love, triumph over his enemies, and retire to the country. Adversity teaches him to distinguish between the complex vices of the urban sophisticates and the simpler but more substantial pleasures of generosity and love in a rural retreat. Despite its picaresque vigor and satisfactory resolution, the novel suffers from a confusion of purposes: Peregrine's arrogance undermines the credibility of his role as a satirist of high society. Thus, Smollett's satiric intentions are blunted by his aspirations to a novel of character.

FERDINAND, COUNT FATHOM

Ferdinand, Count Fathom is remembered today for its dedication, in which Smollett gives his famous definition of the novel, and for its place as the first important eighteenth century work to propose terror as a subject for a novel. In *The Novels of Tobias Smollett* (1971), Paul-Gabriel Boucé finds that the major defect of the novel is the author's "mixture of genres, without any transition brought about by unfolding of the story or the evolution of the characters." Fathom's dark cynicism informs the majority of the work, with the last ten chapters unraveling into a weak melodrama; nevertheless, Smollett's satire remains effective as a bitter denunciation of the hypocrisy and violence of elegant society. As an early contribution to the literature of terror, the novel probes the emotions of a young, virtuous girl who undergoes isolation, deprivation, and sadistic brutality at the hands of a rapacious creature. The figure of Fathom is used to undercut sentimental conventions and show their uselessness when civilized norms are forgotten.

SIR LAUNCELOT GREAVES

Sir Launcelot Greaves completed serialization in December, 1761, and was published as a book in March, 1762. Because of its serial publication, the novel's structure suffers from the frequent contrivance of artificial suspense. Modern criticism, however, has pointed to an underlying thematic unity based on a series of variations on the theme of madness, with minute investigation into the physical, psychological, and moral aspects of the disorder. Greaves, the quixotic hero, launches a noble crusade for reform. His hopeless demand that a corrupted world listen to reason embraces Smollett's social idealism. If moral intention were the only measure of a novel's worth, then the didactic power of *Sir Launcelot Greaves* would guarantee its success; unfortunately, the delicate balance of the genre remains disordered by the force of an overobvious moral preoccupation.

HUMPHRY CLINKER

Smollett's last novel, *Humphry Clinker*, appeared in the bookstalls on June 15, 1771; Smollett had written the three volumes over a five-year period. It is his masterpiece, and it remains among the great English novels. The work was inspired by the epistles of Christopher Anstey's witty and popular *New Bath Guide* (1766).

Using the epistolary method instead of the travel narrative of the early novels, Smollett characterizes his correspondents by means of their wonderfully individual letter-writing styles. Old Matthew Bramble of Brambleton Hall, Wales, travels with his household through Gloucester, Bath, London, Scarborough, Edinburgh, Cameron (Smollett country), Glasgow, Manchester, and home again. Squire Bramble suffers various physical complaints, and his ill health makes him sensitive to the social ills surrounding him on his journey. Bramble searches for a recovery but finds himself becoming worse, not better, yet his compassionate nature remains undiminished. The journey was begun so that Bramble might distract his young niece, Lydia Melford, from a strolling actor named Wilson. The party also includes Tabitha, his aging, narrow-minded, old-maid sister; her malapropic maid, Winifred Jenkins, the classic example of the illiterate servant; and the modishly cynical nephew, Jery. En route, they adopt, much to Tabitha's delight, a Scottish veteran of American Indian warfare, Obadiah Lismahago. Soon, they add Humphry Clinker to the party as a new footman; he turns out to be the natural son of Matthew.

There are three major plots to develop, and numerous minor episodes, all of which hinge on the characteristic picaresque device of the journey; Smollett exchanged the rogue hero for a group of picaros—Bramble and nephew Jery—who analyze and observe society. Through careful stages in letter after letter, Matthew's character is revealed to the reader, who learns to trust him as a reliable observer of society's foibles; in this respect *Humphry Clinker* is much stronger than *Peregrine Pickle*, where the satire was blunted by the protagonist's unreliability.

Smollett's satire strikes not individuals but categories of people and assorted social institutions; in particular *Humphry Clinker* is an exposé of the false attitudes and disordered life of the eighteenth century nouveaux riches. His conservative political views are displayed in Bramble's rages against an unrestricted press, politically biased juries, and the ignorance of the mob, and, as in *Peregrine Pickle*, he contrasts the folly and depravity of urban life with idealized pictures of the country.

Smollett's achievement in *Humphry Clinker* depends on his skillful use of the picaresque and epistolary traditions. His last novel is also distinguished by a warmth and tolerance not found to such a degree in his earlier works. Bramble's cynicism never becomes obnoxious to the reader; the brutality of Roderick is muted here. Smollett allows his hero to accept human society, despite "the racket and dissipation." Finally, for all his burlesque of Samuel Richardson's epistolary method, Smollett's characterization of Lydia has a depth and intensity that raises her above mere romantic convention.

In contrast to many critical reports, *Humphry Clinker* ends on a buoyant note of pure happiness, a happiness that fulfills the eighteenth century dictum of conformity to the universal order. Smollett's novels embrace moral and virtuous methods for pursuing one's goals. Passions and reason must remain in balance, and within this harmony, nature and art can moderate the demands of vice and folly.

Paul J. deGategno

OTHER MAJOR WORKS

PLAYS: *The Regicide: Or, James the First of Scotland, a Tragedy*, pb. 1749; *The Reprisal: Or, The Tars of Old England*, pr. 1757.

NONFICTION: *The History and Adventures of an Atom*, 1749, 1769; *An Essay on the External Use of Water*, 1752; *A Compendium of Authentic and Entertaining Voyages*, 1756; *A Complete History of England*, 1757-1758; *Continuation of the Complete History of England*, 1760-1765; *Travels Through France and Italy*, 1766; *The Present State of All Nations*, 1768-1769; *Letters of Tobias Smollett*, 1970 (Lewis M. Knapp, editor).

TRANSLATIONS: *The Adventures of Gil Blas of Santillane*, 1748 (of Alain René Le Sage's novel); *The History and Adventures of the Renowned Don Quixote*, 1755 (of Miguel de Cervantes' novel); *The Works of M. de Voltaire*, 1761-1774 (35 volumes); *The Adventures of Telemachus, the Son of Ulysses*, 1776 (of François de Salignac de La Mothe-Fénelon's novel).

BIBLIOGRAPHY

Beasley, Jerry C. *Tobias Smollett: Novelist*. Athens: University of Georgia Press, 1998. Beasley devotes separate chapters to an analysis of each of Smollett's five novels, which he interprets as "exercises in the visual imagination," written by an author who believed the private, interior life could be defined by the externally visible.

Bold, Alan, ed. *Smollett: Author of the First Distinction*. New York: Barnes & Noble Books, 1982. A collection of essays about Smollet's work, with four essays discussing general issues and five concentrating on each of the major novels. Includes a bibliography and an index.

Brack, O. M., Jr, ed. *Tobias Smollett, Scotland's First Novelist*. Newark: University of Delaware Press, 2007. Collection of essays on both the fiction and nonfiction, including a discussion "On the External Uses of Water in *The Expedition of Humphrey Clinker*" and a comparison of novels by Smollett and Henry Fielding.

Bulckaen, Denise. *A Dictionary of Characters in Tobias Smollett*. Nancy, France: University Press of Nancy, 1993. A useful way to keep track of the multitude of characters in

Smollett's fiction. Each character is identified; chapter and page number of the character's first appearance are also cited. There is also an index of the main categories of characters.

Gibson, William. *Art and Money in the Writings of Tobias Smollett*. Lewisburg, Pa.: Bucknell University Press, 2007. Gibson analyzes Smollett's novels and nonfiction writing, focusing on issues of aesthetics, commercialism, luxury, and taste, to describe how these works provide insights into the eighteenth century art world.

Grant, Damian. *Tobias Smollett: A Study in Style*. Totowa, N.J.: Rowman & Littlefield, 1977. As the title suggests, Grant ignores questions of realism and moral purpose to concentrate on what he regards as Smollett's three styles: comic, passionate, and, to a lesser extent, lyrical.

Lewis, Jeremy. *Tobias Smollett*. London: Jonathan Cape, 2003. An appreciative look at Smollett's life, written by an acclaimed biographer. Includes a bibliography and an index.

Spector, Robert D. *Smollett's Women: A Study in an Eighteenth-Century Masculine Sensibility*. Westport, Conn.: Greenwood Press, 1994. Organized differently from most books on Smollett, with chapters on society, personality, and literary tradition; heroines, fallen women, and women as victims; and the comic and the grotesque. Includes notes and a bibliography.

_____. *Tobias George Smollett*. 1968. Rev. ed. Boston: Twayne, 1989. The first chapter of the book quickly surveys Smollett's minor works; the rest of the book is a consideration of his novels. Contains an annotated bibliography of secondary criticism.

JONATHAN SWIFT

Born: Dublin, Ireland; November 30, 1667
Died: Dublin, Ireland; October 19, 1745

Principal long fiction
A Tale of a Tub, 1704
Gulliver's Travels, 1726 (originally titled *Travels into Several Remote Nations of the World, in Four Parts, by Lemuel Gulliver, First a Surgeon, and Then a Captain of Several Ships*)

Other literary forms

Jonathan Swift's oeuvre includes a large and important body of verse, best assembled in *The Poems of Jonathan Swift* (1937, 1958), edited by Harold Williams. His letters may be found in *The Correspondence of Jonathan Swift* (1963-1965), also edited by Williams. Outstanding among a variety of political writings are Swift's contributions to *The Examiner* (1710-1711), the treatise called *The Conduct of the Allies and of the Late Ministry, in Beginning and Carrying on the Present War* (1711), and the important *The Drapier's Letters to the People of Ireland* (1735).

His prose writings have been published together in *The Prose Works of Jonathan Swift* (1939-1968), a fourteen-volume collection edited by Herbert Davis.

Achievements

It is generally conceded that Jonathan Swift is the greatest satirist among English-language writers, possibly the most brilliant ironist and acerb wit in any language. The force of his satiric barbs has rendered him controversial, however, and many critics have retaliated against his potent quill by claiming that Swift is reckless, uncontrolled, spiteful, insensate, heathenish, and insane. Such rash responses merely demonstrate the powerful effects of his writing.

Swift is not an overt lampooner, diatribe-monger, or name-caller. Curiously, he never utilizes the direct approach; he almost always speaks through a defective mouthpiece, a flawed, self-incriminating persona who forges a case against himself. Indeed, Swift is to be remembered as a grand satiric mimic, finely shaping and generating the voices of knaves and fools alike (the "modern" hack writer in *A Tale of a Tub*, the ignorant serving-woman Frances Harris, the idiot astrologer Isaac Bickerstaff, the callous and mathematical Modest Proposer, the proud but demented simpleton Lemuel Gulliver).

Swift's ear for clichés and inflections of dullness is almost perfect, and authors such as Herbert Read (in *English Prose Style*, 1928) have hailed Swift as the inevitable and clear master of "pure prose" style. Swift is, without doubt, the major satirist in prose, yet he is also a first-rate light poet (in the manner of Horace and the coarser Samuel "Hudibras"

Jonathan Swift
(Library of Congress)

Butler), and, if anything, his reputation as a poet is rising. Furthermore, Swift wrote political pamphlets with ruthless force, and his prose in sermons, letters, and treatises is virile and direct. Finally, Swift should not be forgotten as wit and jester. He invented a child-language when corresponding with Stella, wrote mock-Latin sayings, devised wicked epigrams, created paraphrases of Vergil and Ovid, and could even toy with versifying when devising invitations to dinner. In a word, Swift is the all-around expert in English in straightforward exposition—especially when it is bent to provoke savage mockery and the *jeu d'esprit*.

Biography

Jonathan Swift was born in Dublin, Ireland, on November 30, 1667, after the death of his father, a lower-middle class Anglo-Irishman. His grandfather, the Reverend Thomas Swift, had been a vicar in Herefordshire. His father, also named Jonathan, had settled in Ireland to work as a steward of the King's Inns in Dublin. His mother was Abigail Erick, the daughter of a Leicestershire clergyman. Swift's mother entrusted her young son to a nurse, who spirited the infant Swift away from Ireland for several years; he was eventually returned, and he was peculiarly linked with Ireland throughout his life. In any case, it was his fancy to picture himself a lonely outcast amid barbarians.

Swift attended Kilkenny School in his youth and Trinity College, Dublin, obtaining a bachelor's degree in 1686. He spent most of the following decade at Moor Park, Surrey, in the household of Sir William Temple, the distinguished Whig statesman. It was at Moor Park that Swift met, in 1689, the child of Esther Johnson (whom Swift later immortalized as "Stella"), the daughter of Temple's widowed housekeeper. Swift helped in supervising her education and inaugurated a lifelong (and little understood) relationship, for Stella later immigrated to Dublin and spent her life near the Anglican Dean Swift. Naturally, under Temple's aegis, Swift hoped for introductions and advancement, but little came of promises and possibilities, and in 1694 he returned to Dublin long enough to be ordained an Anglican priest (in 1695). He subsequently was reunited with Temple until the latter's death in 1699. Thereafter, he returned to Ireland as chaplain to the Earl of Berkeley. His reputation for talent and wit was rapidly growing.

Swift's great political period took place in London from 1708 to 1714. He became the chief spokesman, apologist, and pamphleteer for the powerful Tory leaders then in power, Robert Harley and Henry St. John, first Viscount Bolingbroke. Their fall and disgrace ushered in a lengthy era of Whig dominance that permanently drove Swift back to what he must have considered exile in Ireland. Swift had been finally rewarded (although he would have perceived it as a paltry recognition) with the deanery of St. Patrick's Cathedral in Dublin, where he served for the remainder of his life. His powerful satires had earned him powerful enemies, and significant advancement in the Anglican Church or in England was never permitted to him.

In any event, Swift served with precision, justness, and rectitude as a clergyman and continued throughout his career to be an admirable satirist and wit. He even elected to champion the rights of the maltreated Irish, and he came to be admired as their avatar and protector, a "Hibernian Patriot." In his last years, Swift suffered increasingly from deafness and vertigo (the results of a lifelong affliction by Ménière's syndrome, a disease of the inner ear), which resulted in senility and, most likely, a stroke. Guardians were appointed to oversee his affairs in his last years, and he died in 1745, shortly before his seventy-eighth birthday.

Swift played his last ironic jest on humankind in his will, which committed the bulk of his estate to the founding of a "hospital" for fools and madmen, just as he had pronounced the plan in his *Verses on the Death of Dr. Swift, D.S.P.D.* (1739):

> He gave the little Wealth he had,
> To build a House for Fools and Mad;
> And shew'd by one satyric Touch,
> No Nation wanted it so much

Analysis

It must be noted that Jonathan Swift's "fictions" are nothing like conventional novels. They seldom detail the "adventures" of a hero or even a protagonist and never conclude with a character's romantic achievement of goals or fulfillment of desires. Indeed, Swift is the great master of fictionalizing nonfiction. His satires always purport to be something factual, humdrum, diurnal, unimaginative: a treatise, a travel diary, an annotated edition, a laborious oration, a tendentious allegory, a puffed-out "letter to a friend." Extremist Protestant sects condemned fiction, and "projectors" and would-be investigators in the dawning age of science extolled the prosaic, the plodding, the scholarly, the methodical, and the factual. At the same time, urban population growth and the rise of the middle class created a growing new audience, and printing presses multiplied in accordance with demand. Many "popular" and best-seller art forms flourished: sermons, true confessions, retellings (and second parts) of hot-selling tales and political harangues, news items, hearsay gossip, and science all became jumbled together for public consumption, much of which led to spates of yellow journalism. Throughout his life Swift rebelled against such indelicacies and depravities, and his satiric procedure included the extremist parody of tasteless forms—*reductio ad absurdum*. It was by such means that Swift secured his fame as an author.

A Tale of a Tub

Doubtless his most dazzling prose performance of this kind was his earliest, *A Tale of a Tub*, which appeared anonymously in 1704. (Swift, in fact, published most of his satires anonymously, although his work was usually instantly recognized and acclaimed.) *A Tale of a Tub* is actually a "medley" of pieces imitating the penchant for an author's combining fiction, essays, letters, verse, fragments, or anything else to enable him to amass a book-length manuscript. It contains "The Battle of the Books," a wooden allegorical piece in the manner of *Aesop's Fables*, detailing the "quarrel of ancients versus moderns," and a fragmentary treatise titled "The Mechanical Operation of the Spirit," trussed up in the inept form of a casual letter to a friend.

The treatise mocks the new "scientific" trend of reducing all things to some species of Cartesian (or Newtonian) materialism. Rather comically, it deploys in a blasé manner the language of ancient Greek and Roman atomists—Democritus and Epicurus—as if they were contemporary modernists. Indeed, one pervasive theme throughout this volume is the ridiculousness of the modernist position of "independence"—although the moderns might be ignorant of the past, the ideas and genres of classical antiquity keep recurring in their works, a fact that belies their supposed originality (even while demonstrating that, as a result of solipsism, their form and control disintegrate into chaos).

Clearly, the titular piece, "A Tale of a Tub," is Swift's early masterpiece and one of the great (and most difficult) satires in any language. In its pages, an avowed fanatic "modern" aspires to "get off" an edition, to tout and sell himself, to make money, to demonstrate his uniqueness and, however evanescently, tyrannically to be "the latest modern." He seeks to reedit an old tale of three brothers and their adventures. Naturally, he decorates and updates such a version to give it the latest cut and fashion, the style and wit and jargon of the moment. (It is perhaps an accident that this tale of the dissensions of Peter, Martin, and Jack parallels the vicissitudes of the history of Christianity, as it splinters into differing and quarreling religious sects. The modern appears ignorant of historical sense.)

The new version of the old story, however, is fragmented: Every time the modern's imagination or his fancy supplies him with a spark, he promptly follows his rather meandering muse and travels into an elaboration, an annotation, or a digression. In fact, the opening fifty pages of the work are cluttered with the paraphernalia of "modern" publishing: dedications, publisher's comments, introductions, apologies, notes to the second edition, acknowledgments, prefaces, and forewords. Thereafter, when such a cloud of ephemeral formalities would seem to have been dispensed with, the author still manages to interject a plethora of digressions—afterthoughts, asides, cute remarks apropos of nothing, commentary, snipings at critics, obsequious snivelings for the reader, canting pseudophilosophy for the learned, and pity and adoration for himself. In no time at all, the entire tale is awash in detours, perambulations, and divagations.

This modern storyteller is nothing if not effervescent, boorish, and chronically self-indulgent. He claims that his pipe dreams and diversions are in essence planned excursions and in fact deliberately philosophical meditations, rich with allegorical meanings. The opposite is also true, and the modern's tub is like an empty cart—rattling around most furiously in its vacuity, making the most noise. Furthermore, the digressions become unwieldy. The tale is disrupted more and more frequently, and the digressions become longer and longer. The modern is his most penetrating in the trenchant section IX—a digression in praise of madness—as he coyly confesses that his reason has been overturned, his intellect rattled, and that he has been but recently confined. The continued multiplication of digressions (until they subvert sections of the tale) and the finale, when the modern loses his notes and his ramblings give out entirely, are easily understood as the wanderings of a madman—a modern who suppresses the past, memory, reason, and self-control. If Swift's warning about the growing taste for newness, modernity, and things-of-the-moment appears madcap and farcical, it is nevertheless a painfully close nightmare preview of future fashions, fantasms, and fallacies that subsequently came to be real.

A Tale of a Tub clearly demonstrates several of Swift's most common fictional ploys and motifs. Some representative of the depraved "moderns" is usually present, always crass, irreligious, ignorant, arrogant, proud, self-adulatory, concerned with the events of the moment. Indeed, Swift was fond of scrupulously celebrating every April 1 as All Fools' Day, but he also recognized April 2: All Knaves' Day. He doubtless felt that both halves of humankind deserved some token of official recognition. Swift also favored mixing the two, however: He frequently shows readers that a man who is manipulator, con man, and knave in one set of circumstances is himself conned, befooled, and gulled in another. As such, the modern reveals an unexpected complexity in his makeup; he also illustrates the era (as Swift imagines it) that he inhabits—a period overfull of bad taste and poor writing, which are the broad marks of cultural decadence.

In the work of a satirist, the world is regularly depicted as cyclic in historic periods, and usually in decline. Swift and Sir William Temple both stressed some trend toward decay in the modern era and spoke often of barbarians and invasions; it was a type of satiric myth suitable to the disruptive fictions that the satirist envisions. In section IX of *A Tale of a Tub*, the modern vacillates between viewing all humankind as "curious" or "credulous," as busy probers, analysts, and excavators or as superficial and inert: knaves versus fools. As is typical of Swift, the fool and knave personas are infused with enough familiar traits to suggest that all people partake of either. Further, Swift entraps his reader by implying that there are no other categories: One is either fool or knave or both. His irony is corrosive and inclusive, capturing the reader in its toils. In that sense, Swift is deliberately disruptive; he seeks to startle and to embroil the reader in his fictions about stupidity and depravity. To such an end, he tampers with logic to make his case appear substantial and manipulates paradox to keep his readers off balance. Such techniques lend Swift his volatile force.

These strategies are to be found in Swift's best verse; the same may be said for his two great ironic short-prose pieces: *Argument Against Abolishing Christianity* (1708) and *A Modest Proposal for Preventing the Children of Poor People of Ireland from Being a Burden to Their Parents or the Country, and for Making Them Beneficial to the Public* (1729). Both of these works seek to shock the reader and to propose the discomforting, the alarming, the untenable.

GULLIVER'S TRAVELS

Swift's undisputed masterpiece is *Gulliver's Travels*, originally titled *Travels into Several Remote Nations of the World, in Four Parts, by Lemuel Gulliver, First a Surgeon, and Then a Captain of Several Ships*. This fictional work accommodates all of Swift's perennial themes and does so effectually. First, the work is perhaps the definitive study of new middle-class values, specifically the preoccupation with slang, cash, smug self-righteousness, self-assertion, and self-congratulation. Second, it might not be considered a "novel" in the conventional sense of the term, but it is a delightfully fact-filled simulation of adventure fiction, and it stems assuredly from the satiric picaresque tradition (in Spain and France) that greatly contributed to the formulation of modern novelistic techniques and themes.

Swift's Lemuel Gulliver (a mulish gull) is a model representative of the fool and the knave: He aspires to befool others but nevertheless befuddles himself. His medium is the very popular literary genre of the travelogue, or record of a "voyage of discovery." The genre grew popular through its Cartesian emphasis on an inductive observer-self and the Romantic subject of adventures in far-off lands. Such a travelogue format allows the narrator to take his readers on a vicarious journey of adventure and concludes by suggesting that the traveler has fulfilled the pattern of the bildungsroman and has attained education, growth, experience, and Aristotelian *cognitio* (insight, maturation, the acquisition of new knowledge). As might be expected in an exemplary case manipulated by Swift, Gulliver is anything but the apt learner. He is a crass materialist for whom experiences consist of precise measurements of objects observed, a tedious cataloging of dress, diet, and customs, and an infinite variety of pains in note taking, recording, transcribing, and translating. He is superficiality and rank objectivity incarnate. Naturally, therefore, his everyday mean density prevents his acquisition of any true understanding.

Gulliver is a minor physician, the mediocre little man, anxious, like Daniel Defoe's Robinson Crusoe, to make sightseeing tours and to acquire cash. His first of four voyages carries him to the land of six-inch mites, the Lilliputians, and his second voyage to the land of gargantuan giants, the Brobdingnagians. Gulliver remains myopic in both locations, for he can hardly consider that tiny creatures can (and do) perpetuate monstrous deeds, and, once he perceives that the giants are rather tame, he leaps to the conclusion that they are infinitely superior to other human types (even though their political and social institutions are no better than they should be, given the quirks and flaws of human nature). In sum, the tour from very small to very large merely stimulates in Gulliver a sense of wondrous contrast: He expects in these different worlds wondrous differences.

Amusingly, what the reader finds is much the same—that is, the uneven and imperfect human nature. Equally amusing, Gulliver behaves much the same himself in his attempts to ingratiate himself with his "superiors": He aspires to become a successful competitor in all worlds as a "titled" nobleman, a "nardac," a "courtier" with "connections" at court. Like many middle-class people, he is a man in the middle, aspiring above all for upward mobility, mouthing the commonplaces of the day, utterly incapable of judging people and events. He is also the worst sort of traveler; he is a man who sees no further than his own predilections and preconceptions and who imitates all the manners that he sees around him. Actually, the realms of big and little are merely distortions of the real world. Here, one of the work's central ironies is found in the fact that Gulliver could have learned as much, or as little, if he had stayed at home.

The world of sizes is replaced in Gulliver's third voyage by the world of concepts: The muddled peoples he visits are victims of mathomania and abstraction-worship. At the same time, it is revealed that the world of the past, like the world of the present, has been tainted and corrupt. Even the potentially ideal Struldbruggs, who live forever, are exposed as being far from lucky. They are, rather, especially accursed by the afflictions of impotence, depression, and senility. Swift has, with cartoon facility, carted Gulliver all around the world, showing him the corrosive face of fallen humanity, even among the various robbers, cowards, pirates, and mutineers that had beset him as he traveled in European ships—but Gulliver does not see.

The stage is properly set for the fourth voyage. Utilizing his favorite ploys of reversal and entrapment, Swift puts Gulliver into a land of learned and rational horses (the

Houyhnhnms) and debauched hairy, monkeylike beasts (the Yahoos). Once again, there is no middle ground: All in this world is rational horse or wolfish (and oafish) bestiality. Obviously, Gulliver chooses the equestrian gentlemen as his leaders and masters. (Indeed, throughout all the voyages, Gulliver the conformist is in quest of a staid position and "masters" who will tell him what to do and grant him praise and sustenance for his slavish adulation.)

Slowly it is revealed, however, that the Yahoos are men: Gulliver *is* a debased, gross, and deformed member of the Yahoo tribe; as Swift sweetly and confoundingly phrases it, Gulliver is a "perfect yahoo." The horses themselves rebuff this upstart, and Gulliver, who has undergone every other sort of ignominy in the course of his travels, is finally evicted as an undesirable alien from the horsey paradise. At last, Gulliver thinks he has learned a lesson; he aspires to be a horse, and, back in Europe, he shuns the human species and favors the environs of straw and stables. He has hardly acquired the rationality of his leaders and appears quite mad. Swift's ultimate paradox seems to imply that people can "know" about reason and ideals but can never master or practice them. Even here, however, Swift cruelly twists the knife at the last moment, for Gulliver, several years later, is revealed as slowly forgetting his intense (and irrational) devotion to the Houyhnhnms and slowly beginning to be able to tolerate and accept the lowly human race that he had earlier so intransigently spurned. Gulliver cannot even stick to a lesson painfully and rudely learned during many years; he lacks the brains, drive, ambition, and consistency necessary to keep him on any course. Gulliver's travels eventually get him nowhere.

In sum, *Gulliver's Travels* makes a huge tragicomical case for the absurdity of pretentious humankind. Gulliver is fool enough to believe that he is progressing and knave enough to boast about it and to hope to gain some position and affluence from the event. At his proudest moments, however, he is little more than a driveler, a gibbering idiot who is raveningly insane. Gulliver's painful experiences and the brute instruction his readers acquire are a caustic finale to much of the heady and bold idealism of the Renaissance and a cautionary plea for restraint in an era launched on celebrating reason, science, optimism, and enlightenment. Time has shown that Swift was largely right: Blithe superconfidence in people, their sciences, and their so-called progress is very likely to come enormously to grief. *Gulliver's Travels* speaks to everyone because it addresses crucial issues about the human condition itself.

John R. Clark

OTHER MAJOR WORKS

POETRY: *Cadenus and Vanessa*, 1726; *On Poetry: A Rapsody*, 1733; *Verses on the Death of Dr. Swift, D.S.P.D.*, 1739; *The Poems of Jonathan Swift*, 1937, 1958 (3 volumes; Harold Williams, editor).

NONFICTION: *A Discourse of the Contests and Dissensions Between the Nobles and the Commons in Athens and Rome*, 1701; *The Battle of the Books*, 1704; *The Accomplishment* of the First of Mr. Bickerstaff's Predictions, 1708; *Argument Against Abolishing Christianity*, 1708 (first published as *An Argument to Prove That the Abolishing of Christianity in England May, as Things Now Stand, Be Attended with Some Inconveniences, and Perhaps Not Produce Those Many Good Effects Proposed Thereby*); *Predictions for the Year 1708*, 1708; *A Project for the Advancement of Religion, and the Reformation of Manners by a Person of Quality*, 1709; *A Vindication of Isaac Bickerstaff, Esq.*, 1709; *The Conduct of the Allies and of the Late Ministry, in Beginning and Carrying on the Present War*, 1711; *A Proposal for Correcting, Improving, and Ascertaining the English Tongue, in a Letter to the Most Honourable Robert Earl of Oxford and Mortimer, Lord High Treasurer of Great Britain*, 1712; *The Public Spirit of the Whigs, Set Forth in Their Generous Encouragement of the Author of the Crisis*, 1714; *A Letter from a Lay-Patron to a Gentleman, Designing for Holy Orders*, 1720; *A Proposal for the Universal Use of Irish Manufacture*, 1720; *A Modest Proposal for Preventing the Children of Poor People of Ireland from Being a Burden to Their Parents or the Country, and for Making Them Beneficial to the Public*, 1729; *The Drapier's Letters to the People of Ireland*, 1735; *A Complete Collection of Genteel and Ingenious Conversation, According to the Most Polite Mode and Method Now Used at Court, and in the Best Companies of England, in Three Dialogues*, 1738; *Directions to Servants in General...*, 1745; *The History of the Four Last Years of the Queen, by the Late Jonathan Swift DD, DSPD*, 1758; *Journal to Stella*, 1766, 1768; *Letter to a Very Young Lady on Her Marriage*, 1797; *The Correspondence of Jonathan Swift*, 1963-1965 (5 volumes; Harold Williams, editor).

MISCELLANEOUS: *Miscellanies in Prose and Verse*, 1711; *Miscellanies*, 1727-1733 (4 volumes; with Alexander Pope and other members of the Scriblerus Club); *The Prose Works of Jonathan Swift*, 1939-1968 (14 volumes; Herbert Davis, editor).

BIBLIOGRAPHY

Barnett, Louise. *Jonathan Swift in the Company of Women*. New York: Oxford University Press, 2007. Focuses on Swift's relationships with the women in his life and his attitudes toward the fictional women in his texts. Explores Swift's contradictory views and illustrates how he respected and admired individual women yet loathed the female sex in general. Offers a critical, nonjudgmental discussion of the misogynistic attitude Swift displays in his writing when he expresses contempt and disgust for the female body.

Connery, Brian A., ed. *Representations of Swift*. Newark: University of Delaware Press, 2002. Collection of essays examines, among other topics, Swift's treatments of gender, class, and Ireland. Includes an analysis of *A Tale of a Tub*.

Ehrenpreis, Irvin. *Swift: The Man, His Works, and the Age*. 3 vols. Cambridge, Mass.: Harvard University Press, 1962-1983. Monumental biography rejects long-held myths about Swift and provides much previously unavailable information about the author and his works. Relates Swift to the intellectual and political currents of his age.

Fox, Christopher, ed. *The Cambridge Companion to Jonathan Swift*. New York: Cambridge University Press, 2003. Collection of essays about Swift's life and work includes analysis of *A Tale of a Tub* and *Gulliver's Travels* and discussions of Swift's religion, the language and style of his works, and his representation of women.

Fox, Christopher, and Brenda Tooley, eds. *Walking Naboth's Vineyard: New Studies of Swift*. Notre Dame, Ind.: University of Notre Dame Press, 1995. Collection of essays opens with an introduction that discusses Swift in relation to Irish studies, and the subsequent essays all consider aspects of Swift as an Irish writer.

Glendinning, Victoria. *Jonathan Swift: A Portrait*. New York: Henry Holt, 1998. Biography serves to illuminate Swift's nature as a proud and intractable man. Investigates the main events and relationships of Swift's life, which may be viewed as a tapestry of controversy and paradox.

Hunting, Robert. *Jonathan Swift*. Boston: Twayne, 1989. Good source of biographical information as well as insightful, if general, analysis of Swift's art. Devotes one chapter to *Gulliver's Travels*. Includes chronology, notes and references, bibliography, and index.

Kelly, Ann Cline. *Jonathan Swift and Popular Culture: Myth, Media, and the Man*. New York: Palgrave, 2002. Chronicles the creation of Swift's literary legend in his own time and in succeeding generations. Swift realized that in "a print-contracted world, texts create authors, not the other way around," and Kelly demonstrates how the writer constructed a print persona that differed from the "real" individual.

Nokes, David. *Jonathan Swift, A Hypocrite Reversed: A Critical Biography*. New York: Oxford University Press, 1985. Offers a good introduction for the general reader seeking information about Swift's life and works, drawing heavily on Swift's writings. Nokes views Swift as a conservative humanist.

Palmieri, Frank, ed. *Critical Essays on Jonathan Swift*. New York: G. K. Hall, 1993. Collection of essays is divided into sections on Swift's life and writings, *Gulliver's Travels*, *A Tale of a Tub* and eighteenth century literature, and his poetry and nonfiction prose. Includes index.

Quintana, Ricardo. *The Mind and Art of Jonathan Swift*. 1936. Reprint. New York: Oxford University Press, 1953. One of the standards of Swift criticism, concentrating on the public Swift. Examines his political activities and writings, tracing the intellectual sources of his thought. Includes synopses of his major works and provides historical background.

Rawson, Claude. *The Character of Swift's Satire: A Revised Focus*. Newark: University of Delaware Press, 1983. Presents eleven essays by Swift scholars, including John Traugatt's excellent reading of *A Tale of a Tub*, Irvin Ehrenpreis on Swift as a letter writer, and F. P. Lock on Swift's role in the political affairs of Queen Anne's reign.

VOLTAIRE
François-Marie Arouet

Born: Paris, France; November 21, 1694
Died: Paris, France; May 30, 1778
Also known as: François-Marie Arouet

PRINCIPAL LONG FICTION

Zadig: Ou, La Destinée, histoire orientale, 1748 (originally published as *Memnon: Histoire orientale*, 1747; *Zadig: Or, The Book of Fate*, 1749)
Le Micromégas, 1752 (*Micromegas*, 1753)
Histoire des voyages de Scarmentado, 1756 (*The History of the Voyages of Scarmentado*, 1757; also known as *History of Scarmentado's Travels*, 1961)
Candide: Ou, L'Optimisme, 1759 (*Candide: Or, All for the Best*, 1759; also known as *Candide: Or, The Optimist*, 1762; also known as *Candide: Or, Optimism*, 1947)
L'Ingénu, 1767 (*The Pupil of Nature*, 1771; also known as *Ingenuous*, 1961)
L'Homme aux quarante écus, 1768 (*The Man of Forty Crowns*, 1768)
La Princesse de Babylone, 1768 (*The Princess of Babylon*, 1769)

OTHER LITERARY FORMS

Voltaire (vohl-TAYR) is probably the most prolific and versatile writer of any age. He wrote in all the literary forms, and he wrote in them concurrently. His numerous plays fill 6 volumes, and his correspondence 102 volumes. He was especially active toward the end of his life; living at Ferney in his eighties, he wrote pamphlets, many plays, and one of his best philosophical poems, *Épître à Horace* (1772). He went to Paris at the age of eighty-three, shortly before he died, to see a production of his latest classical tragedy, *Irène* (pr. 1778). At the time of his death, he was at work on a new play and rewriting others.

In many ways, Voltaire wished to be considered as a defender of the classical tradition. His plays are mainly classical, embodying the unities and dealing with highborn heroes. *Œdipe* (pr. 1718; *Oedipus*, 1761) was widely acclaimed in Voltaire's day, as were *Zaïre* (pr. 1732; English translation, 1736) and *Mérope* (1743; English translation, 1744, 1749). He also, however, introduced devices and techniques that ultimately led to the demise of classical theater, including local color, such as red togas for members of the Senate in *Brutus* (pr. 1730; English translation, 1761) and real cannon fire in *Adélaïde du Guesclin* (pr. 1734). Voltaire's later plays include a certain amount of tearful sensibility that was a characteristic of Denis Diderot's bourgeois dramas.

Voltaire composed many kinds of poetry. As a young man, he achieved much acclaim with his epic poem *La Ligue* (1723) and *La Henriade* (1728, a rewriting of *La Ligue*; *Henriade*, 1732). *Henriade*, which narrates Henry IV's successful struggle against the

Voltaire
(Library of Congress)

Catholic League, was reprinted through the beginning of the nineteenth century. Today, these poems have no appeal. Voltaire also wrote satiric and philosophical poetry, including *Le Mondain* (1736; *The Man of the World*, 1764). This poem caused a scandal with its suggestion that a pleasurable life on earth is the only positive happiness one can grasp and that one should enjoy it rather than wait for a life after death. This element of audacious irreverence is a quality that spices all of Voltaire's work and was what his admirers appreciated. Voltaire's *Épître à Horace* is one of the best of Voltaire's philosophical epistles.

Voltaire has some renown as a historian. His *Le Siècle de Louis XIV* (1751; *The Age of Louis XIV*, 1752) reveals meticulous research and a journalistic bent. Voltaire praises the reign of Louis XIV in order to criticize the reign of Louis XV. *Essai sur les mœurs* (1756, 1763; *The General History and State of Europe*, 1754, 1759) presents a philosophical review of historic events. Other nonfiction works popularize the accomplishments of Sir Isaac Newton in science and of John Locke in philosophy (*Éléments de la philosophie de Newton*, 1738; *The Elements of Sir Isaac Newton's Philosophy*, 1738). In *Lettres philosophiques* (1734; originally published in English as *Letters Concerning the English Nation*, 1733; also known as *Philosophical Letters*, 1961), Voltaire, with his powerful satire, praises English customs and institutions as a method of criticizing French society of his day. Censorship, which outlawed much of Voltaire's work, not only added to the satirist's celebrity but also increased the prices charged for his books. The articles that Voltaire wrote for *Dictionnaire philosophique portatif* (1764, enlarged 1769; *A Philosophical Dictionary for the Pocket*, 1765; also known as *Philosophical Dictionary*, 1945, enlarged 1962) were also offensive to the establishment, full of his propaganda on the subject of fanaticism, judicial corruption, and social oppression.

Achievements

Voltaire's career spanned sixty years, and during that time he achieved great fame and even greater notoriety. Voltaire's literary ambitions were revealed when he chose *Œdipe* as the subject of his first tragedy. His ambition was to rival Pierre Corneille, and at the age of twenty-four he was already hailed as a worthy successor to both Jean Racine and Corneille. In the theater, Voltaire considerably delayed the demise of classical tragedy, and he remained an extremely popular dramatist of the age. Between 1745 and 1803, his plays were staged many more times than those of Corneille and Racine. Today, however, Voltaire's plays are no longer of interest to audiences.

Voltaire also enjoyed success in the field of poetry. *La Ligue* was so highly acclaimed that it put epic poetry back in fashion. Voltaire's love of the classical tradition stemmed, no doubt, from his Jesuit education at Louis-le-Grand. His poetry also brought him prestige at court and financial rewards. After the successful production of *La Princesse de Navarre* in 1745, performed at the wedding of Louis XV, Voltaire was given the post of royal historiographer and a pension of two thousand francs a year, and later was made a gentleman of the king's chamber. The following year, 1746, Voltaire achieved another ambition when he was finally elected to the Académie Française. He had been denied this privilege several times before because of the various scandals he had caused. Madame du Châtelet tried to protect him from his own indiscretion; she once locked up his outrageous *La Pucelle d'Orléans* (1755, 1762; *The Maid of Orleans*, 1758; also as *La Pucelle: Or, The Maid of Orleans*, 1785-1786), a scurrilous writing on the subject of Joan of Arc.

Voltaire's philosophical and satiric writings, such as his tales and pamphlets, not only brought him literary fame but also endangered his liberty. For this reason, Voltaire lived much of his life in exile or on the French-Swiss border.

One of the most astonishing aspects of Voltaire is his schizophrenic outlook. He dearly wished to have access to the noble classes (which accounts for his name change), while at the same time he despised the inequality inherent in the privilege of noble birth. A champion of the classical tradition, Voltaire inadvertently eroded its hold on his century by his innovations in drama and the novel. It is surprising that a champion of French classical tragedy and epic poetry should be the prime mover in introducing the latest developments in English literature, philosophy, and science into France. Voltaire's efforts to create a climate for liberty of thought and belief did eventually ameliorate conditions in France. The Encyclopedists, with Voltaire at their head, were ultimately responsible for producing a climate of critical thinking and a desire for reform that culminated in the French Revolution. Voltaire's *Philosophical Letters* were burned in public because they did not display the respect due "authority." Voltaire nevertheless would have been horrified to see the revolutionary tide sweep away this authority, even though it was corrupt. He enjoyed the cultivated nobility and the gracious support this class gave to the arts; he would have had no faith in the judgment of unrefined and poorly educated republicans. Still, the new ideas he had promulgated traveled through France and even to North America. Like John Locke, many of whose ideas are to be found in the American Bill of Rights and the Constitution, Voltaire contributed to political philosophy as it was developing in Europe and even in the United States.

It is through his satiric and philosophical writings that Voltaire exercised that influence. Whereas his effect on literature disappeared at the beginning of the nineteenth century, his emphasis on reason and critical thinking still dominates the French mind. The ideals of liberty of thought and justice are his legacy.

Biography

Voltaire was born François-Marie Arouet in Paris in 1694. His father was a highly placed official and belonged to the upper middle class. Voltaire received an excellent classical education at the Jesuit school of Louis-le-Grand in Paris, where he displayed a talent for writing poetry. He also probably acquired his taste for theater there.

The Abbé de Châteauneuf, Voltaire's godfather, introduced the twelve-year-old boy to the Society of the Temple, which was the domain of worldly libertines. Voltaire's taste for witty irreverence and for luxurious living was definitely encouraged by this company. In 1711, Voltaire became a law student. As early as 1716, his satiric writing, aimed at the king's regent and the poet Antoine Houdar de la Motte, caused Voltaire to be exiled twice to the provinces. In 1717, after writing a second time satirizing the regent, Voltaire was imprisoned (fairly comfortably) in the Bastille for eleven months. During this stay, he completed *Oedipus* and began to write *La Ligue*. Upon leaving prison, he changed his name to de Voltaire. He became famous with the success of *Oedipus* in 1718 and *La Ligue* in 1723, and as a result he was invited to the literary and social circles of the wealthy. He even became a habitué of the court and had three of his plays, *Oedipus*, *Mariamne* (pr. 1724; English translation, 1761), and *L'Indiscret* (pr., pb. 1725) performed as part of the celebrations for Louis XV's marriage in 1725.

Late in 1725, Voltaire had a dispute with the chevalier de Rohan, who ridiculed Voltaire's use of a false aristocratic name. Angered by a beating at the hands of Rohan's men, Voltaire challenged the noble to a duel. None of Voltaire's aristocratic friends supported him in the matter, which increased Voltaire's hatred of the unfairness of privilege. A *lettre de cachet* (a letter of arbitrary arrest issued by the king) sent him to the Bastille. Soon—in May, 1726—Voltaire was allowed to go into exile in England, where he spent three years frequenting the literary circles of the day. There he wrote his *Philosophical Letters*, prepared four tragedies, and published *Henriade*. Voltaire returned to France in 1729 and once again gained access to literary circles. In 1730, his play *Brutus* was produced. The influence of William Shakespeare, acquired in England, is obvious in Voltaire's drama. *Zaïre* was presented in 1732 and *Adélaïde du Guesclin* in 1734. In the same year, Voltaire also took a great risk when he published his highly critical *Philosophical Letters* for the first time in France.

From 1734 to 1744, Voltaire lived in the du Châtelet castle at Cirey, where Madame du Châtelet, Voltaire's mistress, restrained Voltaire's volatile literary indiscretions somewhat. This period proved to be a most productive one. Voltaire wrote several plays during this time, including *Alzire* (pr., pb. 1736; English translation, 1763) and *Mérope*. He also wrote his provocative *The Man of the World* while at Cirey. Both Madame du Châtelet and Voltaire took an interest in physics, chemistry, and astronomy; it is at Cirey that Voltaire wrote *The Elements of Sir Isaac Newton's Philosophy*.

For the three years following 1744, Voltaire was involved in life at court. His protectress, Madame de Pompadour, was, like him, of a humble background. The king and queen always distrusted Voltaire. After a thoughtless remark, Voltaire was obliged to flee the court and go to the summer home of the duchesse du Maine, the Château d'Anet at Sceaux. In *Zadig*, Voltaire satirizes life at court.

In 1747, Madame de Châtelet died in childbirth. Voltaire was extremely pained by this loss. There was no longer a reason to remain in France, and Voltaire spent the years from 1750 to 1753 at the court of Frederick the Great of Prussia. He published *The Age of Louis XIV* in Berlin in 1751. There he also wrote his satiric philosophical tale *Micromegas*. Although he had hoped to discover in Frederick his ideal of the "enlightened" monarch, Voltaire was as independent as Frederick was authoritarian, and the visit soon ended. These two men still respected each other greatly, however, and continued to correspond. In 1755, Voltaire moved to Les Délices, an estate near the Swiss border. He lived there from 1755 to 1760, and it was there that, still in a depressed frame of mind, he wrote *Candide*.

From 1760 until his death, Voltaire resided in Ferney, on French soil, although situated very close to the Swiss border. Voltaire was extremely active during this period. He wrote some six thousand letters, as well as pamphlets, plays, and tales. In closing his letters, he usually wrote "Écrasez l'infâme" (crush the vile), by which he meant that superstition and intolerance must be eliminated. He wrote philosophical tales here, waging his battle against the usual targets; *Ingenuous* appeared at this time, as did many other philosophical tales. Voltaire championed the causes of the Calas and Sirven families and also of La Barre; all three were cases of the miscarriage of justice and of religious persecution.

Voltaire, taking his own advice at the end of *Candide*, did much to improve the region of Ferney. He built a church, installed a tannery, and established a watchmaking industry. He even had his area exempted from the salt tax. In 1778, at the age of eighty-three, Voltaire went to Paris in triumph to watch a production of *Irène*. His popularity was at its highest, and the accolades and honors he received during his sojourn proved too much for him; he died shortly thereafter.

Analysis

Voltaire was the most influential writer in eighteenth century France. He epitomizes the philosopher of the *siècle des lumières*, the Age of Enlightenment; his curiosity embraces all the developments of his day, whether French or otherwise European, scientific or literary. His faith in human reason does not waver, although his optimism about human progress often does. His writings reflect the changing literary tastes of the century as he defends a waning classical tradition while himself introducing the most outrageous innovations. His theater particularly embodies both of these tendencies, whereas his tales tend to exploit traditional literary forms in order to introduce a unique type of satiric philosophical story. Voltaire's long fiction includes many rather short stories, which have been called indiscriminately *romans philosophiques* (philosophical novels) or *contes philosophiques* (philosophical tales). According to Henri Coulet, Voltaire himself used the term *histoire* (story). Because satire such as Voltaire's depends on economy of style and the tales have no real development of plot or character, they are limited in length by the genre itself.

Candide is considered to be the most perfect example of the philosophical novel, revealing Voltaire's brilliant irony and vivacious wit. All the tales are humorous tragicomedies and include incidents that are by turns absurd, grotesque, poetic, romantic, and shocking. The unifying element is always the philosophical theme that Voltaire is stressing. Voltaire began writing his tales at the age of forty-five, when his ideas were firmly established; hence, the concerns and reforms he seeks to address remain fairly constant throughout the tales. Despite the fact that these stories are meant to appeal primarily to the intellect, they are eminently entertaining. Voltaire's writings are rooted firmly in the humanistic rationalism of the first half of his century rather than in the literature of pre-Romantic sensibility, which made its appearance in the late 1700's.

Henri Bénac's suggestion that the tales fall into four chronological groups related to the development of Voltaire's thought is widely accepted. Bénac proposes that the first two groups—of 1747 to 1752 and 1756 to 1759—reveal Voltaire's growing realization that war must be waged against evils such as intolerance, injustice, corruption, and ignorance. The first group includes such stories as *Le Monde comme il va* (1748; revised as *Babouc: Ou, Le Monde comme il va*, 1749; *Babouc: Or, The World as It Goes*, 1754; also known as *The World as It Is: Or, Babouc's Vision*, 1929), *Memnon: Or, Human Wisdom*, and *La Lettre d'un Turc* (1750); *Zadig* and *Micromegas* are the best known of the group. The second group includes *History of Scarmentado's Travels*, which is the outline of *Candide*. In the third group figure *Jeannot et Colin* (1764; *Jeannot and Colin*, 1929), *Le Blanc et le noir* (1764; *The Two Genies*, 1895), and, best known, *Ingenuous*, *The Man of Forty Crowns*, and *The Princess of Babylon*. According to Bénac, the tales in this third group are, like Voltaire's pamphlets, weapons in his war against oppression of all kinds. In the last group, Bénac sees Voltaire searching for a morality on which to base a humane and free society. Tales in this period include *L'Histoire de Jenni* (1775) and *Les Oreilles du Comte de Chesterfield* (1775; *The Ears of Lord Chesterfield and Parson Goodman*, 1826).

ZADIG

The concerns of the early tales recur throughout all the stories, but Voltaire presents the different tales with a rich range of tones. *Zadig*, like other tales of this early group, is imbued with sunny humor and gaiety despite the sardonic irony that underscores the misfortunes of the hero. Voltaire sketches his hero Zadig with an unusually delicate touch, and some passages dazzle momentarily with rare poetry: "He marveled at these vast globes of light which to our eyes appear to be only feeble sparks. . . . His soul flew up into the infinite and, detached from his senses, contemplated the immutable order of the universe."

Memnon: Histoire orientale contained fifteen chapters that reappeared in *Zadig* in 1748. The story of Zadig is in the picaresque tradition, which is to say that the hero, on his travels, meets with many adventures. The plot of such a tale is of necessity episodic and highly imaginative. Zadig, a wealthy, virtuous, and handsome young Babylonian, is about to marry the beautiful young Semire, who loves him "passionately." When a jealous youth, Orcan, attempts to abduct Semire, Zadig bravely rescues his betrothed, receiving a wound that might mean the loss of an eye. Instead of expressing her gratitude, Semire protests that she hates one-eyed men, and she promptly marries Orcan. Zadig recovers quickly and marries another woman, Azora, whose faithfulness he puts to the test by pretending to have died. Unfortunately, Azora fails the test. Zadig encounters difficulties with the law when he makes scientific deductions from observing the tracks of the queen's dog and the king's horse, leading a huntsman to deduce that Zadig stole the animals. Zadig eventually becomes the king's prime minister.

His next misfortune arises through no fault of his own: Queen Astarté falls in love with him. The king, in jealousy, plots to kill them both, and Zadig has to flee. As he arrives in Egypt, he sees an Egyptian beating a woman, who asks Zadig to save her. In the ensuing fight, Zadig kills his adversary. Zadig is arrested and imprisoned for this act, then sold as a slave and taken to Arabia by his master, Sétoc, with whom he becomes close friends. Zadig dissuades a young widow from burning herself on her husband's funeral pyre, as is the religious custom. He also persuades an Egyptian, an Indian, a Chinese, a Greek, and a Celt to worship the same Supreme Being. Zadig is accused of impiety by Arabian priests and condemned to be burned. The young widow whom he saved now helps him escape.

Zadig next goes to the island of Serendib (Ceylon) on behalf of Sétoc. He makes a good impression on the king of the island and helps him to find an honest minister. On his travels, Zadig meets the brigand chief Arbogad and learns that King Moabdar has gone mad and been killed, and Astarté has disappeared. Zadig eventually discovers that Astarté is a captive of Ogul, who is sick with an imaginary illness. Zadig cures Ogul, and the two return to Babylon, where peace is restored. Zadig wins a tournament that is held to decide who shall be the new king of Babylon and marry Astarté. Zadig wins the tournament but is cheated, and his rival claims the victory. In the middle of his despair, Zadig meets a hermit who reveals to him the secret of happiness, and Zadig learns to accept the ways of Providence. Zadig guesses the correct answers to the riddles and finally marries Astarté.

Zadig the hero—whose name in Arabic means "just"—attempts to be happy in a world where goodness is frustrated by absurd and illogical interventions of fate. At one point, Zadig says: "I was sent to execution because I had written verses in praise of the King; I was on the point of being strangled because the Queen had yellow ribbons; and here I am a slave with you because a brute beat his mistress. Come, let's not lose heart; perhaps all this will end."

The absurdity of Zadig's world, which is out of control and beyond the powers of logical explanation, is not the horror evoked in Franz Kafka's fiction; unlike Kafka, Voltaire does not attempt to create a sense of dreamlike but undeniable reality in either setting or characterization. Voltaire's exotic Eastern novel is in the tradition of the fifteenth century *The Arabian Nights' Entertainments*, also known as *The Thousand and One Nights*, translated from the Arabic by Antoine Gallard and much in vogue after the success of Montesquieu's *Lettres persanes* (1721; *Persian Letters*, 1722). The events are as unreal as those of the fairy tale, and the sensibility of the reader is not touched by Zadig's dilemmas. Instead, Voltaire disturbs the comfort of the reader's reason, logic, and innate sense of order and justice; the irony of Voltaire is at work. The frustration of Zadig becomes that of his audience. The knight Itobad steals Zadig's white suit of armor during the night, leaving his green suit in its place so that Zadig cannot claim the hand of Astarté, and Zadig cannot prove that he is the victor of the tournament, because the combatants must conceal their identities until a victor is proclaimed. Zadig has often been punished unjustly for being good, and here he is once again cheated of a happiness that is almost within his grasp. The audience is robbed of an anticipated happy ending and is frustrated by this anticlimax.

Voltaire was a master of the art of satire, and he often made use of anticlimax as an effective satiric technique. Zadig, after bewailing a list of horrifying punishments he has narrowly escaped, says, "Come, let's not lose heart; perhaps all this will end." This anticlimactic statement satirizes both Zadig's naïve optimism and the ridiculous optimism of the philosophers Gottfried Wilhelm Leibniz and Friedrich August Wolf—that "this is the best of all possible worlds"—which was much in vogue in the eighteenth century.

This leitmotif, the attack on optimism, is one of the many minor satiric barbs that Voltaire uses to spice his tale. Other satiric attacks abound in *Zadig* and reappear throughout the tales. Eighteenth century readers, usually members of the nobility and upper middle class, took delight in synthesizing the apparent subject of Voltaire's narrative with the real and often audacious object of its satire. Voltaire makes a dangerous allusion to the court when the fisherman tells Zadig how archers "armed with a royal warrant were pillaging his house lawfully and in good order." The ironic effect is achieved by the surprising juxtaposition of "pillaging" and "lawfully." Voltaire's irony had its basis in reality: He had been forced to flee the court at Versailles after making disparaging remarks about the courtiers being cheats. In *Zadig*, Voltaire also frequently satirizes the judicial system and judges who are "abysses of knowledge," who "prove" Zadig looked out of a window even though Zadig has answered none of their questions.

Voltaire's anticlericalism and antireligious bent often figure in the satire of *Zadig*. Almona the Arab widow intends to burn herself on her husband's funeral pyre, as the Brahman religion demands. Zadig the philosopher reasons her out of this plan, convincing her that she is about to take a ridiculous course in order to satisfy her vanity and not her religious principles. Zadig also persuades Sétoc that it is ridiculous to worship shining lights (the stars), and he demonstrates his reasons by kneeling and appearing to worship lighted candles. The "bonzes," who represent the monks, "chanted beautiful prayers to music, and left the state a prey to the barbarians." Zadig's rationalism (and Voltaire's) is primarily concerned with people's practical problems in society.

Voltaire's primary philosophical theme, however, is people's concern with destiny. Zadig vacillates between hope and despair as fate deals him many adverse blows. Despite his ingenuity and virtue, which he displays when he acts as the prime minister of King Moabdar, Zadig is presented as the plaything of destiny. The fisherman's story and the hermit incident reinforce the supremacy of this philosophical question as the main theme. How do philosophers explain the sufferings of a good person in the hands of a malevolent destiny? Voltaire resolves this problem happily with a deus ex machina ending. The angel Jesrad, representing divine intervention, tells Zadig to stop his questioning and simply worship Providence. Most men, Jesrad explains, form opinions with limited knowledge. Zadig's virtue triumphs, and he wins his queen and rules with "justice and love. Men blessed Zadig and Zadig blessed heaven." The skies of Zadig remain free of the blackness of *Candide*.

MICROMEGAS

Micromegas, which appeared in 1752, is a philosophical tale in a more literal sense, being primarily a vehicle for ideas on relativity. It is a very short tale, with almost no action (in stark contrast to the episodic *Zadig*) and only two main protagonists. Micromegas (which is Greek for "little big one") is a very tall inhabitant of the planet Sirius who has been banned from court for writing a book about insects that the "Mufti" of his planet has found to be heretical. He goes on an interplanetary voyage, finally arriving on the planet Saturn, where he meets a dwarf. (Voltaire intended his readers to recognize in the dwarf a caricature of his own enemy, Bernard le Bovier de Fontenelle.) The two travelers arrive on Earth and finally discover minute humans in a boat. The travelers attend a banquet at which various forms of philosophical credos are represented, allowing Voltaire to launch a satiric attack on the theories of Aristotle, René Descartes, Nicolas Malebranche, and Leibniz. Voltaire approves of the philosophy of the follower of John Locke. A storm develops, and the philosophers fall into the pocket of Micromegas. Although the giant is angry that such small creatures have so much pride, he gives a book to the philosophers; its pages, however, are blank. Voltaire gives the closing line to the dwarf (his enemy, Fontenelle), who, upon receiving the blank book—supposedly a philosophical treatise revealing the final truth about things—says, "Ah . . . that's just what I suspected." This last line was extremely offensive to Fontenelle, because it implied that he agreed that all of his metaphysical speculations over the past years had been wasted effort—that such truths were impossible to discover and prove. This attack on metaphysics is the main thrust of Voltaire's satire in *Micromegas*. Voltaire ridicules the philosophers in the boat, implying that "our little pile of mud" is relatively unimportant when seen in relation to the rest of the cosmos and that the opinions of its inhabitants are hence practically worthless. The philosophers in the boat all talk at once and all have different opinions. Voltaire shows that this kind of truth is "relative" to the person uttering it, and unreliable.

Voltaire's *Micromegas* is in direct imitation of Jonathan Swift's *Gulliver's Travels* (1726), and Montesquieu had previously used this type of travel story in *Persian Letters*. Voltaire, then, used an established subgenre, the fictional travelogue, as a vehicle for social commentary: The traveler in a strange land, seeing things for the first time, has no prejudice and puts into a new perspective situations that have been seen in only a certain way for centuries. This fresh perspective opens the way for critical appraisal and reform.

In *Micromegas*, Voltaire makes little effort to convince the reader of the reality of his story; the tale must be accepted as fantasy. The satire is less complicated, less adroit, and less sparkling than it is in *Zadig*. The main purpose of the satire is to address subjects of great interest to Voltaire's contemporaries; little of the subject matter of *Micromegas* is of interest to the modern reader. These two early works, *Zadig* and *Micromegas*, do, however, share a lighthearted spirit of enjoyment as Voltaire ridicules general stupidity and personal enemies. In these works, too, Voltaire formulated what would become the constant subjects of his satiric attacks throughout his tales.

CANDIDE

Candide belongs to the second group of tales described by Bénac and is distinguished by its radical pessimism and bitter irony, in contrast to the sunny atmosphere of the previous two tales. *Candide* is considered the epitome of the philosophical tale, and it remains highly relevant today. Unlike Voltaire's other writings, *Candide* is still read everywhere. The tale's atmosphere is dark and often despairing. Voltaire was shocked by the horrors and atrocities of the Seven Years' War, which began in August, 1756, when Frederick the Great invaded Saxony. The Lisbon earthquake in 1755 also horrified Voltaire, causing him to reflect on what kind of Providence could inflict death on the innocent and guilty alike. The optimistic philosophy of Leibniz and Wolf seemed totally absurd in the midst of so much human suffering.

The satire in *Candide* is directed above all against this optimistic philosophy, epitomized in the character Pangloss. The characters in this tale are caricatures, deformed so that each represents only one characteristic or outlook. Candide, the hero, represents naïve, good, and reasonable humanity. The philosopher Martin symbolizes a cynical Manichaeanism that acknowledges the power of evil as well as of good in the world. James, who represents real human goodness and charity, is allowed to drown in stormy seas after rescuing a sailor who had attempted to murder him. Such is the bitter mood of the tale.

The form of this novel is basically picaresque, as in *Zadig*, but Voltaire also parodies the novel of adventure and the novel of sentiment. The characters continually die horrible deaths after suffering gruesome tortures in various lands, but they somehow miraculously (and ridiculously) reappear, having been saved or cured. Their tearful reunions are a parody of the sentimental literature that Samuel Richardson's *Pamela: Or, Virtue Rewarded* (1740-1741) introduced to France from England and that infiltrated the bourgeois dramas of Diderot, and indeed of Voltaire's own theater. These reappearances also reinforce the central unity of the novel. A finely orchestrated rhythm unifies the entire tale; it is not simply that the main aim of the satire holds the tale together, as in the other stories. The fates (and philosophies) of secondary characters affect the hero in a rhythmic ebb and flow of alternating hope and despair that echo across the desolate landscape of a sad humanity in the throes of war, persecution, and suffering.

A gloss of the incidents in the tale reveals that there is no development of character or plot as such, and it underlines the rapid and vertiginous pace of the tale's episodes. This brisk pace lightens the seriousness of the atrocities being described, preventing the reader from dwelling on them or taking them to heart. Hence, Voltaire employs a technique of diminution, undercutting the value and dignity of human life.

Candide lives happily in a château in Westphalia with the baron of Thunderten-tronckh. Pangloss, the disciple of the optimistic philosophy of Leibniz, also lives there as tutor, as does Cunegonde, the baron's beautiful daughter, whom Candide loves. Candide agrees with Pangloss that all works out for the best in this wonderful world at the château. The baron, however, discovering the two lovers embracing, chases Candide out of the château. He is carried off forcibly to join an army and fight. After deserting, he goes to Holland, where he meets Pangloss, who has become a beggar and is barely recognizable with the sores of a terrible disease. Candide learns that all the people of the château have been killed.

Candide takes Pangloss to his benefactor, James the Anabaptist, who restores the sick man. The three then set sail for Lisbon, where James has a business engagement. On the way to Lisbon, their ship is wrecked in a storm, and James is drowned, while a sailor who had tried to murder him is saved. In Lisbon, Pangloss and Candide live through an earthquake that kills thirty thousand people. As Candide and Pangloss wander through the destroyed city, Pangloss attempts to comfort the citizens with his philosophy that "all is for the best"—a philosophy that, as Voltaire makes clear in his juxtaposition of Pangloss's theories to the suffering about him, is ludicrous if not cruel. Overhearing Pangloss's remarks, an officer of the Inquisition questions Pangloss about his belief in Original Sin and Free Will. Pangloss, sputtering his rationalizations, is arrested along with Candide—"one for having spoken, the other for having listened with an air of approval." Pangloss is hanged, but Candide is saved by the timely arrival of Cunegonde, who has escaped from the massacre of her family.

As things are beginning to seem more hopeful, Candide is obliged to kill two people, and he has to flee to America. He takes refuge with some Jesuits in Paraguay, where he miraculously meets Cunegonde's brother, who has also escaped the massacre at the château and has become a priest. Although he embraces Candide as a brother, his mood suddenly shifts when Candide announces that he intends to marry Cunegonde, and in the ensuing fight, Candide kills the brother of his beloved. After similar incidents in Eldorado, Surinam, Venice, and Constantinople, Candide finally finds Cunegonde. After all of her suffering, she has become very ugly, but, true to his word, Candide marries her. He then takes the advice of a wise old Turk and installs himself and his companions in an estate. He refuses to ask any more philosophical questions about evil and suffering in favor of hard work and practical reality—thus the novel's famous closing line: " . . . we must cultivate our garden."

In 1759, the year that *Candide* was published, Voltaire bought Ferney, an estate on the French-Swiss border, which has led critics to surmise that Candide's conclusions about work and the happiness to be found in practical progress are those of Voltaire. Once Voltaire was installed at Ferney, he gained confidence and energy and bombarded his public and his enemies with pamphlets, essays, plays, and stories, waging numerous legal battles on behalf of those persecuted for religious reasons. *Ingenuous* was written during this last, very active period of Voltaire's life. Although Voltaire was seventy-three years old when he wrote this work, his incredible intellectual and creative vigor had not diminished.

INGENUOUS

Ingenuous is one of the weapons Voltaire used in his unremitting battle against intolerance and injustice and belongs to the third group of novels delineated by Bénac. Voltaire's confidence had returned, and he wrote with a sure hand; none of the tales that follow *Candide* can rival the grandeur of *Ingenuous*.

Ingenuous is the most romantic of Voltaire's stories, and its plot is narrative rather than episodic. The tone of the story is more naturalistic, as are the characters. The device of a voyage is used again; the religious and social systems of France in the time of Louis XIV are seen through the eyes of the Huron stranger, who, without prejudice and with candid reasoning, questions institutions and beliefs that have been taken for granted and must now be considered from a new perspective.

The character of the Huron is in the tradition of the "noble savage" popularized by a missionary, baron de Lahontan, who praised the uncorrupted American Indian. The unity of the tale lies in the unfolding of the story of two lovers: Hercules Kerkabon (as the Huron is later named) and Mademoiselle de St. Yves. The satire used here also unites with the central love theme, targeting the corrupt Catholic Church and its priests, monks, and practices, which are instrumental in separating the lovers and ruining their chance for happiness. Voltaire also satirizes the court officials and Jansenism.

Voltaire's wit has a somewhat subdued tone throughout *Ingenuous*; the satire resides in the calmly reasoned arguments of the Huron, who questions all the basic doctrines of Jesuit and Jansenist alike. Voltaire, using the Huron as his mouthpiece, explains very simply all of his objections to the two religions. At the time of writing this tale, Voltaire was involved in the trials of the Calas family, the Sirven family, and La Barre, and his hatred of religious persecution and his anger at the injustices meted out by a corrupt judicial system were therefore as intense as they had ever been.

The story reflects the century's taste for cosmopolitanism. The Huron has been reared by a Huron tribe in Canada and arrives on the Lower Brittany coast in 1689. It is "discovered" that he is the lost child of the Abbé Yerkabon and his sister. Their brother went to Canada as a soldier and was killed by the Iroquois. The Abbé claims Hercules as his nephew and baptizes him as a Catholic. The beautiful Mademoiselle de St. Yves acts as his godmother. Hercules later falls in love with Mademoiselle de St. Yves but cannot marry his godmother, because the Church forbids it. Mademoiselle de St. Yves is sent to a convent, and Hercules, who is by now a hero for helping to defend the French against an English attack, goes to Versailles to engage the king's help in his marriage scheme. At Versailles, he is arrested and imprisoned in the Bastille, where he meets Gordon, a Jansenist. After much study and discussion, he converts Gordon to Deism. Now Mademoiselle de St. Yves goes to Versailles to save Hercules, but she must submit to a government minister in order to obtain her lover's release. She never recovers from the shame and dies of her chagrin. Hercules is tempted to take his own life but recovers himself and becomes an excellent officer and philosopher. The tale does not end with the expected happy ending for the lovers, but Voltaire suggests that even if ambitions and ideals cannot be attained, there are compromises that can be made and one can be tolerably happy—a message similar to that of *Candide*.

THE MAN OF FORTY CROWNS

The Man of Forty Crowns, published the year after *Ingenuous*, displays a strong contrast in style. The two tales have in common the underlying interest of Voltaire in practical things. In *Ingenuous*, Voltaire has Hercules recover from his loss and become a good soldier; in *The Man of Forty Crowns*, Voltaire has his protagonist discuss tax reform with a mathematician. There is a great difference, however, between these polemics and those of *Ingenuous*. In the later tale, Voltaire writes for a clever and agile mind able to follow the mathematical bent of his arguments. There is scarcely a plot or an appealing character to enliven the discussion. Voltaire, as usual, satirizes monks (who do not pay taxes), despotic monarchs, unfair judicial systems, and ignorant people who think they know more than they do. This highly polemical tale, amusing for Voltaire's eighteenth century circle, is of little interest today; not even the odd humorous remark, such as the suggestion that smiles and songs be taxed, can redeem the lack of relevance or interest of this story for a modern reader.

Voltaire's tales do suffer a slight impoverishment in translation. The musicality of the

French language offsets the dryness of the succinct, economic prose and the laconic, pointed understatement. Polemical tales such as *The Man of Forty Crowns* particularly suffer in English translation.

Of Voltaire's many tales (some two dozen in all), *Candide* remains the most popular. Perhaps it has universal appeal because the evils it portrays persist in today's world. Wars are still waged in the name of religious causes, and political prisoners continue to be tortured and cast into jail without trial. Unfortunately, Voltaire is no longer here to provoke people's consciences and fire their minds with his energetic fury. Without him, the genre of the philosophical tale lies in disuse.

Avril S. Lewis

OTHER MAJOR WORKS

SHORT FICTION: *Le Monde comme il va*, 1748 (revised as *Babouc: Ou, Le Monde comme il va*, 1749; *Babouc: Or, The World as It Goes*, 1754; also known as *The World as It Is: Or, Babouc's Vision*, 1929); *Memnon: Ou, La Sagesse humaine*, 1749 (*Memnon: Or, Human Wisdom*, 1961); *La Lettre d'un Turc*, 1750; *Le Blanc et le noir*, 1764 (*The Two Genies*, 1895); *Jeannot et Colin*, 1764 (*Jeannot and Colin*, 1929); *L'Histoire de Jenni*, 1775; *Les Oreilles du Comte de Chesterfield*, 1775 (*The Ears of Lord Chesterfield and Parson Goodman*, 1826).

PLAYS: *Œdipe*, pr. 1718 (*Oedipus*, 1761); *Artémire*, pr. 1720; *Mariamne*, pr. 1724 (English translation, 1761); *L'Indiscret*, pr., pb. 1725 (verse play); *Brutus*, pr. 1730 (English translation, 1761); *Ériphyle*, pr. 1732; *Zaïre*, pr. 1732 (English translation, 1736); *La Mort de César*, pr. 1733; *Adélaïde du Guesclin*, pr. 1734; *L'Échange*, pr. 1734; *Alzire*, pr., pb. 1736 (English translation, 1763); *L'Enfant prodigue*, pr. 1736 (verse play; prose translation, *The Prodigal*, 1750?); *Zulime*, pr. 1740; *Mahomet*, pr., pb. 1742 (*Mahomet the Prophet*, 1744); *Mérope*, pr. 1743 (English translation, 1744, 1749); *La Princesse de Navarre*, pr., pb. 1745 (verse play; music by Jean-Philippe Rameau); *La Prude: Ou, La Grandeuse de Cassette*, pr., pb. 1747 (wr. 1740; verse play; adaptation of William Wycherley's play *The Plain Dealer*); *Sémiramis*, pr. 1748 (*Semiramis*, 1760); *Nanine*, pr., pb. 1749 (English translation, 1927); *Oreste*, pr., pb. 1750; *Rome sauvée*, pr., pb. 1752; *L'Orphelin de la Chine*, pr., pb. 1755 (*The Orphan of China*, 1756); *Socrate*, pb. 1759 (*Socrates*, 1760); *L'Écossaise*, pr., pb. 1760 (*The Highland Girl*, 1760); *Tancrède*, pr. 1760; *Olympie*, pb. 1763; *Le Triumvirat*, pr. 1764; *Les Scythes*, pr., pb. 1767; *Les Guèbres: Ou, La Tolérance*, pb. 1769; *Sophonisbe*, pb. 1770 (revision of Jean Mairet's play); *Les Pélopides: Ou, Atrée et Thyeste*, pb. 1772; *Les Lois de Minos*, pb. 1773; *Don Pèdre*, pb. 1775 (wr. 1761); *Irène*, pr. 1778; *Agathocle*, pr. 1779.

POETRY: *Poème sur la religion naturelle*, 1722; *La Ligue*, 1723; *La Henriade*, 1728 (a revision of *La Ligue*; *Henriade*, 1732); *Le Mondain*, 1736 (*The Man of the World*, 1764); *Discours en vers sur l'homme*, 1738 (*Discourses in Verse on Man*, 1764); *Poème de Fontenoy*, 1745; *Poème sur la loi naturelle*, 1752 (*On Natural Law*, 1764); *La Pucelle* d'*Orléans*, 1755, 1762 (*The Maid of Orleans*, 1758; also known as *La Pucelle: Or, The Maid of Orleans*, 1785-1786); *Poème sur la désastre de Lisbonne*, 1756 (*Poem on the Lisbon Earthquake*, 1764); *Le Pauvre Diable*, 1758; *Épître à Horace*, 1772.

NONFICTION: *An Essay upon the Civil Wars of France . . . and Also upon the Epick Poetry of the European Nations from Homer Down to Milton*, 1727; *La Henriade*, 1728 (*Henriade*, 1732); *Histoire de Charles XII*, 1731 (*The History of Charles XII*, 1732); *Le Temple du goût*, 1733 (*The Temple of Taste*, 1734); *Lettres philosophiques*, 1734 (originally published in English as *Letters Concerning the English Nation*, 1733; also known as *Philosophical Letters*, 1961); *Discours de métaphysique*, 1736; *Éléments de la philosophie de Newton*, 1738 (*The Elements of Sir Isaac Newton's Philosophy*, 1738); *Discours en vers sur l'homme*, 1738-1752 (*Discourses in Verse on Man*, 1764); *Vie de Molière*, 1739; *Le Siècle de Louis XIV*, 1751 (*The Age of Louis XIV*, 1752); *Essai sur les mœurs et l'esprit des nations*, 1756, 1763 (*The General History and State of Europe*, 1754, 1759); *Traité sur la tolérance*, 1763 (*A Treatise on Religious Toleration*, 1764); *Commentaires sur le théâtre de Pierre Corneille*, 1764; *Dictionnaire philosophique portatif*, 1764 (enlarged 1769 as *La Raison par alphabet*; also known as *Dictionnaire philosophique*; *A Philosophical Dictionary for the Pocket*, 1765; also known as *Philosophical Dictionary*, 1945, enlarged 1962); *Avis au public sur les parracides imputés aux calas et aux Sirven*, 1775; *Correspondence*, 1953-1965 (102 volumes).

MISCELLANEOUS: *The Works of M. de Voltaire*, 1761-1765 (35 volumes), 1761-1781 (38 volumes); *Candide, and Other Writings*, 1945; *The Portable Voltaire*, 1949; *Candide, Zadig, and Selected Stories*, 1961; *The Complete Works of Voltaire*, 1968-1977 (135 volumes; in French).

BIBLIOGRAPHY

Aldridge, A. Owen. *Voltaire and the Century of Light*. Princeton, N.J.: Princeton University Press, 1975. Reexamines the life and career of Voltaire within the context of European intellectual and political history, providing many useful insights. Presents information in a pleasant style equally suited to specialists and general readers. Also offers stimulating readings of *Candide* and other selected works as well as a valuable bibliography.

Bird, Stephen. *Reinventing Voltaire: The Politics of Commemoration in Nineteenth Century France*. Oxford, England: Voltaire Foundation, 2000. Focuses on the critical response to Voltaire in nineteenth century France, where his legacy was both vilified and venerated. Includes bibliography and indexes.

Cronk, Nicholas, ed. *The Cambridge Companion to Voltaire*. New York: Cambridge University Press, 2009. Collection of essays examines Voltaire's life, philosophy, and works. Includes discussions of Voltaire as a storyteller, Voltaire and authorship, and Voltaire and the myth of England as well as an analysis of *Candide* by Philip Stewart.

Davidson, Ian. *Voltaire in Exile: The Last Years*. New York: Grove Press, 2004. Chronicles Voltaire's life during his exile from France, when he actively campaigned against censorship, war, torture, capital punishment, the alliance between church and state, and other perceived injustices. Includes an analysis of much of Voltaire's personal correspondence.

Gray, John. *Voltaire.* New York: Routledge, 1999. Volume in Routledge's Great Philosophers series provides a concise overview of Voltaire's philosophy.

Havens, George R. *The Age of Ideas.* New York: Henry Holt, 1955. Often reprinted and providing a model and inspiration for many writers, Havens's witty, informed overview of the Enlightenment and its precursors remains authoritative as a guide to trends and thinkers of the period. Contains groups of chapters devoted to Voltaire, Charles de Montesquieu, Denis Diderot, and Jean-Jacques Rousseau; the four chapters devoted to Voltaire provide an excellent introduction to the man and his work, with brief but perceptive readings of such texts as *Zadig* and *Candide.*

Knapp, Bettina Liebowitz. *Voltaire Revisited.* New York: Twayne, 2000. Good introductory study describes Voltaire's life and devotes separate chapters to all of the genres of his works. Includes bibliography and index.

Mason, Haydn Trevor. *"Candide": Optimism Demolished.* New York: Twayne, 1992. Examination of Voltaire's novel is divided into two parts: The first addresses the work's literary and historical context, including its critical reception, and the second provides a reading of the book's view of history, philosophy, personality, structure, and form. Includes notes and annotated bibliography.

_____. *Voltaire.* New York: St. Martin's Press, 1975. Comprehensive monograph (not to be confused with the biography Mason published six years later, cited below) is intended for the interested undergraduate or general reader. Steers clear of the traditional chronological approach in order to present Voltaire's works by genre, treating first his drama and dramatic criticism and then proceeding to historiography, short fiction, poetry, and polemics. Supplemented by a useful if brief bibliography.

_____. *Voltaire: A Biography.* Baltimore: Johns Hopkins University Press, 1981. Presents a concise but lively survey of the subject's life, clearly relating the major works to their contexts, including their inspiration or—as is especially pertinent in the case of Voltaire—provocation. Closely documented, useful both as biography and as criticism, this volume is recommended to students and general readers alike.

Pearson, Roger. *Voltaire Almighty: A Life in Pursuit of Freedom.* London: Bloomsbury, 2005. Account of Voltaire's life focuses on his love of liberty and how that passion informed his life and work. Includes bibliography, index, and illustrations.

Vartanian, Aram. "*Zadig:* Theme and Countertheme." In *Dilemmas du roman,* edited by Catherine Lafarge. Saratoga, Calif.: Anima Libri, 1990. Analyzes Voltaire's novel and argues that its philosophical theme of impersonal fate is counterpoised against a background theme, creating a contrapuntal movement of the narrative structure. Asserts that the story is told in such a way that its overall meaning emerges from a network of tensions felt among its various elements.

JOHN WAIN

Born: Stoke-on-Trent, Staffordshire, England; March 14, 1925
Died: Oxford, England; May 24, 1994

PRINCIPAL LONG FICTION
Hurry on Down, 1953 (also known as *Born in Captivity*)
Living in the Present, 1955
The Contenders, 1958
A Travelling Woman, 1959
Strike the Father Dead, 1962
The Young Visitors, 1965
The Smaller Sky, 1967
A Winter in the Hills, 1970
The Pardoner's Tale, 1978
Young Shoulders, 1982 (also known as *The Free Zone Starts Here*)
Where the Rivers Meet, 1988
Comedies, 1990
Hungry Generations, 1994

OTHER LITERARY FORMS

A complete man of letters, John Wain (wayn) published short stories, poetry, drama, many scholarly essays, and a highly respected biography in addition to his novels. Significant among Wain's writings other than novels are several collections of short stories, including *Nuncle, and Other Stories* (1960), *Death of the Hind Legs, and Other Stories* (1966), *The Life Guard* (1971), and *King Caliban, and Other Stories* (1978); and volumes of poetry, such as *Mixed Feelings* (1951), *A Word Carved on a Sill* (1956), *Weep Before God: Poems* (1961), *Wildtrack: A Poem* (1965), *Letters to Five Artists* (1969), *The Shape of Feng* (1972), *Feng: A Poem* (1975), and *Open Country* (1987). Wain also published criticism that communicates a sensitive and scholarly appreciation of good books. Readers should pay particular attention to *Preliminary Essays* (1957), *Essays on Literature and Ideas* (1963), *A House for the Truth: Critical Essays* (1972), *Professing Poetry* (1977), and his autobiography, *Sprightly Running: Part of an Autobiography* (1962). Most readers believe that *Samuel Johnson* (1974) is the best and most lasting of all Wain's nonfiction. In this monumental biography, many of the commitments reflected in Wain's other writings come through clearly and forcefully.

ACHIEVEMENTS

John Wain is noted for his observance of and compassion for human sorrow. His writing reflects his determination to speak to a wider range of readers than that addressed by many of his modernist predecessors; it reflects his faith in the common reader to recognize and respond to abiding philosophical concerns. These concerns include his sense of the dignity of human beings in the middle of an oftentimes cruel, indifferent, and cynical world. His concern is with a world caught up in time, desire, and disappointment. His novel *Young Shoulders*, an examination of the ramifications of a fatal accident on the people left behind, won the 1982 Whitbread Best Novel Award.

Biography

Although his world was that of the twentieth century, John Wain was very much an eighteenth century man. He delighted in pointing out that he and eighteenth century writer Samuel Johnson were born in the same district ("The Potteries") and in much the same social milieu; that he attended the same university as Johnson (Oxford, where he served from 1973 to 1978 as a professor of poetry); and that he knew, like Johnson, the Grub Street experiences and "the unremitting struggle to write enduring books against the background of an unstable existence." What chiefly interests the critic in surveying Wain's formative years are the reasons for his increasingly sober outlook. Wain's autobiography, *Sprightly Running*, remains the best account of his formative years as well as offering engaging statements of many of his opinions. In it, the reader finds some of the profound and lasting effects on Wain's writing of his childhood, his adolescence, and his years at Oxford.

John Barrington Wain was born on March 14, 1925, in Stoke-on-Trent, Staffordshire, an industrial city given over to pottery and coal mining. Here, as in other English cities, a move upward in social status is signaled by a move up in geographical terms. Therefore, the Wain family's move three years later to Penkhull—a manufacturing complex of kilns and factories and, incidentally, the setting for Wain's third novel, *The Contenders*—marked a step up into the middle-class district.

From infancy, Wain had a genuine fondness for the countryside. He immersed himself in the sights and sounds and colors of rural nature, all of which made an impression on him that was distinctive as well as deep. This impression developed into an "unargued reverence for all created life, almost a pantheism." On holidays, he and his family traveled to the coast and hills of North Wales—an association that carried over into his adult years, when, at the age of thirty-four, he married a Welsh woman. His feeling for Wales—for the independent life of the people, the landscape and mountains, the sea, the special light of the sun—is recorded in *A Winter in the Hills*. Here and elsewhere is the idea that nature is the embodiment of order, permanence, and life. Indeed, the tension between the nightmare of repression in society and the dream of liberation in the natural world is an important unifying theme throughout Wain's work.

The experience of living in an industrial town also left an indelible imprint on Wain's mind and art. His exposure to the lives of the working class and to the advance of industrialism gave him a profound knowledge of working people and their problems, which he depicts with sympathy and humanity in his fiction. Moreover, Wain's experiences at Froebel's Preparatory School and at Newcastle-under-Lyme High School impressed on him the idea that life was competitive and "a perpetual effort to survive." He found himself surrounded and outnumbered by people who resented him for being different from themselves. His contact with older children, schoolboy bullies, and authoritative schoolmasters taught Wain that the world is a dangerous place. These "lessons of life" were carried into his work. The reader finds in Wain's fiction a sense of the difficulty of survival in an intrusive and demanding world. The worst of characters is always the bully, and the worst of societies is always totalitarian. Beginning with *Born in Captivity*, each of Wain's published novels and stories is concerned in some way with the power and control that some people seek to exercise over others.

To cope with these injustices as well as with his own fears and inadequacies during his early years, Wain turned to humor, debate, and music. For Wain, the humorist is above all a moralist, in whose hands the ultimate weapon of laughter might conceivably become the means of liberating humankind from its enslavement to false ideals. Thus, his mimicry of both authorities and students was used as the quickest way to illustrate that something was horrible or boring or absurd. In both *Born in Captivity* and *The Contenders*, the heroes use mockery and ridicule to cope with their unjust world.

Wain's interest in jazz also influenced his personal and literary development. He spoke and wrote often of his lifelong enthusiasm for the trumpet playing of Bill Coleman, and he admitted that Percy Brett, the black jazz musician in *Strike the Father Dead*, was created with Coleman in mind. Accompanying this interest was a growing interest in serious writing and reading. Unlike many youths, Wain did not have to endure the agonizing doubt and indecision of trying to decide what he wanted to do in life. By the age of nine, he knew: He wanted to be an author. He began as a critically conscious writer who delighted in "pastiche and parody for their own sake," although he had problems maintaining steady plot lines. Wain matched his writing with voracious reading. His early interest in the novels of Charles Dickens, Tobias Smollett, Daniel Defoe, and others in the tradition of the English novel influenced his later literary style. Like these predecessors, Wain approached his characters through the conventional narration of the realist, and his concerns were social and moral.

The second major period in Wain's life occurred between 1943, when he entered St. John's College, Oxford, and 1955, when he resigned his post as lecturer in English at Reading University to become a full-time writer. Two friends made in his Oxford period especially influenced his writing. One was Philip Larkin, whose "rock-like determination" provided an inspiring example for Wain. The other friend was Kingsley Amis, whose work on a first novel inspired Wain to attempt writing a novel in his spare time. Wain wrote his first novel, not particularly because he wished to be a novelist, but to see if he could write one that would get into print. In 1953, Frederick Warburg accepted *Born in Captivity*, and its unexpected success quickly established Wain as one of Britain's promising new writers.

Wain's exhilarating experience with his first book was, however, poor preparation for the sobering slump that followed. Ill health, divorce proceedings, and the drudgery of a scholar's life pushed him into a crisis of depression and discouragement. He tried to climb out of this crisis by leaving the university for a year and retreating to the Swiss Alps. There, he let his imagination loose on his own problems. The result was *Living in the Present*, a depressing book of manifest despair and disgust. Out of this period in his life, Wain developed a profound awareness of love and loneliness, union and estrangement. The essential loneliness of human beings, and their more or less successful attempts to overcome their loneliness by love, became major themes in his later fiction.

Although Wain was never sanguine about the human condition or the times in which he lived, his life was to be more fulfilling than he anticipated at this time. As a result of his year of self-assessment, in 1955, Wain did not return to the junior position he had held at the University of Reading but instead began working full time at his writing. Little more than a decade later, his reputation had become so well established that he could reenter the academic world as a visiting professor. Eventually, Wain was appointed a professor of poetry at Oxford University, a post he held from 1973 to 1978.

Sprightly Running, published in 1962, was evidence that Wain was much more contented than he had been seven years before. He was now happily married to Eirian James, an intelligent, insightful woman who provided him with companionship and sometimes help with his work (she coedited *The New Wessex Selection of Thomas Hardy's Poetry* in 1978). The couple had three sons, and their life together ended only with Eirian's death in 1987. The following year, Wain married Patricia Dunn.

Despite ill health and diminished vision, Wain labored on courageously at what proved to be his final project, three novels that together constitute the Oxford trilogy. On May 24, 1994, Wain died of a stroke at the John Radcliffe Hospital in Oxford.

Analysis

As a novelist, John Wain has been described as a "painfully honest" writer who always, to an unusual degree, wrote autobiography. His own fortunes and his emotional reactions to these fortunes are, of course, transformed in various ways. His purpose is artistic, not confessional, and he shaped his material accordingly. As Wain himself stated, this intention is both pure and simple: to express his own feelings honestly and to tell the truth about the world he knew. At his best—in *Born in Captivity*, *Strike the Father Dead*, *A Winter in the Hills*, and *The Pardoner's Tale*—Wain finds a great many ways to convey the message that life is ultimately tragic. Human beings suffer, life is difficult, and the comic mask conceals anguish. Only occasionally is this grim picture relieved by some sort of idealism, some unexpected attitude of unselfishness or tenderness. What is more, in all his writings Wain is a thoughtful, literate man coming to terms with these truths in a sincere and forthright manner.

To understand something of Wain's uniqueness as a novelist, the reader must look back at least to the end of World War II. For about ten years after the war, established writers continued to produce successfully. English novelists such as Aldous Huxley, Graham Greene, Evelyn Waugh, C. P. Snow, and Anthony Powell had made their reputations before the war and continued to be the major literary voices of that time. Most of them were from upper-class or upper-middle-class origins and had been educated in Great Britain's elite public schools, then at Oxford or Cambridge. Their novels were likely to center on fashionable London or some country estate. Often they confined their satire to the intellectual life and the cultural as well as social predicaments of the upper middle class.

A combination of events in postwar England led to the appearance of another group of writers, soon referred to by literary journalists as the Angry Young Men. Among these writers was Wain, who, along with Amis, John Braine, John Osborne, Angus Wilson, Alan Sillitoe, and others, turned away from technical innovations, complexity, and the sensitive, introspective protagonist to concentrate on concrete problems of current society. Thus, in the tradition of the eighteenth century novel, Wain fulfills most effectively the novelist's basic task of telling a good story. His novels move along at an even pace; he relies on a simple, tightly constructed, and straightforward plot; clarity; good and bad characters; and a controlled point of view. The reader need only think of James Joyce and Franz Kafka, and the contrast is clear. What most of Wain's novels ask from the reader is not some feat of analysis, but a considered fullness of response, a readiness to acknowledge, even in disagreement, his vision of defeat.

Wain's typical protagonist is essentially an "antihero," a man at the mercy of life. Although sometimes capable of aspiration and thought, he is not strong enough to carve out his destiny in the way he wishes. Frequently, he is something of a dreamer, tossed about by life, and also pushed about, or at least overshadowed, by the threats in his life. Wain's Charles Lumley (*Born in Captivity*) and Edgar Banks (*Living in the Present*) bear the marks of this type. Often there is discernible in his characters a modern malaise, a vague discontent, and a yearning for some person or set of circumstances beyond their reach. Sometimes, this sense of disenchantment with life as it is becomes so great that the individual expresses a desire not to live at all, as Edgar Banks asserts in *Living in the Present* and as Gus Howkins declares in *The Pardoner's Tale*.

Wain is also accomplished in his creation of place and atmosphere. In *Strike the Father Dead*, he fully captures the grayness of a London day, the grayness of lives spent under its pall, the grayness of the people who wander its streets. When Wain describes an afternoon in which Giles Hermitage (*The Pardoner's Tale*) forces himself to work in the subdued light at home, when Arthur Geary (*The Smaller Sky*) walks the platforms at Paddington Station, when Charles Lumley walks in on a literary gathering, or when Roger Furnivall (*A Winter in the Hills*) makes his way home through the Welsh countryside—at such moments the reader encounters Wain's mastery of setting and atmosphere.

The themes communicated through Wain's novels are, like his method, consistent. It is clear that he sees the eighteenth century as a time of dignity, pride, and self-sufficiency—

qualities lacking in the twentieth century. Like Johnson, Wain defends the value of reason, moderation, common sense, moral courage, and intellectual self-respect. Moreover, his fictional themes of the dignity of the human being, the difficulty of survival in the modern world, and the perils of success have established him principally as a moralist concerned with ethical issues. In later works, the value of tradition, the notion of human understanding, and the ability to love and suffer become the chief moral values. In all his novels, he is primarily concerned with the problem of defining the moral worth of the individual. For all these reasons, Wain is recognized as a penetrating observer of the human scene.

One final point should be noted about Wain's capacities as a novelist. Clearly, the spiritual dimension is missing in the world he describes, yet there is frequently the hint or at least the possibility of renewal, which is the closest Wain comes to any sort of recognized affirmation. Charles Lumley, Joe Shaw, Jeremy Coleman, and Roger Furnivall are all characters who seem to be, by the end of their respective stories, on the verge of rebirth of a sort, on the threshold of reintegration and consequent regeneration. In each case, this renewal depends on the ability of the individual to come to terms with himself and his situation; to confront and accept at a stroke past, present, and future; and to accept and tolerate the contradictions inherent in all three. Wain's sensitive response to the tragic aspects of life is hardly novel, but his deep compassion for human suffering and his tenderness for the unfortunate are more needed than ever in an age when violence, brutality, and cynicism are all too prevalent.

BORN IN CAPTIVITY

In his first novel, *Born in Captivity*, Wain comically perceives the difficulties of surviving in a demanding, sometimes fearful world. Detached from political causes and the progress of his own life, the hero is a drifter, seeking to compromise with or to escape from such "evils" as class lines, boredom, hypocrisy, and the conventional perils of success. Although the novel carries a serious moral interest, Wain's wit, sharp observations, and inventiveness keep the plot moving. His comedy exaggerates, reforms, and criticizes to advocate the reasonable in social behavior and to promote the value and dignity of the individual.

Born in Captivity has the characteristic features of the picaresque novel: a series of short and often comic adventures loosely strung together; an opportunistic and pragmatic hero who seeks to make a living through his wits; and satiric characterization of stock figures rather than individualized portraits. Unlike the eighteenth century picaro, however, who is often hardhearted, cruel, and selfish, Wain's central character is a well-intentioned drifter who compromises enough to live comfortably. His standby and salvation is a strong sense of humor that enables him to make light of much distress and disaster. Lumley's character is revealed against the shifting setting of the picaresque world and in his characteristic response to repeated assaults on his fundamental decency and sympathy for others. He remains substantially the same throughout the novel; his many roles—as window cleaner, delivery driver, chauffeur, and the like—place him firmly in the picaresque tradition. Lumley's versatility and adaptability permit Wain to show his character under a variety of circumstances and in a multiplicity of situations.

Lumley's character is established almost immediately with the description of his conflict with the landlady in the first chapter. The reader sees him as the adaptable antihero who tries to control his own fate, as a jack of all trades, a skilled manipulator, an adept deceiver, an artist of disguises. Wain stresses Lumley's ingenuity rather than his mere struggle for survival; at the same time, he develops Lumley's individual personality, emphasizing the man and his adventures. The role that Lumley plays in the very first scene is one in which he will be cast throughout the story—that of a put-upon young man engaged in an attempt to cope with and outwit the workaday world.

The satire is developed through the characterization. Those who commit themselves to class—who judge others and define themselves by the class structure—are satirized throughout the novel. Surrounding the hero is a host of lightly sketched, "flat," stock figures, all of whom play their predictable roles. These characters include the proletarian girl, the American, the landlady, the entrepreneur, the middle-class couple, and the artist. In this first novel, Wain's resources in characterization are limited primarily to caricature. The comedy functions to instruct and entertain. Beneath the horseplay and high spirits, Wain rhetorically manipulates the reader's moral judgment so that he sympathizes with the hero. In the tradition of Smollett and Dickens, Wain gives life to the grotesque by emphasizing details of his eccentric characters and by indicating his attitude toward them through the selection of specific bodily and facial characteristics.

Wain has also adopted another convention of eighteenth century fiction: the intrusive author. The active role of this authorial impresario accounts for the distance between the reader and the events of the novel; his exaggerations, his jokes, and his philosophizing prevent the reader from taking Lumley's fate too seriously. In later novels, Wain's authorial stance changes as his vision deepens.

Any discussion of comic technique in *Born in Captivity* leads inevitably to the novel's resolution. Ordinarily, readers do not like to encounter "perfect" endings to novels; nevertheless, they are not put off by the unrealistic ending to this novel because they know from the beginning that they are reading a comic novel that depends on unrealistic exaggeration of various kinds. Elgin W. Mellown was correct when he called the novel "a pastiche: Walter Mitty's desire expressed through the actions of the Three Stooges—wish fulfillment carried out through outrageous actions and uncharacteristic behavior." The reader feels secure in the rightness of the ending as a conclusion to all the comic wrongness that has gone on before.

STRIKE THE FATHER DEAD

In *Strike the Father Dead*, Wain further extended himself with a work more penetrating than anything he had written before. Not only is it, as Walter Allen said, a "deeply pondered novel," but it is also a culmination of the promises inherent in Wain's earlier works. Plot, theme, character, and setting are integrated to tell the story of a son who breaks parental ties, thereby freeing himself to make his own way in life as a jazz pianist. Pointing to the foibles of his fellowman and probing the motives of an indignant parent, Wain's wit and sarcastic humor lighten this uncompromising study of the nonconformist's right to assert his nonconformity.

Two later Wain novels—*A Winter in the Hills* and *The Pardoner's Tale*—continue and elaborate on many of the central themes of his fiction, but they surpass the earlier novels in richness and complexity. Both novels exhibit, far more than do his earlier writings, an interest in the tragic implications of romantic love; a greater complexity in character development allows Wain to portray convincingly men whose loneliness borders on self-destruction. Each novel is not simply another story of isolation or spiritual desolation, although it is that. Each hero is cast into a wasteland, and the novel in a sense is the story of his attempts to find the river of life again, or possibly for the first time. One of the themes that develops from this period in Wain's career is that personal relationships are the most important and yet most elusive forces in society.

The plot of *Strike the Father Dead* is arranged in an elaborate seven-part time scheme. Parts 1 and 6 occur sometime late in 1957 or early in 1958, part 2 takes place in the immediate prewar years, and the other divisions follow chronologically up to the last, which is set in 1958. The scene shifts back and forth between a provincial university town and the darker, black-market-and-jazz side of London, with a side trip to Paris.

Wain narrates the story from the points of view of four characters. The central figure, Jeremy Coleman, revolts against his father and the academic establishment in search of self-expression as a jazz pianist. Alfred Coleman, Jeremy's father and a professor of classics, is an atheist devoted to duty and hard work. Eleanor, Alfred's sister and foster mother to Jeremy, is devoted to Jeremy and finds comfort in innocent religiosity. Percy Brett, a black American jazz musician, offers Jeremy his first real parental leadership. Like Ernest Pontifex, in Samuel Butler's *The Way of All Flesh* (1903), Jeremy escapes from an oppressive existence; he has a passion for music, and once he has the opportunity to develop, his shrinking personality changes.

Strike the Father Dead marks a considerable advance over *Born in Captivity* in the thorough rendering of each character and each scene. By employing a succession of first-person narrators, Wain focuses attention more evenly on each of the figures. The result is that the reader comes away knowing Jeremy even better, because what is learned about him comes from not only his own narration but other sources as well. Inasmuch as there are three central characters, *Strike the Father Dead* represents a larger range for Wain. Each interior monologue is a revelation; the language is personal, distinctive, and descriptive of character.

In the manner of a bildungsroman, *Strike the Father Dead* is also a novel that recounts the youth and young manhood of a sensitive protagonist who is attempting to learn the nature of the world, discover its meaning and pattern, and acquire a philosophy of life. Setting plays a vital role in this odyssey. The provincial and London backgrounds and the accurate rendering of the language make the novel come alive. *Strike the Father Dead* moves between two contemporary worlds—a world of rigidity and repression, represented by Alfred, and a world of creativity, international and free, represented by London and Paris. The first world oppresses Jeremy; the second attracts and draws him. He dreams about it and invents fictions about it. Central to this new world is Jeremy's love of jazz. For him, the experience of jazz means beauty, love, life, growth, freedom, ecstasy—the very qualities he finds missing in the routine, disciplined life of Alfred.

Although *Strike the Father Dead* tells the story of a British young man who becomes successful, the success is to a certain extent bittersweet. In his triumphs over his home circumstances, Jeremy loses something as well. There are various names given to it: innocence; boyhood; nature; the secure, predictable life at home. The world beyond the academic life waits for Jeremy, and he, unknowingly, does his best to bring it onstage. With such a life comes a developing sense of injustice, deprivation, and suffering. These concerns become focal points in Wain's subsequent novels, as he turns toward the impulse to define character and dilemma much more objectively and with greater moral responsibility.

A Winter in the Hills

With its setting in Wales, *A Winter in the Hills* marked a departure from Wain's first seven novels, all of which were centered in England. The story expresses, perhaps more comprehensively than any other, Wain's feelings for the provincial world, its cohesion and deep loyalties, and its resistance to innovation from outside. Here the reader finds Wain's sympathy for the underdog, his respect for decency and the dignity of humanity, and his affirmation of life; here, too, is expressed Wain's deep interest in the causes and effects of loneliness and alienation.

The reader's first inclination is to approach the novel as primarily a novel of character, the major interest and emphasis of which is the constantly developing character of Roger Furnivall himself. Using third-person narration, Wain keeps the focus on his main character as he progresses straight through several months that constitute a time of crisis in his life. Through most of the novel, Roger struggles doggedly against a combination of adverse circumstances, always in search of a purpose. Outwardly, he forces himself on Gareth, for example, as a way of improving his idiomatic Welsh. Inwardly, he "needed involvement, needed a human reason for being in the district." The guilt he carries because of his brother's suffering and death helps to propel him into a more active engagement with contemporary life. His conflict with Dic Sharp draws him out of his own private grief because he is helping not only Gareth but also an entire community of people.

The reader learns about Roger in another way, too: Wain uses setting to reveal and reflect the protagonist's emotions and mental states. Roger's walk in the rain down the country roads, as he attempts to resolve his bitterness and disappointment at Beverley's rejection of him, is vividly depicted. It carries conviction because Roger's anxiety has been built up gradually and artistically. The pastoral world is a perpetually shifting landscape, and Wain depicts its shifts and contrasts with an acute eye for telling detail. Especially striking are the sketches of evening coming on in the Welsh hills, with their rocks and timber and vast expanses of green. Such descriptions help to convey Roger's yearning for happiness in a world that seems bent on denying it to him.

One major theme of the book is the invasion of the peaceful, conservative world of Wales by outsiders who have no roots in the region, and therefore no real concern for its inhabitants. These invaders are characterized by a sophisticated corruption that contrasts sharply with the unspoiled simplicity and honesty of the best of the natives. A related theme is the decline of the town: its economic insecurity, its struggle to resist the progressive and materialistic "cruelty, greed, tyranny, the power of the rich to drive the poor to the wall." Through Roger's point of view, Wain expresses his opposition to the pressures—economic, political, cultural—that seek to destroy the Welsh and, by implication, all minority enclaves. Thus, *A Winter in the Hills* is more than a novel about the growth of one human being from loneliness and alienation to mature and selfless love; it is also a powerful study of the quality of life in the contemporary world, threatened by the encroachments of bureaucracy, greed, and materialism.

THE PARDONER'S TALE

The somewhat optimistic resolution of *A Winter in the Hills* stands in stark contrast to that of *The Pardoner's Tale*, Wain's most somber novel. In no other work by Wain are the characters so lonely, so frustrated, or so obsessed with thoughts of mutability, lost opportunities, and death. The novel is really two stories: a first-person tale about Gus Howkins, an aging Londoner contemplating divorce, and a third-person narrative (the framing narrative) about Giles Hermitage, an established novelist and bachelor living in an unnamed cathedral town, who gets involved with the Chichester-Redferns, a woman and daughter, while he is working out the story of Howkins. It is the interplay between these two stories that constitutes the plot of *The Pardoner's Tale*.

Giles Hermitage is obviously the figure with whom Wain is the most intimately involved. He is a highly idiosyncratic figure with very recognizable weaknesses; he is easily discouraged (there is an early thought of suicide), and he resorts to excessive drinking. The root cause of his death wish and of his drinking is loneliness. Like Wain's earlier heroes, he is very much a modern man: vague in his religious and humanitarian aspirations, rootless and alienated from the social life of the community in which he lives, and initially weak and confused in his relationships with women. Plagued by anxiety, depression, vague discontent, and a sense of inner emptiness, he seeks peace of mind under conditions that increasingly militate against it. Add to his problems the ever-growing urge toward self-destruction, and the reader begins to recognize in this novel a truly contemporary pulsebeat. Hermitage is a stranger in a world that does not make sense.

Unlike Wain's earlier heroes, however, Hermitage tries to make sense of the world through the medium of his writing by stepping back into what he calls "the protecting circle of art." His approach to writing is autobiographical, personal, even subjective. The hero of his novel is a mask for himself. The author is creating a character who is in his own predicament, and the agonies he endures enable him to express his deepest feelings about life. In Hermitage, Wain presents a character who tries to create, as artists do, a new existence out of the chaos of his life.

The remaining major characters in *The Pardoner's Tale* bear family resemblances to those in other of Wain's novels. If the part of the lonely, alienated hero so effectively carried in *A Winter in the Hills* by Roger Furnivall is here assigned to Giles Hermitage, then the role of the manipulator is assigned in this novel to Mrs. Chichester-Redfern. Although a good deal less ruthless than Dic Sharp, she nevertheless seeks to exploit the hero.

The process by which Mrs. Chichester-Redfern is gradually revealed through the eyes of Hermitage is subtle and delicate. At first merely a stranger, she comes to seem in time a calculating and educated woman, the innocent victim of a man who deserted her, a seventy-year-old woman grasping for answers to some vital questions about her own life. She summons Hermitage under the pretense of wanting to gain insight into her life. From these conversations, the reader learns that she, like Hermitage, is confronted and dislocated by external reality in the form of a personal loss. Also like the hero, she desires to come to some understanding of her unhappy life through the medium of art. Her true motive is revenge, however, and she wants Hermitage to write a novel with her husband in it as a character who suffers pain. Then, she says, "there will be that much justice done in the world."

In addition to the alienated, lonely hero and the manipulator, most of Wain's fiction portrays a comforter. In his latest novel, the comforter is embodied in Diana Chichester-Redfern, but the happiness Diana offers is only temporary. In this novel, love is reduced to a meaningless mechanical act: Diana, also, is living in a wasteland.

The basic tension of this novel is a simple and classic one—the life-force confronting the death-force. As surely as Mrs. Chichester-Redfern is the death-force in the novel, Diana is the active and life-giving presence. She is depicted as an abrasive, liberated, sensual, innately selfish modern young woman who stands in positive contrast to the deathlike grayness of her mother. She is earthy and fulfilled, accepting and content with her music (playing the guitar satisfies her need for proficiency), her faith (which takes care of "all the moral issues") and her sexuality (which she enjoys because she has no choice). Diana goes from one affair to another, not in search of love (she claims she "can't love anybody") but out of a need for repetition. Diana defines love and meaning as the fulfillment of a man or woman's emotional requirements. To her, love does not mean self-sacrifice; rather, love is synonymous with need.

The world of *The Pardoner's Tale* is thus the archetypal world of all Wain's fiction: random, fragmented, lonely, contradictory. It is a world in which wasted lives, debased sexual encounters, and destroyed moral intelligence yield a tragic vision of futility and sterility, isolation from the community, estrangement from those who used to be closest to one, and loneliness in the middle of the universe itself.

YOUNG SHOULDERS

Amid all this, Wain's unflinching honesty and his capacity for compassion make his definition of the human condition bearable. Both characteristics are evident in *Young Shoulders*. Again, Wain focuses on senseless waste. A plane of English schoolchildren crashes in Lisbon, Portugal, killing everyone aboard. Seventeen-year-old Paul Waterford, whose twelve-year-old sister, Clare, was one of the victims, describes his journey to Lisbon with his parents, their encounters with other grief-stricken relatives, the memorial service they attend, and their return to England. Because he is still untainted by convention, Paul feels free to see the other characters as they are, often even to find them funny; however, he has to admit that he can be wrong about people. The seemingly calm Mrs. Richardson, a teacher's widow, collapses during the memorial service; the restrained Janet Finlayson howls in the hotel lobby that God is punishing them all; Mr. Smithson, whom Paul assessed as a man on his way up, goes crazy on the tarmac; and everyone depends on Paul's parents: the mother Paul saw only as a drunk and the father Paul dismissed as hopelessly withdrawn.

Because Wain has the eighteenth century writer's hunger for universals, we may assume that the real subject of *Young Shoulders* is not how individuals behave in the face of tragedy but what the young protagonist and, by extension, the reader has learned by the end of the novel. Paul comes to see that human beings avoid acknowledging their emotions in so many ways that an outsider's judgment is likely to be inaccurate. He also recognizes the extent to which he deludes himself, whether by imagining a utopian society he will govern or by addressing "reports" to Clare, thus denying that she is dead. By losing his innocence, Paul gains in compassion.

THE OXFORD TRILOGY

With its single plot line, its compressed time scheme, and its limited cast, *Young Shoulders* is much like a neoclassical play. By contrast, the three novels composing the Oxford trilogy have an epic quality, as indeed they must if they are to "describe and dramatize the Oxford that has been sinking out of sight, and fading from memory, for over thirty years," as Wain states in his preface to the final volume. The series does indeed cover three decades.

Where the Rivers Meet introduces the protagonist Peter Leonard and takes him through his undergraduate years at Oxford; *Comedies* begins in 1933, with Leonard's appointment as a fellow, and ends after World War II; and *Hungry Generations* covers Leonard's life from 1947 to 1956. There is a multitude of characters, ranging from Oxford intellectuals to the patrons of the pub that Leonard's parents run, each with definite ideas about local politics, world news, and the progress of society. Wain's honesty is reflected in the way he permits all the characters to speak their minds; his compassion is revealed in his attempt to understand even the least appealing of them. These qualities, along with his creative genius and his consummate artistry, should ensure for John Wain a permanent place in twentieth century literary history.

Dale Salwak
Updated by Rosemary M. Canfield Reisman

OTHER MAJOR WORKS

SHORT FICTION: *Nuncle, and Other Stories*, 1960; *Death of the Hind Legs, and Other Stories*, 1966; *The Life Guard*, 1971; *King Caliban, and Other Stories*, 1978.

PLAYS: *Harry in the Night: An Optimistic Comedy*, pr. 1975; *Johnson Is Leaving: A Monodrama*, pb. 1994.

POETRY: *Mixed Feelings*, 1951; *A Word Carved on a Sill*, 1956; *A Song About Major Eatherly*, 1961; *Weep Before God: Poems*, 1961; *Wildtrack: A Poem*, 1965; *Letters to Five Artists*, 1969; *The Shape of Feng*, 1972; *Feng: A Poem*, 1975; *Poems for the Zodiac*, 1980; *Thinking About Mr. Person*, 1980; *Poems, 1949-1979*, 1981; *Twofold*, 1981; *Open Country*, 1987.

TELEPLAY: *Young Shoulders*, 1984 (with Robert Smith).

RADIO PLAYS: *You Wouldn't Remember*, 1978; *A Winter in the Hills*, 1981; *Frank*, 1982.

NONFICTION: *Preliminary Essays*, 1957; *Gerard Manley Hopkins: An Idiom of Desperation*, 1959; *Sprightly Running: Part of an Autobiography*, 1962; *Essays on Literature and Ideas*, 1963; *The Living World of Shakespeare: A Playgoer's Guide*, 1964; *Arnold Bennett*, 1967; *A House for the Truth: Critical Essays*, 1972; *Samuel Johnson*, 1974; *Professing Poetry*, 1977; *Samuel Johnson, 1709-1784*, 1984 (with Kai Kin Yung); *Dear Shadows: Portraits from Memory*, 1986.

CHILDREN'S/YOUNG ADULT LITERATURE: *Lizzie's Floating Shop*, 1981.

EDITED TEXTS: *Contemporary Reviews of Romantic Poetry*, 1953; *Interpretations: Essays on Twelve English Poems*, 1955; *International Literary Annual*, 1959, 1960; *Fanny Burney's Diary*, 1960; *Anthology of Modern Poetry*, 1963; *Selected Shorter Poems of Thomas Hardy*, 1966; *Selected Stories of Thomas Hardy*, 1966; *Thomas Hardy's "The Dynasts,"* 1966; *Shakespeare: Macbeth, a Casebook*, 1968 (revised 1994); *Shakespeare: Othello, a Casebook*, 1971; *Johnson as Critic*, 1973; *The New Wessex Selection of Thomas Hardy's Poetry*, 1978 (with Eirian James).

BIBLIOGRAPHY

Bayley, John. "Obituary: John Wain." *The Independent*, May 25, 1994. In this biographical sketch of Wain's life and literary career, Bayley compares him with Kingsley Amis and praises his biography of Samuel Johnson.

Burgess, Anthony. *The Novel Now: A Guide to Contemporary Fiction*. 1967. Reprint.

New York: Faber & Faber, 1972. Expanded from an earlier study, Burgess's work groups Wain with other class-conscious British fiction writers.

Gerard, David E. *John Wain: A Bibliography.* Westport, Conn.: Meckler, 1987. Contains a comprehensive, if dated, annotated bibliography of Wain's work. Lists materials of critical and biographical interest, including radio, television, and sound recordings. Also includes other critical and biographical references and reviews of works by Wain.

Gindin, James J. "The Moral Center of John Wain's Fiction." In *Postwar British Fiction: New Accents and Attitudes.* Berkeley: University of California Press, 1962. Gindin's chapter on Wain discusses the writer's use of morality as a thematic and structural device and claims that each novel contains a central statement of the moral worth of the individual.

Hatziolou, Elizabeth. *John Wain: A Man of Letters.* London: Pisces Press, 1997. The first extensive biography to be published after Wain's death. Includes an index.

Heptonstall, Geoffrey. "Remembering John Wain." *Contemporary Review* 266 (March, 1995): 144-146. A brief discussion of Wain's central themes of faithlessness and the assumption that there are no assumptions. Examines Wain's rejection of realism and his intention to speak imaginatively.

Rabinovitz, Rubin. "The Novelists of the 1950's: A General Survey." In *The Reaction Against Experiment in the English Novel, 1950-1960.* New York: Columbia University Press, 1967. Rabinovitz places Wain in the context of novelists who embraced traditional values rather than those who experimented with unconventional ideas or forms, aligning Wain's novels with those of Arnold Bennett and eighteenth century picaresque novelists.

Salwak, Dale. *Interviews with Britain's Angry Young Men.* San Bernardino, Calif.: Borgo Press, 1984. This useful resource characterizes Wain as an "eighteenth century man." Engages Wain in a discussion of the role of criticism in the author's life, his goals as a writer, his response to the phenomenon of the Angry Young Men, and the sources and themes in several of his novels.

_____. *John Wain.* Boston: Twayne, 1981. Part of Twayne's English Authors series, this work is the first book-length study of Wain and is a useful introduction to Wain's life, career, and works.

Taylor, D. J. *After the War: The Novel and English Society Since 1945.* London: Chatto & Windus, 1993. An attempt to define the nature of postwar writing. Wain is grouped with William Cooper and Kingsley Amis as antiromantic and as antimodernist, that is, opposed to the psychological emphasis and stylistic complexity of James Joyce and Virginia Woolf.

Bibliography

Every effort has been made to include studies published in 2000 and later. Most items in this bibliography contain a listing of secondary sources, making it easier to identify other critical commentary on novelists, movements, and themes.

Theoretical, thematic, and historical studies

Altman, Janet Gurkin. *Epistolarity: Approaches to a Form*. Columbus: Ohio State University Press, 1982. Examines the epistolary novel, explaining how novelists use the letter form to develop characterization, further their plots, and develop meaning.

Beaumont, Matthew, ed. *Adventures in Realism*. Malden, Mass.: Blackwell, 2007. Fifteen essays explore facets of realism, which was critical to the development of the novel. Provides a theoretical framework for understanding how novelists attempt to represent the real and the common in fiction.

Brink, André. *The Novel: Language and Narrative from Cervantes to Calvino*. New York: New York University Press, 1998. Uses contemporary theories of semiotics and narratology to establish a continuum between early novelists and those of the postmodern era in their conscious use of language to achieve certain effects. Ranges across national boundaries to illustrate the theory of the development of the novel since the seventeenth century.

Brownstein, Rachel. *Becoming a Heroine: Reading About Women in Novels*. New York: Viking Press, 1982. Feminist survey of novels from the eighteenth century through the latter half of the twentieth century. Examines how "becoming a heroine" defines for women a sense of value in their lives. Considers novels by both men and women, and discusses the importance of the traditional marriage plot.

Bruzelius, Margaret. *Romancing the Novel: Adventure from Scott to Sebald*. Lewisburg, Pa.: Bucknell University Press, 2007. Examines the development of the adventure novel, linking it with the medieval romance tradition and exploring readers' continuing fascination with the genre.

Cavallaro, Dani. *The Gothic Vision: Three Centuries of Horror, Terror, and Fear*. New York: Continuum, 2005. Study of the gothic novel from its earliest manifestations in the eighteenth century to the early twenty-first century. Through the lenses of contemporary cultural theories, examines readers' fascination with novels that invoke horror, terror, and fright.

Doody, Margaret Anne. *The True Story of the Novel*. New Brunswick, N.J.: Rutgers University Press, 1996. Traces the roots of the novel, traditionally thought to have been developed in the seventeenth century, to classical Greek and Latin texts that exhibit characteristics of modern fiction.

Hale, Dorothy J., ed. *The Novel: An Anthology of Criticism and Theory, 1900-2000*. Malden, Mass.: Blackwell, 2006. Collection of essays by theorists and novelists. Includes commentary on the novel form from the perspective of formalism, structuralism, poststructuralism, Marxism, and reader response theory. Essays also address the novel through the lenses of sociology, gender studies, and feminist theory.

_____. *Social Formalism: The Novel in Theory from Henry James to the Present*. Stanford, Calif.: Stanford University Press, 1998. Emphasizes the novel's special ability to define a social world for readers. Relies heavily on the works of contemporary literary and cultural theorists. Provides a summary of twentieth century efforts to identify a theory of fiction that encompasses novels of many kinds.

Hart, Stephen M., and Wen-chin Ouyang, eds. *A Companion to Magical Realism*. London: Tamesis, 2005. Essays outlining the development of Magical Realism, tracing its roots from Europe through Latin America to other regions of the world. Explores the political dimensions of the genre.

Hoffman, Michael J., and Patrick D. Murphy, eds. *Essentials of the Theory of Fiction*. 2d ed. Durham, N.C.: Duke University Press, 1996. Collection of essays by influential critics from the late nineteenth century through the twentieth century. Focuses on the essential elements of fiction and the novel's relationship to the world it depicts.

Lodge, David. *The Art of Fiction: Illustrated from Classic and Modern Texts*. New York: Viking Press, 1993. Short commentaries on the technical aspects of fiction. Examples from important and minor novelists illustrate literary principles and techniques such as point of view, suspense, character introduction, irony, motivation, and ending.

Lynch, Deirdre, and William B. Walker, eds. *Cultural Institutions of the Novel*. Durham, N.C.: Duke University Press, 1996. Fifteen essays examine aspects of long fiction produced around the world. Encourages a redefinition of the genre and argues for inclusion of texts not historically considered novels.

Moretti, Franco, ed. *The Novel*. 2 vols. Princeton, N.J.: Princeton University Press, 2006. Compendium exploring the novel from multiple perspectives, including as an anthropological, historical, and sociological document; a function of the national tradition from which it emerges; and a work of art subject to examination using various critical approaches.

Priestman, Martin, ed. *The Cambridge Companion to Crime Fiction*. New York: Cambridge University Press, 2003. Essays examine the nature and development of the genre, explore works by writers (including women and ethnic minorities) from several countries, and establish links between crime fiction and other literary genres. Includes a chronology.

Scaggs, John. *Crime Fiction*. New York: Routledge, 2005. Provides a history of crime fiction, explores key subgenres, and identifies recurring themes that suggest the wider social and historical context in which these works are written. Suggests critical approaches that open crime fiction to serious study.

Shiach, Morag, ed. *The Cambridge Companion to the Modernist Novel*. New York: Cambridge University Press, 2007. Essays explaining the concept of modernism and its influence on the novel. Detailed examination of works by writers from various countries, all influenced by the modernist movement. Includes a detailed chronology.

Vice, Sue. *Holocaust Fiction*. New York: Routledge, 2000. Examines controversies generated by novels about the Holocaust. Focuses on eight important works, but also offers observations on the polemics surrounding publication of books on this topic.

Zunshine, Lisa. *Why We Read Fiction: Theory of Mind and the Novel*. Columbus: Ohio State University Press, 2006. Applies theories of cognitive psychology to novel reading, explaining how experience and human nature lead readers to constrain their interpretations of a given text. Provides numerous examples from well-known novels to illustrate how and why readers find pleasure in fiction.

THE PICARESQUE NOVEL

Reed, Walter L. *An Exemplary History of the Novel: The Quixotic Versus the Picaresque*. Chicago: University of Chicago Press, 1981. Systematic study of the novel that examines its unique qualities and contrasts it with older forms of discourse. Offers close readings of several texts, explaining how the English novel fits within the larger developments in European fiction.

Laurence W. Mazzeno

GLOSSARY OF LITERARY TERMS

absurdism: A philosophical attitude, pervading much of modern drama and fiction, that underlines the isolation and alienation that humans experience, having been thrown into what absurdists see as a godless universe devoid of religious, spiritual, or metaphysical meaning. Conspicuous in its lack of logic, consistency, coherence, intelligibility, and realism, the literature of the absurd depicts the anguish, forlornness, and despair inherent in the human condition. Counter to the rationalist assumptions of traditional humanism, absurdism denies the existence of universal truth or value.

allegory: A literary mode in which a second level of meaning, wherein characters, events, and settings represent abstractions, is encoded within the surface narrative. The allegorical mode may dominate an entire work, in which case the encoded message is the work's primary reason for being, or it may be an element in a work otherwise interesting and meaningful for its surface story alone. Elements of allegory may be found in Jonathan Swift's *Gulliver's Travels* (1726) and Thomas Mann's *Der Zauberberg* (1924; *The Magic Mountain*, 1927).

anatomy: Literally the term means the "cutting up" or "dissection" of a subject into its constituent parts for closer examination. Northrop Frye, in his *Anatomy of Criticism* (1957), uses the term to refer to a narrative that deals with mental attitudes rather than people. As opposed to the novel, the anatomy features stylized figures who are mouthpieces for the ideas they represent.

antagonist: The character in fiction who stands as a rival or opponent to the *protagonist*.

antihero: Defined by Seán O'Faoláin as a fictional figure who, deprived of social sanctions and definitions, is always trying to define himself and to establish his own codes. Ahab may be seen as the antihero of Herman Melville's *Moby Dick* (1851).

archetype: The term "archetype" entered literary criticism from the psychology of Carl Jung, who defined archetypes as "primordial images" from the "collective unconscious" of humankind. Jung believed that works of art derive much of their power from the unconscious appeal of these images to ancestral memories. In his extremely influential *Anatomy of Criticism* (1957), Northrop Frye gave another sense of the term wide currency, defining the archetype as "a symbol, usually an image, which recurs often enough in literature to be recognizable as an element of one's literary experience as a whole."

atmosphere: The general mood or tone of a work; atmosphere is often associated with setting but can also be established by action or dialogue. A classic example of atmosphere is the primitive, fatalistic tone created in the opening description of Egdon Heath in Thomas Hardy's *The Return of the Native* (1878).

bildungsroman: Sometimes called the "novel of education," the bildungsroman focuses on the growth of a young *protagonist* who is learning about the world and finding his or her place in life; typical examples are James Joyce's *A Portrait of the Artist as a*

Young Man (1914-1915, serial; 1916, book) and Thomas Wolfe's *Look Homeward, Angel* (1929).

biographical criticism: Criticism that attempts to determine how the events and experiences of an author's life influence his or her work.

bourgeois novel: A novel in which the values, preoccupations, and accoutrements of middle-class or bourgeois life are given particular prominence. The heyday of the bourgeois novel was the nineteenth century, when novelists as varied as Jane Austen, Honoré de Balzac, and Anthony Trollope both criticized and unreflectingly transmitted the assumptions of the rising middle class.

canon: An authorized or accepted list of books. In modern parlance, the literary canon comprehends the privileged texts, classics, or great books that are thought to belong permanently on university reading lists. Recent theory—especially feminist, Marxist, and poststructuralist—critically examines the process of canon formation and questions the hegemony of white male writers. Such theory sees canon formation as the ideological act of a dominant institution and seeks to undermine the notion of canonicity itself, thereby preventing the exclusion of works by women, minorities, and oppressed peoples.

character: Characters in fiction can be presented as if they were real people or as stylized functions of the plot. Usually characters are a combination of both factors.

classicism: A literary stance or value system consciously based on the example of classical Greek and Roman literature. While the term is applied to an enormous diversity of artists in many different periods and in many different national literatures, "classicism" generally denotes a cluster of values including formal discipline, restrained expression, reverence for tradition, and an objective rather than a subjective orientation. As a literary tendency, classicism is often opposed to *Romanticism*, although many writers combine classical and romantic elements.

climax/crisis: The term "climax" refers to the moment of the reader's highest emotional response, whereas "crisis" refers to a structural element of plot, a turning point at which a resolution must take place.

complication: The point in a novel when the *conflict* is developed or when the already existing conflict is further intensified.

conflict: The struggle that develops as a result of the opposition between the *protagonist* and another person, the natural world, society, or some force within the self.

contextualist criticism: A further extension of *formalist criticism*, which assumes that the language of art is constitutive. Rather than referring to preexistent values, the artwork creates values only inchoately realized before. The most important advocates of this position are Eliseo Vivas (*The Artistic Transaction*, 1963) and Murray Krieger (*The Play and Place of Criticism*, 1967).

conventions: All those devices of stylization, compression, and selection that constitute the necessary differences between art and life. According to the Russian Formalists, these conventions constitute the "literariness" of literature and are the only proper concern of the literary critic.

deconstruction: An extremely influential contemporary school of criticism based on the works of the French philosopher Jacques Derrida. Deconstruction treats literary works as unconscious reflections of the reigning myths of Western culture. The primary myth is that there is a meaningful world that language signifies or represents. The deconstructionist critic is most often concerned with showing how a literary text tacitly subverts the very assumptions or myths on which it ostensibly rests.

defamiliarization: Coined by Viktor Shklovsky in 1917, this term denotes a basic principle of Russian Formalism. Poetic language (by which the Formalists meant artful language, in prose as well as in poetry) defamiliarizes or "makes strange" familiar experiences. The technique of art, says Shklovsky, is to "make objects unfamiliar, to make forms difficult, to increase the difficulty and length of perception. . . . Art is a way of experiencing the artfulness of an object; the object is not important."

detective story: The so-called classic detective story (or mystery) is a highly formalized and logically structured mode of fiction in which the focus is on a crime solved by a detective through interpretation of evidence and ratiocination; the most famous detective in this mode is Arthur Conan Doyle's Sherlock Holmes. Many modern practitioners of the genre, however, such as Dashiell Hammett, Raymond Chandler, and Ross Macdonald, have de-emphasized the puzzlelike qualities of the detective story, stressing instead characterization, theme, and other elements of mainstream fiction.

determinism: The belief that an individual's actions are essentially determined by biological and environmental factors, with free will playing a negligible role. (See *naturalism.*)

dialogue: The similitude of conversation in fiction, dialogue serves to characterize, to further the *plot*, to establish *conflict*, and to express thematic ideas.

displacement: Popularized in criticism by Northrop Frye, this term refers to the author's attempt to make his or her story psychologically motivated and realistic, even as the latent structure of the mythical motivation moves relentlessly forward.

dominant: A term coined by Roman Jakobson to refer to that which "rules, determines, and transforms the remaining components in the work of a single artist, in a poetic canon, or in the work of an epoch." The shifting of the dominant in a *genre* accounts for the creation of new generic forms and new poetic epochs. For example, the rise of *realism* in the mid-nineteenth century indicates realistic conventions becoming dominant and *romance* or fantasy conventions becoming secondary.

doppelgänger: A double or counterpart of a person, sometimes endowed with ghostly qualities. A fictional character's doppelgänger often reflects a suppressed side of his or her personality. One of the classic examples of the doppelgänger motif is found in

Fyodor Dostoevski's novella *Dvoynik* (1846; *The Double*, 1917); Isaac Bashevis Singer and Jorge Luis Borges, among others, offer striking modern treatments of the doppelgänger.

epic: Although this term usually refers to a long narrative poem that presents the exploits of a central figure of high position, the term is also used to designate a long novel that has the style or structure usually associated with an epic. In this sense, for example, Herman Melville's *Moby Dick* (1851) and James Joyce's *Ulysses* (1922) may be called epics.

episodic narrative: A work that is held together primarily by a loose connection of self-sufficient episodes. *Picaresque novels* often have episodic structure.

epistolary novel: A novel made up of letters by one or more fictional characters. Samuel Richardson's *Pamela: Or, Virtue Rewarded* (1740-1741) is a well-known eighteenth century example. In the nineteenth century, Bram Stoker's *Dracula* (1897) is largely epistolary. The technique allows for several different points of view to be presented.

euphuism: A style of writing characterized by ornate language that is highly contrived, alliterative, and repetitious. Euphuism was developed by John Lyly in his *Euphues, the Anatomy of Wit* (1578) and was emulated frequently by writers of the Elizabethan Age.

existentialism: A philosophical, religious, and literary term, emerging from World War II, for a group of attitudes surrounding the pivotal notion that existence precedes essence. According to Jean-Paul Sartre, "Man is nothing else but what he makes himself." Forlornness arises from the death of God and the concomitant death of universal values, of any source of ultimate or a priori standards. Despair arises from the fact that an individual can reckon only with what depends on his or her will, and the sphere of that will is severely limited; the number of things on which he or she can have an impact is pathetically small. Existentialist literature is antideterministic in the extreme and rejects the idea that heredity and environment shape and determine human motivation and behavior.

exposition: The part or parts of a fiction that provide necessary background information. Exposition not only provides the time and place of the action but also introduces readers to the fictive world of the story, acquainting them with the ground rules of the work.

fantastic: In his study *The Fantastic* (1970), Tzvetan Todorov defines the fantastic as a *genre* that lies between the "uncanny" and the "marvelous." All three genres embody the familiar world but present an event that cannot be explained by the laws of the familiar world. Todorov says that the fantastic occupies a twilight zone between the uncanny (when the reader knows that the peculiar event is merely the result of an illusion) and the marvelous (when the reader understands that the event is supposed to take place in a realm controlled by laws unknown to humankind). The fantastic is thus essentially unsettling, provocative, even subversive.

feminist criticism: A criticism advocating equal rights for women in political, economic, social, psychological, personal, and aesthetic senses. On the thematic level, the feminist reader should identify with female characters and their concerns. The object is to provide a critique of phallocentric assumptions and an analysis of patriarchal ideologies inscribed in a literature that is male-centered and male-dominated. On the ideological level, feminist critics see gender, as well as the stereotypes that go along with it, as a cultural construct. They strive to define a particularly feminine content and to extend the *canon* so that it might include works by lesbians, feminists, and women writers in general.

flashback: A scene in a fiction that depicts an earlier event; it may be presented as a reminiscence by a character in the story or may simply be inserted into the narrative.

foreshadowing: A device to create suspense or dramatic irony in fiction by indicating through suggestion what will take place in the future.

formalist criticism: Two particularly influential formalist schools of criticism arose in the twentieth century: the Russian Formalists and the American New Critics. The Russian Formalists were concerned with the conventional devices used in literature to defamiliarize that which habit has made familiar. The New Critics believed that literary criticism is a description and evaluation of its object and that the primary concern of the critic is with the work's unity. Both schools of criticism, at their most extreme, treated literary works as artifacts or constructs divorced from their biographical and social contexts.

genre: In its most general sense, this term refers to a group of literary works defined by a common form, style, or purpose. In practice, the term is used in a wide variety of overlapping and, to a degree, contradictory senses. Tragedy and comedy are thus described as distinct genres; the novel (a form that includes both tragic and comic works) is a genre; and various subspecies of the novel, such as the *gothic* and the *picaresque*, are themselves frequently treated as distinct genres. Finally, the term "genre fiction" refers to forms of popular fiction in which the writer is bound by more or less rigid conventions. Indeed, all these diverse usages have in common an emphasis on the manner in which individual literary works are shaped by particular expectations and conventions; this is the subject of genre criticism.

genre fiction: Categories of popular fiction in which the writers are bound by more or less rigid conventions, such as in the *detective story*, the *romance*, and the *Western*. Although the term can be used in a neutral sense, it is often used dismissively.

gothic novel: A form of fiction developed in the eighteenth century that focuses on horror and the supernatural. In his preface to *The Castle of Otranto* (1765), the first gothic novel in English, Horace Walpole claimed that he was trying to combine two kinds of fiction, with events and story typical of the medieval romance and character delineation typical of the realistic novel. Other examples of the form are Matthew Gregory

Lewis's *The Monk: A Romance* (1796; also known as *Ambrosio: Or, The Monk*) and Mary Wollstonecraft Shelley's *Frankenstein: Or, The Modern Prometheus* (1818).

grotesque: According to Wolfgang Kayser (*The Grotesque in Art and Literature*, 1963), the grotesque is an embodiment in literature of the estranged world. Characterized by a breakup of the everyday world by mysterious forces, the form differs from fantasy in that the reader is not sure whether to react with humor or with horror and in that the exaggeration manifested exists in the familiar world rather than in a purely imaginative world.

Hebraic/Homeric styles: Terms coined by Erich Auerbach in *Mimesis: The Representation of Reality in Western Literature* (1953) to designate two basic fictional styles. The Hebraic style focuses only on the decisive points of narrative and leaves all else obscure, mysterious, and "fraught with background"; the Homeric style places the narrative in a definite time and place and externalizes everything in a perpetual foreground.

historical criticism: In contrast to *formalist criticism*, which treats literary works to a great extent as self-contained artifacts, historical criticism emphasizes the historical context of literature; the two approaches, however, need not be mutually exclusive. Ernst Robert Curtius's *European Literature and the Latin Middle Ages* (1940) is a prominent example of historical criticism.

historical novel: A novel that depicts past historical events, usually public in nature, and features real as well as fictional people. Sir Walter Scott's Waverley novels established the basic type, but the relationship between fiction and history in the form varies greatly depending on the practitioner.

implied author: According to Wayne Booth (*The Rhetoric of Fiction*, 1961), the novel often creates a kind of second self who tells the story—a self who is wiser, more sensitive, and more perceptive than any real person could be.

interior monologue: Defined by Édouard Dujardin as the speech of a character designed to introduce the reader directly to the character's internal life, the form differs from other kinds of monologue in that it attempts to reproduce thought before any logical organization is imposed on it. See, for example, Molly Bloom's long interior monologue at the conclusion of James Joyce's *Ulysses* (1922).

irrealism: A term often used to refer to modern or postmodern fiction that is presented self-consciously as a fiction or a fabulation rather than a mimesis of external reality. The best-known practitioners of irrealism are John Barth, Robert Coover, and Donald Barthelme.

local colorists: A loose movement of late nineteenth century American writers whose fiction emphasizes the distinctive folkways, landscapes, and dialects of various regions. Important local colorists include Bret Harte, Mark Twain, George Washington Cable, Kate Chopin, and Sarah Orne Jewett. (See *regional novel*.)

Marxist criticism: Based on the nineteenth century writings of Karl Marx and Friedrich Engels, Marxist criticism views literature as a product of ideological forces determined by the dominant class. However, many Marxists believe that literature operates according to its own autonomous standards of production and reception: It is both a product of ideology and able to determine ideology. As such, literature may overcome the dominant paradigms of its age and play a revolutionary role in society.

metafiction: This term refers to fiction that manifests a reflexive tendency, such as Vladimir Nabokov's *Pale Fire* (1962) and John Fowles's *The French Lieutenant's Woman* (1969). The emphasis is on the loosening of the work's illusion of reality to expose the reality of its illusion. Other terms used to refer to this type of fiction include "irrealism," "postmodernist fiction," "antifiction," and "surfiction."

modernism: An international movement in the arts that began in the early years of the twentieth century. Although the term is used to describe artists of widely varying persuasions, modernism in general was characterized by its international idiom, by its interest in cultures distant in space or time, by its emphasis on formal experimentation, and by its sense of dislocation and radical change.

motif: A conventional incident or situation in a fiction that may serve as the basis for the structure of the narrative itself. The Russian Formalist critic Boris Tomashevsky uses the term to refer to the smallest particle of thematic material in a work.

motivation: Although this term is usually used in reference to the convention of justifying the action of a character from his or her psychological makeup, the Russian Formalists use the term to refer to the network of devices that justify the introduction of individual *motifs* or groups of motifs in a work. For example, "compositional motivation" refers to the principle that every single property in a work contributes to its overall effect; "realistic motivation" refers to the realistic devices used to make a work plausible and lifelike.

multiculturalism: The tendency to recognize the perspectives of those traditionally excluded from the canon of Western art and literature. In order to promote multiculturalism, publishers and educators have revised textbooks and school curricula to incorporate material by and about women, members of minority groups, persons from non-Western cultures, and homosexuals.

myth: Anonymous traditional stories dealing with basic human concepts and antinomies. According to Claude Lévi-Strauss, myth is that part of language where the "formula *tradutore, tradittore* reaches its lowest truth value.... Its substance does not lie in its style, its original music, or its syntax, but in the story which it tells."

myth criticism: Northrop Frye says that in myth "we see the structural principles of literature isolated." Myth criticism is concerned with these basic principles of literature; it is not to be confused with mythological criticism, which is primarily concerned with finding mythological parallels in the surface action of the *narrative*.

narrative: Robert Scholes and Robert Kellogg, in *The Nature of Narrative* (1966), say that by "narrative" they mean literary works that include both a story and a storyteller. The term "narrative" usually implies a contrast to "enacted" fiction such as drama.

narratology: The study of the form and functioning of *narratives*; it attempts to examine what all narratives have in common and what makes individual narratives different from one another.

narrator: The *character* who recounts the *narrative*, or story. Wayne Booth describes various dramatized narrators in *The Rhetoric of Fiction* (1961): unacknowledged centers of consciousness, observers, narrator-agents, and self-conscious narrators. Booth suggests that the important elements to consider in narration are the relationships among the narrator, the author, the characters, and the reader.

naturalism: As developed by Émile Zola in the late nineteenth century, naturalism is the application of the principles of scientific *determinism* to fiction. Although it usually refers more to the choice of subject matter than to technical conventions, those conventions associated with the movement center on the author's attempt to be precise and scientifically objective in description and detail, regardless of whether the events described are sordid or shocking.

New Criticism: See *formalist criticism*.

novel: Perhaps the most difficult of all fictional forms to define because of its multiplicity of modes. Edouard, in André Gide's *Les Faux-monnayeurs* (1925; *The Counterfeiters*, 1927), says the novel is the freest and most lawless of all *genres*; he wonders if fear of that liberty is the reason the novel has so timidly clung to reality. Most critics seem to agree that the novel's primary area of concern is the social world. Ian Watt (*The Rise of the Novel*, 2001) says that the novel can be distinguished from other fictional forms by the attention it pays to individual characterization and detailed presentation of the environment. Moreover, says Watt, the novel, more than any other fictional form, is interested in the "development of its characters in the course of time."

novel of manners: The classic examples of this form might be the novels of Jane Austen, wherein the customs and conventions of a social group of a particular time and place are realistically, and often satirically, portrayed.

novella, novelle, nouvelle, novelette, novela: Although these terms often refer to the short European tale, especially the Renaissance form employed by Giovanni Boccaccio, the terms often refer to that form of fiction that is said to be longer than a short story and shorter than a novel. "Novelette" is the term usually preferred by the British, whereas "novella" is the term usually used to refer to American works in this *genre*. Henry James claimed that the main merit of the form is the "effort to do the complicated thing with a strong brevity and lucidity."

phenomenological criticism: Although best known as a European school of criticism practiced by Georges Poulet and others, this so-called criticism of consciousness is also propounded in the United States by such critics as J. Hillis Miller. The focus is less on individual works and *genres* than it is on literature as an act; the work is not seen as an object but rather as part of a strand of latent impulses in the work of a single author or an epoch.

picaresque novel: A form of fiction that centers on a central rogue figure, or picaro, who usually tells his or her own story. The plot structure is normally *episodic*, and the episodes usually focus on how the picaro lives by his or her wits. Classic examples of the mode are Henry Fielding's *The History of Tom Jones, a Foundling* (1749; commonly known as *Tom Jones*) and Mark Twain's *Adventures of Huckleberry Finn* (1884).

plot/story: "Story" refers to the full *narrative* of *character* and action, whereas "plot" generally refers to action with little reference to character. A more precise and helpful distinction is made by the Russian Formalists, who suggest that "plot" refers to the events of a narrative as they have been artfully arranged in the literary work, subject to chronological displacement, ellipses, and other devices, while "story" refers to the sum of the same events arranged in simple, causal-chronological order. Thus story is the raw material for plot. By comparing the two in a given work, the reader is encouraged to see the narrative as an artifact.

point of view: The means by which the story is presented to the reader, or, as Percy Lubbock says in *The Craft of Fiction* (1921), "the relation in which the narrator stands to the story"—a relation that Lubbock claims governs the craft of fiction. Some of the questions the critical reader should ask concerning point of view are the following: Who talks to the reader? From what position does the narrator tell the story? At what distance does he or she place the reader from the story? What kind of person is he or she? How fully is he or she characterized? How reliable is he or she? For further discussion, see Wayne Booth, *The Rhetoric of Fiction* (1961).

postcolonialism: Postcolonial literature emerged in the mid-twentieth century when colonies in Asia, Africa, and the Caribbean began gaining their independence from the European nations that had long controlled them. Postcolonial authors, such as Salman Rushdie and V. S. Naipaul, tend to focus on both the freedom and the conflict inherent in living in a postcolonial state.

postmodernism: A ubiquitous but elusive term in contemporary criticism, "postmodernism" is loosely applied to the various artistic movements that followed the era of so-called high modernism, represented by such giants as James Joyce and Pablo Picasso. In critical discussions of contemporary fiction, the term "postmodernism" is frequently applied to the works of writers such as Thomas Pynchon, John Barth, and Donald Barthelme, who exhibit a self-conscious awareness of their modernist predecessors as well as a reflexive treatment of fictional form.

protagonist: The central *character* in a fiction, the character whose fortunes most concern the reader.

psychological criticism: While much modern literary criticism reflects to some degree the impacts of Sigmund Freud, Carl Jung, Jacques Lacan, and other psychological theorists, the term "psychological criticism" suggests a strong emphasis on a causal relation between the writer's psychological state, variously interpreted, and his or her works. A notable example of psychological criticism is Norman Fruman's *Coleridge, the Damaged Archangel* (1971).

psychological novel: A form of fiction in which *character*, especially the inner lives of characters, is the primary focus. This form, which has been of primary importance at least since Henry James, characterizes much of the work of James Joyce, Virginia Woolf, and William Faulkner. For a detailed discussion, see *The Modern Psychological Novel* (1955) by Leon Edel.

realism: A literary technique in which the primary convention is to render an illusion of fidelity to external reality. Realism is often identified as the primary method of the novel form: It focuses on surface details, maintains a fidelity to the everyday experiences of middle-class society, and strives for a one-to-one relationship between the fiction and the action imitated. The realist movement in the late nineteenth century coincides with the full development of the novel form.

reception aesthetics: The best-known American practitioner of reception aesthetics is Stanley Fish. For the reception critic, meaning is an event or process; rather than being embedded in the work, it is created through particular acts of reading. The best-known European practitioner of this criticism, Wolfgang Iser, argues that indeterminacy is the basic characteristic of literary texts; the reader must "normalize" the text either by projecting his or her standards into it or by revising his or her standards to "fit" the text.

regional novel: Any novel in which the character of a given geographical region plays a decisive role. Although regional differences persist across the United States, a considerable leveling in speech and customs has taken place, so that the sharp regional distinctions evident in nineteenth century American fiction have all but disappeared. Only in the South has a strong regional tradition persisted to the present. (See *local colorists*.)

rhetorical criticism: The rhetorical critic is concerned with the literary work as a means of communicating ideas and the means by which the work affects or controls the reader. Such criticism seems best suited to didactic works such as satire.

roman à clef: A fiction wherein actual people, often celebrities of some sort, are thinly disguised.

romance: The romance usually differs from the novel form in that the focus is on symbolic events and representational characters rather than on "as-if-real" characters and events. Richard Chase says that in the romance, character is depicted as highly stylized, a function of the plot rather than as someone complexly related to society. The romancer is more likely to be concerned with dreamworlds than with the familiar world, believing that reality cannot be grasped by the traditional novel.

Romanticism: A widespread cultural movement in the late eighteenth and early nineteenth centuries, the influence of which is still felt. As a general literary tendency, Romanticism is frequently contrasted with *classicism*. Although many varieties of Romanticism are indigenous to various national literatures, the term generally suggests an assertion of the preeminence of the imagination. Other values associated with various schools of Romanticism include primitivism, an interest in folklore, a reverence for nature, and a fascination with the demoniac and the macabre.

scene: The central element of *narration*; specific actions are narrated or depicted that make the reader feel he or she is participating directly in the action.

science fiction: Fiction in which certain givens (physical laws, psychological principles, social conditions—any one or all of these) form the basis of an imaginative projection into the future or, less commonly, an extrapolation in the present or even into the past.

semiotics: The science of signs and sign systems in communication. According to Roman Jakobson, semiotics deals with the principles that underlie the structure of signs, their use in language of all kinds, and the specific nature of various sign systems.

sentimental novel: A form of fiction popular in the eighteenth century in which emotionalism and optimism are the primary characteristics. The best-known examples are Samuel Richardson's *Pamela: Or, Virtue Rewarded* (1740-1741) and Oliver Goldsmith's *The Vicar of Wakefield* (1766).

setting: The circumstances and environment, both temporal and spatial, of a *narrative*.

spatial form: An author's attempt to make the reader apprehend a work spatially in a moment of time rather than sequentially. To achieve this effect, the author breaks up the *narrative* into interspersed fragments. Beginning with James Joyce, Marcel Proust, and Djuna Barnes, the movement toward spatial form is concomitant with the *modernist* effort to supplant historical time in fiction with mythic time. For the seminal discussion of this technique, see Joseph Frank, *The Widening Gyre* (1963).

stream of consciousness: The depiction of the thought processes of a *character*, insofar as this is possible, without any mediating structures. The metaphor of consciousness as a "stream" suggests a rush of thoughts and images governed by free association rather than by strictly rational development. The term "stream of consciousness" is often used loosely as a synonym for *interior monologue*. The most celebrated example of stream of consciousness in fiction is the monologue of Molly Bloom in James Joyce's *Ulysses* (1922); other notable practitioners of the stream-of-consciousness technique include Dorothy Richardson, Virginia Woolf, and William Faulkner.

structuralism: As a movement of thought, structuralism is based on the idea of intrinsic, self-sufficient structures that do not require reference to external elements. A structure is a system of transformations that involves the interplay of laws inherent in the system itself. The study of language is the primary model for contemporary structuralism. The structuralist literary critic attempts to define structural principles that operate intertextually throughout the whole of literature as well as principles that operate in *genres* and in individual works. One of the most accessible surveys of structuralism and literature available is Jonathan Culler's *Structuralist Poetics* (1975).

summary: Those parts of a fiction that do not need to be detailed. In *Tom Jones* (1749), Henry Fielding says, "If whole years should pass without producing anything worthy of . . . notice . . . we shall hasten on to matters of consequence."

thematics: According to Northrop Frye, when a work of fiction is written or interpreted thematically, it becomes an illustrative fable. Murray Krieger defines thematics as "the study of the experiential tensions which, dramatically entangled in the literary work, become an existential reflection of that work's aesthetic complexity."

tone: The dominant mood of a work of fiction. (See *atmosphere*.)

unreliable narrator: A narrator whose account of the events of the story cannot be trusted, obliging readers to reconstruct—if possible—the true state of affairs themselves. Once an innovative technique, the use of the unreliable narrator has become commonplace among contemporary writers who wish to suggest the impossibility of a truly "reliable" account of any event. Notable examples of the unreliable narrator can be found in Ford Madox Ford's *The Good Soldier* (1915) and Vladimir Nabokov's *Lolita* (1955).

Victorian novel: Although the Victorian period extended from 1837 to 1901, the term "Victorian novel" does not include the later decades of Queen Victoria's reign. The term loosely refers to the sprawling works of novelists such as Charles Dickens and William Makepeace Thackeray—works that frequently appeared first in serial form and are characterized by a broad social canvas.

vraisemblance/verisimilitude: Tzvetan Todorov defines vraisemblance as "the mask which conceals the text's own laws, but which we are supposed to take for a relation to reality." Verisimilitude refers to a work's attempts to make the reader believe that it conforms to reality rather than to its own laws.

Western novel: Like all varieties of *genre fiction*, the Western novel—generally known simply as the Western—is defined by a relatively predictable combination of *conventions*, *motifs*, and recurring themes. These predictable elements, familiar from many Western films and television series, differentiate the Western from *historical novels* and idiosyncratic works such as Thomas Berger's *Little Big Man* (1964) that are also set in the Old West. Conversely, some novels set in the contemporary West are regarded as Westerns because they deal with modern cowboys and with the land itself in the manner characteristic of the *genre*.

Charles E. May

Guide to Online Resources

Web Sites

The following sites were visited by the editors of Salem Press in 2009. Because URLs frequently change, the accuracy of these addresses cannot be guaranteed; however, long-standing sites, such as those of colleges and universities, national organizations, and government agencies, generally maintain links when sites are moved or updated.

American Literature on the Web
http://www.nagasaki-gaigo.ac.jp/ishikawa/amlit

Among this site's features are several pages providing links to Web sites about specific genres and literary movements, southern and southwestern American literature, minority literature, literary theory, and women writers, as well as an extensive index of links to electronic text collections and archives. Users also can access information for five specific time periods: 1620-1820, 1820-1865, 1865-1914, 1914-1945, and since 1945. A range of information is available for each period, including alphabetical lists of authors that link to more specific information about each writer, time lines of historical and literary events, and links to related additional Web sites.

Books and Writers
http://www.kirjasto.sci.fi/indeksi.htm

This broad, comprehensive, and easy-to-use resource provides access to information about hundreds of authors throughout the world, extending from 70 b.c.e to the twenty-first century. Links take users from an alphabetical list of authors to pages featuring biographical material, lists of works, and recommendations for further reading about individual authors; each writer's page also includes links to related pages on the site. Although brief, the biographical essays provide solid overviews of the authors' careers, their contributions to literature, and their literary influences.

The Canadian Literature Archive
http://www.umanitoba.ca/canlit

Created and maintained by the English Department at the University of Manitoba, this site is a comprehensive collection of materials for and about Canadian writers. It includes an alphabetical listing of authors with links to additional Web-based information. Users also can retrieve electronic texts, announcements of literary events, and videocasts of author interviews and readings.

A Celebration of Women Writers
http://digital.library.upenn.edu/women

This site presents an extensive compendium of information about the contributions of women writers throughout history. The "Local Editions by Authors" and "Local Editions by Category" pages include access to electronic texts of the works of numerous writers, including Louisa May Alcott, Djuna Barnes, Grazia Deledda, Edith Wharton, and Virginia Woolf. Users can also access biographical and bibliographical information by browsing lists arranged by writers' names, countries of origin, ethnicities, and the centuries in which they lived.

Contemporary Writers
http://www.contemporarywriters.com/authors

Created by the British Council, this site offers "up-to-date profiles of some of the U.K. and Commonwealth's most important living writers (plus writers from the Republic of Ireland that we've worked with)." The available information includes biographies, bibliographies, critical reviews, news about literary prizes, and photographs. Users can search the site by author, genre, nationality, gender, publisher, book title, date of publication, and prize name and date.

Internet Public Library: Native American Authors
http://www.ipl.org/div/natam

Internet Public Library, a Web-based collection of materials, includes this index to resources about writers of Native American heritage. An alphabetical list of authors enables users to link to biographies, lists of works, electronic texts, tribal Web sites, and other online resources. The majority of the writers covered are contemporary Indian authors, but some historical authors also are featured. Users also can retrieve information by browsing lists of titles and tribes. In addition, the site contains a bibliography of print and online materials about Native American literature.

LiteraryHistory.com
http://www.literaryhistory.com

This site is an excellent source of academic, scholarly, and critical literature about eighteenth, nineteenth, and twentieth century American and English writers. It provides numerous pages about specific eras and genres, including individual pages for eighteenth, nineteenth, and twentieth century literature and for African American and postcolonial literature. These pages contain alphabetical lists of authors that link to articles, reviews, overviews, excerpts of works, teaching guides, podcast interviews, and other materials. The eighteenth century literature page also provides access to information about the eighteenth century novel.

Literary Resources on the Net
http://andromeda.rutgers.edu/~jlynch/Lit

Jack Lynch of Rutgers University maintains this extensive collection of links to Internet sites that are useful to academics, including numerous Web sites about American and English literature. This collection is a good place to begin online research about the novel, as it links to hundreds of other sites with broad ranges of literary topics. The site is organized chronically, with separate pages for information about the Middle Ages, the Renaissance, the eighteenth century, the Romantic and Victorian eras, and twentieth century British and Irish literature. It also has separate pages providing links to Web sites about American literature and to women's literature and feminism.

LitWeb
http://litweb.net

LitWeb provides biographies of more than five hundred world authors throughout history that can be accessed through an alphabetical listing. The pages about each writer contain a list of his or her works, suggestions for further reading, and illustrations. The site also offers information about past and present winners of major literary prizes.

The Modern Word: Authors of the Libyrinth
http://www.themodernword.com/authors.html

The Modern Word site, although somewhat haphazard in its organization, provides a great deal of critical information about writers. The "Authors of the Libyrinth" page is very useful, linking author names to essays about them and other resources. The section of the page headed "The Scriptorium" presents "an index of pages featuring writers who have pushed the edges of their medium, combining literary talent with a sense of experimentation to produce some remarkable works of modern literature." The site also includes sections devoted to Samuel Beckett, Umberto Eco, Gabriel García Márquez, James Joyce, Franz Kafka, and Thomas Pynchon.

Novels
http://www.nvcc.edu/home/ataormina/novels/default.htm

This overview of American and English novels was prepared by Agatha Taormina, a professor at Northern Virginia Community College. It contains three sections: "History" provides a definition of the novel genre, a discussion of its origins in eighteenth century England, and separate pages with information about genres and authors of nineteenth century, twentieth century, and postmodern novels. "Approaches" suggests how to read a novel critically for greater appreciation, and "Resources" provides a list of books about the novel.

Outline of American Literature
http://www.america.gov/publications/books/outline-of-american-literature.html

This page of the America.gov site provides access to an electronic version of the ten-chapter volume *Outline of American Literature,* a historical overview of prose and poetry from colonial times to the present published by the U.S. Department of State. The work's author is Kathryn VanSpanckeren, professor of English at the University of Tampa. The site offers links to abbreviated versions of each chapter as well as access to the entire publication in PDF format.

Voice of the Shuttle
http://vos.ucsb.edu

One of the most complete and authoritative places for online information about literature, Voice of the Shuttle is maintained by professors and students in the English Department at the University of California, Santa Barbara. The site provides thousands of links to electronic books, academic journals, association Web sites, sites created by university professors, and many, many other resources about the humanities. Its "Literature in English" page provides links to separate pages about the literature of the Anglo-Saxon era, the Middle Ages, the Renaissance and seventeenth century, the Restoration and eighteenth century, the Romantic age, the Victorian age, and modern and contemporary periods in Britain and the United States, as well as a page focused on minority literature. Another page on the site, "Literatures Other than English," offers a gateway to information about the literature of numerous countries and world regions.

ELECTRONIC DATABASES

Electronic databases usually do not have their own URLs. Instead, public, college, and university libraries subscribe to these databases, provide links to them on their Web sites, and make them available to library card holders or other specified patrons. Readers can visit library Web sites or ask reference librarians to check on availability.

Canadian Literary Centre

Produced by EBSCO, the Canadian Literary Centre database contains full-text content from ECW Press, a Toronto-based publisher, including the titles in the publisher's Canadian fiction studies, Canadian biography, and Canadian writers and their works series, *ECW's Biographical Guide to Canadian Novelists,* and *George Woodcock's Introduction to Canadian Fiction.* Author biographies, essays and literary criticism, and book reviews are among the database's offerings.

Literary Reference Center

EBSCO's Literary Reference Center (LRC) is a comprehensive full-text database designed primarily to help high school and undergraduate students in English and the humanities with homework and research assignments about literature. The database contains massive amounts of information from reference works, books, literary journals, and other materials, including more than 31,000 plot summaries, synopses, and overviews of literary works; almost 100,000 essays and articles of literary criticism; about 140,000 author biographies; more than 605,000 book reviews; and more than 5,200 author interviews. It also contains the entire contents of Salem Press's MagillOnLiterature Plus. Users can retrieve information by browsing a list of authors' names or titles of literary works; they can also use an advanced search engine to access information by numerous categories, including author name, gender, cultural identity, national identity, and the years in which he or she lived, or by literary title, character, locale, genre, and publication date. The Literary Reference Center also features a literary-historical time line, an encyclopedia of literature, and a glossary of literary terms.

MagillOnLiterature Plus

MagillOnLiterature Plus is a comprehensive, integrated literature database produced by Salem Press and available on the EBSCO*host* platform. The database contains the full text of essays in Salem's many literature-related reference works, including *Masterplots, Cyclopedia of World Authors, Cyclopedia of Literary Characters, Cyclopedia of Literary Places, Critical Survey of Long Fiction, Critical Survey of Short Fiction, World Philosophers and Their Works, Magill's Literary Annual,* and *Magill's Book Reviews.* Among its contents are articles on more than 35,000 literary works and more than 8,500 writers, poets, dramatists, essays, and philosophers, more than 1,000 images, and a glossary of more than 1,300 literary terms. The biographical essays include lists of authors' works and secondary bibliographies, and almost four hundred overview essays offer information about literary genres, time periods, and national literatures.

NoveList

NoveList is a readers' advisory service produced by EBSCO. The database provides access to 155,000 titles of both adult and juvenile fiction as well information about literary awards, book discussion guides, feature articles about a range of literary genres, and "recommended reads." Users can search by author name, book title, or series title or can describe the plot to retrieve the name of a book, information about the author, and book reviews; another search engine enables users to find titles similar to books they have enjoyed reading.

Rebecca Kuzins

GEOGRAPHICAL INDEX

AUSTRIA
    Kafka, Franz, 129

BRAZIL
    Machado de Assis, Joaquim Maria, 153

CANADA
    Bellow, Saul, 18

CZECH REPUBLIC
    Kafka, Franz, 129

ENGLAND
    Defoe, Daniel, 57
    Fielding, Henry, 88
    Rushdie, Salman, 175
    Wain, John, 240

FRANCE
    Diderot, Denis, 74
    Lesage, Alain-René, 141
    Voltaire, 224

GERMANY
    Grimmelshausen, Hans Jakob Christoffel von, 115

INDIA
    Rushdie, Salman, 175

IRELAND
    Swift, Jonathan, 214

RUSSIA
    Aleichem, Sholom, 12
    Gogol, Nikolai, 104

SCOTLAND
    Smollett, Tobias, 204

SPAIN
    Cervantes, Miguel de, 46

UKRAINE
    Aleichem, Sholom, 12

UNITED STATES
    Bellow, Saul, 18
    Boyle, T. Coraghessan, 36
    Prokosch, Frederic, 166
    Saroyan, William, 191

SUBJECT INDEX

Actual, The (Bellow), 32
Adventure novels, 1, 4
   Miguel de Cervantes, 49
   Daniel Defoe, 64
   Jonathan Swift, 219
Adventures of Augie March, The (Bellow), 22
Adventures of Wesley Jackson, The (Saroyan), 197
Adventurous Simplicissimus, The (Grimmelshausen), 120
Aestheticism, 77
Aleichem, Sholom, 12-17
Allegory
   Daniel Defoe, 59
   Frederic Prokosch, 170
   Salman Rushdie, 179
   Jonathan Swift, 217
Amerika (Kafka), 132
Amis, Kingsley, 242, 244
Angry Young Men, 244
Antiheroes, 5
   T. Coraghessan Boyle, 40
   John Wain, 244
Archetypes, 5
Aristotle, 232
Arouet, François-Marie. *See* Voltaire
Asiatics, The (Prokosch), 170
Atmosphere, 244
Atwood, Margaret, 9
Auden, W. H., 167
Auster, Paul, 7

Barca, Pedro Calderón de la, 142
Barth, John, 37
Beckett, Samuel, 21
Bellarosa Connection, The (Bellow), 32

Bellow, Saul, 18-35
Biblical themes, 63, 65
Bildungsromans, 1
   Hans Jakob Christoffel von Grimmelshausen, 116
   Jonathan Swift, 220
   John Wain, 247
Blake, William, 25
Bloody Hoax, The (Aleichem), 16
Borges, Jorge Luis, 53
Born in Captivity (Wain), 245
Bourgeois novel, 3, 150
Boyle, T. Coraghessan, 36-45
Boys and Girls Together (Saroyan), 200
Braine, John, 244
Brecht, Bertolt, 126
Brod, Max, 129
Budding Prospects (Boyle), 38
Bunyan, John, 99

Candide (Voltaire), 233
Carpio, Lope de Vega, 46, 143
Cary, Joyce, 6
Castle, The (Kafka), 137
Catholic themes
   Hans Jakob Christoffel von Grimmelshausen, 119, 123
   Voltaire, 235
Censorship
   Salman Rushdie, 175
   Voltaire, 225
Cervantes, Miguel de, 46-56, 143
Cheever, John, 37
Chekhov, Anton, 13
Cibber, Colley, 95
Coleridge, Samuel Taylor, 25

Colonel Jack (Defoe), 67
Comedies (Wain), 251
Continuation, The (Grimmelshausen), 125
Corneille, Pierre, 79, 226
Counselor Ayres' Memorial (Machado de Assis), 161
Courage (Grimmelshausen), 125

Dahl, Roald, 178
Dangling Man (Bellow), 22
Dead Souls (Gogol), 106
Dean's December, The (Bellow), 30
Defoe, Daniel, 4, 57-73
Descartes, René, 232
Devil upon Two Sticks, The (Lesage), 145
Dickens, Charles, 107, 205
Didactic novels, 99
Diderot, Denis, 74-87, 224
Dom Casmurro (Machado de Assis), 160
Don Quixote de la Mancha (Cervantes), 49, 206
Doppelgängers, 22
Dostoevski, Fyodor, 104
Drop City (Boyle), 44

East Is East (Boyle), 40
Eckhart, Meister, 28
Enchantress of Florence, The (Rushdie), 188
Epistolary novels
    Sholom Aleichem, 15
    Tobias Smollett, 211
Epitaph of a Small Winner (Machado de Assis), 158
Euripides, 166

Fantastic
    Saul Bellow, 24
    Franz Kafka, 132
Feminist fiction, 9
Ferdinand, Count Fathom (Smollett), 210
Fiddler on the Roof (Aleichem), 13

Fielding, Henry, 4, 88-103, 141, 205
Flashbacks, 7
Fortunate Mistress, The. See *Roxana*
France, Anatole, 150
Fraser, George MacDonald, 8
Free Zone Starts Here, The. See *Young Shoulders*
Friend of the Earth, A (Boyle), 43

Gay, John, 95
Gay and lesbian novels, 9
Gil Blas (Lesage), 146
Gogol, Nikolai, 104-114
Goldsmith, Oliver, 207
Goncharov, Ivan, 107
Gothic novel, 111
Grimmelshausen, Hans Jakob Christoffel von, 3, 115-128
Grotesque
    Daniel Defoe, 63
    Nikolai Gogol, 107
    Franz Kafka, 137
    Voltaire, 229
    John Wain, 246
Gulliver's Travels (Swift), 219

Henderson the Rain King (Bellow), 25
Herzog (Bellow), 26
Historical novels
    Nikolai Gogol, 112
    Frederic Prokosch, 169
History of Gil Blas of Santillane, The. See *Gil Blas*
History of the Great Plague in London, The. See *Journal of the Plague Year, A*
Hölderlin, Friedrich, 166
Holocaust literature
    Sholom Aleichem, 13
    Saul Bellow, 34
Homer, 183, 197

Subject Index

Hugo, Victor, 142
Human Comedy, The (Saroyan), 197
Humboldt's Gift (Bellow), 29
Humphry Clinker (Smollett), 211
Hungry Generations (Wain), 251
Hurry on Down. See *Born in Captivity*

Impressionism, 14
In the Storm (Aleichem), 15
Indiscreet Toys, The (Diderot), 81
Ingenuous (Voltaire), 235
Interior monologues, 247
Irving, John, 37
Islam, 179

Jacques the Fatalist and His Master (Diderot), 84
Johnson, Samuel, 99, 245
Jonathan Wild (Fielding), 99
Jong, Erica, 9
Joseph Andrews (Fielding), 97
Journal of the Plague Year, A (Defoe), 62

Kafka, Franz, 129-140
Keats, John, 30
King, Stephen, 178
Kundera, Milan, 178

La Fayette, Madame de, 142
Larkin, Philip, 242
Laughing Matter, The (Saroyan), 199
Lazarillo de Tormes (1554), 1
Le Carré, John, 178
Leibniz, Gottfried Wilhelm, 231
Lesage, Alain-René, 3, 141-152
Letter to His Father (Kafka), 130
Local color
    Denis Diderot, 80
    Voltaire, 224
Locke, John, 232

McCarthy, Cormac, 7
Machado de Assis, Joaquim Maria, 153-165
McInerney, Jay, 7
McMurtry, Larry, 7
Mailer, Norman, 178
Malebranche, Nicolas, 232
Man of Forty Crowns, The (Voltaire), 236
Marivaux, 142
Micromegas (Voltaire), 232
Midnight's Children (Rushdie), 179
Modern novel
    Saul Bellow, 19, 21
    Franz Kafka, 129
Moll Flanders (Defoe), 67
Moor's Last Sigh, The (Rushdie), 186
More Die of Heartbreak (Bellow), 31
More, Sir Thomas, 99
Mother Courage and Her Children (Brecht), 126
Motifs
    Hans Jakob Christoffel von Grimmelshausen, 120
    Salman Rushdie, 181
    Jonathan Swift, 218
Mr. Sammler's Planet (Bellow), 28
My Name Is Aram (Saroyan), 196

Nabokov, Vladimir, 43, 53
Nashe, Thomas, 4
Naturalism, 157
New Novel, 77
Nine Days to Mukalla (Prokosch), 171
Novel of manners, 146
Novel of sensibility, 77, 142
Nun, The (Diderot), 82

Odyssey (Homer), 197
O'Neill, Eugene, 131
Osborne, John, 244
Oxford trilogy (Wain), 251

Pardoner's Tale, The (Wain), 249
Peregrine Pickle (Smollett), 209
Philosophes, 77
Philosophical novels
   Denis Diderot, 79
   Voltaire, 229
Picaresque novel, 1-11
   Sholom Aleichem, 14
   T. Coraghessan Boyle, 38
   Nikolai Gogol, 107
   Hans Jakob Christoffel von
      Grimmelshausen, 116
   Franz Kafka, 133
   Alain-René Lesage, 148
   Joaquim Maria Machado de Assis, 158
   William Saroyan, 198
   Tobias Smollett, 209
Picaros, 1, 38, 160, 209
Point of view
   Nikolai Gogol, 108
   Hans Jakob Christoffel von
      Grimmelshausen, 118
   Franz Kafka, 132
   William Saroyan, 196
   John Wain, 244
Political novels, 179
Pope, Alexander, 95
Posthumous Memoirs of Brás Cubas, The.
   See *Epitaph of a Small Winner*
Prokosch, Frederic, 166-174
Psychological novel, 26
Pupil of Nature, The. See *Ingenuous*
Pynchon, Thomas, 37

Racine, Jean, 226
Rameau's Nephew (Diderot), 83
Ravelstein (Bellow), 33
Realism
   Saul Bellow, 20
   T. Coraghessan Boyle, 38

Daniel Defoe, 58
Nikolai Gogol, 104
Joaquim Maria Machado de Assis, 157
Salman Rushdie, 186
Tobias Smollett, 205
Religious novels
   Daniel Defoe, 63
   Hans Jakob Christoffel von
      Grimmelshausen, 119
   Salman Rushdie, 183
Richardson, Samuel, 77, 93, 142, 205, 234
Riven Rock (Boyle), 42
Road to Wellville, The (Boyle), 41
Robinson Crusoe (Defoe), 64
Rock Wagram (Saroyan), 198
Roderick Random (Smollett), 208
Romanticism
   Denis Diderot, 77
   Joaquim Maria Machado de Assis, 154
Rousseau, Jean-Jacques, 78, 142
Roxana (Defoe), 67
Rushdie, Salman, 175-190

Saroyan, William, 191-203
Satanic Verses, The (Rushdie), 183
Satire
   T. Coraghessan Boyle, 39
   Denis Diderot, 83
   Henry Fielding, 94
   Nikolai Gogol, 107
   Alain-René Lesage, 143
   Salman Rushdie, 181
   Tobias Smollett, 208
   Jonathan Swift, 217
   Voltaire, 229
   John Wain, 246
Seize the Day (Bellow), 23
Sentence, The (Kafka), 131
Seven Sisters, The (Prokosch), 171
Seven Who Fled, The (Prokosch), 170